Peace Operations and International Criminal Justice

This new volume provides the first thorough examination of the involvement of peace enforcement soldiers in the detention of indicted war criminals.

The book first addresses why peace enforcement missions need to be involved in detaining indicted war criminals. This discussion includes an analysis of how the securing of justice and transitional justice is incorporated into the UN's approach to peace-building. It also explores IFOR's, SFOR's and KFOR's activities in this regard, before turning to an analysis of how these detentions are incorporated into peace enforcement doctrines, mandates and rules of engagement. The book then outlines the mechanisms that need to be established in order to enable peace enforcers to arrest war criminals effectively in the areas where they are deployed. It concludes with a discussion of the prospects for the involvement of peace enforcement soldiers in the detention of indicted war criminals, and of the lessons future peace enforcement missions can learn from the experience of IFOR, SFOR and KFOR.

This book will be of much interest to students of peace operations, war crimes and humanitarian law, transitional justice and IR/Security Studies in general.

Majbritt Lyck was formerly a lecturer in the Department of Peace Studies at the University of Bradford. She has a PhD in Conflict Resolution from the University of Bradford.

Contemporary security studies

Series Editors: James Gow and Rachel Kerr
King's College London

This series focuses on new research across the spectrum of international peace and security, in an era where each year throws up multiple examples of conflicts that present new security challenges in the world around them.

NATO's Secret Armies
Operation Gladio and terrorism in
Western Europe
Daniele Ganser

**The US, NATO and Military
Burden-Sharing**
*Peter Kent Forster and
Stephen J. Cimbala*

**Russian Governance in the
Twenty-First Century**
Geo-strategy, geopolitics and new
governance
Irina Isakova

**The Foreign Office and Finland
1938–1940**
Diplomatic sideshow
Craig Gerrard

Rethinking the Nature of War
*Edited by Isabelle Duyvesteyn and
Jan Angstrom*

**Perception and Reality in the
Modern Yugoslav Conflict**
Myth, falsehood and deceit
1991–1995
Brendan O'Shea

**The Political Economy of
Peacebuilding in Post-Dayton
Bosnia**
Tim Donais

The Distracted Eagle
The rift between America and
old Europe
Peter H. Merkl

The Iraq War
European perspectives on politics,
strategy, and operations
*Edited by Jan Hallenberg and
Håkan Karlsson*

Strategic Contest
Weapons proliferation and war in the
greater Middle East
Richard L. Russell

Peace Operations and International Criminal Justice

Building peace after mass atrocities

Majbritt Lyck

Routledge
Taylor & Francis Group

LONDON AND NEW YORK

First published 2009
by Routledge
2 Park Square, Milton Park, Abingdon, Oxon OX14 4RN

Simultaneously published in the USA and Canada
by Routledge
270 Madison Ave, New York, NY 10016

Routledge is an imprint of the Taylor & Francis Group, an informa business

Transferred to Digital Printing 2009

Typeset in Times by Wearset Ltd, Boldon, Tyne and Wear

British Library Cataloguing in Publication Data
A catalogue record for this book is available from the British Library

Library of Congress Cataloging in Publication Data
A catalog record for this book has been requested

ISBN10: 0-415-44459-4 (hbk)
ISBN10: 0-415-57533-8 (pbk)
ISBN10: 0-203-89159-7 (ebk)

ISBN13: 978-0-415-44459-0 (hbk)
ISBN13: 978-0-415-57533-1 (pbk)
ISBN13: 978-0-203-89159-9 (ebk)

Contents

Acknowledgements

First of all I would like to thank my fiancé Ceri M. Bowen for all his help and support. I would also like to thank my family and friends for their support and encouragement. My sincere thanks also go to the people I interviewed in Kosovo and Bosnia-Herzegovina and the people who helped me set up the interviews and made my stay there a very enjoyable time.

For the PhD project that this book is partly built on I received financial support from the following sources: British Council (British Chevening Scholarship), Højgaard's Fond, Frimodt Heineke Fonden, Thea og Thorkild Rosenvold's Fond, Unibank Danmark Fonden, Greve Schack's Fond and the European Union (Marie Curie Research Fellowship). I have also benefited from the help and support of my PhD supervisor Professor Tom Woodhouse and Dr John Allcock from the Department of Peace Studies, University of Bradford and Dr Hans Joachim Heintze from the Institute for International Law on Peace and Armed Conflict, Ruhr University Bochum, Germany. My thanks also go to the anonymous reviewers of my PhD thesis.

Abbreviations

AI	Amnesty International
AU	African Union
CIVPOL	civilian police
DDR	disarmament, demobilisation and reintegration
DPA	Dayton Peace Agreement
DRC	Democratic Republic of Congo
ECOMOG	Military Observer Group of the Economic Community of West African States
ECOWAS	Economic Community of West African States
EU	European Union
EUFOR	European Union Force
EUPM	European Union Police Mission
FRY	Former Republic of Yugoslavia
HQ	headquarters
HRW	Human Rights Watch
ICC	International Criminal Court
ICG	International Crisis Group
ICTR	International Criminal Tribunal for Rwanda
ICTY	International Criminal Tribunal for the Former Yugoslavia
IFOR	Implementation Force
IPTF	International Police Task Force
ISAF	International Security Assistance Force
KFOR	Kosovo Force
KPS	Kosovo Police Service
MICIVIH	International Civilian Mission in Haiti
MINOPUH	United Nations Civilian Police Mission in Haiti
MINUGUA	United Nations Verification Mission in Guatemala
MINUSTAH	United Nations Stabilisation Mission in Haiti
MND	multinational division
MNF	multinational force
MONUA	United Nations Observer Mission in Angola
MONUC	United Nations Organisation Mission in the Democratic Republic of Congo

MSU	Multinational Specialised Unit
NATO	North Atlantic Treaty Organisation
NATO SG	North Atlantic Treaty Organisation Secretary General
NGO	non-governmental organisation
ONUC	United Nations Operation in Congo
ONUMOZ	United Nations Operation in Mozambique
ONUSAL	United Nations Observer Mission in El Salvador
SC-SL	Special Court for Sierra Leone
SFOR	Stabilisation Force
UN	United Nations
UNAMID	United Nations–African Union Mission in Darfur
UNAMIR	United Nations Assistance Mission in Rwanda
UNAMSIL	United Nations Mission in Sierra Leone
UNAVEM I	United Nations Angola Verification Mission I
UNAVEM II	United Nations Angola Verification Mission II
UNAVEM III	United Nations Angola Verification Mission III
UNGA	United Nations General Assembly
UNITA	União Nacional para a Independência Total de Angola
UNMIBH	United Nations Mission in Bosnia-Herzegovina
UNMIH	United Nations Mission in Haiti
UNMIK	United Nations Mission in Kosovo
UNMIL	United Nations Mission in Liberia
UNMIS	United Nations Mission in Sudan
UNMISET	United Nations Mission of Support to East Timor
UNOCI	United Nations Mission in Côte d'Ivoire
UNOMIL	United Nations Observer Mission in Liberia
UNOMSIL	United Nations Observer Mission in Sierra Leone
UNOSOM II	United Nations Operation in Somalia II
UNPROFOR	United Nations Protection Force
UNSC	United Nations Security Council
UNSG	United Nations Secretary General
UNSMIH	United Nations Support Mission in Haiti
UNTAC	United Nations Transitional Administration in Cambodia
UNTAES	United Nations Transitional Administration in Eastern Slavonia, Baranja and Western Sirmium
UNTAET	United Nations Transitional Administration in East Timor
UNTAG	United Nations Transition Assistance Group
UNTMIH	United Nations Transition Mission in Haiti
US	United States of America

Introduction

In the end of 2007 in her final speech to the United Nations Security Council (UNSC) the outgoing Prosecutor for the International Criminal Tribunal for the Former Yugoslavia (ICTY) Carla Del Ponte reiterated her disappointment at not having been able to bring the former political leader Radovan Karadžić and the former military commander Ratko Mladić to justice (Del Ponte 10 December 2007). The ICTY was established in 1993 in order to help ensure accountability for serious violations of international humanitarian law committed during the violent conflict in the territory of the Former Yugoslavia, which was seen as a precondition for establishing sustainable peace in the area. Two years after its establishment Richard Goldstone, who was the Prosecutor of the ICTY at the time, indicted Karadzic and Mladic, accusing them of bearing the main responsibility for some of the worst atrocities committed during the violent conflict in Bosnia-Herzegovina. Despite being on top of the ICTY's most wanted list, the two men remain at large twelve years after their indictments were announced and they are far from the only indicted war criminals who have managed to stay at large after indictment by the ICTY. Especially in the beginning, this failure to arrest individuals sought for prosecution seriously threatened the tribunal's prospects for success. Even ten years after the establishment of the ICTY, sixteen men in addition to Mladic and Karadzic were still at large (President of the ICTY 2003). The failure to arrest Karadzic, Mladic and other indicted war criminals has exposed the Achilles' heel of international criminal tribunals, namely their current dependence on the cooperation of national and international authorities outside their control to carry out vital tasks such as arrests. In contrast to national courts, the ICTY like other international criminal tribunals, does not have its own police force to carry out the arrest warrants that it issues. Instead the initial idea was that national authorities in the states where the indicted war criminals were residing would be responsible for their arrest and transfer to the ICTY. However, it soon became apparent that not all national authorities were eager to provide that kind of assistance. Whereas the national authorities in the Federation of Bosnia and Herzegovina have been fairly cooperative, the national authorities in Republika Srpska, the mainly Serb part of Bosnia-Herzegovina, have refused to carry out any requests for arrests despite strong criticism for their inaction on numerous occasions (President of the

ICTY, 1995, 1996, 1997, 1998, 1999, 2000, 2001, 2002, 2003, 2004). Hence, it soon became clear that, unless alternative arrangements were made, the areas in which national authorities refused to cooperate would be safe havens for indicted war criminals. In the case of Bosnia-Herzegovina a possible alternative solution was to request the peace enforcement mission deployed in the country at the time to carry out the arrest warrants. The peace enforcement mission consisted of the UN-led United Nations Mission in Bosnia-Herzegovina (UNMIBH), which was in charge of implementing the civilian parts of the Dayton Peace Agreement (DPA) and the NATO-led Implementation Force (IFOR), which was responsible for assisting the national authorities in implementing the military parts of the DPA. Thus the Prosecutor of the ICTY began to pass on arrest warrants to IFOR, requesting that the peace enforcement soldiers detain the individuals indicted by the ICTY (President of the ICTY 1996). However, although 60,000 IFOR soldiers were deployed all over Bosnia-Herzegovina, they never managed to detain a single indicted war criminal. IFOR's successor, the similarly NATO-led Stabilisation Force (SFOR), did eventually manage to detain some indicted war criminals but, throughout SFOR's mission, others remained at large within SFOR's area of operation despite the presence of thousands of international soldiers. The lack of detentions led actors such as the Prosecutor of the ICTY and human rights organisations to heavily criticise the peace enforcement missions for not doing enough to detain indicted war criminals on numerous occasions.

In Kosovo soldiers from the NATO-led Kosovo Force (KFOR) who had been deployed in 1999 in order to help the UN Mission in Kosovo (UNMIK) administrate the province, were also eventually requested to assist the ICTY with detaining the indicted individuals. KFOR soldiers were more successful than their colleagues in Bosnia-Herzegovina since they managed to secure custody of three out of the four individuals that they had been requested to detain. However, the Prosecutor of the ICTY still criticised KFOR for having allowed the fourth indicted war criminal to pass unhindered through an airport that the soldiers guarded before escaping to Slovenia.

Though the lack of detentions of indicted war criminals has been one of the most serious threats to the ICTY's successful prosecution of these individuals and despite the many controversies surrounding the involvement of IFOR, SFOR and KFOR in such detentions, extensively addressed in the international media, remarkably few studies and analyses have focused on the involvement of peace enforcement missions in this matter. So far only a few studies have focused on the legality of employing peace enforcement soldiers to detain indicted war criminals and a few other studies have analysed and assessed IFOR's and SFOR's activities aimed at detentions.[1] This paucity of studies on the question is especially problematic because the International Criminal Court (ICC), established in 2002 in order to ensure accountability for atrocities committed during violent conflict, now faces the same problem. The ICC has issued arrest warrants against individuals who are allegedly responsible for mass atrocities committed in Sudan but so far the Sudanese national authorities have refused to carry out the detention warrants. Hence, in order to ensure the arrest of these individuals, soldiers from the UN Mission in Sudan (UNMIS) or from the new joint African Union/UN operation in Darfur (UNAMID) may have to detain the fugitives. Similarly, it is also not unlikely that soldiers from the United Nations Organisation Mission in the Democratic Republic of Congo (MONUC) will become involved in detaining individuals indicted by the ICC. Hence a thorough analysis of the issue of the involvement of peace enforcement missions in the detention of indicted war criminals is imminent and that is what this book sets out to provide. The book addresses why these missions need to be involved in the detention process. It also analyses the incorporation of measures to ensure justice and transitional justice into the UN's approach to peace-building. Furthermore it analyses IFOR's, SFOR's and KFOR's activities aimed at detaining indicted war criminals before turning to an analysis of the incorpo-ration of detention operations into peace enforcement doctrines, mandates and rules of engagement. The book also discusses what practices peace enforcement missions should implement and what training the soldiers should receive in order to be able to detain indicted war criminals successfully. In addition it also debates some of the political considerations concerning involving peace enforce-ment soldiers in these detentions before addressing which actors should assist the soldiers in apprehending indicted war criminals. Finally, the book examines the prospects of the involvement of peace enforcement soldiers in the detention of indicted war criminals and the lessons future peace enforcement missions can learn from the experience of IFOR, SFOR and KFOR.

The book is partly based on interviews with senior military officers from SFOR and KFOR and senior police officers from UNMIK that the author con-ducted in Kosovo and Bosnia-Herzegovina in 2003. In order to ensure the anonymity of the interviewees they will just be referred to as SFOR, KFOR and UNMIK interviews respectively.

Definition of key concepts

The key concepts of this book are defined as follows:

humane law Serves as a generic term for human rights law and humanitarian law. Mary Kaldor recommends that human rights law be combined with humanitarian law because the distinction between human rights law that is generally applicable in times of peace and humanitarian law that is applicable in times of war is not suitable in the context of contemporary violent conflict, since these conflicts have eradicated the line between peace and war. She also pointed out that violations of humanitarian law are at the same time often vio-lations of human rights. See Kaldor 2001: 116.

indicted war criminal Used to refer to an individual who has been indicted by an international criminal tribunal.

justice Refers to efforts aiming at securing accountability for crimes commit-ted after the violent conflict has officially ended.

peace enforcement mission   Used to describe a peace mission with a Chapter VII of the UN Charter mandate that allows the mission to employ force not only in strict self-defence but also in order to defend its mandate.

peace mission   Applies generically to all UN authorised missions regardless of whether the missions have been established on the basis of Chapter VI or Chapter VII of the UN Charter.

transitional justice   Refers to efforts aimed at addressing mass atrocities committed during the violent conflict including not only prosecution in order to ensure individual accountability but also alternative mechanisms such as truth and reconciliation processes, vetting programmes and reparations.

Structure of the book

Part I: peace missions, global order and transitional justice

The two chapters in Part I focus on the two main reasons why peace missions should be involved in detaining indicted war criminals.

The first reason why international peace missions need to be involved in these detentions is that it will assist in the enforcement of humane law that is an important part of a new cosmopolitan world order (Held 1993, 1995, 1996, Held *et al.* 1999, Kaldor 2001). It is only within the last five years that the relations between peace missions and global order have seriously entered the peacekeeping research agenda. Contributions to this new debate have come from peacekeeping theorists such as Alex Bellamy and colleagues, David Chandler, Oliver Richmond and Michael Pugh, who have all addressed how peace missions contribute to upholding a current global order that is based on the prevalence of liberal democratic states and that mainly benefits Western states (Bellamy *et al.* 2004, Chandler 2004, Pugh 2004, Richmond 2004). Chapter 1 briefly presents some of these arguments and contends that the debate needs to include not only what kind of global order peace missions support but also what kind of global order is desirable. The chapter goes on to detail one alternative to the present global order, namely, a cosmopolitan global order and the potential role of peace missions in the transformation of the current world order into a cosmopolitan global order.

The other main reason why international peace missions need to be involved in detaining indicted war criminals is that it will help the implementation of transitional justice, a precondition for the establishment of sustainable peace. There is an increasing consensus both in the academic and political spheres that, if societies are to successfully recover from war or internal violent conflict, then mass atrocities committed during the war or violent conflict need to be addressed, if not earlier, then at least once the violence has ended. However, it is still contentious how societies which have been through conflict or war best address mass violations of humane law. So far the debate has to a high degree focused mainly on two possible solutions, namely, the establishment of a criminal tribunal based on the idea of retributive justice or a truth and reconciliation commission based on the concept of restorative justice. Chapter 2 gives a brief overview of the debate and argues that, though there is no unanimous support for retributive justice in the form of a criminal trial process, indicators still point towards the importance of at least holding the worst perpetrators accountable for their deeds, if possible in a criminal trial process. It should be underlined that this does not rule out putting individuals who have committed less serious atrocities through a truth and reconciliation process. The chapter then provides a brief overview of the history of international criminal tribunals and the obstacles that they have faced. One of the most serious obstacles recent tribunals have encountered is failure to arrest the individuals facing prosecution. In contrast to national courts, which can normally rely on the local police to arrest individuals, international criminal tribunals have no police force at their disposal to make arrests. Instead they rely mainly on national authorities for arrests. However, in many states recovering from internal violent conflict the national police are often either unable or unwilling to detain indicted war criminals. These individuals are often still in power or boast strong links to influential politicians and hence they are not transferred to the tribunals. Thus, in order for international criminal tribunals to be successful in prosecutions, alternative ways of securing the detention and arrest of indicted war criminals need to be implemented. Some alternatives to reliance on national authorities have already been suggested and these are also briefly presented and discussed in Chapter 2. Finally, the chapter suggests that mandating international peace missions to detain indicted war criminals represents a viable solution.

Part II: UN peace missions' involvement in securing justice and transitional justice

Chapters 3 and 4 in Part II examine the involvement of UN peace missions in assisting societies recovering from internal violent conflict in securing justice and transitional justice.

Chapter 3 focuses on the inclusion of activities intended to establish justice through securing accountability for crimes committed in the post-conflict phase in the UN's peace-building approach. First, the chapter examines the kind of activities recent UN peace missions have been authorised to implement and the actions missions have actually carried out to help post-conflict states secure accountability for crimes committed after the signing of the peace agreement. In addition the chapter assesses the results of these efforts and identifies some of the main reasons why the missions have succeeded or failed to build institutions and structures that can ensure accountability for crimes committed after the violent conflict has ended. Furthermore, the chapter examines recent UN debates and reports in order to establish what role they envisage for UN peace missions in the development of institutions and structures aiming at preventing future crimes and securing accountability for crimes committed in the post-conflict period.

Chapter 4 focuses on the inclusion of activities aimed at establishing transitional justice through ensuring individual accountability for atrocities committed during the violent conflict in the UN's approach to post-conflict peace-building.

First, the chapter examines what transitional justice-related activities recent peace missions have been involved in. It also assesses the efforts of the peace missions and it identifies some of the main reasons why peace missions have failed or succeeded in assisting societies to implement a transitional justice process. Finally, the chapter examines recent UN reports and debates in order to establish their views on the role of peace missions in establishing transitional justice after violent conflicts.

Part III: The experience of IFOR, SFOR and KFOR

The Implementation Force (IFOR) and the Stabilisation Force (SFOR) that were deployed in Bosnia-Herzegovina from 1995 to 2004 and the Kosovo Force (KFOR) that has been deployed in Kosovo since 1999 have all been involved in attempts to detain indicted war criminals. Hence, in Part III, Chapters 5, 6 and 7 focus on the efforts of these three peace missions in this regard.

Chapter 5 looks at how IFOR interpreted its mandate concerning the detention of indicted war criminals and how this influenced its actions. The chapter also discusses why IFOR failed to detain any indicted war criminals. Chapter 6 outlines SFOR's results concerning the detention of indicted war criminals and discusses SFOR's failures and successes. The chapter also discusses which factors contributed to SFOR changing its policy and practice concerning these detentions and why it never fully committed to the process. Finally, Chapter 7 outlines KFOR's results concerning such detentions and discusses KFOR's response to its involvement in the detention of indicted war criminals and why it chose a reactive rather than a proactive response to detaining indicted war criminals.

Part IV: Preparing, authorising and ensuring the detention of indicted war criminals

If peace enforcement soldiers are to successfully detain indicted war criminals, it is important that they are prepared and authorised to carry out the task and that they know what actions are recommended to ensure successful detention. Hence these issues form the focus of Chapters 8, 9 and 10 in Part IV.

If peace enforcement soldiers are to be properly prepared for involvement in detention operations, it is vital that this task is not just included but also thoroughly incorporated into peace enforcement military doctrines. Hence, chapter 8 examines the dominant doctrines to determine if such incorporation has already begun and, if so, how far it has progressed. Based on the experience of IFOR, SFOR and KFOR, the chapter also discusses any further developments needed to fully integrate the detention of indicted war criminals into the doctrines.

It is also important that the task is not only included in the mandates granted to peace enforcement missions but also in their rules of engagement. Therefore, based on the experience of IFOR, SFOR and KFOR, Chapter 9 discusses what the mandates and specific rules of engagement of peace enforcement missions need to include concerning the detention of indicted war criminals.

Finally, if peace enforcement missions are to be successful in this task, the soldiers need to implement some recommended practices. Thus, based on the experience of IFOR, SFOR and KFOR, Chapter 10 identifies and discusses some of these practices.

Part V: Peace missions and politics

The experience of the peace missions in Bosnia-Herzegovina in particular, where both IFOR and SFOR were very reluctant to become involved in detaining indicted war criminals, shows that political considerations play an important role in this regard.

Thus Chapter 11 in Part V identifies some of the most significant political considerations that impacted on the involvement of IFOR and SFOR in detentions. The chapter also discusses these considerations in their temporal and territorial as well as in a contemporary context.

Part VI: Assisting peace enforcement missions in the apprehension of indicted war criminals

If peace enforcement soldiers are to successfully detain indicted war criminals, they need help from other local as well as international actors. Hence Chapters 12 and 13 in Part VI discuss which actors can provide peace enforcement soldiers with important assistance in the process of apprehending indicted war criminals.

Experience, especially from SFOR, indicates that, just like national police forces, peace enforcement missions can significantly benefit from help from international and local actors who are not a part of the peace mission and not involved in the detention operations but, through living and working in the peace mission's area of deployment, may potentially have vital information about the whereabouts of the indicted. Thus, based on experience from Bosnia-Herzegovina, Chapter 12 discusses which local and international actors can potentially assist the peace enforcement missions in locating indicted war criminals and some of the barriers that can potentially impact negatively on the cooperation between missions and these other actors.

Finally, Chapter 13 discusses which actors other than peace enforcement soldiers should be involved in apprehending indicted war criminals. The chapter also instigates the development of a framework for cooperation between the various actors involved in such apprehensions.

Conclusion

The book concludes with a discussion of the prospects for peace missions supporting a more cosmopolitan global order and becoming more involved in transitional justice activities and in detaining indicted war criminals. The lessons future missions can learn from the experience of IFOR, SFOR and KFOR are also examined.

Part I

Peace missions, global order and transitional justice

1   Peace missions and global order

Introduction

Until recently the literature on peacekeeping predominantly focused on the failures and successes and strengths and weaknesses of peace missions without reflecting on the reciprocal relations between peace missions and global politics and order. However, within the last five years peacekeeping scholars have begun to discuss how peace missions influence and are influenced by global order. Some of the most interesting contributions to this debate have come from Alex Bellamy *et al.*, David Chandler, Michael Pugh and Oliver Richmond (Bellamy *et al.* 2004, Chandler 2004, Pugh 2004, Richmond 2004). This chapter briefly presents some of the arguments these scholars have put forward and argues that the debate should not only focus on what world order peace missions support but also on what world order it is desirable that they and how they can do this. The chapter contends that a more cosmopolitan world order is a preferable alternative to the current global order. One of the main pillars of a cosmopolitan global order is the enforcement of cosmopolitan humane law, including securing accountability for violations of humane law in order to prevent further atrocities and thereby also prevent internal violent conflict and wars (Kaldor 2001). Hence, a cosmopolitan world order would involve the transformation of international humane law into cosmopolitan humane law, upholding human rights and humanitarian law, with prosecution of violations seen as a cosmopolitan rather than an international matter. Finally, the chapter identifies some potential roles that peace missions can play in the transformation of the current world order into a cosmopolitan one.

The debate on peace missions and global order

In their recent book *Understanding Peacekeeping* Bellamy *et al.* argue that global order can be divided into a Westphalian and post-Westphalian order (Bellamy *et al.* 2004: 11–33). The Westphalian order is characterised by the dominance of state sovereignty and the non-intervention norm, which implies that what happens inside states is entirely a state matter that no other state has the right to intervene in (ibid.). International law is kept to a minimum, aimed at facilitating coexistence between sovereign states; and the role of international institutions is reduced to forums where states can peacefully resolve their disputes (ibid.). Peacekeeping under the Westphalian order is based on the principles of consent, impartiality and non-use of force and aims to support the upholding of a cease-fire and help prevent further violence in order to facilitate space to allow the parties to the conflict to negotiate a peace agreement (Bellamy *et al.* 2004: 95–110). In contrast, the post-Westphalian order is dominated by a strong belief in the prevalence of liberal democratic states that trust each other and trade and cooperate with each other (Bellamy *et al.* 2004: 11–33). In accordance with the liberal democratic peace theory, the post-Westphalian order is built on the assumption that liberal democratic states do not fight each other (ibid.). Hence, one of the main roles of peacekeepers is to intervene in states torn apart by violent conflict and help them become liberal democratic states, thereby reducing the chance of war and violent conflict (ibid.). In some cases such as Cambodia, El Salvador and Namibia the parties to the violent conflict have invited peacekeepers to assist them in establishing a liberal democracy (ibid.). In other cases such as Haiti and Sierra Leone the United Nations Security Council (UNSC) has assessed that the overthrow of an elected government constituted a threat to peace and security and therefore authorised a peace mission to help restore democracy (ibid.). Finally, in some cases like Bosnia-Herzegovina, Kosovo and East Timor the UN and its regional partner organisations have attempted to install liberal democracy in states that have fallen apart due to internal violent conflict (ibid.). Bellamy *et al.* argue that there is an ongoing struggle between, on the one hand, China and many developing countries and on, the other hand, Western states (ibid.). China and her allies think that peace missions should support a Westphalian order because they believe that only respect for state sovereignty and peace between states is the way forward (ibid.). In contrast, Western states prefer peace missions to support a post-Westphalian order because they believe that only liberal democratic states can bring peace and that upholding sovereignty allows human rights violations in states to go unaddressed (ibid.).

The assumption that Western states prefer the post-Westphalian order partly because it means that human rights are better protected has been seriously questioned by other authors. In his article *The Responsibility to Protect? Imposing the 'Liberal Peace'*, David Chandler argued against the assumption that the so-called humanitarian interventions in the late 1990s such as NATO's intervention in the Kosovo conflict constitute a moral shift towards international intervention in order to protect individual human rights rather than international intervention because it is in the interest of dominating states (Chandler 2004). Instead he claimed that the interventions were based on the liberal peace thesis that states: 'that international peace and individual rights are best advanced through cosmopolitan frameworks whereby democratic and peaceful states take a leading responsibility for ensuring the interests of common humanity' (Chandler 2004: 60). Chandler also contended that the current dominance of the liberal peace thesis replicates the new balance of power in the sphere of international politics since humanitarian interventions are still only conducted if in the interests of the most powerful states (Chandler 2004). Rather than advancing international order in the direction of cosmopolitanism, where individual rights are respected regardless of the individual's nationality, Chandler claimed that the humanitarian interventions in fact underpinned the current international order of sovereign states that only act if it is in their own self-interest (ibid.). Hence, peacekeeping and peace enforcement missions support the upholding of the current world order and the dominance of Western states (ibid.).

In line with Chandler and Bellamy *et al.*, Oliver Richmond has also contended that UN peacekeeping missions add to the construction of an international order that is made up of liberal democratic states (Richmond 2004). He focused on the nature of the peace that peacekeeping missions promote and argued that peace operations have significant implications for both local and global order (ibid.). He contended that peace missions use their concept of peace as a justification for deep and long interventions in zones of violent conflict and that an international presence in the conflicting area is seen as a vital component in the pursuit of peace (ibid.). Therefore the peace is conditional, since it relies on the presence of the peace operations and it thereby contributes to upholding the present global order (ibid.). Richmond argued that Cold War peacekeeping approaches: 'revolved around the protection of the Wesphalian international system and addressed the shortcomings of that system through Westphalian tools ultimately replicating that system and its explicit legal positivism' (ibid.: 86). Therefore these approaches were status quo-oriented; they provided grey areas that allowed for regular atrocities and they created a negative peace that was not beneficial to the local actors but rather to regional and international actors (Richmond 2004). Like Bellamy *et al.*, Richmond claimed that the understanding of peace changed with the introduction of the post-Cold War period (ibid.). Now: 'peace is understood to lie in the establishment of reconstructive and transformative processes that culminate in states that mirror the liberal-democratic state' (ibid.: 87). Thus Richmond argued that peace is an outside vision rather than a concept defined by the local actors and that any opposition to the outside idea of peace is repressed through external actors taking over governance functions among other measures (Richmond 2004). Finally, Richmond contended that: 'what has run through all attempts to make peace and create order has been an attempt by hegemonic actors to preserve their own value system and to freeze the world's cartographies in their favour' (ibid.: 88).

Michael Pugh has also analysed peace missions from a critical theory perspective, focusing especially on the relations between international order, international norms and peace missions (Pugh 2004). Pugh contended that: 'a deconstruction of the role of peace support operations suggests that they sustain a particular order of world politics that privileges the rich and powerful states in their efforts to control or isolate unruly parts of the world' (ibid.: 39). Pugh clarified that: 'the received view of peacekeeping in global governance is not neutral but serves the purpose of an existing order (ibid.: 41) and that: 'the orthodoxy has been to police the liberal peace and the US dominated conception of world order' (ibid.: 44). Pugh also argued that: 'the elevation of PSOs and humanitarianism in global governance is accompanied by representations that attempt to legitimatise the right to use military force to protect populations within states' (ibid: 48) and that: 'governments have adapted their representations of PSOs to the discourses of ethics, humanitarianism, justice and the will of the international community' (ibid.: 48). Furthermore, Pugh also criticised the common contemporary understanding of humanitarianism since: 'it promotes moral values and responses that demonstrate and reinforce the superiority of liberal ideology whilst avoiding having to deal with the structured injustices that foster instabilities in the system' (ibid.: 49). He also contended that: 'political and military elites are not especially heroic about humanitarianism but rather nervous about incurring casualties, cautiously weighing up a range of variables including intangibles such as credibility and prestige' (ibid.: 50). Thus Pugh concluded that: 'PSOs replicate the normative and ideological assumptions that enable dominant states to manage the system in their own image' (ibid.: 54). Finally, he also questioned 'the extent to which the statist structure and neo-liberal value system fosters the kinds of political and social instability that require policing, protection and exclusion' (ibid.: 54).

Hence, the current debate among peace mission scholars about the relations between peace missions and global order have so far mainly focused on how peace missions support the upholding of the post-Westphalian order by means of assisting states recovering from internal violent conflict in implementing liberal democracies. There is a general agreement that the post-Westphalian order is dominated by Western states and that their decisive motive behind the deployment of peace missions is serving their own self-interest in upholding the current global order.

Expanding the debate to desirable alternatives to the current world order

So far the debate on the relations between peace missions and global order has mainly focused on how peace missions support the current global order. However, this is not adequate if current peace missions support the upholding of a global order that is primarily benefiting Western states rather than engendering more desirable aims such as promoting human rights around the world. If current peace missions uphold an undesirable world order then it is not enough that the debate merely criticises the current global order. It is also necessary that the debate suggests how peace missions can support more desirable alternatives and the transformation to these alternatives. So far this discussion has been almost completely absent from the debates on peace missions and global order.[2] Nevertheless, alternative global orders have been discussed in other fields such as international relations and, as pointed out by Roland Paris, it is always important to consider how theoretical debates in other subfields can improve peacekeeping theory (Paris 2003). It is well beyond the scope of this chapter to discuss all suggested alternatives to the current world order. Instead focus will be on one of the most widely debated alternatives, namely, the development of a more cosmopolitan world order.

A cosmopolitan global order

The idea of a cosmopolitan world order builds on recent observations put forward by Robert Keohane and Joseph Nye on the concept of transnationalism. International relations theorists Keohane and Nye developed the concept of transnationalism in the beginning of the 1970s (Keohane and Nye 1972, 1974). During this time the research field of international relations was dominated by the realist approach that among others took the nation-state as its primary unit of analysis. In their studies of political economy Keohane and Nye argued that a state-centric approach like realism was inadequate because the state did not have full control over the international economy and its role in the international economic system (ibid.). Keohane and Nye claimed that the international political system was highly influenced by actors operating within nation-states who had horizontal relations to similar actors in other nation-states and the networks of actors cut across the border of states so were therefore transnational (ibid.). They went on to broaden the scope of influential factors in international relations even further by arguing that nation-states deal with a multiplicity of issues, such as the environment, culture and migration that cut across the borders of nation-states. Both national and international networks of actors influence the behaviour of nation-states regarding these issues with interests and powers in these areas. Some of these networks are embedded on the national level in the institutions of the nation-states and on the international level in international formal institutions. Other networks are more informal without any affiliation to an organisation as such. Keohane and Nye named these systems of influential interests and powers *complex interdependence* (Keohane and Nye, 1977).

Over the last decade especially scholars from the London School of Economics have further developed the theory of transnationalism. David Held has argued that the international system of states is slowly but steadily being taken over by a transnational system where the nation-state is no longer the defining unit of analysis (Held 1995). The point of departure for Held's discussion is the interstate system that was established after the Second World War which he has named the *UN Charter Model* (ibid.). According to this model, the world community is made up of sovereign states that are connected through a partly institutionalised, partly ad-hoc network of relations (ibid.). Individuals are regarded as legitimate actors in international relations but their role is very limited (ibid.). Attempts to control the actions of states have been by means of international rules and regulations, with steps towards international law enforcement taken and international law intended to protect the fundamental rights of the individual also developed (ibid.). Though the UN Charter model envisaged cooperation between states, it was still based on the assumption that the international system is made up of sovereign states that have the right and means to decide what happens within their borders (ibid.). Nevertheless, according to

Held, it soon became apparent that these basic assumptions about the character-istics of the international system were too simplistic (ibid.). The distinction between external/international and internal/domestic was not viable for a number of reasons: first, the activities of the growing body of international and transnational organisations cut across the borders of states; second, the increas-ing interconnectedness restricted the amount of political instruments available for states; and finally, an increasing number of issues such as the environment cut across borders and therefore could not be adequately dealt with by the indi-vidual states (ibid.). Held identified five specific areas: world economy, inter-national organisation, regional and global institutions, international law and military alliance, which illustrate that the state is no longer able to fully control its own destiny and that it should not therefore be the only unit of analysis in the examination of international politics and relations (ibid.: 99). Held *et al.* have also identified a range of factors that they argue indicate interconnectedness and enmeshment of nation-states in global and regional processes (Held *et al.* 1999). These include political-legal factors such as diplomatic relations between nation-states and the establishment of customary international law; military factors such as security treaties and peacekeeping missions; economic factors such as international trade and multinational corporations and cultural factors such as worldwide television stations and telecommunications (ibid.).

The increase in these transnational networks has led to more and more decisions and actions being implemented beyond the reach of states and thereby resulting in transnational actors slowly gaining more power at the expense of states (ibid.). This necessarily raises concerns about how these transnational actors can and should be controlled and this is one of the reasons why cosmopol-itan theorists such as David Held argue in favour of the development of a cosmopolitan world order. Held has argued that one of the ways these trans-national powers can be controlled is by means of cosmopolitan democracy, which entails that the structures of democratic states are expanded to regional and global levels (Held 1993, 1995, 1996 and Held *et al.* 1999). Basically the rules and regulations that regulate behaviour within states need to be extended to cover behaviour between states and across the borders of states (ibid.). Held argues that the foundation for the development of such a global order was laid with the adoption of the UN Charter (ibid.). Since then a system of various inter-national laws governing the behaviour of both states and individuals, through granting rights and duties has been developed. Held argues that this system of international laws is well on the way to becoming cosmopolitan law since viola-tions of these laws become less and less legitimate (ibid.). Held claims that it is both likely and desirable that this system of cosmopolitan laws will be further expanded to include not only more regulations but also law enforcement institu-tions (ibid.). Furthermore, Held also contends, that simultaneously with the developments within international law, the support for democracy has also steadily grown to become an overall collective priority. From the local to the global level, institutions are therefore also slowly becoming more and more democratic. Democracy is therefore well on the way to becoming cosmopolitan in the sense that it is seen as the most legitimate form of governance at all levels (ibid.). Held anticipates that these developments will occur in two stages (ibid.). In the short term current international institutions will slowly adapt to these new ideals. Held, for example, foresees the creation of a UN second chamber and a reform of the UNSC to make it more representative and its decision-making capacity more effective. Regarding the enforcement of cosmopolitan law, Held predicts compulsory jurisdiction before the International Court of Justice, the creation of a new international human rights court and the establishment of an effective international military force in the short term. In the longer term, Held pictures that cosmopolitan democratic law will become entrenched into the political, economic and social power domains and that a global parliament will be implemented. He also envisions a global legal system that embraces elements of both criminal and public law and that has its own court, also a shift away from national military forces to regional and global military forces (Held 1993, 1995, 1996). Finally, it has to be underlined that for Held this is not just a normative theory; he argues that this is the way development is going at the moment (Held 1996, 2001).

The critical theorist Andrew Linklater has also argued in favour of alternative structures of governance because he claims that the Westphalian state system is too particularistic and therefore excludes or marginalises various groups of people (Linklater 1998). Rather than basing the structures of governance on sovereignty, nationalism, citizenship and territory such as the present state system does, Linklater argues in favour of more cosmopolitan forms of governance (ibid.). The idea is not necessarily to totally abandon the state system but rather to be open towards the idea that authority, power and loyalty do not need to be monopolised by a single unit of governance (ibid.). It is a matter of moving power and authority away from the state towards more inclusive and wide-ranging communities of dialogue (ibid.). Linklater has identified three tendencies that he argues indicate that the world is already moving towards a cosmopolitan political community. These three tendencies are: growing support for universalising legal, moral and political principles; increasing promotion of a reduction in material inequality; and rising requests for consideration of cultural and ethnic differences (ibid.). Linklater argues that, since states can no longer intercede in the multiple various identities and interests that transnationalism and globalisation have brought along, the state needs to redefine its role in the international system (ibid.). Linklater identifies three alternatives. The first is a pluralist society of states where states accept and respect the presence of other independent political communities. The second is a solidarist society of states that have decided on a common set of moral principles. The third is a post-Westphalian model where states agree to give up on some of their sovereign power in exchange for an institutionalisation of their shared political and moral norms. These three alternatives share the assumption that outsiders such as other states or civil society will be involved in decision-making processes and that therefore the scope of political community will be widened (ibid.). Finally, Linklater promotes what he calls *thin cosmopolitanism*, a system of multiple levels and types of political community that recognises political associations from the local to the supranational level (ibid.).

Mary Kaldor has also focused on the prospects and desirability of developing a cosmopolitan world order (Kaldor 2001). Her point of departure is the international community's response to contemporary violent conflict. She argues that this contemporary conflict is significantly different from the interstate and post-colonial wars prevalent during the Cold War (ibid.). She claims that the main contending issue in many current conflicts is politics of identity (ibid.). Today people mobilise around ethnic, racial or religious identity in movements that aim at taking over state power. These movements are very exclusive, since a precondition for membership is the bearing of the ethnic, racial or religious label that is innate and therefore cannot be acquired. The support of these movements is to a high degree based on fear, which means that the policies these movements use rank from discrimination to genocide, since they induce a culture of fear that is a precondition for further mobilisation. Kaldor points out that the characteristic atrocities of this new kind of warfare are those which international humanitarian law and international human rights law aim to protecting human beings from (ibid.). Kaldor also argues that these conflicts are neither internal nor interstate since they have both internal and external actors (ibid.). The internal actors are necessarily the identity-based movements that fight for control over the authority of the state (ibid.). These internal actors are either directly or indirectly supported by a wide variety of external actors such as diaspora, foreign mercenaries, transnational organisations, etc. (ibid.). Finally, Kaldor argues that contemporary violent conflicts take place in states that are rapidly disintegrating and therefore lose their importance as the conflicts intensify (ibid.). Therefore these violent conflicts demands a response that is radically different from the state-centred approach adopted by the international community to address conflicts during the Cold War (ibid.). Kaldor argues that the response to these new violent conflicts needs to be based on what she calls cosmopolitan politics (ibid.). Her understanding of cosmopolitan politics is broader than its Kantian predecessor since it encompasses: 'a positive political vision embracing tolerance, multiculturalism, civility and to a more legalistic respect for certain overriding universal principles which should guide political communities at various levels including the global level' (Kaldor 2001: 115–116). According to Kaldor an implementation of cosmopolitan politics includes making local, regional and global levels of governance more open, accessible and democratic (ibid.). She recognises that cosmopolitan politics are already on the international political agenda but she argues that, rather than being peripheral, they need to underpin all policies and actions of the international community (ibid.). In addition Kaldor also argues that cosmopolitan politics need to be embedded in a cosmopolitan political consciousness that represents an appreciation of the multiple overlapping global identities and simultaneously a commitment to treating all human beings equally (ibid.). She identifies two sources of cosmopolitan political consciousness: one from above and one from below (ibid.). The one from above is the increasing multitude of international organisations, some of which are developing supranational power structures. The one from below is the increasing multitude of transnational nongovernment organisations (NGOs) concerned with global issues such as the environment, human rights and peace. In line with John Paul Lederach, Kaldor also argues that these two levels form the basis for cosmopolitan political mobilisation (Kaldor 2001, Lederach 1998). In order to properly address contemporary violent conflict, the international community needs to work together with the local population in the areas of conflict, since these people possess knowledge and resources that are valuable assets for the peace process (Kaldor 2001).

Kaldor also addresses the development of cosmopolitan human rights and humanitarian law (ibid.). She contends that a cosmopolitan regime is already in the process of being established, since NGOs and the media are already making the public aware of violations of humane law and since governments and international institutions respond by means of measures ranging from pressure to cautious enforcement (ibid.). Kaldor also argues that especially the establishment of the ICTY, ICTR and ICC are visible steps towards an operative cosmopolitan regime (ibid.).

In conclusion, a cosmopolitan global order where international humane law has been transformed into cosmopolitan humane law and enforced globally would mean fewer international wars and internal violent conflicts because abuse of power and armed aggression can only be contained by means of regulations of warfare and prevention of violations of human rights (Held 2001, Held and McGrew 2000). Humane law is now already not merely an international matter between states but rather a transnational body of laws that applies to all human beings (Held 1995, Held and McGrew 2000). This change was instigated in the aftermath of the Second World War when the Nuremberg trials established that international law must prevail over state law when state law fails to protect fundamental humanitarian values (Held 2000). All individuals now have obligations and rights beyond the ones laid down in their own national authority and judicial systems, leading to rules that restrict the extent of collective and individual action within the associations and organisations of civil society, economy and state, meaning that there are now certain standards for the treatment of all human beings that political regimes cannot legitimately violate (Held 1995, Held and McGrew 2000). Held has also pointed out that international law has expanded rapidly in both scope and depth in recent years and he contends that these developments are the basis of a new emerging framework of cosmopolitan law that changes and regulates the relations between individuals and their political leaders and thereby limits the political power of states (Held and McGrew 2000). States are no longer allowed to deal with their citizens any way they like because these new laws establish fundamental standards that no one should be able to infringe (ibid.).

However, David Held has also acknowledged that there is an inconsistency between the claim of a universal human rights regime and the frequent limited impact of this regime (Held 2001). Fundamentally, the development of a cosmopolitan world order is still ongoing and the enforcement of cosmopolitan humane law is still incoherent and insufficient (Held 1995).

The role of peace missions in the development of a cosmopolitan global order

The first attempts to link peace missions with the development of a cosmopolitan global order have already been made. Pugh has suggested 'releasing peace support operations from the state-centric control system and making them answerable to more transparent, more democratic and accountable multinational institutions' (Pugh 2004: 39). This would 'entail a permanent military volunteer force recruited directly among individuals predisposed to cosmopolitan rather than patriotic values' (ibid.: 53). However, Pugh did not provide any detail as to what roles the permanent military volunteer force would have.

Woodhouse and Ramsbotham have also argued in favour of a cosmopolitan world order and contended that cosmopolitan peacekeeping bridges the critical theorists' call for radical transformation of the current world order with peace support operations' potential to reform (Woodhouse and Ramsbotham 2005: 153). They called for the development of a UN Emergency Peace Service (UNEPS) (Woodhouse and Ramsbotham 2005). According to Woodhouse and Ramsbotham UNEPS 'would include a robust military composition, capable of deterring belligerents and of defending the mission as well as civilians at risk' (ibid.: 153). They also contended that:

> the future roles and potential tasks of the new service should include the provision of: reliable early warning with on-site technical reconnaissance; rapid deployment for preventive action and protection of civilians at risk; and prompt start-up of diverse peace operations, including policing, peace-building and humanitarian assistance.
>
> (ibid.)

Hence:

> the UNEPS force proposal includes a balanced integration of military capacity and a range of civilian expertise, recognizing that from the initiation of a mission at first deployment, there will be a need for prompt disaster relief and humanitarian assistance, as well as conflict resolution teams, medical units, peace-building advisory teams and environmental crisis response teams.
>
> (ibid.)

In addition Anthony McGrew has also argued that, in order to enforce cosmopolitan law, the support of coercive forces at all stages of governance is a necessity and so therefore is the establishment of new supranational military structures (McGrew 2000). In accordance with McGrew, Kaldor has also made a case for the formation of a cosmopolitan law enforcement mechanism that can enforce cosmopolitan law worldwide (Kaldor 2001). Building on the experience of peacekeeping forces, Kaldor argues that cosmopolitan law enforcement needs to be able to perform both typical soldiering tasks, such as maintaining cease-fires and separating belligerents and typical policing tasks, such as capturing war criminals and ensuring freedom of movement (ibid.). Kaldor has contended that an examination of new wars indicates that the enforcement of cosmopolitan norms, that is the enforcement of humane law, is the best way of addressing contemporary violent conflict rather than the deployment of ordinary peacekeeping troops (ibid.). To Kaldor, cosmopolitan law enforcement forces are somewhere in between policing and soldiering and she contends that cosmopolitan law enforcement necessitates a reformulation of the three traditional basic peacekeeping principles of consent, impartiality and use of force (ibid.). Regarding consent, Kaldor argues that unqualified consent is impossible and she points out that if, for example, the delivery of humanitarian aid was always based on full consent, then peacekeeping troops would not be needed to protect the convoys since they would not be under threat (ibid.). She also argues that it is impossible to gain consent from both the local population and all the warring parties (ibid.). The consent from the local population depends upon the performance of the international troops (ibid.). If the international troops are not able to protect the local population and if they are not able to arrest perceived war criminals, they lose the consent of the local population (ibid.). If the international troops on the other hand use force against the warring parties who threaten the local population, they lose the consent of the warring parties (ibid.). Kaldor argues that what is important for the international troops is the consent of the local population. Consent from the warring parties at both the operational and tactical level is desirable but only as long as it does not compromise the mission. Regarding impartiality, Kaldor emphasises the importance of distinguishing between neutrality and impartiality (ibid.). She argues that cosmopolitan law enforcement requires troops to act impartial, which means not to discriminate on the basis of ethnicity, religion, etc. but that they should not be neutral, since that would entail staying passive towards individuals who violate cosmopolitan law (Kaldor 2001).

Hence, the debate on how peace missions can support the development of an alternative cosmopolitan world order has already been initiated though it is still in its infancy. Several potential roles for peace missions have already been suggested but these are yet to be explored and examined in detail. In line with Kaldor's suggestion, this book will contribute to this debate by exploring and examining the role of peace missions in detaining indicted war criminals, which is an important part of the enforcement of cosmopolitan humane law as part of the development of a cosmopolitan global order.

2   Peace missions and transitional justice

Introduction

Though millions of civilians have lost their lives as a consequence of violent conflicts throughout human history, it is only recently that the question of how societies recovering from conflict should address mass atrocities committed during the
conflict has entered the agendas of researchers as well as politicians. Especially
since the establishment of the Truth and Reconciliation Commission in South
Africa and the International Criminal Tribunal for the Former Yugoslavia in the
beginning of the 1990s, different ways of obtaining transitional justice have been
extensively debated. The debate has particularly focused on whether restorative
justice through a truth and reconciliation commission or whether retributive justice
by means of a criminal tribunal is the most preferable solution, though other
means such as lustrations[3] or victims compensation[4] have also been discussed.
This chapter provides a brief overview of this debate and argues that, if possible, it
is important to hold at least the individuals responsible for the worst atrocities
accountable for their deeds in a criminal trial procedure. However, this does not
exclude the possibility of less serious atrocities being dealt with through a truth
and reconciliation process. In states recovering from violent conflict, the national
judicial system is often not able or willing to hold individuals who have committed atrocities during the violent conflict accountable. Although the use of local
traditional justice mechanisms should not be ruled out, the chapter argues that
these have some important weaknesses. Therefore international criminal tribunals
are a necessary alternative in cases where the national system is either unable or
unwilling to hold individuals accountable. Hence, the chapter briefly examines the
history of international criminal tribunals and the obstacles that they have faced.
One of the most serious problems recently encountered is that of arresting and
detaining indicted war criminals because local authorities have been either unwilling or unable to carry out the tribunals' arrest orders. This is a problem that the
new International Criminal Court has also already faced and is very likely to
encounter again in the future. Hence, the chapter briefly discusses possible
alternatives to reliance on local authorities in this regard and suggests that one
viable solution is to enable international peace missions to detain indicted war
criminals in their areas of deployment.

Restorative or retributive justice?

Especially during the last decade the question as to how societies should come to terms with mass atrocities committed during war or internal violent conflict has been extensively debated. The academic contributors to the debate generally agree that some form of transitional justice is a precondition for sustainable peace (See for example Brito 2001, Huyse 1995, Kaye 1997, Mani 1998, McAdams 1997, Teitel 2001). Some authors have argued that transitional justice is a prerequisite because it helps restore the rule of law while others have underlined that transitional justice promotes the development and upholding of new democratic states and helps prevent further similar atrocities (ibid.). In contrast, there is less agreement on what kind of transitional justice policy states recovering from mass atrocities should implement. The debate has particularly focused on whether perpetrators should be put on trial and thereby exposed to retributive justice or whether they should participate in a restorative justice process in the form of a truth and reconciliation commission.

Among the most prominent supporters of truth commissions are co-founder of the International Centre for Transitional Justice, Priscilla Hayner, Professor of Law at Harvard Law School, Martha Minow and Archbishop Desmond Tutu (Hayner 1994, 2001, Minow 1998, Tutu 1999, 2000). Based on a comparison of twenty truth commissions from around the world, Priscilla Hayner has argued that, since neither national nor international courts can deal with the extensive demands for accountability after mass atrocities and since they cannot address the needs for acknowledgement, reform and reparation, truth and reconciliation commissions should be recommended (Hayner 1994, 2001). Martha Minow has claimed that trials have proven too frail and insufficient and that compensation is not enough to heal victims either (Minow 1998). Instead she promoted the idea of restorative justice and argued in favour of the kind of public acknowledgement of the utter wrongness of the atrocities that truth commissions can provide (ibid.). Desmond Tutu has also defended the South African Truth and Reconciliation Commission's amnesty in exchange of truth principle and argued that the relatively peaceful transition to democracy in South Africa would not have taken place if bringing perpetrators to retributive justice had been a precondition for the transition (Tutu 1999). Tutu also contended that the Commission was able to establish the truth in cases where the courts had failed to do so and that the commissioners and the truth-telling process helped victims come to terms with what had happened to them (ibid.). Theissen has also contended that a truth commission can

> break the silence about past human-rights violations, and encourage people to speak out about past atrocities, since the risk of repression decreases as more people go public; expose past atrocities from a victim perspective, turn the public against the perpetrators and thus decrease their credibility and power in society [and] provide a comprehensive and well-written

account of past human-rights abuses, and encourage public debate as to how peaceful co-existence can be secured in the future.

(Theissen 2003: 6)

Among the fiercest defenders of trials are Professor Emeritus of Political Science at the University of Nevada, Richard Lewis Siegel and Professor of Law at Washington College of Law, American University in Washington, Diane Orentlicher (Orentlicher 1995, Siegel 1998). Siegel has rejected the arguments against trials and contended that, in addition to securing accountability, a trial process can provide invaluable experience in the building and maintenance of both national and international judicial institutions (Siegel 1998). He has also pointed out that the judicial systems in transitional states are weak because the former regime made them weak and it would be inappropriate for the former regimes to benefit from this (ibid.). Diane Orentlicher has also argued that prosecution of perpetrators is crucial if a society is to recover from internal violent conflict since failure to do so will promote a culture of impunity and fail to prevent future repression (Orentlicher 1995). Theissen has also evaluated the use of trials as a means of transitional justice policy and argued that trials:

> may break the culture of impunity, prevent future human-rights abuses and increase awareness of human-rights and humanitarian law; send a clear message that past atrocities are not legitimate (as is often claimed by the relevant parties to the conflict) but rather criminal acts; may provide victims with a certain satisfaction and prevent them from taking the law into their own hands and individualise accountability and guilt.

(Theissen 2003: 3)

Akhavan and Steadman have also argued that, if suspected war criminals are not removed from their powerful positions and held accountable, they could constitute a significant threat to the peace-building process (Akhavan 2001, Steadman 1997).

The practical experience from around the world adds to the uncertainty as to how societies recovering from internal violent conflict best confront past human rights violations. In contrast to the general support for the need to somehow deal with past human rights violations in the academic literature amnesty still enjoys support in the international political sphere. In some places, such as Cambodia, Chile and South Africa, amnesty has been seen as a precondition for the participation in the peace process of the parties to the violent conflict (Amnesty International 1996, Neou and Gallup 1997, Slovo 2002). In other cases such as Argentina and Afghanistan, amnesty has served to consolidate a fragile peace in the aftermath of violent conflict (Amnesty International 2003a, BBC 20 February 2007, Nino 1995). In other cases trials and truth-seeking mechanisms have been implemented with very mixed results. Some trial processes, such as the International Criminal Tribunal for the Former Yugoslavia (ICTY) and the Special Court for Sierra Leone (SC-SL) and truth-seeking processes such as the

Chilean Truth Commission and the South African Truth and Reconciliation Commission have at least partly been hailed as successes and others, such as the truth commissions in for example Uganda and Ecuador, have been assessed as failures (Barsalou 2005, Hayner 1994, 2001, Kritz 1995). Hence, experience from around the world offers no definite answers as to whether truth commissions, criminal tribunals or even a third alternative is the best way of addressing mass atrocities committed during violent conflict. In addition, it is also widely acknowledged that transitional justice policies need to be closely adapted to the needs of the people and the society in question. Furthermore, even if the best transitional justice policy was identified, it might not be possible to implement it in a given society due especially to political constraints limiting possible options. As Mani has pointed out, transitional justice is a politicised matter and consequently, due consideration of the political context needs to be undertaken, with the chosen methods carefully adapted to the specific situation (Mani 1998). Harris and Reilley have also discussed under which circumstances trials should be preferred and under which they should be avoided (Harris and Reilley 1998). In addition Brito has also shown how institutional, political and social constraints and the international community's perceptions of the different policy options influence the policy a transitional regime chooses (Brito 2001). Finally, Siegel has also contended that the decision-makers should base their choice of policy on an assessment of the probability of provoking the old elite to attempt to regain power and the probability of positively influencing national reconciliation, the rule of law and democracy (Siegel 1998).

However, despite the disagreement among academics debating transitional justice and the mixed results in practice, there are at least two strong arguments supporting the criminal prosecution of the individuals responsible for the worst atrocities. First, parts of humane law demand criminal accountability for certain violations of the laws such as genocide and hence these atrocities need to be prosecuted. Second, it is noteworthy that even the most successful truth commissions such as the ones in Chile, Argentina and South Africa have not been able to silence the victims' demand for retributive justice (Human Rights Watch 2006a, 2006b, Nullis 2006). Hence, though the choice of transitional justice policy is a politicised matter, which means that trials are not always possible and that in those cases alternative mechanisms such as truth commissions should be used to address past gross violations of human rights, it still seems that, if trials of at least the most culpable individuals can be successfully implemented, then they should be initiated.

Which judicial institution should hold individuals accountable for mass atrocities committed during violent conflict?

The next contentious question is then *where* individuals who have committed mass atrocities during violent conflict should be held accountable for their deeds. Normally when a crime has been committed, the alleged criminal is put on trial in the local or national court. However, as further addressed in the next chapter, the national judicial system in post-conflict states has often totally broken down and is therefore unable to hold individuals accountable. In some states, such as Mozambique and Rwanda, local traditional justice systems have been used to bring individuals to justice and, though this solution needs to be taken into consideration, it also presents some serious drawbacks. First, local traditional justice systems might reflect the new post-conflict power structure dominated by groups that were heavily involved in the violent conflict rather than the pre-violent conflict traditional power structure (Theissen 2003). Local traditional justice systems might also not operate in accordance with human rights standards and not adequately include women and young people because they are based on traditional patriarchal structures (ibid.). There might also not be any mechanisms to supervise the local traditional justice systems and use of such systems might also further alienate the already weak formal judicial system, making it more difficult to build a strong national judicial system (ibid.).

Hence, if individuals are to be held accountable and the national judicial system is not able to cope with these cases, some kind of external involvement is probably necessary.

The development of international criminal prosecution

Already after the First World War, when international humane treaty law was still in its infancy, attempts were made to prosecute violators of international humanitarian treaty law. On the one hand, these trials pointed towards the possibility of international prosecution of violators of international humane treaty law in cases where the national judicial systems were either unwilling or unable to prosecute. On the other hand, the trials also revealed the vast amount of obstacles such trials encounter in their attempt to hold individuals accountable for such violations. In fact these early trials were so flawed that it can be argued that it was not until the end of the Second World War and the establishment of the Nuremberg and Tokyo Trials that the foundation for international prosecution of violators of international humane treaty law was laid.

During the final years of the war, while fierce fighting was still occurring in large parts of Europe and Asia, the dominant states of Britain, the US and Russia decided that, if they were to win the war, the worst criminals from the defeated states Germany and Japan should be held accountable for their deeds. Based on the negative experience from the First World War, where it had largely been left to the national judicial systems of the defeated states to hold violators accountable for their crimes and where these systems had often failed miserably, the victorious powers opted to make the prosecution process international. Consequently statutes based on what was considered to be international law were drafted and international military tribunals were set up in Nuremberg and Tokyo. The Nuremberg Tribunal had subject matter jurisdiction over crimes against peace, war crimes and crimes against humanity and lasted about a year from November 1945 to October 1946. The Tokyo Tribunal had subject jurisdiction over crimes against peace, crimes against humanity and war crimes and was operated from May 1946 to November 1948.

Hence, with these trials, these crimes became subject to prosecution by an international judicial mechanism operating in cases where the national system proved either unwilling or unable to prosecute and thus the foundation for international criminal law was laid. However, as had been the case with the trials after the First World War, the Nuremberg and Tokyo Trials also encountered various serious obstacles. The most discouraging feature of the Nuremberg and Tokyo Trials was undoubtedly that they only prosecuted individuals from the defeated states, which prompted grave questions as to whether they represented international prosecution of violations of international humane law or merely victors' justice. The interpretation of the trials as not being an example of a nascent international community committed to prosecute violators of international humane treaty law in cases where the states involved failed to do so was further supported by the international community's failure to follow up on the experiences of the Nuremberg and Tokyo Trials.

In the years following the end of the Second World War, a lot of treaties were added to international humane treaty law. States routinely signed and ratified such treaties, thereby promising to attempt to uphold some basic humanitarian and human rights standards. Unfortunately, many states were not that eager to implement and enforce all these various treaties. Consequently gross violations of international humane law still took place every day in many places around the world. Since national judicial systems were either unable or unwilling to prosecute the violators, the vast majority were never brought to justice, which meant that accountability was the exception rather than the rule. At the same time states were not ready to relinquish responsibility for enforcement of the treaties to a supranational body outside their national domain and control. Soon after the final verdicts at Nuremberg and Tokyo, an international congress in Paris called for the adoption of an international criminal code that would prohibit crimes against humanity and for the establishment of an international criminal court. Separately, certain UN member states asked the International Law Commission to investigate the prospect of setting up a permanent international criminal tribunal. During the years 1949–1954 the International Law Commission drafted statutes for such a court but opposition from powerful parties on both sides of the Cold War hindered progress towards its actual establishment. Disagreement on the content of an international code of crimes and especially on the definition of crimes of aggression led the UN General Assembly to at least temporarily abandon the idea. It was another twenty years before the UN General Assembly finally agreed on a shared definition of aggression and it was not until 1981 that the Assembly asked the International Law Commission to readdress the problem of establishing a common code of crimes.

The reasons for the states' failure to commit to the idea of a permanent international criminal court responsible for prosecuting violators of international humane law from the end of the Second World War to the end of the Cold War have been widely debated. Benjamin Ferencz has analysed the debates and international politics during this period and concluded that the time was not yet ripe for the project, due to factors such as the tense relationship between the two major powers, the US and the Soviet Union (Ferencz 1980). In addition Michael Scharf has argued that there are three main reasons why agreement could not be reached during the Cold War period (Scharf 1997). First, there had been no war with an obvious winner as was the case with the Second World War. Second, prosecution on the grounds of aggressive warfare by an international criminal court was seen as a threat to state's vital national sovereignty. Finally, the various drafts of a statute for an international criminal court were so ambitious that most of the states quickly abandoned the idea completely (ibid.).

In 1989 the UN General Assembly, at the request of Trinidad and Tobago, asked the International Law Commission to recommence the development of an international criminal court. While the commission was still drafting a possible statute for the court the UNSC established two ad hoc criminal tribunals, one for the Former Yugoslavia in 1993 and one for Rwanda in 1995. The International Criminal Tribunal for the Former Yugoslavia (ICTY) was set up as a response to the threat to international peace and security that the serious violations of international criminal law committed in the former Yugoslavia constituted. UNSC resolution 827 (1993) declared the objectives of the ICTY to be: to bring to justice persons allegedly responsible for violations of international humanitarian law; to render justice to the victims; to deter future crimes and to contribute to the restoration of peace by promoting reconciliation in the former Yugoslavia. The ICTY's territorial jurisdiction covers the territory of the former Yugoslavia and its temporal jurisdiction covers crimes committed from 1991 until the UNSC decides that peace has been restored. The subject jurisdiction of the ICTY covers four clusters of international crimes namely: grave breaches of the Geneva Conventions; violations of the laws or customs of war; genocide; and crimes against humanity. Up until September 2007, the ICTY has indicted 161 persons (ICTY 28 September 2007).[5] Twenty-six of the accused are currently on trial, twelve others are at the pre-trial stage and a further seven individuals are being dealt with in the Appeals Chamber (ibid.). Fifty-two individuals have been sentenced and thirty-six have either been withdrawn or have died (ibid.). Four of the accused, namely Goran Hadžić, Radovan Karadžić, Ratko Mladić and Stojan Župljanin are currently at large (ibid.).

The UNSC established the International Criminal Tribunal for Rwanda (ICTR) in response to the 1994 genocide in Rwanda that left approximately 800,000 people dead. The ICTR has subject jurisdiction over genocide, crimes against humanity and violations of Article 3 common to the Geneva Conventions and their Additional Protocol II. The ICTR's territorial jurisdiction covers the territory of Rwanda and its neighbouring states in cases where the perpetrator is Rwandan. If the perpetrator is not Rwandan, the tribunal only has territorial jurisdiction over Rwanda. The tribunal's temporal jurisdiction covers the year 1994. As of September 2007, the ICTR had handed down twenty-seven judgments involving thirty-three of the accused, with eleven trials still in progress, dealing with a further twenty-seven accused (ICTR 2007). Nine detainees were awaiting trial and eighteen indicted war criminals were still at large (ibid.).

Several observers of the prosecution of international criminal law have proposed explanations as to why states began to see humanitarianism, human rights and the prosecution of international criminal law as matters of not only national but also international interest and concern. Peskin and Boduzynski have argued that:

> In the 1980s and the early 1990s efforts by newly democratizing countries to seek accountability for atrocities committed by their authoritarian predecessors played a key role in the development of the global human rights movement and in turn are important background factors in the establishment of the ICTY and ICTR.
>
> (Peskin and Boduzynski 2003: 1121)

In addition John Hagan has pointed out that:

> In the early 1990s nearly fifty years after Nuremberg, the geopolitics of international criminal law changed. The catalysts were the demise of the Soviet Union and the end of the cold war. A new public awareness also resulted from televised and eyewitness accounts of atrocities in the Balkans and later in Rwanda. The tacit acceptance of human rights violations of both sides of the cold war divide became simultaneously more visible and less tolerable.
>
> (Hagan 2003: 29)

Other authors such as Aleksandar Fatic have more cynically argued that setting up international criminal tribunals was far cheaper than initiating a proper military operation aimed at ending the violence (Fatic 2000). Accordingly, the establishment of the tribunals did not necessarily signify greater commitment to the international prosecution of violations of international humane law but rather represented a tolerable compromise, that would relatively cheaply give the impression that the international community was committed to end violent conflicts that included genocide and ethnic cleansing.

In July 2002 the temporary international criminal tribunals were joined by the International Criminal Court (ICC), based on the Rome Statute from 1998. In Rome 160 states, thirty-three intergovernmental organisations and 236 nongovernmental organisations had participated in meetings and, after long and extensive negotiations, 120 states had voted in favour of the Statute, seven against and twenty-one abstained. After sixty states had ratified the Rome Statute the ICC began its operations. The ICC's temporal jurisdiction covers crimes committed after the Rome Statute entered into force. The ICC has subject jurisdiction over genocide, war crimes, crimes against humanity and crimes of aggression once the state parties to the ICC have agreed on a definition of crimes of aggression. However, due to certain limitations in its jurisdiction, the inclusion of all these crimes in its subject jurisdiction does not mean that the ICC can hold all individuals accountable for committing these crimes. First, though substantive parts of international humanitarian treaty law (such as the four Geneva Conventions and their Additional Protocols) and of international human rights treaty law (such as the conventions against genocide and torture) have been included in the subject jurisdiction of the ICC, important parts of international humane law have also been left out. Second, the temporal jurisdiction limits the ICC to only dealing with crimes committed after the ICC Statute entered into force, that is after July 2002. Third, regarding the territorial aspects of jurisdiction, unless the UNSC has referred the case to the prosecutor of the ICC, the ICC only has jurisdiction over violations within its subject jurisdiction in cases where the perpetrator is a national of a state party or when the crime was committed on the territory of a state party. Fourth, the UNSC can halt the investigation and prosecution of a case for a year if it deems that the judicial process is a threat to international peace and security under Chapter VII of the UN Charter. An order to halt can be repeated as long as the UNSC considers the situation to represent such a threat. Fifth, the ICC, unlike the ICTY and the ICTR, can only handle cases that cannot be dealt with in the national judicial systems. Sixth, the ICC is based on a statute and not a UN Chapter VII decision, which means that only states that have signed and ratified the Statute are bound by it. If the ICC had been based upon a UN Chapter VII decision such as is the case with the ICTY and ICTR, then all states, regardless of whether they had signed and ratified the Rome Statute, would have been bound by it. This is especially problematic since important states such as China, Russia and the US have not ratified the Statute and are therefore not bound by it.

In February 2003 the Assembly of State Parties to the Rome Statute elected the first eighteen judges[6] to the serve the ICC after a long and thorough selection procedure. The judges were sworn in a month later. In April 2003 the Argentinean Luis Moreno Ocampo, well known for his role as deputy prosecutor in the trials of Argentina's former military junta, was elected prosecutor of the ICC. The prosecutor has so far indicted eight suspected war criminals from Sudan, the Congo and Uganda.[7]

In addition to the international criminal tribunals, in recent years these have been joined by part-international and national criminal tribunals established in Sierra Leone,[8] East Timor[9] and Cambodia.[10]

Obstacles to holding individuals accountable for atrocities committed during the violent conflict in international criminal tribunals

All the international criminal tribunals have encountered numerous serious obstacles in their attempts to hold individuals accountable for atrocities committed during wars or internal violent conflicts. The Nuremberg and Tokyo Tribunals and the ICTY suffered from a lack of adequately developed international criminal treaty law and international criminal legal and procedural experience (see

Askin 2003, Maogoto 2004, Ratner and Abrams 2001). From the very beginning limitations on jurisdiction have also been problematic for the tribunals. In particular the personal jurisdiction of the Nuremberg and Tokyo trials and the temporal jurisdiction of the ICTR and the ICC have either created or are still creating serious obstacles to the tribunals' success in ensuring transitional justice (see Bald 2002, Beigbeder 1999, Bourgon 2002, Chris 1997, Chuter 2003, Haines 2003, Juma 2002, Maogoto 2004, Penrose 1999, Strain and Keyes 2003, Ward 2003). From the very beginning all the way up to the latest attempts to prosecute individuals factors such as a lack of support, evidence, witness testimony and proper investigation have also hindered prosecutors' efforts to build cases against the violators of international criminal law (see Akhavan 2001, Askin 2003, Baroni 2000, Bass 2000, Beigbeder 1999, Chuter 2003, Cogan 2000, Fatic 2000, Forsythe 1996, Gray 2003, Hagan 2003, Haines 2003, International Crisis Group 2003a, 2003b, Juma 2002, Kamatali 2003, Maogoto 2004, McCormack 1997, Miskowiak 2000, Nizich 2001, Penrose 1999, Robertson 2000, Schabas 2001, Ward 2003). The various international criminal tribunals have also encountered such problems as witnesses who are unwilling to testify, the presence of unqualified and/or inexperienced staff, mismanagement by judges and even cases where the whole trial process was accused of being partial (see Beigbeder 1999, Chuter 2003, Hagan 2003, International Crisis Group 2003a, Juma 2002, Kamatali 2003, Maogoto 2004, McCormack 1997, Miraldi 2003, Penrose 1999, Robertson 2000, Schocken 2002, Strain and Keyes 2003, Udombana 2003). Yet another area where difficulties have been encountered is in securing the rights of the defendants. In some of the tribunals the defendant has had no right to appeal; there has been no provision on double jeopardy; unqualified and inexperienced defence lawyers have represented the defendants and the tribunals have relied on anonymous witnesses and hearsay (see Beigbeder 1999, Chuter 2003, Human Rights Watch 2004, Maogoto 2004, Penrose 1999, Petrovic 1998, Robertson 2000, Scharf 1997, Schvey 2003, Strain and Keyes 2003). Furthermore, the tribunals have also experienced a wide variety of other problems. The most noteworthy of these have been a lack of adequate funding, securing the cooperation of states, the location and working languages of some of the tribunals and inconsistent sentencing (see Akhavan 2001, Askin 2003, Beigbeder 1999, Blakesley 1997, Chuter 2003, Haines 2003, International Crisis Group 2003a, 2003b, McDonald 2002, Nizich 2001, Penrose 1999, Petrovic 1998, Ratner and Abrams 2001, Schocken 2002, Schvey 2003, Udombana 2003). Finally, and most importantly in this context, some tribunals have also encountered serious problems regarding the arrest of indicted individuals because states have been unwilling to hand these individuals over (see Askin 2003, Baroni 2000, Bass 2000, Beigbeder 1999, Hagan 2003, Kolodkin 1996, Maogoto 2004, Nizich 2001, Penrose 1999, Peskin and Boduzynski 2003, Petrovic 1998, Ratner and Abrams 2001, Robertson 2000, Schvey 2003).

The problem of detaining and arresting indicted war criminals

All of the recent international or partly international criminal tribunals have encountered difficulties in securing the detention and arrest of the indicted individuals. The Special Court for Sierra Leone during the period 2003–2006 was prevented from bringing the former President of Liberia Charles Taylor to trial because he managed to flee to Nigeria and the Nigerian authorities refused to hand him over. Furthermore, the success of the part-national, part-international criminal tribunal in East Timor was severely hampered by Indonesia's refusal to hand over more than 300 individuals indicted by the tribunal (Reiger and Wierda 2006). Also the ICTR is still missing fourteen individuals wanted for prosecution for atrocities committed during the Rwandan genocide (President of the ICTR 2007). The failure to detain and arrest indicted war criminals has also seriously threatened the success of the ICTY. The two most notorious alleged war criminals from the conflict in Bosnia-Herzegovina, Ratko Mladić and Radovan Karadžić are still at large twelve years after being indicted. Finally, the ICC has come up against national authorities that are reluctant to hand over indicted war criminals. In, for example, the case of Sudan, the ICC has indicted two individuals whom the Sudanese authorities refuse to arrest and transfer to the court.

Alternative ways of securing detention and arrest

Several alternatives to reliance on national authorities for detention have already been suggested and discussed. Among the more radical suggestions is that from Beverly Izes, the research editor of the *Columbia Journal of Law and Social Problems*, namely, a proposal to allow state-sanctioned abduction of indicted war criminals; also the American Major Christopher Supernor's suggestion of legalising international bounty hunters to make arrests (Izes 1997, Supernor 2001). The proposition for state-sanctioned abduction has already been dismissed on the grounds that it violates both the UN Charter and international customary law (Supernor 2001). Though international bounty hunters have apparently already been involved in apprehending indicted war criminals Dragan Nikolic and Stevan Todorovic, this idea has also been rejected on the grounds of questionable legality, risk of legal liability and illegitimacy in view of the aims of international justice (Kalinauskas 2002).

International economic sanctions and inducements aiming to convince states to hand over indicted war criminals have also been suggested and tried out, particularly in the case of the ICTY (United States Institute of Peace 1997). Although there is disagreement as to whether the prospects of economic assistance programmes or the threat of withholding financial aid are the most effective ways of persuading states to surrender indicted war criminals, experience from especially the ICTY indicates that both these means have only a limited effect (Kalinauskas 2002, Meernik 2003). Political and diplomatic sanctions and inducements, such as the EU making talks of Serbian membership of the EU conditional on the arrest and transfer of indicted war criminals have also proved to be inadequate to secure full state cooperation in handovers (Associated Press 19 September 2007). Though Serbia has recently handed over the indicted war criminal Zdravko Tolimir, it is still accused of harbouring indicted war criminals Goran Hadžić, Stojan Župljanin and Ratko Mladić (ibid.). Finally, it has also been suggested that international peace missions deployed in areas where indicted war criminals are at large should be authorised to detain them (Kalin-auskas 2002, United States Institute of Peace 1997). Building on the experience of the ICTY and the peace missions in the former Yugoslavia, which have managed to detain about thirty of the indicted whom the local authorities have been unwilling or unable to arrest, this seems to represent a potentially viable solution to the problem. Hence, this book will further explore this option.

Part II

UN peace missions' involvement in securing justice and transitional justice

3 UN peace missions, peace-building and justice

Introduction

Since the end of the Cold War UN peace missions have become increasingly involved in helping states recovering from internal violent conflict establish the rule of law in order to obtain long-term peace. Peace missions have been involved in two sets of activities aimed at securing accountability for crimes committed after the signing of the peace agreement and ensuring accountability for atrocities committed during the violent conflict. This chapter focuses on the incorporation of activities aimed at securing accountability for crimes committed after the signing of the peace agreement and the deployment of the peace mission, in the UN's approach to peace-building. It examines these activities, assesses their results and examines why the missions have failed or succeeded in building structures and institutions that can help ensure accountability for such crimes. Finally, it also examines recent UN reports and debates in order to establish their views on the role of UN peace missions in this regard.

The immediate aftermath of the Cold War: getting involved

Though civilian police were already introduced in peace missions in the Congo (ONUC) and Cyprus (UNFICYP) in the 1960s and continued to assist military observers monitoring local police forces up until the end of the Cold War, it was not until the late 1980s that UN peace missions became considerably involved in securing accountability for crimes committed in the post-conflict era (Peace-keeping Best Practices Unit 2003: 84).

The first of these missions, the United Nations Transition Assistance Group (UNTAG), was deployed in Namibia from April 1989–March 1990 after decades of UN involvement in negotiating peace between the belligerent parties in order to facilitate Namibia's independence in accordance with UNSC resolution 632 (1989). UNTAG's peacekeepers were required to monitor the disarmament, demobilisation and reintegration (DDR) process and to help revoke discriminatory laws and secure the release of detainees and prisoners (DPKO, Namibia – UNTAG: Background). UNTAG also included an international civilian police force that was authorised to monitor the national police and hence, these international officers accompanied local police on patrol and observed how investigations were carried out (ibid.). The responsibility for enforcing the rule of law remained with the local police as the international officers had no powers of arrest but they were allowed to patrol on their own when the national police was either unable or unwilling to do so (ibid.).

In 1991 the United Nations Angola Verification Mission (UNAVEM) II took over from UNAVEM I, which had been deployed in 1988 after a civil war between the Angolan government and União Nacional para a Independência Total de Angola (UNITA) in order to verify the withdrawal of Cuban troops from Angola. When the first mission had fulfilled its mandate, it was replaced by UNAVEM II, requested to monitor the cease-fire through UNSC resolution 696 (1991). Together with members of UNITA and Angolan government forces, UNAVEM police observers were also supposed to monitor police activities and facilities and investigate possible political rights violations (DPKO Angola – UNAVEM II: Background).

A mixed beginning

The UN experienced mixed results from its first attempts to help ensure accountability for crimes committed in the post-conflict phase. UNTAG's international civilian police officers set up police stations and monitored the work of the local police and thereby helped create an environment suitable for the conduct of elections and maintainable without the deployment of further UN peace missions (Sismanidis 1997). However, the impact on long-term Namibian policing standards was questionable (ibid.). In Angola UNAVEM II did not have much success in disarming and demobilising the combatants and, though joint national and international teams monitoring the national police were set up, they did not have much impact (DPKO Angola – UNAVEM II: Background, Jett 1999).

Explaining the initial results

The UNTAG mission in Namibia constituted an important step towards the development of a comprehensive UN approach to peace-building with many new features, signalling a more active role for UN peace missions and an increase in personnel, including 1,500 international civilian police officers (Sismanidis 1997). However, though generally considered a success, it also suffered from being the first mission with a significantly expanded mandate (Broer and Emery 1998, DPKO Namibia – UNTAG: Background). The large number of international civilian police officers needed to carry out UNTAG's mandate meant that resources had to be drawn from many different states, which resulted in the deployment of a force with very diverse training standards and varied experience in policing in international peace operations (Broer and Emery 1998, Sismanidis 1997). The mission also had logistical problems resulting, for example, in officers having to borrow vehicles from their national Namibian colleagues (Sismanidis 1997). Finally UNTAG's international police officers were also only mandated to monitor the local police and therefore they had a limited influence on the establishment of a functional and fair national police force.

Spurred on by the relatively successful mission in Namibia, the UN decided that their peace missions in Angola did not need to be as extensive, costly and resource-demanding (Paulo 2004). Hence, though the violent conflict had been much more brutal and the parties to the Angolan conflict were significantly more hostile and reluctant to take part in the peace process, UNAVEM II was a relatively small mission with considerably fewer police observers, a fact which seriously limited its actions (ibid.). In addition, UNAVEM II had no powers to force the parties to comply with agreements, which meant that, when the two parties to the conflict refused to participate in the joint monitoring of the national police, there was very little the mission could do about it (DPKO Angola – UNAVEM II: Background, Jett 1999).

UN reports: An Agenda for Peace

In light of the gradually expanding role of UN peace missions and the new possibilities that the end of the Cold War stand-off between the US and the Soviet Union and their respective allies had brought to the UNSC, the UNSG was asked to develop a report on how the UN could strengthen its preventive diplomacy, peacemaking and peacekeeping at a UNSC meeting in 1992 (Boutrous-Ghali 1992: paragraph 1). The report, named *An Agenda for Peace*, became the first influential UN report on post-conflict peace-building. It contended that a range of actions, such as restoring order, disarming former militants and advising and training security personnel, aimed at supporting the structures that underpin peace were needed if peace operations were to be successful (Boutrous-Ghali 1992: paragraph 55). In addition it also emphasised the importance of establishing the rule of law and protecting human rights for the development of peace (Boutrous-Ghali 1992: paragraph 55 and 59).

Summing up

The UN's first post-Cold War experiences in helping states secure accountability for crimes committed in the post-conflict era raised more questions than answers. The mission in Namibia showed that UN peace missions could help national police forces uphold law and order during elections and thereby help a country move towards sustainable peace. In contrast the mission in Angola showed that, without the cooperation of the parties to the conflict and a strong mandate backed by adequate resources, UN personnel could do very little to stop the violence and help build sustainable peace. Therefore it was still unsure what role the UN should and would be willing to play in the whole process.

The new, but yet mostly unexplored opportunities, the initial mixed results on the ground and the uncertainty about the most suitable role of UN peace missions were evident in the UNSG's *Agenda for Peace*. The report hinted that UN operations intending to help establish long-term peace needed to include activities such as disarming former combatants, protecting human rights and establishing the rule of law. However, the report was still very vague about what actions peace operations should carry out in order to ensure accountability for crimes committed in the post-conflict period.

The troubled years: failures and disillusions

While the United Nations Secretary General (UNSG) was preparing his *Agenda for Peace* two more UN peace missions, United Nations Protection Force (UNPROFOR) in the former Yugoslavia and United Nations Transitional Administration in Cambodia (UNTAC) were launched. UNPROFOR was deployed while the violent conflict in the Former Yugoslavia was still ongoing and hence it is outside the focus of this chapter. During the next three years a further five UN peace missions, with elements aimed at ensuring accountability for crimes committed in the post-conflict period, were deployed. These missions were: United Nations Operation in Mozambique (ONUMOZ), United Nations Operation in Somalia (UNOSOM) II, United Nations Assistance Mission for Rwanda (UNAMIR), United Nations Mission in Haiti (UNMIH) and United Nations Observer Mission in Liberia (UNOMIL). In addition two missions, UNAVEM II and the United Nations Observer Mission in El Salvador (ONUSAL), which like UNPROFOR had been deployed while the violent conflict was still ongoing, continued.

In Angola UNAVEM II continued to support the disarming and demobilisation process and a small group of international police officers, attempting to monitor the neutrality of the local police, also became involved in patrolling areas and conducting its own investigations (DPKO Angola – UNAVEM II: Background).

In El Salvador ONUSAL had been deployed since May 1991 while peace negotiations were still ongoing. Initially ONUSAL focused on human rights including observing, promoting, informing and educating about human rights, investigating allegations of human rights violations, monitoring actions taken to ensure accountability, recommending how these violations could be stopped and reporting to the UNSG (DPKO El Salvador – ONUSAL: Background, DPKO El Salvador – ONUSAL: Mandate). After the signing of the peace agreement UNSC resolution 729 (1992) expanded ONUSAL's mandate to include monitoring how the newly formed National Civil Police maintained public order and hence, international police officers were added to ONUSAL (DPKO El Salvador – ONUSAL: Background). They helped establish a new police academy, evaluated and supported the new national police force and helped locate illegal arms, while international military personnel monitored the disarmament and demobilisation process (ibid.). ONUSAL's human rights unit also actively supported national institutions in charge of protecting human rights and administrating justice through for example training judges and military personnel, following investigations into sensitive human rights violations and helping the government implement the changes that the Commission on the Truth[11] had recommended (ibid.).

At the same time the UN through UNSC resolution 745 (1992) also deployed UNTAC in order to help ensure the implementation of the Cambodian peace agreement that had been signed in Paris in 1991. One of the largest peace missions ever deployed, UNTAC carried out a wide range of tasks. UNTAC's military unit confirmed compliance with and violations of DDR agreements and its human rights unit taught human rights to a wide range of people, also monitoring and investigating allegations of violations of human rights (DPKO Cambodia – UNTAC: Background). The administration also helped build a legal system, trained personnel in the new judiciary, inspected prisons and investigated allegations of politically motivated detentions (ibid.). UNTAC's civilian police unit also trained and supervised local police officers in order to ensure that they maintained law and order impartially, effectively and in accordance with human rights standards (ibid.). Finally, in a response to politically motivated violence, UNTAC also founded a rapid response mechanism focusing on investigations into alleged violations of human rights (ibid.).

Based on UNSC resolution 797 (1992), ONUMOZ was also deployed in 1992 in order to help implement a peace agreement aimed at bringing an end to the violent conflict in Mozambique (DPKO Mozambique – ONUMUZ: Background). Initially ONUMOZ was only requested to monitor and verify the DDR process, however; the UNSG left open the possibility of adding an international civilian police component to ONUMOZ if both parties to the violent conflict would later agree to it (ibid.). This happened in September 1993 when the UN was requested to observe that the rights of citizens were upheld and that all policing activities were carried out in accordance with the peace agreement and to assist the new police commission (ibid.). Subsequently, in accordance with UNSC resolution 898 (1994), a significant international civilian police component was added to ONUMOZ. In addition to the initial tasks, international police officers also confirmed the location and power of the national police, observed the retraining and reorganisation of the rapid reaction police and carried out their own investigations (ibid.).

In March 2003, on the basis of UNSC resolution 814 (1993), UNOSOM II took over from UNOSOM I, which had been sent to Somalia in 1992 to monitor a cease-fire and, with assistance from the US-led United Task Force (UNITAF), to safeguard the delivery of humanitarian aid (DPKO Somalia – UNOSOM II: Background). The fact that there were no national government, army and police force meant that no secure environment prevailed, so that UNOSOM II was granted Chapter VII powers and requested to help build a democratic state with a sound economy, infrastructure and social and political structures and obtain national reconciliation (ibid.). UNOSOM II was also asked to be significantly involved in the DDR process, to prevent further violence and to assist in the reestablishment of the national police force, judiciary and correction system (Thomas and Spataro 2002, UNSC resolution 865, 1993). UNOSOM II managed to train and support the local police, to initiate activities focusing on rebuilding the judicial and penal systems and to prepare for the establishment of a human rights office to investigate violations of international humanitarian law (ibid.). In the middle of the mission, in a response to widespread violence and UNSC resolution 897 (1994), UNOSOM II also attempted to step up its efforts in the judicial, correctional, human rights and crime prevention areas as well as its police training (ibid.).

In October 1993, on the basis of UNSC resolution 872 (1993), UNAMIR was launched to assist in the implementation of the Arusha Peace Agreement in Rwanda (DPKO Rwanda – UNAMIR: Background, DPKO Rwanda – UNAMIR: Mandate). Initially UNAMIR was only requested to assist with the DDR process and help maintain public security through observing and verifying the actions of the local police (ibid.). Not long after international civilian police observers had arrived in Rwanda, the violence escalated, culminating in a widespread genocide in the spring of 1994. In the midst of the genocide a Special UN Rapporteur and a Commission of Experts were asked to monitor the human rights situation and after the genocide more international human rights officers were sent to Rwanda to help rebuild the judicial system and educate on human rights (ibid.). UNAMIR's civilian police officers were also asked to assist in the development of a new national multiethnic police force.

In addition, based on UNSC resolution 867 (1993), UNMIH was also launched after the democratically elected Haitian President Aristide was overthrown in a military coup in the autumn of 1991, in order to assist in the implementation of the Governors Island Agreement (DPKO Haiti – UNMIH: Background). Prior to UNMIH's deployment, the International Civilian Mission in Haiti (MICIVIH) had been sent to Haiti to confirm respect for human rights (ibid.). UNMIH was asked to help modernise the army and develop, monitor and supervise a new national police (ibid.). The ongoing violent conflict initially prevented the deployment of UNMIH and led to the partial withdrawal of MICIVIH in October 1993 (ibid.). After international sanctions, increased tensions and diplomatic negotiations, the UNSC decided to deploy a multinational force (MNF) with Chapter VII powers sanctioning the use of all means necessary to reinstate the legitimate president and deploy UNMIH (ibid.). The MNF included international police monitors who assisted in training, assessing and supervising national police officers and conducted joint patrols with them (ibid.). In the autumn of 1994 UNMIH finally began deployment and MICIVIH was also able to continue its activities (ibid.).

Finally, after the regional organisation the Economic Community of West African States (ECOWAS) had attempted to end a violent conflict through facilitating negotiations and deploying the peacekeeping mission, the Military Observer Group (ECOMOG), UNSC resolution 866 (1993) established UNOMIL in Liberia in order to assist in the implementation of the peace agreement (DPKO Liberia – UNOMIL: Background). UNOMIL was authorised to observe and confirm the DDR process and to report on violations of international humanitarian law to the UNSG (ibid.). In the spring of 1994 UNOMIL military observers were deployed and began monitoring and verifying the disarmament and demobilisation process; however, their work was hampered by continued violence and threats to their own security and hence, their presence was reduced towards the end of 1994 (ibid.).

Many more failures than successes

The impact of the activities of these peace missions aimed at securing accountability for crimes committed after the signing of the peace agreement varied considerably and there were undeniably more failures than successes.

In Angola, although some international police officers occasionally managed to monitor the local police, patrol areas and conduct investigations, the failures dominated (DPKO Angola – UNAVEM II: Background). The disarmament and demobilisation of the warring factions was disproportionate and slow, the joint police monitoring mechanism collapsed when the warring parties withdrew their participation and hardly any progress was made towards establishing a national police force (Human Rights Watch 1999a, DPKO Angola – UNAVEM II: Background). Instead UNAVEM's deployment signified a disagreement and lack of commitment from the parties to the violent conflict, who preferred to keep on fighting.

In Somalia, although some progress was made in training and deploying the national police force and setting up courts, due mainly to an unsuccessful DDR process, the police were often left defenceless against the heavy armed parties to the violent conflict (DPKO Somalia – UNOSOM II: Background, Thomas and Spataro 2002). UNOSOM II's deployment was marred by continued fierce violence that also led to the death of several US and UNOSOM II soldiers and halted police patrols (Thomas and Spataro 2002). Hence, when UNOSOM II was withdrawn, Somalia did not have a well-functioning government or national armed force nor a fair and effective judiciary and police force (ibid.).

In Rwanda efforts towards disarming and demobilising the warring factions failed miserably and UNAMIR's police officers and military units could only stand by while thousands of people were brutally slaughtered (Dorn *et al.* 2000, Feil 1998). Despite attempting to implement numerous new initiatives after the genocide, civilians were still killed and many of UNAMIR's investigations into human rights violations made little difference because of a lack of regular reporting procedures and data either not being made public or being inadequate for prosecution (Human Rights Watch 1996a).

In Haiti and Liberia continued violence prevented UNMIH and UNOMIL from effectively carrying out most of their planned activities.

ONUMOZ enjoyed some success in policing human rights and reporting on human rights violations and international police officers were praised for ensuring that national police officers acted appropriately during the elections (Amnesty International 1998, Woods 2002). However, the setting up of a commission in charge of handling alleged human rights violations committed by national police was very slow and it never became very effective, which meant that the international officers' investigations were not followed up (Woods 2002). Poor training of, and a problematic relationship with, national police officers and the dearth of mechanisms ensuring accountability for inappropriate police behaviour also meant that police officers continued to commit human rights violations after the withdrawal of ONUMOZ (Amnesty International 1998, Woods 2002).

ONUMOZ also failed to establish an effective judicial system, address over-crowded prisons and ensure disarmament and demobilisation (ibid.).

In Cambodia UNTAC did not have the means to fully supervise and control the local police in all areas of the country and national authorities often failed to act on UNTAC's investigations, resulting in widespread impunity (Schear and Farris 2002). However, during the election campaign UNTAC's civilian police officers, together with the military component of UNTAC, managed to keep the level of violence at an acceptable level though politicians were still targeted and voters intimidated (ibid.). During UNTAC's mission Cambodia also signed and ratified many international human rights conventions and drafted a new penal code but it was not completely in accordance with international human rights standards and UNTAC did not manage to set up strong judicial institutions able to ensure the implementation of the conventions and thereby ensure respect for human rights (Amnesty International 2002). Hence, UNTAC did not manage to establish justice in Cambodia (Schear and Farris 2002).

In El Salvador ONUSAL was more successful since the mission managed to disarm and demobilise the former combatants without causing violations of the cease-fire. However the reintegration part of the process was less successful, resulting in waves of crimes committed by former combatants (Montgomery 1995, Stanley and Loosle 2002). ONUSAL also succeeded in increasing the respect for human rights, in maintaining public safety, reforming the judicial system and establishing a new national police force (ibid.). Although important steps towards enforcing the rule of law were taken, new national police officers were still reported to be committing violations of human rights (ibid.).

Explaining the successes and failures

One of the most important factors that contributed to the relatively limited success of the peace missions was that key parties to the violent conflict were not committed to implementing the peace agreement and therefore also not interested in cooperating with the peace mission (Jett 1999, Mackinlay and Alao 1995, Schear and Farris 2002, Thomas and Spataro 2002, Woods 2002). This meant that the peace missions were often deployed in the midst of ongoing violent conflicts with no powers and resources to stop the violence and force the parties to cooperate.

Many of the mandates were also very vague concerning what peace missions were expected to do in order to secure accountability for crimes committed after a peace agreement (Schear and Farris 2002, Stanley and Loosle 2002). All the missions had also been given a limited and often inadequate mandate that con-siderably constrained their role in the implementation of the peace agreement. For international police officers this meant that they were allowed to monitor and verify the activities of their national counterparts and in some cases also to investigate human rights violations but they had no authority to carry out arrests, which often meant that culprits could walk free because the local police were either unwilling or able to make the arrests (Mackinlay and Alao 1995, O'Neill

2005, Paulo 2004, Schear and Farris 2002, Stanley and Loosle 2002, Thomas and Spataro 2002, Woods 2002). The inadequate mandates also meant that there was often no coherent approach to ensuring justice. In some cases the peace agreements, mandates and lack of resources hindered the development of effective national police forces (Thomas and Spataro 2002). In other cases where efforts were put into developing national police forces, their impact was significantly limited by vague mandates and peace agreements and a lack of resources to help establish effective and fair judicial and correctional systems, leaving states without the means to deliver justice (Bailey *et al.* 2002, Human Rights Watch 1996, O'Neill 2005, Stanley and Loosle 2002, Thomas and Spataro 2002). Some of the missions also faced considerable resistance when attempting to assist in the DDR process (Human Rights Watch 1999a, Mackinlay and Alao, 1995).

In addition, many missions suffered from inadequate financial resources, personnel and equipment and from delayed deployments and inadequate planning (Dorn *et al.* 2000, Human Rights Watch 1996a, Human Rights Watch 1999a, Mackinlay and Alao 1995, Paulo 2004, Schear and Farris 2002, Thomas and Spataro, 2002). Furthermore, many suffered from inadequately skilled, trained and experienced personnel and in some missions, differences within civilian police (CIVPOL), such as different national ranking systems, command and control structures and varied ideas and methods on policing also had a negative impact on the way the peace mission performed its task (Bailey *et al.* 2002, Schear and Farris 2002, Stanley and Loosle 2002, Thomas and Spataro 2002, Woods 2002). Moreover, tense relations and a lack of coordination and cooperation between different parts of the peace missions also negatively affected outcomes (Mackinlay and Alao 1995, Montgomery 1995, Schear and Farris 2002, Stanley and Loosle, 2002, Thomas and Spataro 2002). Finally, many missions were also hampered by different, often underestimated, interpretations and assessments of the situation on the ground in the countries where they were deployed (Human Rights Watch 1999a, Mackinlay and Alao 1995, Schear and Farris 2002).

The opposite of many of the factors contributing to the failure of many of the peace missions enabled ONUSAL to be fairly successful. The parties to the violent conflict in El Salvador generally supported the peace agreement and ONUSAL's mandate, which meant that, by and large, ONUSAL received the necessary local cooperation (Montgomery 1995). A timely deployment and fairly generous resources also contributed to its success (Stanley and Loosle 2002). Finally, ONUSAL also benefited from sufficient equipment and personnel with the right qualifications, training, experience and skills (Montgomery 1995, Stanley and Loosle 2002).

UN reports: Supplement to an Agenda for Peace

In the beginning of 1995 UNSG Boutrous-Ghali published a follow-up report to *An Agenda of Peace*. The successor, named *Supplement to an Agenda for Peace*, pointed out that one of the features of the emerging internal violent conflicts was a breakdown of law and order due to a collapse in state institutions including the police and judiciary (Boutrous-Ghali 1995: paragraph 13). Hence, the report argued that improving judicial and policing institutions and structures is an important part of post-conflict peace-building and that the UN had already been involved in establishing new civilian police forces and planning and supervising the implementation of judicial reforms (Boutrous-Ghali 1995: paragraphs 21–22 and 47). In addition to disarming former warring factions, the report also argued that observing, promoting and verifying respect for human rights were similarly important (ibid.). Finally, it emphasised that the UN prefers to assist the former warring parties develop structures and institutions to maintain law and order rather than take full responsibility for this itself (Boutrous-Ghali 1995: paragraph 14).

Summing up

During the years 1992–1994 the activities UN personnel were expected to carry out to help state authorities ensure accountability for post-conflict crimes committed were significantly expanded. All peace operations were involved in DDR processes. International civilian police officers able to monitor and supervise, train and reform and restructure new or already existing national police forces also gained significance. Some peace operations also extended to strengthening local judicial systems through training of personnel, initiating the adoption of new laws and procedures, reviewing criminal cases and setting up local mechanisms for the resolution of civil disputes. A couple of peace operations also became involved in activities to improve correctional systems, such as inspecting prisons, improving their administration and promoting respect for the rights of the accused and convicted. Finally, peace missions were also involved in human rights issues. These included supporting the establishment of national human rights institutions, training police officers, judicial personnel and politicians in human rights, educating the general public, monitoring human rights, investigating and reporting violations of human rights and international humanitarian law to help deter violations.

Despite all these activities, the successes were few and far between. In most states where they were deployed, the missions failed to help develop national structures and institutions able to ensure accountability for crimes committed after the violent conflict once the peace mission had ended. In some cases the parties to the violent conflict refused to cooperate with the peace mission and, since they were dependent on this cooperation, these missions were not able to initiate the activities in their mandate. Instead, they found themselves deployed in the middle of ongoing violent conflict with a mandate based on parties to the conflict complying with the peace agreement developed prior to the peace mission's deployment. In other cases, though both parties were ready to cooperate with the peace mission, it was evident that helping states secure accountability for crimes was still something that the UN had very little experience in carrying out. Inadequate mandates and incoherent approaches meant limited positive results. Negative experiences and uncertainty about how UN peace missions could be successful meant that states were reluctant to contribute personnel and resources to the missions, leaving them with so few means that failure was inevitable.

The failure of many of the peace operations to protect human rights and prevent human rights violations was reflected in the *Supplement to an Agenda for Peace*, where the original *Agenda's* promise that peace operations would participate in protecting human rights had been changed to merely promoting and observing human rights, implying a lowering of expectations as to what these missions could achieve. Mirroring the fact that efforts towards disarmament and strengthening the rule of law structures and institutions had been included in all peace operations, the report also acknowledged these to be important means towards ensuring accountability for crimes committed after the end of violent conflict and preventing crimes being committed in the future. The very mixed and often disappointing results of peace missions' efforts and the wide variety of activities included in their mandates in such an incoherent way were also reflected in the fact that the report failed to detail the activities peace missions should be involved in. Finally, the report also echoed the fact that many of the peace missions had been marred by a lack of political will and cooperation from both the authorities and the parties to the conflicts, since it emphasised that the UN continued to rely on national authorities and that the UN operations preferred to support activities in the peace process rather than bear responsibility for them.

The intermediate years: learning from past mistakes?

During this period UNMIH and UNOMIL continued their missions in Haiti and Liberia. In Angola first the United Nations Angola Verification Mission III (UNAVEM III) and later the United Nations Observer Mission in Angola (MONUA) took over from UNAVEM II. In Haiti UNMIH was also in quick succession replaced by three new missions, namely, the United Nations Support Mission in Haiti (UNSMIH), United Nations Transition Mission in Haiti (UNTMIH) and United Nations Civilian Police Mission in Haiti (MINOPUH). In addition eight new missions, namely, the United Nations Mission in Bosnia-Herzegovina (UNMIBH), the United Nations Transitional Administration in Eastern Slavonia, Baranja and Western Sirmium (UNTAES), United Nations Verification Mission in Guatemala (MINUGUA), United Nations Observer Mission in Sierra Leone (UNOMSIL), United Nations Mission in Sierra Leone (UNAMSIL), United Nations Mission in Kosovo (UNMIK), United Nations Transitional Administration in East Timor (UNTAET) and United Nations Organisation Mission in the Democratic Republic of Congo (MONUC) were also established.

In Haiti in March 1995 UNMIH finally took over power from the multinational force. UNMIH's 800 international civilian police officers became involved in monitoring, supervising and extensively training the new national police force, in helping run prisons, in guarding national authority buildings and in investigating particularly serious murder cases (Bailey *et al.* 2002). UNMIH continued these activities until it was replaced by UNSMIH in the summer of 1996.

In the summer of 1995 the parties to the violent conflict in Liberia signed a new peace agreement. In response UNSC resolution 1020 (1995) adapted UNOMIL's mandate to include assisting local human rights activists in raising resources for logistics and training and investigating and reporting human rights violations to the UNSG (DPKO Liberia – UNOMIL: Background). However, the situation on the ground deteriorated again and UNOMIL was forced to evacuate most of its personnel, leaving only a small group of monitors to report and investigate human rights violations, observe the status of prisoners of war and examine ways in which Liberia's judicial system could be improved (ibid.). DDR began in November 1996 overseen by UNOMIL's military observers and, though the security situation remained unstable, elections were held in August 1997 and hence UNOMIL was terminated in September 1997 (ibid.).

The UN also deployed a new peace mission in Angola named UNAVEM III, based on UNSC resolution 976 (1995), 1008 (1995), 1045 (1996) and 1055 (1996) that was mandated to assist in the implementation of the Peace Accord for Angola signed in May 1991 and the Lusaka Protocol signed in November 1994 (DPKO Angola – UNAVEM III). UNAVEM III's mandate included assisting in the DDR of UNITA, government forces and civilians and in monitoring and verifying the neutrality of the Angolan national police. It also encompassed human rights specialists that observed the implementation of the national reconciliation provisions (ibid.).

Following the signing of the Dayton Peace Agreement and the termination of UNPROFOR the UNSC established UNMIBH in December 1995.[12] UNMIBH included a UN civilian office and the UN International Police Task Force (IPTF) and its mandate was expanded several times during its deployment.[13] The IPTF aimed to help transform the local police from an oversized highly monoethnic force into a professional and effective multiethnic one (DPKO Bosnia-Herzegovina – UNMIBH: Background). Hence, the IPTF assisted in recruiting, training and deploying new police officers from minority groups, in training returning officers in policing in accordance with human rights and in training senior police officers (ibid.). The IPTF also offered special training courses to national police officers on drugs control, organised crime and crowd control and carried out prison and weapons inspections (ibid.). UNMIBH's human rights unit attempted to implement measures ensuring that only qualified police officers carried out police duties and it investigated cases where police officers were thought to have violated human rights and observed that these police officers were held accountable (ibid.). UNMIBH also observed and evaluated the Bosnian court system, developed recommendations on how it could be improved, observed court cases, facilitated cooperation between the judiciary and the police and trained local police officers in criminal procedures (ibid.).

Simultaneously with UNMIBH, the UN also established UNTAES through adopting UNSC resolution 1037 (1996) on the basis of Chapter VII of the UN Charter in order to help the Croatian government and the local Serb authorities to implement the Basic Agreement that both had signed two months earlier. UNTAES was requested to assist and supervise the demilitarisation process, to observe the parties to the violent conflict's obligation to respect human rights, to oversee the prison system and to found and train a temporary national police force (DPKO Croatia – UNTAES: Background). International civilian police officers were also requested to set up a provisional police force, to develop and monitor the implementation of training programmes for police officers and to patrol and conduct investigations, though they were not allowed to arrest suspects (ibid.). UNTAES also carried out human rights training and observed the upholding of human rights (ibid.).

In July 1996, acknowledging that the new national police force in Haiti was still not ready to take full responsibility for ensuring security, the UNSC decided in resolution 1063 (1996) to establish UNSMIH (DPKO Haiti – UNSMIH: Background). In addition to assisting in improving the national police, UNSMIH was also asked to help maintain stability and security and to coordinate the UN's activities towards promoting economic recovery, national reconciliation and institution-building (ibid.). Some 300 international civilian police officers continued to assist the national police while they carried out their daily tasks and to train national officers in, for example, conflict resolution, general police work, human rights and community policing until the end of the mission in July 1997 (ibid.).

Originally MINUGUA was a civilian and humanitarian mission that the UN General Assembly (UNGA) had established while the violent conflict in Guatemala was still ongoing but, in January 1997, after the signing of a peace agreement, the UNSC decided to add a military component to MINUGUA (DPKO Guatemala – MINUGUA: Background). Originally MINUGUA included human rights observers, native specialists and police officers and legal experts who were deployed around Guatemala in order to confirm the implementation of the peace agreement and to respond to problems by making recommendations to the parties to the conflict (ibid.). MINUGUA was also requested to probe into whether national institutions properly investigated allegations of human rights violations and, if this was not the case, to investigate complaints and to advise the national institutions on necessary action (ibid.). The 155 military observers added to MINUGUA were asked to verify the cease-fire and disarmament and demobilisation process (ibid.).

In addition, in 1997 MONUA replaced UNAVEM III in Angola. In MONUA UN military personnel were replaced by an international civilian mission that, as well as the tasks inherited from UNAVEM II, was mandated to pay special notice to respect for political and civil rights, to do joint patrols with the Angolan National Police, to monitor the disarmament of the civilian population and to inspect prisons (DPKO Angola – MONUA: Background, DPKO Angola – MONUA: Mandate). MONUA also included a human rights unit that was requested to assist in the development of national human rights institutions and NGOs, to investigate allegations of abuse and instigate proper actions and to contribute to promoting human rights and preventing human rights violations (ibid.). Finally, MONUA's military and humanitarian components were also supposed to support and monitor the DDR of former soldiers (ibid.).

The UN also authorised two more peace missions in Haiti in 1997 because the national police force was still not ready to take responsibility for ensuring public order. UNSC resolution 1123 (1997) established UNTMIH and requested the deployment of 250 international civilian police officers and 50 military personnel, who were no longer supposed to carry out patrols but merely support the work of the civilian police officers and to train three special units (DPKO Haiti – UNSMIH: Background, DPKO Haiti – UNTMIH). After four months UNTMIH was replaced by MINOPUH, consisting of international civilian police officers who were asked to help further develop the national police force (ibid.). MINOPUH continued to run training courses for specialised police units and to support senior police officers until its mandate was terminated in March 2000 (ibid.).

After the UN had been involved in negotiating a peace agreement in Sierra Leone, the UNSC launched UNOMSIL through resolution 1181 (1998) in the middle of 1998 (DPKO Sierra Leone – UNOMSIL: Background). UNOMSIL's seventy military observers were requested to monitor respect for international humanitarian law and the DDR process and its civilian unit was supposed to inform on violations of international humanitarian law and human rights and to assist the government in dealing with human rights (ibid.). UNOMSIL was also mandated to guide and observe the reform and restructuring of the national police and to give advice on training, practices, recruitment and equipment (ibid.). Using ECOMOG for protection, unarmed UNOMSIL personnel managed to develop reports on human rights violations against civilians (ibid.). However, the violence still continued, leading to most of UNOMSIL's personnel leaving the country in early 1999. Further UN-led negotiations ended with a new peace agreement and a strengthened human rights unit and peace mission that included 210 military observers (ibid.).

During the summer of 1999, on the basis of UNSC 1244 (1999), the UN also deployed UNMIK as the transitional administrator of Kosovo. UNMIK's mandate included supporting the establishment of local provisional institutions, promoting and protecting human rights and maintaining law and order by means of international police officers executing policing tasks until a local police force had been established and trained (UNSC resolution 1244, 1999). In the beginning maintaining law and order was left to the Kosovo Force (KFOR), with international police officers in an advisory role (UNMIK – Civilian Police – Mandate & Tasks). A year after UNMIK had been deployed, its international police officers took over responsibility for upholding law and order by means of patrols, investigating crimes, collecting evidence and carrying out arrests (ibid.). UNMIK also supported the establishment of a police academy that began training local police officers and, after this basic training, international officers then observed, advised and trained local police (ibid.).

The UN also launched a peace operation in East Timor named UNTAET under Chapter VII of the UN by UNSC resolution 1272 (1999). The aim of UNTAET was to administrate East Timor during its transition to independence and, to fulfil that aim, the UNSC resolution granted the mission wide powers, including the right to carry out all executive and legislative authority over the territory. Concerning law and order, a UN police unit with more than 1200 international civilian police officers was included in UNTAET (DPKO East Timor – UNTAET: Law and Order). Its job was to found and train a national police force and to maintain law and order. UNTAET also initiated activities aimed at developing an effective and fair judiciary and legal system (DPKO East Timor – UNTAET: Background). The human rights unit observed and received complaints about human rights violations, helped find a solution to human rights concerns and monitored especially women's rights and their access to justice (DPKO East Timor – UNTAET: Human Rights). In addition the unit also assessed and advised local authorities on how to prevent human rights violations and it provided human rights education and the backing of civil society (ibid.).

Furthermore, the UN also launched a new and stronger peace mission in Sierra Leone to assist in the implementation of the new peace agreement (DPKO Sierra Leone – UNAMSIL: Background). Originally UNSC resolution 1270 (1999) requested UNAMSIL military to facilitate the DDR process and to support the activities of the civilian component (DPKO Sierra Leone – UNAMSIL: Mandate). The mandate was expanded to include providing security in connection with the DDR process, protecting civilians from imminent threats of violence within UNAMSIL's capabilities and coordinating and helping national law enforcement authorities to carry out their daily tasks (ibid.). The number of international soldiers and police officers was also significantly increased. In May 2000 hundreds of peacekeepers were kidnapped by one of the parties to the violent conflict, which also withdrew its consent to the cease-fire. Responding to the incident, UNAMSIL initiated a new mediation process, increased its personnel and stepped up disarmament and demobilisation efforts (DPKO Sierra Leone – UNAMSIL: Background).

Finally in November 1999 the UN agreed to deploy MONUC to facilitate the implementation of a cease-fire agreement in the Democratic Republic of Congo. Three months later MONUC's mandate was expanded under Chapter VII of the UN Charter to include protecting civilians if they were in danger of becoming victims of serious physical violence, developing a plan for the disarmament, demobilisation and reintegration process and monitoring human rights especially for vulnerable groups (DPKO Democratic Republic of Congo – MONUC: Mandate)

Still many more failures than successes

As had been the case in the previous period, the UN's peace missions achieved very mixed results.

In Angola neither UNAVEM III nor MONUA managed to prevent the parties to the violent conflict from taking up arms and continuing fighting (Human Rights Watch 1999a, Paulo 2004). Serious threats to the security of the mission personnel, including the shooting down of UN planes and harassment of UN personnel, seriously impaired their work (ibid.). The peace missions continued to monitor human rights but, due to fear of the reactions from the parties to the violent conflict, the publication of the results of the observations was often kept to a minimum and monitoring activities were generally given very little priority (Human Rights Watch 1999a). Under MONUA the investigations and reporting improved, however these activities came to an end when the violence intensified and hence, neither UNAVEM III nor MONUA managed to create much awareness of the importance of human rights and accountability for human rights atrocities (ibid.).

In Haiti, despite the deployment of several peace missions, the UN failed to ensure justice (Bailey *et al.* 2002, Gantz 2004, Khouri-Padova 2004). The missions were mainly focused on developing an effective national police force and, though they managed to rebuild many police stations and train many police officers, they did not manage to establish a national force able to guarantee security to its people in a fair and effective manner (Bailey *et al.* 2002, Bailey 2006, Gantz 2004, Khouri-Padova 2004). In addition none of the missions managed to substantially improve the Haitian judicial system, leaving it in a nascent state (Bailey *et al.* 2002, Gantz 2004, Khouri-Padova 2004).

In Bosnia-Herzegovina the results of UNMIBH's efforts towards ensuring justice were also mixed. The IPTF did manage to train many local police officers and to initiate some police reforms (Dziedzic and Barr 2002, International Crisis Group 2002a). UNMIBH also helped set up a constitutional court, develop a training programme for lawyers and prosecutors, found an organisation for judges and held a conference on support for an independent judiciary (Dziedzic and Barr 2002). Still the national police and judiciary were not able to uphold the rule of law without international assistance (International Crisis Group 2002a, 2002b).

In Croatia UNTAES managed to establish a transnational multiethnic police force that generally followed the correct procedures and kept security at an acceptable level after the peace mission had withdrawn (Human Rights Watch 1999b). However, when UNTAES left, intimidation of and attacks on the Serb minority rose and there were complaints that crimes committed against Serbs were not properly investigated and prosecuted (ibid.).

In Guatemala MINUGUA's human rights monitors continued to observe the human rights situation until 2004 despite violent incidents and serious threats to the safety of the international human rights monitors (Human Rights Watch 1999c). The human rights monitors were fairly successful in investigating and reporting on human rights violations but, since they had no enforcement powers, serious violations continued to occur (ibid.). Many were never properly investigated by the local police, who also continued to breach these rights themselves (ibid.).

UNOMIL's activities were severely influenced by the continued fighting and hence the peace mission's results were very limited. UNOMIL assisted in the implementation of the disarmament and demobilisation process but the programme largely failed to disarm and demobilise the warring factions and no attempts were made to reintegrate those soldiers that had given up arms (Aning 2000). In addition, only a few international human rights observers were deployed, their investigations very limited and often ignored by both UNOMIL and the UN Secretariat, which were preoccupied with the continued fighting between the parties (Human Rights Watch 1998).

In Sierra Leone UNOMSIL was also struggling to make a difference in the midst of the conflict. Its attempts to disarm and demobilise the warring factions were hampered by a lack of cooperation (Aning 2000). UNOMSIL human rights observers monitored human rights, ran workshops on international human rights law for judicial personnel, police officers and local NGOs, observed court cases in the capital and provided the courts with information on fair trials (Human Rights Watch 1999d, O'Neill, 2002). However, the impact of these activities remained very limited, as fighting continued throughout the mission and UNOMSIL personnel were often threatened. In the beginning UNOMSIL's successor UNAMSIL was not much more successful. Like UNOMSIL, UNAMSIL was initially not granted a Chapter VII mandate, which meant that the peace mission could do very little to prevent the warring factions from continuing their struggle. UNAMSIL was initially a bit more successful than UNOMSIL in disarming and demobilising the combatants but once again, the fragile peace broke down and many of the disarmed weapons filtered back into the conflict (Aning 2000). Even when UNAMSIL was finally granted a Chapter VII mandate in the beginning of 2000, lack of personnel and resources meant that the disarmament and demobilisation remained very slow and the impact of UNAMSIL very limited (Malan *et al.* 2002).

In the beginning UNTAET in East Timor only made slow progress but soon the mission established a police academy and developed and trained a new national police force (Babo-Soares 2001, Human Rights Watch 2001). It also established a new court system and instated local lawyers, prosecutors and judges (ibid.). However, UNTAET only made slow progress in other areas of the judicial system such as the development of a provisional criminal procedure code which the courts needed to operate (Human Rights Watch 2001). UNTAET also failed to establish adequate prison facilities, which meant that in the beginning UNTAET's own police could not make use of their executive powers because there was no place to keep the criminals (Aucoin 2007, Babo-Soares 2001, Human Rights Watch 2001). Hence, though the rate of crime was reduced, human rights violations continued (Babo-Soares 2001, Human Rights Watch 2001).

In Kosovo progress was also slow in the beginning. KFOR troops that were supposed to carry out policing until international police officers were ready to take over failed to patrol the streets adequately, leaving the crime rate high and the local population feeling unsafe (International Crisis Group 1999). A police academy was fairly quickly established but the intake in the training programme was relatively slow at the start so that it took a long time to establish a national force (ibid.). Though it only took about a year to set up functioning courts, develop a new criminal code and training institutions for judicial personnel, the justice system remained weak (International Crisis Group 1999, 2002b). Hence, justice was still far from being upheld in Kosovo despite UNMIK's many activities.

Finally, in the Democratic Republic of Congo fierce fighting between the parties to the violent conflict prevented MONUC from carrying out any relevant activities.

Explaining the successes and failures

A broad range of factors affected the peace missions' results.

One of the most serious obstacles to success was that the parties to the conflict preferred to continue fighting rather than cooperate in the implementation of the peace agreement (Aning 2000, Human Rights Watch 1998, 1999a, Paulo 2004). The problems were exacerbated by the Chapter VI mandate of many missions, which meant that they depended on the consent and cooperation of the parties and lacked the means to force them to comply and cooperate. The assumptions behind many of the mandates were therefore significantly compromised but mandates were also often not adapted in a swift manner to reflect new conditions on the ground. Another main factor impeding the peace missions' attempts to secure accountability for crimes is the lack both of an appropriate mandate and a coherent approach to its implementation. Many had no coordinated and coherent approach, which should have included establishing a national police force and a national judiciary as well as a national correctional system (Bailey *et al.* 2002, Gantz 2004, International Crisis Group 1999, Khouri-Padova 2004, Samuels 2006). Insufficient focus and funding meant that, even if the national police officers managed to detain criminals, the lack of a functional and fair judiciary and prison system meant that the rule of law was still not upheld. Some missions, such as the one in Bosnia-Herzegovina, also suffered from inadequate powers, since they were only mandated to monitor and train local police but not to execute arrests of ordinary criminals or national police officers responsible for human rights violations (Dziedzic and Barr 2002, International Crisis Group 2002a). A couple of the missions also suffered from international personnel's unwillingness to carry out the mandate they had been granted (Human Rights Watch 2001, International Crisis Group 1999). Some of the missions' human rights efforts were also impeded by a deficient support within the mission for human rights issues (Human Rights Watch 1998, 1999a, 2001).

The outcome of the missions was also negatively affected by some general problems. Some, such as those in East Timor and Bosnia-Herzegovina, suffered from insufficient planning and others, especially in Bosnia-Herzegovina, Liberia and Sierra Leone, were disadvantaged by slow and delayed deployment (Dziedzic and Barr 2002, Malan *et al.* 2002, Samuels 2006). Inadequate allocated resources and coordination within the peace missions also negatively influenced their activities (Aning 2000, Babo-Soares 2001, Bailey *et al.* 2002, Dziedzic and Barr 2002, Human Rights Watch 1999a, 2001, International Crisis Group 1999, Khouri-Padova 2004, Malan *et al.* 2002, O'Neill 2002). Some missions also suffered from the UN's failure to commit to long-term deployment along with unqualified and inexperienced staff, who might not speak the local language or know about the local culture in states marred by human rights violations and who were used to very different police practices and cultures (Aucoin 2007, Babo-Soares 2001, Dziedzic and Barr 2002, Human Rights Watch 2001, International Crisis Group 2002a, Khouri-Padova 2004, Malan *et al.* 2002). Especially in Bosnia-Herzegovina and Kosovo, attempts to establish an independent police and judiciary were also hampered by political interference (International Crisis Group 2002a, 2002b). Finally, several missions were hindered by a lack of local engagement and plans for the transfer of responsibility from international to national ownership (Aucoin 2007, Babo-Soares 2001, Khouri-Padova 2004, Samuels 2006).

Some noteworthy factors can also help explain why the peace mission in Croatia especially was fairly successful in carrying out its mandates. In Croatia a fairly clear mandate, a rigorous timetable and plans for the post-deployment phase helped UNTAES achieve results (Harston 2000, Shitakha 1998). In addition, adequate resources, good planning and coordination and a unified civilian and military structure with a strong leadership helped the peace mission succeed (Harston 2000, Shitakha 1998). Finally, UNTAES also by and large enjoyed the cooperation from the parties to the conflict and, even when this was not the case, it was possible to pressure the parties to comply (Shitakha 1998).

UN report: the Report of the Panel on the United Nations Peace Operations

This report from 2000, also known as the Brahimi report, noted that, following violent internal conflict the local judicial system is often not functioning or is considered illegitimate by key groups (Brahimi 2000: paragraph 79). Therefore, establishing structures and institutions such as local police forces, an independent judiciary and well-functioning penal systems to strengthen the rule of law constitute important goals in peace-building meriting UN involvement (ibid.: paragraph 13). Hence, when required, peace operations need to include sufficient judicial specialists and international civilian police to assist in strengthening the structures and institutions responsible for upholding the rule of law (ibid.: paragraph 39). The report states that international civilian police are required to train, restructure and reform local police forces and to respond to civil disorder (ibid.). Processes aimed at DDR of former combatants are also necessary for upholding law and order (ibid.: paragraph 42). The report also underlined that the UN's commitment to peace-building should include enhancing respect for human rights through monitoring, educating and investigating present abuses (ibid.: paragraph 13). In addition, the report's enhanced focus on strengthening the rule of law led to a doctrinal shift in the use of human rights experts, rule-of-law components and civilian police (ibid.: paragraph 40). This included a shift in the role of international civilian police, which encompassed not only advising, monitoring and training local police officers, but also restructuring and reforming local forces (ibid.: paragraph 119). Brahimi also underlined the need for judicial, policing and human rights experts to work together in accordance with a shared approach to upholding the rule of law (ibid.: paragraph 40). Finally, the report concluded that demand for international civilian police officers able to monitor and train local police in future peace operations is likely to be high (ibid.: paragraph 118).

Summing up

Although these peace missions carried out many activities, including assisting in the DDR process and monitoring, advising, training, reforming and restructuring national police forces and, to a lesser degree, training the personnel of, and rebuilding, reforming and monitoring national judicial and correctional systems, none managed to establish structures and institutions able to uphold law and order in a fair and effective way. For some, inherited problems such as inadequate resources and personnel prevented the missions from carrying out their mandates successfully. A coherent approach that placed equal weight on establishing a national police force, judiciary and penal system was also lacking. Often the missions concentrated on establishing a national police force without acknowledging that it would not be able to make much difference if not supported by well-functioning and fair judiciary and penal institutions. Some missions initiated activities to strengthen the judiciary and penal system but insufficient resources and experience in what works and what does not often left these systems weak and unable to support the police. Similarly with the DDR process, the focus was often on disarmament and demobilisation rather than reintegration, meaning that former combatants left without jobs or hope for the future were prone to take up arms again. Peace missions were also still to a high degree dependent on the cooperation of the parties to the violent conflict and often left powerless if the parties refused to cooperate. All in all, by the end of millennium, myriad activities aimed at securing accountability for crimes committed after the conflict were added to the peace missions' remit but the recipe for success had yet to be developed.

The Brahimi report emphasised the importance of upholding the rule of law for post-conflict peace-building and argued that the UN was committed to assist states in developing structures and institutions to do this. The report reflected experience from some of the peace missions that had shown that monitoring, advising and training national police forces were not enough and that restructure and reform were necessary too. However, the report failed to acknowledge that this is a long-term project that leaves an important gap in the upholding of law and order from when the peace agreement is signed to when the new national police force is ready to act without external assistance. Hence, the report did not envisage a more prominent role for international police officers, entailing the execution of policing tasks until the national police force is ready to do so. Reflecting the experience of several missions, which had indicated that a strong police force needs the support of well-functioning and fair judicial and correctional systems to be able to uphold the rule of law, the report did acknowledge the importance of peace missions supporting the development of judicial and penal structures and institutions. Thus it identified the need for a shared approach and the inclusion of international judicial experts able to help societies develop fair judicial and penal systems. Nevertheless and also reflecting the experiences of the peace missions, the report did not provide much detail on precise actions peace operations should undertake in order to achieve this, although it did indicate a need to rethink the role of peace operations in establishing the rule of law in post-conflict societies. Finally, concerning human rights, it is striking that the report only committed peace missions to monitor human rights, to educate about human rights and to investigate violations though experience had shown that this did not stop the parties involved from failing to respect human rights and committing atrocities.

Post-Brahimi: still not getting it right

After the turn of the millennium, UNMIBH, UNMIK, UNTAET, UNAMSIL and MONUC continued their missions. In East Timor and Liberia UNTAET and UNIMIL were replaced by the United Nations Mission of Support to East Timor (UNMISET) and United Nations Mission in Liberia (UNMIL) respectively. Three new missions, namely, the United Nations Mission in Côte d'Ivoire (UNOCI), United Nations Stabilisation Mission in Haiti (MINUSTAH) and United Nations Mission in Sudan (UNMIS) were also deployed.

In Bosnia-Herzegovina UNMIBH continued to reform and train national police forces and attempt to improve the local judiciary.

In Kosovo UNMIK's justice department's responsibility for running courts has entailed hiring international lawyers and judges (Human Rights Watch 2006c). UNMIK's international police officers have also trained and supervised the new national police force and helped the local officers to uphold law and order through taking part in everyday policing tasks (UNMIK – Police & Justice (Pillar I) – Police). Finally, UNMIK police has also established a border police unit and a special unit focusing on handling public disorder and controlling crowds (ibid.).

In East Timor UNTAET continued efforts to maintain law and order and to train national police. As more national officers came through the training and gained experience, the number of international civilian police was gradually reduced (DPKO East Timor – UNTAET: Law and Order). UNTAET also continued to improve East Timor's judicial system by setting up ordinary courts, appeal courts and defence counsel services and endeavoured to reform the police, judiciary and prisons through the development of new regulations (DPKO East Timor – UNTAET: Justice and Serious Crimes, Human Rights

Watch 2002). Finally, UNTAET also went on promoting the protection of human rights (Human Rights Watch 2002, DPKO East Timor – UNTAET: Human Rights).

In Sierra Leone UNAMSIL assisted in the implementation of the DDR process until it was officially ended in 2004 (DPKO Sierra Leone – UNAMSIL: Disarmament, Demobilisation and Reintegration). UNAMSIL also helped develop a new national police force through observing police activities, establishing police stations and police training facilities and recruiting and training (DPKO Sierra Leone – UNAMSIL: Human Rights and Rule of Law). UNAMSIL personnel also rebuilt courts and other judicial institutions, monitored both courts and prisons and established human rights committees to train local human rights activists, among others.

So far MONUC has helped plan the DDR process, advised and provided technical assistance to local courts and lawyers, assessed the national police force's institutional capacity and advised, assisted and trained the national police (DPKO Democratic Republic of Congo – MONUC: Police Activities and DPKO Democratic Republic of Congo – MONUC: DDDRR Activities). MONUC human rights unit also monitors and documents human rights violations and identifies and lobbies for justice in symbolic cases of serious violations (DPKO Democratic Republic of Congo – MONUC: Human Rights Mandates and Activities). Recently, MONUC has also assessed the prison system and advised on prison administration (Action Aid 2006a). Finally, MONUC also facilitates the protection of especially witnesses, victims and human rights advocates who are in imminent physical danger (DPKO Democratic Republic of Congo – MONUC: Human Rights Mandates and Activities).

In May 2002 UNMISET took over from UNTAET on the basis of UNSC resolution 1410 (2002) under Chapter VII of the UN Charter. UNMISET was asked to maintain security, including ensuring public security through law enforcement and the development of a national police force and supporting administrative structures underpinning local political stability. As the security situation improved and local authorities were able to take over leadership, UNMISET's role was reduced. However, it continued to support and advise courts and governmental authorities and to observe the development of a legal framework, judicial system and the rule of law in East Timor (DPKO East Timor – UNMISET: Branches Legal Affairs). In May 2004 the international police ceased to execute policing tasks leaving the maintenance of law and order to the new national police but the mission continued to provide training courses for the new force (DPKO East Timor – UNMISET: Branches UN Police). In addition, UNMISET also initiated a range of human rights-focused activities such as providing assistance to the government, making authorities aware of their human rights violations and assisting local NGOs to strengthen their human rights advocacy capacities (DPKO East Timor – UNMISET: Branches Human Rights).

In September 2003 UNMIL was established through UNSC resolution 1509 (2003) in order to support the peace process and the implementation of the cease-fire agreement in Liberia and originally the mission consisted of 15,000 military personnel and more than 1,000 international civilian police officers (DPKO Liberia – UNMIL: About UNMIL History). UNMIL has been and still is involved in attempting to implement the DDR process and in restructuring, recruiting, vetting and training the new national police force (DPKO Liberia – UNMIL: Operations Disarmament Process, DPKO Liberia – UNMIL: Operations UN Police). In addition, the mission is involved in training judicial and prison personnel, monitoring court proceedings, advising courts and prisons and supporting the national judiciary and justice authorities (DPKO Liberia – UNMIL: Operations Corrections, DPKO Liberia – UNMIL: Operations Legal & Judicial Coordination). Finally, UNMIL's human rights unit monitors and reports on human rights violations, advises the government on the development of national legislation, policy and institutions and helps local authorities build capacity for the promotion and protection of human rights (DPKO Liberia – UNMIL: Operations Human Rights).

Six months after the deployment of UNMIL, the UNSC also established UNOCI[14] through UNSC resolution 1528 (2004) based on Chapter VII of the UN Charter. Since its deployment, UNOCI has helped the local government in Côte d'Ivoire implement a DDR programme, observed and reported on human rights, helped local authorities intervene in order to protect civilians and provided training on and raised awareness of human rights (UNOCI – Human Rights, UNOCI – Working for Peace in a Country in Crisis). Moreover, UNOCI has also monitored legal reforms and sensitive court cases, identified and analysed challenges in the correctional and judicial systems and offered support and training of prison personnel (UNOCI – Rule of Law, UNOCI – Working for Peace in a Country in Crisis).

In June 2004 the UNSC established MINUSTAH through resolution 1542 (2004) under Chapter VII of the UN Charter in order to help develop the national police force, restore and maintain the rule of law, re-establish the prison system, implement the DDR process and promote and protect human rights (DPKO Haiti – MINUSTAH: Mandate). Continued violence has hindered MINUSTAH's efforts in many areas. However, the mission has assisted in vetting and training police officers, in advising local courts, in training judicial personnel and in developing the prison system (Action Aid 2006b, International Crisis Group 2007).

Finally, in March 2005, the UNSC established UNMIS through UNSC resolution 1590 (2005) to support the implementation of the peace agreement. So far UNMIS has begun preparing for the DDR programme and initiated some activities towards demobilising and reintegrating children (UNMIS – DDR Achievements). UNMIS has also established human rights offices, trained local NGOs and, in cooperation with local NGOs, started to prepare for the establishment of a national human rights commission (UNMIS – Human Rights Office). Furthermore, UNMIS has also trained Sudanese police officers, rebuilt policing facilities, monitored and assessed the local police, monitored the parties' adherence to their rule of law-related obligations in the peace agreement, provided policy advice to correctional institutions and assisted and supported judicial institutions

(UNMIS – Police Operations, UNMIS – Police Reform and Restructuring, UNMIS – Police Training, UNMIS – Rule of Law and Judicial Systems Advisory).

Successes and failures

In Bosnia-Herzegovina UNMIBH managed to establish a national police force that was reasonably able to deal with small-scale crime but not ethnicity-related, serious and organised crime and this force remained underpaid, underqualified and politicised (International Crisis Group 2002a). In addition, despite the IPTF's screening efforts, some police officers who had allegedly been heavily involved in the violent conflict managed to keep their jobs. Also, the judicial system remained plagued by numerous expensive, incompetent and corrupt courts that were both inefficient and politicised and many reforms were only partly implemented (International Crisis Group 2002a, 2002b). Hence, though some progress was made concerning the establishment of a functional national police force, UNMIBH left without having developed a national police force and judiciary able to dispense justice without international assistance (Dziedzic and Barr 2002, International Crisis Group 2002a, 2002b). UNMIBH was replaced by a new peace mission led by the European Union.

In Kosovo a new national police force that includes minorities is now in charge of policing, leaving international police officers in a monitoring and advising role (Human Rights Watch 2006c, International Crisis Group 2006a). The national police are able to carry out basic policing tasks but its officers are still accused of using too much force, not responding to ethnically motivated crime in particular, failing to deal with organised crime, especially that involving politicians and being prone to political pressure (Amnesty International 2007a, Human Rights Watch 2006c, International Crisis Group 2006a). Ministries for justice and the interior have been founded and local courts set up but, despite these international activities, the justice system is still considered the weakest institution in Kosovo and impunity for ethnically motivated crimes in particular still prevails (Amnesty International 2007a, Human Rights Watch 2006c, 2007a, 2007b, International Crisis Group 2006a).

In East Timor UNTAET managed to establish a national police force but policing was still carried out jointly by international and local officers until the end of UNTAET's mission (Human Rights Watch 2006d). Notable progress was made towards establishing a legal framework to protect human rights although especially vulnerable groups were still not adequately protected (Amnesty International 2001, Human Rights Watch 2002). UNTAET was much less successful in establishing a well-functioning and fair judicial system in East Timor (ibid.). Though district courts had been established, they did not function in accordance with international human rights standards and they also suffered from paucity of resources and well-qualified personnel (Amnesty International 2001, Human Rights Watch 2003). No independent mechanism able to assess the workings of the judicial system had been established, leaving the courts vulnerable to political interference, Civilians' confidence in the courts was low and discrimination, illegal detentions, threats and assaults allegedly carried out by unofficial security groups were also still rife (Amnesty International 2001).

In Sierra Leone UNAMSIL was generally considered a success but the results of prosecutions of crimes in the post-conflict phase were more ambiguous. Thousands of combatants have been disarmed, demobilised and reintegrated into their communities but unemployment among ex-combatants remains a major problem (Refugees International 2004). Though UNAMSIL managed to recruit and train a national police force, its impact on establishing justice has been hampered by a lack of equipment and facilities and impunity for human rights violations committed by police officers (Human Rights Watch 2004, Refugees International 2004). While some court buildings have been established and are working, insufficient courts and personnel means that the judicial system is very slow and still plagued by corruption, discrimination, illegal detentions and abuse of power (ibid.). Long pre-trial detentions and overcrowded prisons are also common and human rights violations still occur (ibid.). Hence, UNAMSIL has not managed to ensure that justice is upheld in Sierra Leone.

In the Congo serious human rights atrocities are still common (Amnesty International 2007b, Human Rights Watch 2007a). Whereas the DDR of foreign combatants has been relatively successful, the process focusing on Congolese fighters is only partly completed, leaving many still armed, opportunities for recruiting new soldiers open and demobilised soldiers without financial support or job prospects (Action Aid 2006a, Amnesty International 2007b). The plans for establishing a national united police force are yet to be implemented and the police are often accused of using too much force, being corrupt and being involved in violations (Action Aid 2006a, Amnesty International 2007b, Human Rights Watch 2007a). Though some courts are working, the reconstruction and reform of the judicial system is still slow and impunity dominates. Prisons are also heavily overcrowded and in very poor condition (ibid.). Hence, justice is still far from prevailing despite years of international involvement.

In East Timor the national police grew in expertise and strength and in May 2004 UNMISET handed over responsibility for policing to the national government (Human Rights Watch 2005b, 2006d). Still the national police remained fragile, underdeveloped and inadequately trained and not able to maintain law and order in accordance with international human rights standards. The judiciary and correctional system also remained unable to deliver justice (Human Rights Watch 2005b, Samuels 2006).

In Liberia UNMIL has been fairly successful in monitoring and reporting on human rights and in disarming and demobilising combatants (Henry L. Stimson Centre 2007). However, the reintegration of former combatants has been hampered by an inability to tackle high unemployment, with demobilised combatants voicing their discontent in violent demonstrations (Henry L. Stimson Centre 2007, Human Rights Watch 2007b). Though 2,600 national police officers had completed their training programme by March 2007, the force remained weak since it still lacks adequate logistics and transport facilities, its deployment outside the capital remains limited and many police officers still behave unprofessionally and illegally (ibid.). Human rights violations still occur and alleged criminals are still being attacked by mobs trying to impose their own version of justice (Human Rights Watch 2007b). Though some prison personnel have been trained and some prison facilities refurbished, most regions still lack prisons, whereas in other areas the prisons are overcrowded, understaffed and afford poor sanitation and nutrition (Henry L. Stimson Centre 2007, International Crisis Group 2006b). Finally, though a law school has been established, some judicial personnel trained and some courts rebuilt, the Liberian judicial system remains very weak since some regions still have no judge, judicial personnel are inadequately trained and skilled and the infrastructure is poor, resulting in a very slow and at times corrupt judicial system (Henry L. Stimson Centre 2007, Human Rights Watch 2007b, International Crisis Group 2006b).

Despite years of UN involvement in Haiti, progress in the country is negligible. Though some advances have been made in reforming, recruiting and training the national police force, the implementation of the vetting programme has only just begun and the force remains corrupt, abusive, criminal and politicised (Action Aid 2006b, International Crisis Group 2007). The implementation of the DDR process has largely failed and organised crime and gang violence continues and has even escalated (Action Aid 2006b). The justice system is still plagued by poorly trained and corrupt personnel, inadequate infrastructure and lack of up-to-date laws and procedures. There has only been very limited progress in the development of a functioning prison system, with prisons overcrowded and marked by abuse and riots (Action Aid 2006b, International Crisis Group 2007). Hence, Haiti still lacks a functional and fair national police force, judiciary and correctional system.

In Côte d'Ivoire the DDR programme has still not been implemented, the judicial system is still not working, resulting in impunity and UNOCI has not been able to stop serious human rights violations being committed on a regular basis (Amnesty International 2007c, Human Rights Watch 2007c). Hence, international efforts to establish justice have completely failed.

Likewise in the Sudan, the violent conflict also continues and horrendous human rights violations are committed on a daily basis (Amnesty International 2007d, Human Rights Watch 2007d). The UNMIS human rights unit manages to report violations regularly to the UNSC, and a human rights commission for the south has also been set up (ibid.). However, a national commission is yet to be established; arbitrary arrests and detentions, torture and violations of the rights of the defendant still prevail in cases brought to court, and the justice system is far from able to deal with all the crimes committed (ibid.). Hence justice is still very far away.

Explaining the successes and failures

The results of the peace missions deployed in the new millennium have been negatively influenced by many of the same general factors as their predecessors.

One of these main negative factors, impacting the results of several of the peace missions, including those in the Congo, Liberia, Haiti and Sudan, is the ongoing and often severe violence, which mission mandates have failed to consider adequately. Missions have also suffered from an often total lack of cooperation from the parties. In addition, the outcome of many, including those in Bosnia-Herzegovina, Haiti, Liberia and Sierra Leone, has also been negatively affected by a lack of adequate funding and long-term mandates so that they have tended to focus on short-term needs rather than comprehensive and coherent approaches aimed at building sustainable structures and institutions (Dziedzic and Barr 2002, Human Rights Watch 2004, International Crisis Group 2004, 2006b, 2007). Some missions' unwillingness to consult local actors and ensure local involvement, cooperation and ownership in their activities also had a negative impact on results (Action Aid 2006b, International Crisis Group 2004, 2007). Finally, the peace missions have also suffered from a lack of adequately trained and experienced international personnel (Action Aid 2006a, 2006b, International Crisis Group 2003a, 2004).

Several factors also hindered many of the peace missions in developing effective national police forces that were able to ensure justice, including the lack of a coordinated and coherent long-term plan for the development of a new national unified police force (Action Aid 2006a, 2006b, Human Rights Watch 2006c, 2006d). In general, focus has concentrated on training national police officers at the expense of other factors, such as basic equipment, facilities and logistics, also vital for a well-functioning force (Action Aid 2006a, 2006b, Human Rights Watch 2006c, 2006d, 2007a, 2007e, International Crisis Group 2003a, 2004, 2006a, 2006c, Refugees International 2004). Despite this focus on training, the training programmes have often been inadequate and uncoordinated (Action Aid 2006b, Human Rights Watch 2006c, 2006d, 2006f). In Bosnia-Herzegovina, Haiti, Congo and Liberia, inadequate or total lack of vetting of candidates has also meant that many new officers had been heavily involved in the violent conflict and continue to carry out violations as police officers (Action Aid 2006a, 2006b, International Crisis Group 2002a, Human Rights Watch 2007a, 2007b). This has been especially problematic in, for example, the Congo and East Timor, since in these cases no accountability mechanism for police officers guilty of human rights violations has been established (Action Aid 2006a, Human Rights Watch 2006d). The relatively low salary offered to new police in, for example, Haiti, Congo and Sierra Leone, has also left them prone to corruption (Action Aid 2006a, 2006b, International Crisis Group 2003a). Finally, the peace missions have also failed to develop sustainable capacity-building in the national police forces including not only failing to establish plans and secure resources for future reforms and recruitment and training but also failing to induce an institutional culture of fair policing methods and confidence and pride in belonging to the new national force (Action Aid 2006b, Human Rights Watch 2006c, 2006d, International Crisis Group 2004).

Numerous factors have contributed to the peace missions' failure to develop fair and well-functioning national judicial systems. Many missions have focused much less on this goal than on, for example, policing, resulting in inadequate allocation of resources to judicial reform (Action Aid 2006a, 2006b, Dziedzic and Barr 2002, Human Rights Watch 2006d, International Crisis Group 2004, 2006b, 2006c, Samuels 2006, Henry L. Stimson Centre 2007). In addition, many missions had no coordinated, comprehensive and coherent plan to establish a sustainable, fair and well-functioning national judicial system (Action Aid 2006a, 2006b, Dziedzic and Barr 2002, Human Rights Watch 2007a, 2007b, 2007c, 2007d, 2007e, International Crisis Group 2003a, 2003b, Samuels 2006). Hence, the provision of basic infrastructure and resources, such as court rooms and office supplies, essential for a well-functioning justice system, has not been forthcoming (Action Aid 2006a, 2006b, Henry L. Stimson Centre 2007, International Crisis Group 2006b). Furthermore, some missions have also failed to build local sustainable capacity in the system by vetting and adequately training enough personnel for the national courts to be able to work fairly and effectively, both while the peace missions were still deployed and beyond (Action Aid 2006a, 2006b, Human Rights Watch 2004, 2007a, 2007b, 2007e, International Crisis Group 2006b, 2006c, Henry L. Stimson Centre 2007, Samuels 2006). Finally, the peace missions in Liberia and the Congo especially have failed to secure adequate pay to national judicial personnel, leaving judges prone to corruption; and the peace missions in Bosnia-Herzegovina and Haiti have also not been able to curb political influence on the judiciary (Action Aid 2006a, 2006b, International Crisis Group 2002a, 2006b. 2006c).

Furthermore, several factors also contributed to some peace missions' failure to disarm, demobilise and reintegrate former combatants. In some cases, the demobilisation phase has been too short and the waiting time between demobilisation and reintegration too long (Action Aid 2006a, International Crisis Group 2004). The missions in Liberia, Sierra Leone and the Congo also failed to implement an approach focusing on long-term reintegration rather than on immediate needs and to allocate adequate efforts and resources for reintegration and especially securing employment (Henry L. Stimson Centre 2007, International Crisis Group 2004, Malan *et al.* 2002, Refugees International 2004). Finally, some missions have also failed to convince vital actors, such as the national governments, the parties to the violent conflict and civil society groups to support the DDR process (Action Aid 2006a, 2006b).

Lastly, all the peace missions also failed to pay adequate attention to reforming and reconstructing the national correctional system (Action Aid 2006a, 2006b, Aucoin 2007, Henry L. Stimson Centre 2007, Human Rights Watch 2006e, 2006f, 2006g, Refugees International 2004), especially regarding the building and refurbishing of prisons and the staffing of these with trained personnel (ibid.).

UN reports

The Rule of Law and Transitional Justice in Conflict and Post-conflict Societies

The UNSG presented this report to the UNSC in August 2004. The report contended that establishing the rule of law is an important part of post-conflict peace-building that national authorities in societies affected by violent conflict are often not able to develop without the help of the UN (Annan 2004: 1, 3(2–3), 6(14–15), 10(27)). The report admitted that, though many recent missions had been involved in addressing the rule of law, it was still not routinely included in all missions (Annan 2004: 5(11)). The report also mentioned the numerous ways in which peace operations can help national authorities strengthen the rule of law, including establishing a national police force, judiciary and correctional systems; disarming, demobilising and reintegrating former combatants; and it underlined the importance of a comprehensive strategy (Annan 2004: 5–6(11–12), 9(23–24), 10–11(29–32), 12(35)). However, the report was also a reminder that international assistance should be tailored to the needs of the particular society and that ownership of and the main participation in the complex process towards establishing the rule of law should remain national (Annan 2004: 6(14–15)). Furthermore, the report emphasised that strengthening the rule of law is as much a political as it is a judicial process and that local consultation and support are vital (Annan 2004: 8(19–21)). It also contended that, when necessary, rule-of-law activities need to be included and integrated in peace operations (Annan 2004: 1, 6(13), 21(64a), 22(65b)). Finally, it pointed out a need to rethink the role of international soldiers and police officers in the establishment of the rule of law (Annan 2004: 10(28)).

Uniting Our Strengths: Enhancing United Nations Support for the Rule of Law

In 2006 the UNSG published this report, which set out proposals for implementing the recommendations from the previous report on enhancing UN capacity for supporting the rule of law (Annan 2006: 3(2)). The report confirmed the central position of the rule of law in the approach to post-conflict peace-building and the commitment of UN peace missions to help implement the rule of law through establishing effective and fair police, prison and judicial institutions (Annan 2006: 1, 4(7), 5(10), 17(53)). It also contended that many more UN funds, programmes and departments have now become involved in efforts aiming at establishing the rule of law and it outlined the role of UN peace missions in this regard (Annan 2006: 4 (7), 5(10), 7(17), 13(42)). Finally, the report also admitted that, adequate staff are still not allocated to dealing with these issues and the substantial deficiencies in the UN's coherence, capacities and coordination efforts also indicate a need for rationalisation and deepening of the UN's rule-of-law activities (Annan 2006: 1–2, 5(9)).

UN debates

The role of the UN and its peace missions in ensuring justice has also been debated in various UN meetings, including UNSC meetings on 24 and 30 September 2003, 6 October 2004 and 22 June 2006 (United Nations Security Council 24 September 2003, 30 September 2003, 6 October 2004a, 6 October 2004b, 22 June 2006a, 22 June 2006b). The vast majority of the participants in these debates has agreed that establishing justice is very important and that the UN needs to support and participate in the process towards making the rule of law prevail in states recovering from internal violent conflict (ibid.). Many representatives also emphasised the need for a sequenced, coordinated and comprehensive approach that includes DDR and the development of a fair and well-functioning national police force, judiciary and correctional system (ibid.). Many also stressed the importance of basing international assistance on national needs, of securing the support and involvement of local citizens and of ensuring local ownership and capacity-building (ibid.). However, the representatives from Egypt and Venezuela also claimed that the responsibility for establishing the rule of law should remain national and that the efforts of peace missions should be based on consent from the parties and impartiality (United Nations Security Council 22 June 2006b). Some participants also linked the rule of law with need for social, economic and political reforms and with international justice between states, particularly in connection with economic development and territorial disputes (United Nations Security Council 24 September 2003, 30 September 2003, 6 October 2004a, 6 October 2004b). Finally, calls were made for a rethink of the role of the UN and its peace missions in the establishment of the rule of law (United Nations Security Council 30 September, 22 June 2006a).

Summing up

Since the turn of the millennium peace missions deployed around the world have initiated a whole range of activities intended to help societies recovering from conflict establish justice and the rule of law. These missions have been involved in reforming, restructuring and training new national police forces and, in the cases of Kosovo and East Timor, even been directly involved in providing justice through executing policing tasks while national forces were established. They have been active in reforming and restructuring national justice systems, establishing national courts and monitoring and training national judicial personnel. In addition, peace missions have engaged in disarming, demobilising and reintegrating former combatants, helping promote and increase respect for human rights and in efforts to improve national correctional systems. Despite all these activities, the results have often failed to impress. In some states, such as Liberia, Côte d'Ivoire, the Congo and Sudan and to a lesser degree Haiti, continuing violence and atrocities have seriously hindered the missions from making a positive impact on the establishment of justice and the rule of law. In other places, such as Bosnia-Herzegovina, Sierra Leone, Kosovo and East

Timor, the missions have been successful in ending the violence and able to carry out their activities fairly unhindered, with general cooperation of national actors. These peace missions have also managed to establish national police forces that are reasonably able to carry out basic policing tasks but the national forces remain fragile, prone to using excessive force and unable or unwilling to deal with ethnic and organised crime. Despite the attempts to reform and restructure justice systems and to recruit and train judicial personnel, the national systems remain weak, ineffective and still in need of better infrastructure and trained and experienced personnel. In addition, despite some attempts to improve correctional systems, these often remain in desperate need of reform, improved infrastructure and trained personnel. What is worrying is that many of the same factors behind failures in the 1990s are still valid explanations of contemporary missions' limited success in the area of ensuring justice and the rule of law. They are still plagued by inadequate mandates, insufficient resources and superficial, incoherent and uncoordinated approaches. Considerably greater emphasis is still placed on establishing a national police force than on developing national justice and correction systems. This seriously limits efforts to establish justice, because even when national police are able to detain criminals, their efforts are often not supported by national judicial processes and decent imprisonment facilities.

Contemporary peace missions' involvement in establishing justice and the rule of law has been reflected in recent UN publications and debates. The UNSG report *The Rule of Law and Transitional Justice in Conflict and Post-conflict Societies* confirmed that peace operations need to help establish the rule of law in societies torn apart by violent conflict. Reflecting the experience on the ground, the report outlined a detailed, expanded role for peace missions in establishing judicial structures and institutions. It also underlined the importance of international civilian police being able to execute policing tasks if the local police proved unable to as well as the need for peace operations to take part in building correction systems and disarming, demobilising and reintegrating former combatants in order to help prevent further atrocities being committed in the future. Furthermore, reflecting one of the main reasons as to why peace missions have failed to establish national institutions and structures able to provide justice, the report emphasised the need for a comprehensive strategy encompassing all structures and institutions dealing with establishing justice, thus implying a very wide-ranging role for peace missions. Again reflecting the experience on the ground, the report also underscored the importance of adapting the international approach to local needs, of maintaining local ownership of the process and ensuring local political and public support for the process. Finally, the report admitted that the UN still lacks all the resources needed to be able to offer adequate support and that there is still therefore a need to strengthen the UN's efforts towards helping societies establish justice and the rule of law. This also included a more general need to further rethink the role of the UN.

Moreover, though the report *Uniting Our Strengths: Enhancing United Nations Support for the Rule of Law* mainly focused on the UN's general rule-of-law capacities and how these can be strengthened, it also touched upon the role of the UN in establishing the rule of law as a part of an approach to post-conflict peace-building. The report reiterated the UN's commitment to assisting states to achieve this, arguing that the rule of law had now become an integral part of the UN's approach to peace-building. Although outlining the very considerable role of UN peace operations in this process, the report admitted that the UN's activities were still constrained by significant deficiencies and that improved capacities, coherence and coordination are needed to strengthen the UN's ability to help states establish the rule of law.

The importance of establishing justice in societies recovering from violent conflict has also been on the agenda of several recent UN debates. Here the participants have generally agreed that the UN, through its peace missions, should be involved in helping such states establish national structures and institutions able to ensure justice and the rule of law. Reflecting experience from recent missions, numerous participants have underlined the need for a coherent approach based on national needs and considerate of local culture and traditions. Numerous participants have underscored the importance of gaining the support of local people, involving local people in the activities and securing local capacity-building and ownership.

UN peace missions, peace-building and justice

Since the end of the Cold War, assisting societies recovering from violent conflict to ensure justice for crimes committed in the post-conflict period has been increasingly adopted in the UN's approach to building peace. UN peace missions have gradually become engaged in activities such as disarmament, demobilisation and reintegration of former combatants, promoting respect for human rights, and establishing national police forces, judicial and correctional systems to help prevent crimes and ensure justice for post-conflict crimes. Peace missions have gone from merely monitoring national police force efforts to enforce the law, with no influence on the judicial system in Namibia and Angola, to executing policing tasks and being actively involved in rebuilding the judicial system in Kosovo and East Timor. The importance of ensuring justice for building peace in post-conflict communities and of peace missions assisting in this task has been increasingly recognised in recent UN publications and debates. However, so far the role of missions in this regard has varied considerably. In recent cases, such as the Congo, Sudan and Côte d'Ivoire as well as older missions such as Angola, Haiti, Rwanda and Somalia, missions have been deployed in the midst of ongoing conflict, rendering them unable to carry out many of the activities focusing on ensuring justice envisaged by their mandates. In other cases such as Kosovo and East Timor peace missions have been granted extensive roles in implementing programmes for establishing justice with rather more success.

However, though peace missions have at times experienced some successes in helping communities establish justice after violent conflict, these have proved relatively few and far between. Considering how much effort missions have put into these endeavours, it is as striking as it is worrying that none has managed to develop sustainable national structures and institutions able to ensure justice in a fair and effective manner and without external support and involvement. It is also remarkable that some of the basic reasons behind the failure of early peace missions in places such as Angola, Rwanda and Somalia in this regard can still help explain why some contemporary missions also fail to make an impact. Among these basic reasons is an important discrepancy between the mainly post-conflict based mandates dependent on the cooperation of the parties and the realities of a still ongoing violent conflict in the area of deployment such as is the case with the present peace missions in the Congo, Sudan and Côte d'Ivoire. Another reason is the lack of a coherent approach to not only ensuring justice but also to implementing the various parts of a coherent justice programme. Though it has been increasingly recognised in recent UN publications and debates that the development of, not only a national police force, but also functioning and fair judicial and correctional systems are preconditions for establishing justice, contemporary peace missions such as MINUSTAH and MONUC still focus much more on police improvements than they do on building judicial and correctional systems. In addition, whereas contemporary peace missions focus on disarming and demobilising former combatants, less emphasis is placed on reintegrating the soldiers to discourage them from taking up arms again. Furthermore, the stress on, for example, training police rather than on vetting candidates leaves the new national force prone to committing further human rights violations and being infiltrated by the former warring groups. A lack of adequate resources and well-equipped, trained and experienced international personnel also continues to mar the efforts of peace missions to ensure justice. Despite the importance of local participation, ownership and capacity-building, as recognised in recent UN reports and debates, contemporary missions still suffer from an inability to turn these intentions into reality. Hence, though ensuring justice has become an aim that peace missions are expected to help societies achieve, the recipe for the most suitable role of peace missions is yet to be determined.

4   UN peace missions, peace-building and transitional justice

Introduction

In order to establish sustainable peace in societies suffering the consequences of violent conflict, it is not enough to ensure accountability for crimes committed in the post-conflict phase. If reconciliation and the rule of law are to be obtained, atrocities committed during the conflict also have to be addressed. Hence, if UN peace missions are to succeed in helping recovering societies establish the rule of law, then it is not enough that they rebuild and reform the national police force, the justice system and correctional systems to secure accountability for post-conflict crimes. They also need to assist these societies to implement transitional justice processes to secure accountability for atrocities committed during the conflict. This chapter focuses on the inclusion of these processes in the UN's post-conflict peace-building approach. It examines activities that peace missions have been involved in and assesses the results of these efforts. The chapter also examines why the missions have failed or succeeded in carrying out transitional justice-related activities. Finally, it also looks at recent UN reports and debates in order to establish their views of the role of peace missions in securing accountability for serious crimes committed during the violent conflict in the areas where they are deployed.

The first attempts to introduce transitional justice processes into peace missions

The first post-Cold War peace missions in Namibia and Angola did not include any provisions for establishing transitional justice.

In contrast, ONUSAL, which was deployed during ongoing conflict in El Salvador in 1991 boasted a human rights division. This was supposed to actively monitor the human rights situation and investigate specific violations and the mission was also expected to support the work of the UN-supported Commission on the Truth (Doggett and Kircher 2005, DPKO El Salvador – ONUSAL: Background, DPKO El Salvador – ONUSAL: Mandate).

In addition, a couple of years later the UNSC through resolution 965 (1994) also expanded the mandate of UNAMIR to include a request that UNAMIR would use its good office to help achieve national reconciliation and provide security for human rights officers and the personnel of the International Criminal Tribunal for Rwanda (ICTR), who were investigating atrocities committed during the genocide in order for the ICTR to be able to prosecute the worst perpetrators (DPKO Rwanda – UNAMIR: Background).

Though the mandates of the peace missions in Somalia and Haiti also stated that they should support national reconciliation the missions apparently did not carry out any activities aimed at securing accountability for atrocities committed during the conflict.

Limited support to other institutions

In El Salvador ONUSAL managed to set up offices from where human rights officers monitored the human rights situation, investigated violations and reported their findings to the United Nations Secretary General (Doggett and Kircher 2005). However, the peace mission's reports were accused of understating the seriousness of the violations in an attempt to encourage better behaviour rather than secure accountability (ibid.). ONUSAL was also criticised for merely verifying that the atrocities had been committed rather than also lobbying for accountability (ibid.). The downgrading of human rights issues after the signing of the peace agreement also implied that ONUSAL sacrificed human rights concerns for achieving a political solution to the conflict (ibid.). ONUSAL did hand over all the information it had collected about human rights violations to the Ombudsman for Human Rights when it left El Salvador but then it was left to the national institution to follow this up (Ter Horst 2006). ONUSAL also provided support to investigators from the Commission of the Truth and monitored the El Salvadorian government's progress in implementing the recommendations developed by the Commission (DPKO EL Salvador – ONUSAL: Background). Hence, ONUSAL was fairly successful in investigating human rights violations but the mission did very little to help ensure accountability. Accountability was sacrificed in order to secure an end to the violence; and it was left to the national authorities to hold individuals accountable for the violations that they had committed during the conflict. The El Salvadoran government failed to implement many of the truth commission's recommendations and it granted amnesty to perpetrators responsible for atrocities during the conflict (Doggett and Kircher 2005). Hence, ONUSAL's efforts did not secure accountability.

In Rwanda UNAMIR's role in helping secure accountability was also confined to affording limited support to other institutions. Upon the establishment of the new Office of the Prosecutor of the ICTR, UNAMIR provided the new institutions with basic equipment such as vehicles and computers. However, since the equipment had already been well used by UNAMIR, it was not much help (DPKO Rwanda – UNAMIR: Background, President of the ICTR 1997). UNAMIR also provided security for international human rights officers and investigators from the Office of the Prosecutor of the ICTR for a short period of time before leaving Rwanda (President of the ICTR 1997). Hence, though

UNAMIR did manage to support the work of the human rights officers and investigators, the efforts of the peace mission had little positive impact and therefore its contribution to ensuring accountability was very minimal.

A lack of support, powers, resources and commitment

In Rwanda UNAMIR generally suffered from a lack of financial resources and hence, it is hardly surprising that the equipment left behind was well used and not really suitable for recycling by the personnel of the Office of the Prosecutor of the ICTR. Disagreement between the UN and the Rwandan government over the role of UNAMIR and a lack of support from the main troop-contributing countries led to the termination of UNAMIR's mission at a time when the Prosecutor of the ICTR had just begun her investigations and hence the positive impact of UNAMIR was very limited (DPKO Rwanda – UNAMIR: Background).

Several factors also contributed to ONUSAL's limited success in helping El Salvador address violations committed during the violent conflict. There was tension between the UN's political role as mediator of the peace agreement and its dependence on the cooperation of the parties to the violent conflict and ONUSAL's human rights role as observer and investigator of human rights violations committed by the parties to the conflict (Doggett and Kircher 2005). In the beginning ONUSAL's monitoring and investigation of atrocities also suffered from a paucity of guidelines from headquarters, which meant that the work was carried out differently in the various regions of El Salvador (ibid.). ONUSAL also failed to involve the local population and local NGOs in its monitoring and investigative activities (ibid.). ONUSAL's lack of powers to force national institutions such as the Ombudsman for Human Rights and the El Salvadoran government to act on its investigations and the recommendations of the Truth Commission also considerably limited its impact on the process of securing accountability.

UN reports

An Agenda for Peace

The 1992 report, *An Agenda for Peace* did not anticipate transitional justice becoming a part of UN peace missions. It did argue that a precondition for a successful peacekeeping operation was the inclusion of wide-ranging efforts intended to support structures to help strengthen peace and that these activities needed to include efforts towards protecting human rights (Boutrous-Ghali, 1992: paragraph 55). However, the report did not specify the actions that peace operations should take in this regard or that these actions should also focus on holding individuals accountable for violations during the conflict.

A Supplement to an Agenda for Peace

A Supplement to an Agenda for Peace stated that international interventions should include the promotion of national reconciliation without specifying what this entailed (Boutrous-Ghali 1995: paragraph 13). Concerning human rights issues, the report apparently only addressed the importance of upholding human rights after the conflict, since it contended that observing, verifying respect of and promoting human rights represent important parts of post-conflict peace-building (Boutrous-Ghali 1995: paragraphs 21, 22, 47). Hence, like its predecessor, the report did not include transitional justice in its approach to post-conflict peace-building.

Summing up

The UN's first attempts to mandate its peace missions to contribute to securing accountability for atrocities committed during the violent conflict were fairly half-hearted. In Rwanda, UNAMIR merely provided basic support to the investigators of the ICTR and in El Salvador, though the peace mission successfully monitored and investigated human rights violations, few attempts were made to ensure accountability. This lack of commitment to the task of assisting societies in ensuring accountability for crimes committed during the violent conflict was also evident in the two UN reports, *An Agenda for Peace* and *A Supplement to an Agenda for Peace*, neither of which included transitional justice processes among the tasks the reports expected peace missions to be involved in.

Further steps towards including transitional justice processes in peace missions

After the first initial attempts to help societies recovering from violent conflict address atrocities committed during conflict, UN peace missions slowly became more involved in supporting transitional justice processes though the involvement remained limited and incoherent.

In Bosnia-Herzegovina UNMIBH[15] was expected to support the work of the International Criminal Tribunal for the Former Yugoslavia (ICTY) that had been set up prior to UNMIBH's deployment. UNMIBH was also expected to help implement a vetting process to prevent individuals responsible for atrocities from joining the new national police force (DPKO Bosnia-Herzegovina – UNMIBH: Background).

UNSC resolution 1037 (1996) also requested that UNTAES assist the ICTY in holding individuals accountable by protecting ICTY staff while they carried out investigations and guarding mass grave sites during excavation.

In Guatemala more than 250 human rights officers from the original civilian-led peace mission MINUGUA were also involved in observing and verifying atrocities (DPKO Guatemala – MINUGUA: Background). MINUGUA also set up a Coordination Committee to strengthen MINUGUA's cooperation with the

Guatemalan Ombudsman for Human Rights and the peace mission trained the staff of the Ombudsman institution in carrying out investigations (Dodson and Jackson 2004). Finally, MINUGUA was also expected to support the National Truth Commission (Human Rights Watch 1999b).

Furthermore, UNSC resolution 1244 (1999) also demanded that UNMIK[16] fully cooperate with the ICTY and hence, UNMIK assisted the ICTY in its crime scene and exhumations programme (President of the ICTY 2000). In December 1999 UNMIK suggested the setting up of a Kosovo War and Ethnic Crimes Court with both national and international judges and prosecutors able to hold individuals accountable for atrocities committed during the violent conflict that were not serious enough to be dealt with by the ICTY (International Crisis Group 2002b). UNMIK also established a Victim Recovery and Identification Commission to recover and identify bodies, dispose of bodies, provide support to the families and manage data and related legal issues (President of the ICTY 2000).

Finally, in East Timor UNTAET's Human Rights Unit initiated investigations into the atrocities committed during the conflict (Reiger and Wierda 2006). Though its mandate did not specifically authorise UNTAET to set up mechanisms able to secure accountability for these crimes, UNTAET established the Special Panels under the Dili District Court in the summer of 2000 (ibid.). The Special Panels were requested to try cases of atrocities committed between 1 January and 25 October 1999 and consisted of one national and two international judges (ibid.). UNTAET also established a Serious Crimes Unit to investigate the atrocities committed during the same period (DPKO East Timor – UNTAET: Justice and Serious Crimes).

More success supporting other institutions than in carrying out own initiatives

In Bosnia-Herzegovina UNMIBH managed to successfully assist the ICTY in carrying out search warrants and providing accommodation, logistics and communication to the personnel of the Office of the ICTY Prosecutor (President of the ICTY 1999).[17] During 1995–1998 UNMIBH initiated a police vetting programme in the Federation part of Bosnia-Herzegovina but this was abandoned again before any results and, due to resistance from national authorities, it was never even introduced in Republika Srpska (International Centre for Transitional Justice 2004). Hence, UNMIBH's first attempt to vet the national police ended in complete failure. In 1999 it initiated a second attempt, with more success, though some officers, who had allegedly been heavily involved in the conflict, still managed to keep their jobs (International Centre for Transitional Justice 2004, International Crisis Group 2002a, President of the ICTY 1998, 1999).

In Croatia UNTAES soldiers successfully guarded mass graves while they were being exhumed by specialists from the ICTY and, at the end of June 1997, UNTAES assisted agents from the ICTY to arrest indicted war criminal Slavko Dokmanovic (DPKO Croatia – UNTAES: Brief Chronology).

In Guatemala MINUGUA managed to investigate and document human rights violations committed while the violent conflict was still ongoing and in its aftermath (Human Rights Watch 1999b, Wilson 1997). MINUGUA also supported the work of the National Truth Commission, which managed to document 42,000 victims of atrocities during the conflict and recommended reforms of the judiciary and security apparatus (Human Rights Watch 1999b). However, since the Truth Commission only had limited investigatory powers, it was not allowed to name any perpetrators and its findings could not be used in court. Hence its ability to ensure accountability for atrocities was highly constrained (Wilson 1997). MINUGUA's attempts to support the Guatemalan Ombudsman for Human Rights also largely failed since the procurator refused to cooperate and many of the local investigators trained by MINUGUA were fired (Dodson and Jackson 2004). Furthermore, MINUGUA did not manage to prevent the parties to the violent conflict from agreeing to implement amnesty provisions in late 1996 (Wilson 1997). The weak national judicial system that was largely unable to hold perpetrators accountable and the failure to establish an international mechanism able to hold Guatemalan individuals accountable also meant that impunity for human rights violations committed during the violent conflict continued (Human Rights Watch 1999b, Kauffman 2005, Wilson 1997).

In Kosovo UNMIK successfully supported the work of the ICTY through assisting in its crime scene investigations and exhumations and in cooperating in the Victim Recovery and Identification Commission (Risley 10 May 2000, President of the ICTY 2000). However, UNMIK was less successful in helping ensure accountability through establishing a national mechanism able to prosecute alleged war criminals whose deeds were not serious enough to be dealt with by the ICTY, since UNMIK decided to rely instead on prosecution in the ordinary emerging national judicial system (International Crisis Group 2002b). The reasons behind this decision were allegedly that UNMIK considered a special court with international highly paid personnel and high administrative costs was too expensive (ibid.). In addition, UNMIK pointed out that international judges and lawyers were already a part of the emerging national system and that dealing with the cases within this system would build more local capacity than a separate tribunal would (ibid.). The national system, with the help of international judges and lawyers, managed to successfully carry out some reasonably fair trials, thereby contributing to ensuring some accountability (ibid.). However, especially in the beginning, this contribution was limited by the fact that few cases were raised against former KLA fighters (ibid.).

Finally, in East Timor international police investigators working for the Serious Crimes Unit began investigating crimes from during the conflict and recruitment also began for the Special Panels (DPKO East Timor – UNTAET: Justice and Serious Crimes, Reiger and Wierda 2006). However, the slow progress and questionable quality of the investigations questioned UNTAET's commitment to bringing perpetrators to justice (Amnesty International 2001).

Still lacking support, commitment and resources

A wide variety of factors contributed to the peace missions' mixed results.

Several factors contributed to UNMIBH, UNTAES and UNMIK being moderately able to provide the requested support to the ICTY. First, their expected roles were limited to fairly simple and uncontroversial tasks and, even when UNTAES supplied the ICTY with probably the most controversial support, namely, assistance in the arrest of indicted war criminal Slavko Dokmanovic, its role was limited.[18] The missions also had relatively many resources and personnel, together with support from international military personnel, enabling a reasonable level of security. This meant that the civilian parts of the mission enjoyed a fairly secure working environment.

In Bosnia-Herzegovina UNMIBH's first attempt to vet national police officers ended in complete failure, mainly due to a lack of cooperation from national authorities and initially also a lack of clear authorisation to undertake the process despite resistance from those authorities (International Centre for Transitional Justice 2004, United Nations Development Programme 2006). A lack of sufficient time and qualified staff and inadequate resources also contributed to UNMIBH's failure to vet the force (United Nations Development Programme 2006). The second attempt was more successful because UNMIBH had gained clearer authorisation and increased time and resources (ibid.).

In Guatemala MINUGUA was fairly successful in investigating and reporting on human rights abuses due partly to generous donors, enabling the mission to employ many national and international staff (Beruto 2006). It is also likely that MINUGUA's lack of power to hold any individuals accountable for the violations investigated made it easier to investigate allegations of human rights abuses, since the perpetrators knew that, regardless of what MINUGUA found out, the amnesty laws and the lack of a functioning national judicial system or an alternative international criminal tribunal, meant that they would not face repercussions for their deeds. However, it is also likely that MINUGUA's double role as, on the one hand, a mediator of the peace process and, on the other, supporter of the National Truth Commission and investigator of human rights violations, illustrated by the Mincho[19] case, negatively affected its work (Wilson 1997). Finally, a failure in the political will of the national authorities to follow up MINUGUA's investigations and a lack of cooperation from national authorities and the parties to the violent conflict also negatively impacted MINUGUA's ability to ensure accountability for human rights violations (Human Rights Watch 1999c, Kauffman 2005, Wilson 1997).

In Kosovo UNMIK's contribution to holding lower-level war criminals accountable for their atrocities was negatively impacted by a lack of resources for the establishment of a special national war crimes tribunal and an overrated belief in the national judicial system's ability to deal with offenders (International Crisis Group 2002b).

Finally, in East Timor several factors also contributed to UNTAET's initial problems concerning the establishment of the Serious Crimes Unit and the

Special Panels. First the two institutions represented an ad hoc solution rather than the outcome of a well-planned and integrated transitional justice process (Järvinen 2004, Reiger and Wierda 2006). Both the Special Panels and the Serious Crimes Unit also lacked qualified staff and resources (ibid.). Both also failed to consult and involve local NGOs and local judicial personnel, despite for example, the local NGOs possessing a lot of potentially useful information. This negatively affected the progress of the investigations as well as relations with the local community (Reiger and Wierda 2006). Furthermore, UNTAET's lack of explicit powers to initiate a transitional justice process; a slow start that made the collection of evidence more difficult; and a dearth of political support also negatively impacted UNTAET's attempt to hold individuals accountable (Järvinen 2004).

UN report

Report of the Panel on the United Nations Peace Operations

The Brahimi report underlined the UN's commitment to peace-building including promoting reconciliation and enhancing respect for human rights through investigating past abuses (Brahimi 2000: paragraph 13). The report contended that, whenever necessary, experts, forensic specialists and criminal investigators should take part in peace operations in order to assist international criminal tribunals in apprehending and prosecuting indicted war criminals (Brahimi 2000: paragraph 39). Finally, it recommended that the enhanced focus on improving respect for human rights should lead to a doctrinal shift in the use of human rights experts, rule-of-law components and civilian police (Brahimi 2000: paragraph 40).

Summing up

In the latter part of the 1990s the role of peace missions in assisting societies address past atrocities varied considerably, from no involvement at all in cases such as the peace missions in Haiti, Liberia and Angola, through to a consolidating role in the case of MINUGUA and an expanding role in the case of UNMIBH and UNTAES, to a significantly expanded role in the cases of UNMIK and UNTAET. In Guatemala MINUGUA's role resembled that of ONUSAL's in El Salvador, consolidating the task of investigating human rights violations and attempting to support national institutions in securing some kind of accountability for the atrocities committed during the violent conflict. The fairly diverse roles of UNMIBH, UNTAES and UNMIK in helping the ICTY, which included not only providing security for ICTY personnel but also assisting in investigations and, in UNTAES's case, in the apprehension of indicted war criminals, pointed towards peace missions being increasingly expected to actively support and participate in international institutions' attempts to ensure accountability for atrocities committed during conflicts. UNMIBH's involvement in vetting the national police force also indicated that different transitional justice tools were gradually becoming a part of the UN's approach to post-conflict peace-building. The peace missions in Kosovo and East Timor went even further than just supporting the efforts of other international institutions, since they initiated their own trial processes for individuals allegedly responsible for atrocities. Hence, peace missions went from merely supporting national and international attempts to hold individuals accountable for past abuses to attempting to ensure accountability through courts they set up themselves.

The peace missions were generally fairly successful in investigating human rights violations and in providing the required support to international institutions to hold individuals accountable. However, they were less successful in carrying out new tasks, such as vetting the police and establishing tribunals able to hold individuals accountable for past atrocities. Even in the successful cases, the missions' contribution to ensuring accountability for past human rights violations was still limited since, for example, in the case of MINUGUA, the national authorities refused to initiate criminal prosecutions and, in the cases of UNMIBH and UNTAES, though they fairly successfully supported the work of the ICTY, the international criminal tribunal dealt with relatively few cases. Finally, UNTAET's and UNMIK's initial attempts to hold individuals accountable in courts set up by the peace missions were not very successful and therefore their contribution to ensuring accountability for atrocities committed during the violent conflict was relatively limited.

A variety of factors influenced the missions' results in activities to helping societies ensure accountability for past abuses. In some cases a reasonable level of security, a fairly limited role and adequate staff and resources contributed to successful outcomes. In other cases a lack of cooperation especially from national authorities and the parties to the conflict, an inadequate personnel and resources and a failure to consult and involve local people and NGOs negatively impacted the missions' ability to implement their activities. In addition, though the role of peace missions in implementing transitional justice programmes was significantly expanded during this period, they were still far from being requested to implement a coherent transitional justice approach, which limited their contribution to securing transitional justice.

Peace missions' increased involvement in assisting societies address past atrocities was also reflected in the Brahimi report's statement that this was an important goal of post-conflict peace-building. However, also reflecting the experiences of the peace missions, all of which had been involved in implementing rather autonomous and diverse transitional justice, means, the report did not specify which transitional justice activities peace missions should be involved in. It emphasised the importance of investigating human rights violations but did not explicitly include the task of securing individual accountability for these. In addition, the report did acknowledge the importance of peace operations supporting international criminal tribunals' efforts to apprehend and prosecute indicted war criminals but did not specify the type of support intended. Nevertheless, the report did call for a rethink of the role of peace operation personnel in the improvement of respect for human rights.

Hence during this period the inclusion of transitional justice in the UN's approach to peace-building was still in its infancy. UN peace missions had become involved in implementing transitional justice processes but their role was still very unclear and their approach incoherent.

Post-Brahimi: the expanded yet still incoherent approach of UN peace missions in transitional justice processes

In Bosnia-Herzegovina UNMIBH kept implementing its vetting programme and assisting the ICTY until the end of the mission in 2002 (International Centre for Transitional Justice 2004).

In Kosovo UNMIK also continued to assist the Prosecutor of the ICTY in her investigations (The President of the ICTY 2001, 2002, 2003, 2004, 2005, 2006, 2007). UNMIK also acknowledged that it was it's responsibility to investigate and prosecute past atrocities not severe enough to fall under ICTY jurisdiction (International Crisis Group 2002b). Recognising that the national judicial system with national judges and prosecutors that it had established was not able to conduct fair trials, UNMIK began employing international judges and prosecutors able to secure fair and effective trials (Human Rights Watch 2006c, International Centre for Transitional Justice 2006, International Crisis Group 2002b). UNMIK police also began arresting individuals, including former KLA fighters and members of the Kosovo Protection Corps, who had allegedly committed atrocities during the violent conflict (International Crisis Group 2002b).

In East Timor UNTAET and later UNMISET also remained involved in securing accountability for atrocities committed during the violent conflict. UNTAET's Serious Crimes Unit continued to investigate these crimes and the Special Panels began hearing cases (DPKO East Timor – UNTAET: Justice and Serious Crimes). In January 2002 UNTAET also established a Commission for Reception, Truth and Reconciliation in East Timor (CAVR) to obtain reconciliation and justice (DPKO East Timor – UNTAET: Truth and Reconciliation). The commission was not authorised to grant amnesty and it was expected to hand over any evidence about serious violations of human rights to the national prosecutor (ibid.).

In Sierra Leone UNAMSIL helped set up the Special Court for Sierra Leone (SC-SL), authorised to try those individuals most responsible for the atrocities committed during the violent conflict (DPKO Sierra Leone – UNAMSIL: Background). UNAMSIL has also provided security during hearings in the SC-SL and helped promote and raise awareness of the court's work through, for example, airing weekly summaries of this on the mission's radio station (Human Rights Watch 2004, International Crisis Group 2003a). UNAMSIL has also helped the Sierra Leone government establish the Truth and Reconciliation Commission (TRC) and provided the TRC with logistical capacities, supported and promoted its work and helped raise awareness about the TRC through, for example, transmitting TRC hearings on UNAMSIL's radio (DPKO Sierra Leone – UNAMSIL: Background, Human Rights Watch 2004, International Crisis Group 2002d).

In the Democratic Republic of Congo UNSC resolution 1565 (2004)[20] requested MONUC to assist in ending impunity by investigating human rights violations and to participate in the process of holding those accountable for their deeds in close cooperation with other UN agencies (DPKO Democratic Republic of Congo – MONUC: Mandate). Hence, MONUC has established a Human Rights Division to monitor and document violations of humane law (DPKO Democratic Republic of Congo – MONUC: Human Rights Mandates and Activities). MONUC also has a Special Investigations Unit that conducts investigations into alleged gross violations of human rights and a Justice Support Unit that also aims at bringing perpetrators to justice (DPKO Democratic Republic of Congo – MONUC: Human Rights Justice Support Unit, DPKO Democratic Republic of Congo – MONUC: Human Rights Special Investigations Unit). The Justice Support Unit identifies symbolic cases of mass atrocities and lobbies for justice in these cases in local and national courts as well as supporting the establishment of special tribunals to deal with the cases (DPKO Democratic Republic of Congo – MONUC: Human Rights Justice Support Unit). The unit also supports the Truth and Reconciliation Commission (ibid.).

In Liberia UNMIL is also expected to support national attempts to ensure accountability for atrocities committed during the violent conflict and hence UNMIL has supported the establishment of Liberia's Truth and Reconciliation Commission (TRC) (DPKO Liberia – UNMIL: Operations Human Rights). The commission is charged with investigating gross violations of human rights during the violent conflict in Liberia between January 1979 and October 2003, focusing especially on the use of child soldiers and sexual violence (ibid.). The TRC is authorised to recommend amnesty in cases that do not involve serious violations of international humanitarian law and prosecution for the most severe atrocities (Human Rights Watch 2007b). UNMIL has also supported the establishment of the Independent National Commission for Human Rights, which is not only supposed to investigate human rights violations but also to help implement the recommendations of the TRC once the commission has finished its work (Amnesty International 2007e). During 2004–2005 UNMIL was also involved in vetting the new national police force (Human Rights Watch 2006b). Finally, UNSC resolution 1638 (2005) also requested UNMIL to detain the former President of Liberia Charles Taylor and transfer him to the Special Court for Sierra Leone if he returned to Liberia from his exile in Nigeria.

Furthermore, in Haiti MINUSTAH is expected to assist national authorities in vetting police officers. Until recently MINUSTAH has only been involved in vetting new recruits since June 2005 but now the implementation of a new police reform that includes vetting all serving officers has begun (International Crisis Group 2006c, 2007). In addition, UNSC resolution 1542 (2004) requested that MINUSTAH support the national government and national human rights institutions in their attempts to ensure accountability for human rights atrocities and reparation for victims (DPKO Haiti – MINUSTAH: Mandate). So far attempts to hold individuals accountable for past atrocities have been confined to the highly dysfunctional national judicial system apparently without MINUS-TAH involvement (Human Rights Watch 2006f, 2007, International Crisis Group 2006c).

In Sudan UNSC resolution 1590 (2005) requested UNMIS to help the parties to the peace agreement protect human rights by means of a coordinated and comprehensive strategy aim to combat impunity (DPKO Sudan – UNMIS: Mandate). So far UNMIS has set up a Human Rights Office to observe, report and investigate allegations of human rights violations in Darfur and assess the human rights situation in the rest of the country (UNMIS – Human Rights Office). The Human Rights Office also monitors the local and national police, prosecution and judicial institutions that are responsible for holding offenders accountable for their deeds (UNMIS – Human Rights Office).

In Côte d'Ivoire UNSC resolution 1739 (2007) requested UNOCI to monitor and assist in the investigation of human rights violations in order to put an end to impunity. So far UNOCI's human rights division has managed to observe and report on the human rights situation and to participate in the investigation of abuses (UNOCI – Human Rights).

Improvements still needed

In Bosnia-Herzegovina UNMIBH managed to vet 24,000 police officers before the mission ended in 2002 (International Centre for Transitional Justice 2004). Still, some officers apparently slipped through the net and were allowed to keep working despite not fulfilling the requirements of the vetting programme (International Crisis Group 2002a). The vetting process was also criticised for being unfair and failing to institutionalise a vetting procedure for future recruitment (International Centre for Transitional Justice 2004, United Nations Development Programme 2006).

In Kosovo UNMIK satisfactorily supported the work of the Prosecutor of the ICTY up until 2006, when there was serious disagreement between UNMIK and the Prosecutor concerning the handling of the case against the former President of Kosovo Ramush Haradinaj, mainly over the role of UNMIK in securing Haradinaj provisional release[21] (President of the ICTY 2001, 2002, 2003, 2004, 2005, 2006, 2007). The Prosecutor of the ICTY was also discontented with the level of protection UNMIK provided for witnesses testifying in the Haradinaj case (President of the ICTY 2007). UNMIK has had mixed results when prosecuting war criminals in the national judicial system. The national system has been able to deal with some war crime cases satisfactorily but there have also been accusations of highly questionable acquittals of Kosovo Albanians and guilty verdicts of Serb defendants (Human Rights Watch 2006c, Perriello and Wierda 2006). The system also failed to deal with cases where the victims were not Kosovo-Albanians and it failed to secure the detention of many suspects who were no longer living in Kosovo (International Crisis Group 2002b, Human

Rights Watch 2006c). Finally, despite many investigations, only relatively few cases have made it into the national courts and hence, accountability for past crimes has in many cases not yet been secured (Human Rights Watch 2006c).

In East Timor both the Serious Crimes Unit and the Special Panels struggled to deal with all the atrocities committed during the violent conflict (Reiger and Wierda 2006). When UNTAET was replaced by UNMISET after East Timor had become independent, the accountability process became a part of the national East Timor judicial system though many of the staff and much of the funding remained international (International Centre for Transitional Justice 2007). Though the investigation of cases had not finished and it was considered unlikely that the new national judiciary would be able to take over the investigations without international assistance, the UN decided to terminate the work of the Special Crimes Unit in May 2005 (ibid.). At that time the Special Crimes Unit had indicted 391 individuals and ensured 88 convictions of mainly minor perpetrators but 339 indicted individuals were still at large outside the territorial jurisdiction of UNMISET (International Centre for Transitional Justice 2007, Reiger and Wierda 2006). After UNMISET left the Special Panels were also terminated, mainly because the process had lost the support of the East Timorese government, which favoured a good relationship with Indonesia over securing accountability (International Centre for Transitional Justice 2007). Finally, the Truth and Reconciliation Commission managed to document more than 100,000 deaths and develop many recommendations but the report was not released until after UNMISET had left and it was largely ignored by the East Timorese authorities (Human Rights Watch 2006d).

In Sierra Leone UNAMSIL was fairly successful in providing the requested support to the SC-SL and the Sierra Leonean TRC (Human Rights Watch 2004, International Crisis Group 2002c, 2003a). The SC-SL has successfully finished two cases against alleged war criminals with two still ongoing, including the trial against the former President of Liberia Charles Taylor, which has been moved to The Hague for security reasons. The TRC has successfully carried out public hearings around Sierra Leone with perpetrators, victims and witnesses; it has collected more than 7,500 statements; and developed a thorough report that featured recommendations to the Sierra Leone government (Amnesty International 2004, 2005, 2006a). However, many of these recommendations are yet to be implemented (Amnesty International 2007f). In addition, the amnesty provisions of the Lome Peace Agreement and the weak national judicial system have also prevented ensuring accountability for atrocities committed by lower-level perpetrators. Hence, though very important steps towards securing accountability have already been taken, many perpetrators who have not taken part in the SC-SL or the TRC processes are yet to be held accountable for their deeds.

In the Congo, though MONUC has helped deter human rights violations and investigated and reported on offences, these atrocities still occur frequently (DPKO Democratic Republic of Congo – MONUC: Human Rights Mandates and Activities, Human Rights Watch 2006g). Some individuals have been brought to justice but, despite MONUC's support and lobbying, in the vast majority of cases the national judicial system has not been able to ensure accountability (Amnesty International 2006b, 2007, Human Rights Watch 2006g, 2007a). In addition, individuals who took part in the conflict have been allowed to join the new army and take up positions in the local and national transitional institutions (ibid.). Hence, there is still very little accountability for atrocities committed during the violent conflict in the Democratic Republic of Congo.

In Liberia, UNMIL apprehended Charles Taylor upon his arrival in Liberia from Nigeria and transferred him to Sierra Leone (UNMIL 30 March 2006). However, it was much less successful in vetting the new national police force and hence, many individuals who had been heavily involved in the conflict were allowed to join the force, resulting in some new officers engaging in criminal and unprofessional behaviour (Human Rights Watch 2006e). The UNMIL-supported TRC has had an ambiguous beginning: it has been quite successful in collecting statements from victims and witnesses but has not been able to begin its public hearings (Amnesty International 2007e, McConnell 16 March 2007). In addition, the Liberian government and the international community have so far failed to develop plans to hold individuals guilty of the most serious atrocities accountable (Human Rights Watch 2006e, 2007b). Hence, accountability in this regard is still far away.

Since June 2005 MINUSTAH has managed to vet new recruits for the national police force but has only very recently begun to implement the vetting of serving officers. Hence it is still too early to assess whether the vetting process will be a success (International Crisis Group 2006c, 2007). So far the national judicial system has been unable to prosecute individuals responsible for atrocities during the conflict and, since no international mechanism has been established either, these atrocities have not been addressed in Haiti (Amnesty International 2006c, Human Rights Watch 2006f, 2007e, International Crisis Group 2006c).

In Sudan UNMIS's efforts have so far not resulted in ensuring accountability for atrocities committed during the violent conflict. Many violations are still occurring every day and the national judicial system has so far proven unable to carry out fair trials in cases of gross human rights abuses (Amnesty International 2007d).

Finally, in Côte d'Ivoire atrocities also continue to be committed (Amnesty International 2007c). So far no national or international attempts have been made to hold any individuals responsible accountable for their deeds and hence so far UNOCI's efforts have not led to accountability (Human Rights Watch 2006h, 2007c).

Still a lack of cooperation and resources

One of the main reasons why recent peace missions have had very limited success in securing accountability for atrocities committed during the violent conflict is that, rather than being deployed in post-conflict situations where the affected societies are ready for transitional justice, missions have been deployed in the middle of ongoing violence. Failure to develop a transitional justice process sustainable once the mission has terminated has also negatively impacted some peace missions' contribution to helping to ensure accountability for past crimes, such as those committed during conflicts in Liberia, Sierra Leone and East Timor. Several factors, such as the lack of a coherent sustainable inclusive approach that is widely supported, clear criteria based on national legislation and sufficient organisation and resources have also contributed to recent peace missions' failure to vet new national police forces as in the Democratic Republic of Congo, Haiti, Liberia and Bosnia-Herzegovina (Human Rights Watch 2006e, International Centre for Transitional Justice 2004, International Crisis Group 2006c, 2007, Rumin 2007, United Nations Development Programme 2006). Like their predecessors, the peace missions also suffered from a lack of sufficiently trained and experienced staff (International Crisis Group 2002a, Perriello and Wierda 2006). In addition, concerns for personal security, a lack of translators and interpreters and a high turnover of staff have also hampered some of the missions' efforts (DPKO East Timor – UNTAET: Justice and Serious Crimes, Perriello and Wierda 2006, Reiger and Wierda 2006). Furthermore, in some cases, such as Sudan, Kosovo and the Congo, reliance on national judicial systems ability to hold individuals accountable for atrocities has also seriously influenced the peace missions' ability to help ensure accountability, since none of the missions has managed to establish national systems able to carry out fair trials of even ordinary crimes. Most missions also lacked adequate funding for their transitional justice activities, resulting in, for example, low wages to local staff, investigation units working with limited capacity and no financial resources for essential support staff such as defence lawyers, court clerks and translators (DPKO East Timor – UNTAET: Justice and Serious Crimes, International Centre for Transitional Justice 2006, International Crisis Group 2002b, Perriello and Wierda 2006, Reiger and Wierda 2006). In Kosovo and East Timor the peace missions' efforts to bring suspected war criminals to justice were also hampered by many of the suspects having left their area of deployment (Human Rights Watch 2006c, 2006d, International Centre for Transitional Justice 2007, International Crisis Group 2002b, Reiger and Wierda 2006). Finally, some missions also failed to ensure local involvement in their transitional justice activities (Perriello and Wierda 2006, Reiger and Wierda 2006).

UN document

The Rule of Law and Transitional Justice in Conflict and Post-conflict Societies

This report emphasised that peace cannot be obtained unless past atrocities are addressed through legitimate structures and hence a transitional justice process is required (Annan 2004: page 1, page 3(paragraph 2), page 8(paragraphs 19, 21)). International law now also prohibits amnesty for certain serious crimes (Annan 2004: 5 (10)). Claiming that the UN increasingly acknowledges the importance of being involved in transitional justice processes, the report also admitted that this involvement is still not consistent (Annan 2004: 1, 5–6 (11, 12)). The report emphasised that the UN prefers national authorities to deal with transitional justice processes but that, due to a lack of political will and financial and human resources, societies recovering from violent conflict often need international assistance (Annan 2004: 1, 3(3), 6(14, 15), 10(27)). It also recognised the important role of international criminal tribunals and especially the new International Criminal Court and alternative mechanisms such as truth commissions, vetting processes and reparation programmes (Annan 2004: 2, 13–14(39, 40), 16 (49)). The report also emphasised the importance of consulting victims and national authorities, of complementing rather than replacing national efforts, of basing an international approach on national needs, of ensuring national participation and of considering the political climate in which the transitional justice process will take place (Annan 2004: 1, 6(14, 15), 7(17), 8(21), 9(25), 13(39)). The report also identified some factors, such as a lack of available international staff and adequately trained and skilled soldiers, that constrain the UN's contribution to implementing transitional justice processes (Annan 2004: 6(13), 8(21), 10(28)). Finally, the report argued that, when required, transitional justice activities need to be included and integrated into UN peace missions (Annan 2004: 1, 21(64a.), 22(65a/b.).

UN debates

Transitional justice has also been discussed in various UNSC meetings especially on 24 and 30 September 2003, 6 October 2004 and 22 June 2006 (United Nations Security Council 24 September 2003, 30 September 2003, 6 October 2004a, 6 October 2004b, 22 June 2006a, 22 June 2006b). The participants in the debates generally agreed that transitional justice is an important part of peacebuilding and that the UN needs to support and assist in transitional justice processes (ibid.). In cases where national authorities are not able to prosecute individuals, the vast majority of the representatives taking part in the debates also expressed support for ad hoc international criminal tribunals such as the ICTY and ICTR and mixed tribunals such as the SC-SL and the Khmer Rouge Trials (ibid.). With the notable exception of the US, the majority also expressed support for the ICC and some representatives even urged the UNSC to refer cases of alleged atrocities that national authorities are unable or unwilling to deal with to the ICC (ibid.). Many representatives also emphasised the need for a coordinated and comprehensive transitional justice approach based on national needs and supported by the local population and the importance of securing local participation, ownership and capacity-building (ibid.). Finally, in the last meeting some participants also supported mandating UNMIL to assist in the transfer of Charles Taylor into the custody of the SC-SL; the representative from

Peru contended that the UNSC should support the apprehension of five indicted war criminals sought by the ICC; and the participants from France and Austria argued that is it not acceptable that individuals indicted for serious atrocities should remain at large (ibid.).

Summing up

Contemporary peace missions have engaged in several different activities to help societies recovering from violent conflict obtain transitional justice. The missions in Bosnia-Herzegovina, Haiti and Liberia have all been involved in vetting new national police forces. Many missions including those in the Democratic Republic of Congo, Sudan and Côte d'Ivoire, have also helped investigate atrocities committed during the violent conflict. When it comes to ensuring individual accountability for these crimes, the involvement of peace missions has varied significantly. In Haiti MINUSTAH has apparently not been involved in holding individuals accountable. In Côte d'Ivoire UNOCI's investigations have so far also not led to the peace mission calling for the establishment of individual accountability. However, in Congo MONUC has lobbied for perpetrators to be held accountable for their deeds and in Sudan UNMIS has monitored local attempts to hold individuals accountable. In Bosnia-Herzegovina, Kosovo, East Timor, Sierra Leone and Liberia the peace missions have been actively engaged in securing accountability. In Bosnia-Herzegovina and Kosovo UNMIBH and UNMIK have continued to support the ICTY in bringing the worst alleged war criminals to justice and UNMIL has helped the SC-SL by detaining one of its indicted war criminals, Charles Taylor. The peace missions in Sierra Leone and East Timor have supported the establishment of part-national, part-international criminal tribunals to ensure individual accountability, whereas UNMIK has supported prosecution of alleged war criminals in the national judicial system. Finally, the missions in East Timor, Sierra Leone and Liberia have also all assisted in the establishment of TRCs. Hence the role of peace missions in assisting societies to secure accountability for atrocities has been significantly expanded.

The results of the peace missions' efforts have varied considerably. UNMIBH was fairly successful in vetting the national police force, despite some officers slipping through the net; there being no appeal for rejected police officers; and the vetting process not being institutionalised. In contrast, UNMIL's and MINUSTAH's initial efforts to vetting the new national police forces completely failed. The missions in Bosnia-Herzegovina and Kosovo have generally been successful in supporting the work of the ICTY, though UNMIK's involvement in the Haradinaj case has seriously questioned the mission's commitment to supporting the ICTY's quest for justice. The SC-SL set up by the peace mission in Sierra Leone managed to implement fair trials against the worst perpetrators, whereas the criminal tribunal established by the mission in East Timor only managed to deal with a few cases and was terminated before all cases had been tried. The peace missions' attempts to secure individual accountability through national judicial systems have not been very successful. In the Congo and Sudan MONUC and UNMIS respectively have only been successful in lobbying for individual accountability through a trial in the national judicial system in a few cases and in Kosovo UNMIK has also only succeeded in securing accountability in the new national system in relatively few cases. Finally, whereas it is as yet too early to fully assess the impact of UNMIL on the Liberian TRC, the peace missions in Sierra Leone and East Timor have been relatively successful in supporting the work of the national TRCs, which have both been able to document testimonies from many victims, conduct public hearings and develop comprehensive reports including recommendations for the national authorities. However, in both Sierra Leone and East Timor, the peace missions left the countries before the national governments had addressed the TRCs' recommendations and in both cases the national authorities have not shown much interest in following the recommendations.

Several factors have affected the outcome of the peace missions' activities. The transitional justice activities of some were hampered by the ongoing conflict in their area of deployment. A failure to obtain the involvement and cooperation of the local population and national authorities also negatively impacted results. Like their predecessors, several missions also suffered from insufficient funding and inadequately trained and inexperienced personnel. Reliance on national judicial systems that were not able to carry out fair trials and a lack of cooperation from states where alleged war criminals are hiding have also hindered efforts to render individuals accountable. Untimely termination of the peace missions and a failure to develop sustainable institutions have also significantly negatively impacted some of these transitional justice activities. In addition, the continued want of a coherent approach to transitional justice can also help explain the limited impact of missions' activities. This want of a coherent approach has meant that, even in cases where missions have been reasonably successful in fulfilling their mandates, such as was the case especially with UNAMSIL but also to a lesser degree UNMIBH and UNMIK, their contribution to securing accountability has still been relatively limited. The most successful case is undoubtedly Sierra Leone, where UNAMSIL was able to assist both the SC-SL and the TRC although not able to build a national judicial system able to hold those individuals not taking part in the SC-SL or TRC processes accountable for their deeds. In Bosnia-Herzegovina and Kosovo UNMIBH and UNMIK respectively have been fairly good at supporting the work of the ICTY but the two missions have been much less successful in dealing with individuals whose crimes are not serious enough for the ICTY, either through a national trial process or a TRC. Among the least successful cases is MINUSTAH in Haiti where, though a vetting process has now been initiated, very little has been done to address all the atrocities committed during the conflict. Also in Liberia UNMIL's support of the TRC has not been followed up with any plan to hold individuals responsible for serious atrocities or who refuse to take part in the TRC process accountable for their deeds (Amnesty International 2006d, 2006e). In addition, in contrast to the recommendations of the UNSG, UNMIL's mandate does not include a mechanism focusing on the investigation of crimes despite the need for this in Liberia, also demanding international support for the national police, judiciary and prosecution (Amnesty International 2006d, 2007e). In other cases, such as the Democratic Republic of Congo, Sudan and Côte d'Ivoire, an approach to transitional justice is yet to be developed.

A recent UN publication has also addressed the involvement of peace missions in transitional justice processes (Annan 2004). *The Rule of Law and Transitional Justice in Conflict and Post-conflict Societies* underlined that the UN cannot support amnesty for mass atrocities and that past atrocities need to be addressed in order to obtain peace. The report also contended that the UN is increasingly recognising the importance of transitional justice and that many contemporary peace missions are mandated to address human rights abuses. However, it also admitted that not all UN peace missions are mandated to assist in implementing transitional justice processes. Reflecting the experience of some missions, the report also recognised some of the factors that have hindered peace missions in successfully assisting communities implement such processes. It also contended that transitional justice cannot be externally imposed and that international assistance should be based on national needs and participation and complement rather than replace national transitional justice mechanisms. Furthermore, the report also admitted that the UN has not always adequately considered the circumstances of the particular community or sufficiently consulted national authorities and victims before deciding on the role of the peace mission. However, the report failed to address what peace missions should do if national authorities or the parties to the violent conflict refuse to address atrocities, such as has often been the case in states where recent peace missions have been deployed. Keeping in mind that international criminal tribunals are only meant to deal with the worst perpetrators, the report also failed to acknowledge that so far peace missions have not been very successful in using national judicial systems to hold individuals accountable even when international personnel have been called in to strengthen such systems. In addition, the report did not acknowledge that peace missions have so far only been involved in implementing fairly autonomous transitional justice activities rather than attempting to implement a coherent transitional justice approach and hence the impact of these activities on ensuring individual accountability has often been limited. Finally, concerning the detention of indicted war criminals, the report emphasised that it is essential that governments hand over indicted war criminals upon request (Annan 2004: 21(64j.)). However, the report did not address what should be done if governments are unable or unwilling to transfer indicted war criminals to national or international criminal tribunals it did not call for peace missions to be involved in detaining these criminals. Nevertheless, the report did call for a need to rethink the role of international soldiers and police officers, which could potentially include requesting them to participate in such detentions(Annan 2004: 10(28)).

In recent UN debates the participants have generally agreed that transitional justice is important so that the UN needs to support transitional justice processes. The majority of the representatives has also voiced their support for international and part-international criminal tribunals and, excepting the US, representatives have also expressed their support for the ICC. Some participants have also recommended that the UNSC refer cases to the ICC. Furthermore, reflecting the experience of several of the peace missions, some representatives have also contended that it is unacceptable for some indicted war criminals to remain at large and expressed support for UNMIL being specifically mandated to arrest indicted war criminal Charles Taylor. Also reflecting some of the mistakes recent peace missions have made, participants have called for international interventions based on national needs, securing local ownership and cooperation and building local capacity. Calls have also been made for the implementation of coordinated and comprehensive transitional justice approaches.

Peace missions, peace-building and transitional justice

Since the end of the Cold War transitional justice has slowly but steadily been integrated into the UN's approach to peace-building. Peace missions have become increasingly involved in assisting societies recovering from violent conflict ensure accountability for atrocities committed during that conflict and the importance of establishing transitional justice for sustainable peace-building has also been recognised in UN publications and debates. Peace missions have gone from merely verifying that atrocities have been committed and providing basic logistical and security support to other international institutions attempting to ensure individual accountability to actively investigating atrocities, lobbying for individual accountability and detaining individuals whom international and part-international criminal tribunals want to prosecute. Transitional justice has also gone from not being mentioned at all in early post-Cold War UN reports such as *An Agenda for Peace* and *A Supplement to an Agenda for Peace* to being the main focus in the recent report *The Rule of Law and Transitional Justice in Conflict and Post-conflict Societies*. Transitional justice has also been the main topic in several recent UN debates, where the vast majority of the representatives expressed support for UN peace missions supporting post-conflict societies ensure individual accountability for atrocities committed during the conflict. However, many obstacles still remain. Though some peace missions have successfully assisted some societies addressing past abuses, many have also failed to carry out transitional justice activities successfully, rendering their impact in this regard minimal. A wide range of factors, from a lack of cooperation from the national government and the parties to the conflict to a lack of resources and qualified and experienced international personnel can help explain these failures. Many other obstacles and dilemmas are also yet to be properly addressed.

First, though both recent UN publications and debates have recognised the importance of transitional justice for post-conflict peace-building and the vital support peace missions can potentially provide, not all missions are mandated to assist societies in implementing a transitional justice. Among those engaged in transitional justice activities, the tasks involved have also varied considerably.

For example, in the cases of Bosnia-Herzegovina, Haiti and Liberia, the peace missions have all been involved in implementing vetting processes, whereas in the Democratic Republic of Congo the mission has not hindered former combatants from joining the new army and taking up positions in the local and national administration. In addition in Sierra Leone the peace mission has supported the implementation of a fairly comprehensive transitional justice approach that includes both an internationally supported criminal tribunal and a Truth and Reconciliation Commission, whereas in neighbouring Liberia, the mission has only supported the setting up of a Truth Commission, which means that even the worst alleged war criminals have not yet been held accountable in a trial process. Furthermore, in neighbouring Côte d'Ivoire the peace mission has so far made no attempt to support the establishment of individual accountability. Moreover, the peace mission in Liberia has been explicitly mandated to arrest indicted war criminal Charles Taylor, whereas those in Sudan and the Congo have so far not been explicitly mandated to arrest the Sudanese and Congolese individuals that the ICC wants arrested and transferred. Hence, there is still a considerable difference between the declarations in various UN documents and debates and the political will to authorise and enable peace missions to support societies recovering from violent conflict implement transitional justice processes.

In addition, though it is generally agreed that the peace missions' approach to transitional justice needs to be coherent, there is no consensus on what such an approach should entail. Whereas there is general consensus that ensuring justice for post-conflict crimes necessitates a national police force, judicial and correctional systems, there is much more uncertainty about how individual accountability for crimes should be obtained. There is still no consensus on the most appropriate mix of retributive and restorative justice and which crimes are serious enough to be dealt with in a court room and which by a truth and reconciliation commission. There is also no consensus on which crimes are so serious as to preclude membership of the new post-conflict national army and police force. Furthermore, despite general agreement that atrocities should preferably be dealt with in national institutions, there is disagreement as to how to proceed if national institutions prove either unable or unwilling to raise the cases. Recent UN debates have revealed that some states are still reluctant to authorise international institutions to deal with atrocities committed in internal violent conflict and, within the group of states that support international criminal prosecution, there is disagreement whether the prosecution should take place in ad hoc institutions or in the new permanent ICC.

Moreover, both recent publications and debates have recognised the importance of sequencing transitional justice processes, how this should be done has yet to be properly addressed. Questions such as when is a peace no longer so fragile that the initialisation of a transitional justice process will threaten it and what role peace missions should play in the intermediate period still need answering.

Furthermore, all the consequences of involving peace missions in pursuing transitional justice are yet to be fully recognised. Though it has been recognised in some of the recent UN debates and publications that the UN cannot support peace agreements that contain amnesty provisions for serious atrocities, it has not been acknowledged that in most cases the individuals involved in UN peace negotiation efforts are also those responsible for the worst atrocities. In some cases, rather than attempting to hold these individuals accountable, the UN has even allowed them to become prominent legitimate politicians in the post-conflict phase. An example of the first case scenario is the Dayton Peace Agreement, where the three individuals, Franjo Tudjman, Alija Izetbegović and Slobodan Milosevic, who took part in the peace negotiations and signed the peace agreement, all bore political responsibility for atrocities committed during the violent conflict. An example of the latter is Kosovo where former KLA fighters such as Hashim Thaci, Agim Ceku and Ramush Haradinaj have been allowed to transform themselves into influential politicians. Thus, since in many cases the people constituting the national authorities whose cooperation peace missions have had to rely on are the people responsible for some of the worst atrocities, it is hardly surprising that missions have found it difficult to convince national authorities to cooperate in the implementation of its transitional justice activities.

It has also been emphasised in recent UN debates and publications that the UN's involvement in transitional justice processes should be based on national needs. However, it is yet to be established how the national needs of a particular society are to be determined and who should determine them. What, for example, should happen if a state not under the jurisdiction of the ICC decides to deal with via a truth and reconciliation process, though this would contravene humane law mandating certain crimes to be so atrocious as to demand individual criminal accountability in a court room? Should a peace mission still support the truth and reconciliation process or insist that assistance will only be provided if a trial is included in the transitional justice process? Moreover, keeping in mind that, in contrast to the ICTY and the ICTR, the ICC only has complementary powers, what should happen in a situation where a state claims that it is able to prosecute individuals in its own national judicial system and the UN disagrees in this assessment? Should peace missions still support the state's attempt to use its own system or should the UN insist that the ICC or another international or mixed tribunal be set up to deal with the atrocities?

Furthermore, both recent UN publications and debates have emphasised that the local population needs to be involved in the missions transitional justice activities and that the peace missions' need to ensure local ownership and capacity-building. So far the peace missions have not been very successful in achieving any of these objectives but what exactly should the peace missions do differently? Experience from, for example, Bosnia and Sierra Leone, has shown that even the worst war criminals often continue to enjoy a level of support among parts of the local population (Dougherty 2004, Larson 2004). How is a peace mission supposed to engage local people who think that alleged war criminals are heroes who legitimately defended the interests of their people in their transitional justice activities to hold these same individuals accountable for their deeds? Moreover, many contemporary peace missions are deployed in states where the most basic needs of the local population are not met. How is a mission supposed to involve local people who are so poor that they have to spend every minute of every day worrying about how to avoid going to bed hungry? Furthermore, how is a peace mission supposed to build local capacity for holding individuals accountable for past atrocities in a national judicial system that the peace mission so far has not been able to support adequately enough to enable it to deal with such crimes? In addition, considering that peace missions are often only deployed for a short while, whereas achieving transitional justice is a long-term process, how do missions prevent national authorities abandoning the process once the peace mission has left, such as was the case in East Timor?

Some important moral dilemmas concerning the implementation of transitional justice processes remain to be fully recognised. For example, it is still unclear whether attempting to ensure individual accountability for atrocities committed during the conflict prolongs the violence because it takes away the incentives for parties to the conflict to stop the violence and enter the peace negotiation process. If this is the case, then the question is whether it is morally defensible to pursue transitional justice if it means more suffering for civilians. Another moral dilemma concerns the amount of funding available for peace missions. The vast majority of missions have suffered from and continue to be negatively influenced by a lack of funding. In many cases the local population is suffering from starvation and a lack of proper accommodation and health care and it is debatable whether in these cases it is morally defensible to spend money on transitional justice processes while the most essential needs of the local population are not met.

In conclusion, though important steps towards including transitional justice in the UN's approach to post-conflict peace-building have been taken, a long row of obstacles and dilemmas still need to be addressed before UN peace missions will be able to successfully help a society recovering from violent conflict implement a transitional justice process that will ensure individual accountability for atrocities committed during the violent conflict. The rest of the book focuses on one of these obstacles, namely the problem of detaining indicted war criminals.

Part III

The experiences of IFOR, SFOR and KFOR

5 IFOR and the detention of indicted war criminals

Introduction

After more than three years of violence the three parties to the violent conflict in Bosnia-Herzegovina finally signed the Dayton Peace Agreement (DPA) at the end of 1995. UN Security Council resolution 1031 put the United Nations Mission in Bosnia-Herzegovina (UNMIBH) in charge of implementing the civilian parts of the DPA and the resolution also requested NATO to ensure implementation of the military aspects of the peace agreement. Hence, NATO established a multinational peace enforcement mission called the Implementation Force (IFOR). IFOR's 60,000 international soldiers entered Bosnia-Herzegovina in December 1995 on a one-year mandate. At this time the International Criminal Tribunal for the Former Yugoslavia (ICTY) was in its third year and it was finally ready to begin its first trial (President of the ICTY 1996). The Prosecutor was developing numerous indictments but the tribunal was not very successful in securing the detention and transfer of the indicted individuals (ibid.). The ICTY apparently issued the first international arrest warrant to IFOR in December 1995 for the detention of Milan Kovacevic and Simo Drljaca (President of the ICTY 1997). During 1996 the ICTY forwarded a further seven arrest warrants to IFOR (ibid.). In addition the ICTY announced more than 50 other indictments during IFOR's deployment (ibid.). However, IFOR failed to detain any indicted war criminals during its mission.

This chapter looks at how IFOR interpreted its mandate concerning the detention of indicted war criminals and how this influenced its actions.[22] The chapter also discusses why IFOR did not manage to detain any indicted war criminals.

A cautious and confused beginning

From the outset of IFOR's mission it was clear that IFOR commanders took a very cautious approach to detaining indicted war criminals and that confusion abounded as to what IFOR was authorised to do to attain detentions. From the beginning IFOR spokesmen agreed that the mandate did not authorise a hunt for indicted war criminals but merely their detention if encountered during ordinary duties (Col Kirkwood 13 February 1996, Lt Col Rayner 11 February 1996).

However, there was disagreement about how committed to this task the mandate dictated IFOR to be. At one press conference Lt Col Rayner argued that IFOR troops were authorised but not obliged to detain indicted war criminals when they came across them while carrying out their ordinary duties (Lt Col Rayner 12 February 1996). However, at a press conference the day after Col Kirkwood stated that IFOR soldiers should detain these individuals when the situation permitted (Col Kirkwood 13 February 1996). Hence there was seemingly confusion over whether or not IFOR soldiers were obliged to detain such criminals or merely authorised to do so if they felt the need.

The cautious approach to and confusion over the interpretation of IFOR's mandate in this regard influenced the discussions as to actions IFOR could carry out in order to detain indicted war criminals within the limits of its mandate. First, the narrow interpretation of the mandate resulted in very vague rules of engagement concerning IFOR soldiers' involvement in these detentions. At the start of IFOR's mission the rules of engagement were allegedly limited to the general instruction that international soldiers were supposed to apprehend any indicted war criminals encountered while executing their normal duties (Lt Col Rayner 11 February 1996). The instructions only dictated that the situation had to permit detention without specific guidelines as to what this involved (Col Kirkwood 13 February 1996, Lt Col Reddin 13 February 1996). Instead IFOR relied on the common sense of soldiers to decide when it was suitable to attempt detention (Col Kirkwood 13 February 1996). Asked if an IFOR soldier could call for reinforcement if he felt that the situation did not permit him to detain an indicted war criminal on his own, Col Kirkwood responded that he was uncomfortable with the creation of individual scenarios and that he was not aware of any specific rules of engagement on that (Col Kirkwood 13 February 1996). Two weeks later Lt Col Rayner confirmed that the criteria deciding whether to attempt a detention, was whether or not such a detention would endanger the lives of IFOR soldiers and civilians. But he also underlined that fact that it was up to the soldier on the ground to make the decision (Lt Col Rayner 29 February 1996). Hence, IFOR soldiers only received very vague rules of engagement which did not encourage them to take any actions at all to carry out detentions.

Second, and related to the first point, it was contentious whether or not IFOR soldiers on patrols and guarding checkpoints should be actively engaged in detaining war criminals. This debate was stirred up after it was reported that Radovan Karadzic had driven unhindered through several IFOR checkpoints in his large Mercedes on his way from Pale to Banja Luka (Anonymous questioner 11 February 1996). On the one hand Lt Col Rayner argued against using IFOR soldiers at checkpoints to detain people because he contended that that would be hunting the accused and therefore outside IFOR's mandate (Lt Col Rayner 11 February 1996). When offered a description of this Mercedes and its licence plate number, Major Moyer claimed that giving the number to IFOR soldiers would imply that they should look at and stop every vehicle they came across and that would be outside their mandate (Major Moyer 12 February 1996). Col Kirkwood also contended that even Radovan Karadžić had to be guaranteed freedom of movement and that checking every car for indicted war criminals was a police function and therefore not a job for IFOR (Col Kirkwood 13 February 1996). When asked if a convoy of BMWs and Mercedes with tinted windows (such as the one Karadžić had been seen in) would be stopped at a roadblock, Col Kirkwood answered that almost anybody could be travelling in such a convoy (ibid.). On the other hand Lt Col Rayner also contended that IFOR soldiers at checkpoints had been instructed to detain individuals such as Radovan Karadžić if they walked up to a checkpoint and introduced themselves (Lt Col Rayner 11 February 1996). In addition, Col Kirkwood confirmed that IFOR soldiers had been instructed to detain indicted war criminals when they encountered them. He expressed surprise when told that some IFOR soldiers at a checkpoint had not been able to recognise Karadžić when a journalist had shown them his photo (Col Kirkwood 17 February 1996). Thus at the beginning of the mission uncertainty prevailed over whether or not IFOR soldiers at checkpoints should be called on to detain these individuals, the result being that they did not do so.

Third, it was discussed whether or not IFOR soldiers should be provided with photographs of the indicted individuals to enable them to identify them. At a press conference on 11 February 1996 Lt Col Rayner argued that this would send a confusing message to the soldiers, who had been instructed not to hunt indicted war criminals, by giving them photos to help them do just that (Lt Col Rayner 11 February 1996). However, Rayner also acknowledged that, if the photographs were not distributed, to IFOR soldiers would probably not be able to recognise the indicted criminals (Lt Col Rayner 11 February 1996). At a press conference the day after Rayner and Major Moyer argued that the photos had not been distributed because they were of such bad quality that they would not help soldiers to identify the accused (Lt Col Rayner 12 February 1996, Major Moyer 12 February 1996). Nevertheless, Lt Col Rayner did acknowledge that, although IFOR had good-quality photographs of Ratko Mladić and Radovan Karadžić, these had not been given to IFOR soldiers (Lt Col Rayner 12 February 1996). At another press conference the day after it was announced that the ICTY would provide IFOR with 36 good-quality photographs of indicted war criminals (Lt Col Reddin 13 February 1996). During this press conference it was again underlined that IFOR commanders were very confused as to whether or not such photographs should be distributed to IFOR soldiers. At the beginning of the press conference both Lt Col Reddin and Col Kirkwood argued that the available photos should be disseminated to soldiers (Col Kirkwood 13 February 1996, Lt Col Reddin 13 February 1996). However, when asked whether this meant that IFOR had changed its policy on the distribution of photos, both spokesmen backtracked by contending that they had not said that all soldiers would be given the photos (Col Kirkwood 13 February 1996, Lt Col Reddin 13 February 1996). Col Kirkwood also argued against the assumption that the distribution of photos would be the first step towards hunting the accused as argued by Lt Col Rayner a couple of days earlier (Col Kirkwood 13 February 1996). Four days later Col Kirkwood again argued that the available photos were of bad quality and that he did not know the specific guidelines regarding their distribution (Col Kirkwood 17 February 1996). However, he also acknowledged that it was in the interest of IFOR to obtain better photos (Col Kirkwood 17 February 1996). Thus in the beginning confusion surrounded the availability of photos and disagreement was rife as to whether or not they should be given to IFOR soldiers. Hence in the beginning IFOR soldiers were not able to identify indicted war criminals at large.

It was also discussed whether IFOR soldiers should be supplied with basic personal characteristics of the indicted allegedly at large in their area of operation. According to Lt Col Rayner, details of the fifty-two indicted war criminals were not distributed to international soldiers because IFOR had only received limited information from the ICTY (Lt Col Rayner 12 February 1996, 14 February 1996). Major Moyer also contended that, since IFOR only had the name, age, weight, height, eye and hair colour of the indicted, the soldiers would not be able to identify them anyway (Major Moyer 12 February 1996). However, a couple of days later Col Kirkwood admitted that IFOR had thirty-three biographies of accused individuals and that more information should be amassed about the others (Col Kirkwood 17 February 1996). Hence, there was confusion as to how much information IFOR had and whether it should be distributed to soldiers. The result was that in the beginning IFOR soldiers were not given any individual's personal characteristics and hence had no means of identifying them.

Thus from the outset of IFOR's mission it was clear that detaining indicted war criminals was not very high on IFOR's agenda (Col Kirkwood 13 February 1996). IFOR interpreted its mandate very narrowly and even the narrow interpretation that IFOR soldiers were only authorised to detain such criminals when they came across them while carrying out their ordinary duties was not supported by any means. IFOR soldiers were given no personal characteristics or photos of indicted war criminals and received only very vague rules of engagement. This all meant that in effect indicted war criminals could move freely around Bosnia-Herzegovina without fear that IFOR soldiers on patrol or at roadblocks might recognise and detain them.

Slight improvements

Though its spokesmen continued to claim that IFOR's mandate did not authorise IFOR to hunt indicted war criminals but merely to detain them when encountered, IFOR slowly improved its efforts towards detention (Major Haselock 16 May 1996). Eventually photographs of the indicted in question were allegedly distributed to IFOR soldiers (Major Haselock 1 July 1996). However, a CNN survey of IFOR soldiers at the end of June 1996 still showed that many were unable to recognise the most wanted individual Radovan Karadžić (ibid.). This led IFOR to reissue posters with photographs of the indicted war criminals and to order each division and each commander at all levels to ensure that soldiers were given the photographs to enable them to recognise them (ibid.). In May

1996 IFOR forces also increased their presence throughout Bosnia-Herzegovina. Spokesmen for IFOR contended that this would limit the freedom of movement of the indicted and thereby also increase the likelihood of detaining them (Captain Van Dyke 6 June 1996, Major Haselock 27 May 1996). However, IFOR also emphasised that soldiers on patrol had not been given new instructions and that they would not specifically target the alleged places of residence of indicted war criminals (Captain Van Dyke 6 June 1996, Major Haselock 27 May 1996, 4 June 1996). IFOR also underlined that, if an indicted war criminal drove through a checkpoint, he would be detained if the situation permitted it (Major Haselock 27 May 1996). It was also confirmed that IFOR soldiers at checkpoints now had very clear instructions on a card explaining their exact duties if they encountered an indicted war criminal (General Walker 22 May 1996, Major Haselock 20 June 1996). The cards were reissued to include the caution to be read aloud upon detention (Major Haselock 1 July 1996). The new criteria apparently contradicted those set out at the beginning of the mission, since IFOR now never ruled out taking action in any circumstances and did not insist that endangering the lives of soldiers was to be a justifiable reason against detention operations (Major Haselock 27 May 1996). Despite this apparent strengthening of IFOR's actions, journalists still reported that Radovan Karadžić had been seen 100 metres from an American checkpoint (Major Haselock 20 June 1996).

IFOR also dismissed setting up more checkpoints to increase the likelihood of detentions, arguing that this would amount to the same as hunting the indicted (Captain Van Dyke 6 June 1996). Finally, IFOR also continued to refuse to search for these criminals or to carry out special operations to detain them (Major Boudreau 3 July 1996). Hence, though IFOR soldiers were provided with personal characteristics of wanted individuals; more soldiers were patrolling; and the rules of engagement concerning detentions were improved and more widely dispersed to soldiers, IFOR was still not very committed to this task.

Still no results in the end

Towards the end of its mission IFOR maintained that its mandate did not allow IFOR soldiers to hunt indicted war criminals but merely to detain them when encountered (Major Haselock 12 September 1996). At the end of October it was reconfirmed that all IFOR soldiers had been given a poster with photos of the wanted criminals (Major Haselock 30 October 1996). Still, by the end of the mission, IFOR was criticised for not distributing photographs of new indicted war criminals to its soldiers (Anonymous questioner 5 December 1996). Eventually, IFOR soldiers were also given posters with basic information about the indicted individuals, sometimes even including their addresses (Ivanko 12 December 1996). In addition, it was pointed out that IFOR checkpoint soldiers now checked whether people stopped matched any on the posters and that all soldiers had a card detailing their obligations when encountering an indicted war criminal (Major Haselock 30 October 1996). However, it was also still emphasised that checkpoints did not stop all vehicles and that it was therefore still possible for indicted war criminals to pass through (Major Boudreau 11 December 1996).

IFOR also maintained that its soldiers on patrol would detain indicted war criminals encountered during ordinary duties (Major Boudreau 29 November 1996, Major Haselock 30 October 1996). However, IFOR still had to respond to claims that Italian IFOR soldiers were patrolling 200 metres from Radovan Karadžić's office where he worked on a regular basis and that the soldiers deliberately avoided running into indicted war criminals (Major Haselock 12 September 1996). IFOR maintained until the end of its mission that IFOR soldiers had never seen Radovan Karadžić despite reports that Karadžić was being escorted around the country by the local police (Major Boudreau 11 December 1996). IFOR also admitted that they did not maintain surveillance on the whereabouts of the indicted war criminals (Major Boudreau 13 August 1996, 29 November 1996). Instead IFOR relied on information about their whereabouts from the ICTY (Major Boudreau 29 November 1996). IFOR linked this lack of maintaining intelligence with its interpretation of its mandate that did not allow IFOR soldiers to hunt indicted war criminals (Major Boudreau 11 December 1996). A couple of incidents also indicated that other international agencies did not provide IFOR with information about the whereabouts of indicted war criminals. In August 1996 Radovan Stanković entered an IPTF office to file a report of harassment against the local police in Bosnia-Herzegovina, who had attempted to arrest him (President of the ICTY 1997). The IPTF did not inform IFOR about the sighting in time for IFOR to attempt to detain him (ibid.). Another incident was uncovered at the end of October when it became apparent that the IPTF had not swiftly reported to IFOR that several indicted war criminals were still working as police officers in police stations in Prijedor and Omarska (Anonymous questioner 29 October 1996, Murphy 30 October 1996). On that occasion Commissioner Fitzgerald from the IPTF contended that, should the IPTF come across indicted war criminals, they would report it to IFOR. However, he also admitted that they would not immediately call IFOR but rather inform the force about it, presumably at a later stage (Commissioner Fitzgerald 31 October 1996). Finally in the middle of December some IPTF officers spotted Karadžić driving around in a police-guarded convoy of cars. It took them a couple of hours to report the sighting to IFOR (Major Boudreau 11 December 1996). According to IPTF spokesman Ivanko, it took such a long time because the IPTF officers were surprised to see Karadžić driving around in the open and because their radios could only report back to the IPTF station and not directly to IFOR (Ivanko 11 December 1996). Ivanko admitted that communication had been too slow and that that had to be looked into (Ivanko 12 December 1996). He also acknowledged that IPTF had received posters of the indicted war criminals but that he was not sure how widely they had been distributed and how many had actually been put up on walls (ibid.). Hence, at the end of IFOR's mission, it was apparent that IFOR still did very little to detain indicted war criminals.

In conclusion, IFOR interpreted its mandate concerning the detention of indicted war criminals very narrowly and consequently did very little in this regard. IFOR maintained this interpretation until the end of its mission but the top military commander of IFOR, General Crouch, admitted that there was a need for all troops throughout Bosnia-Herzegovina to review their policies and standing operating procedures regarding such detentions and to ensure that all soldiers were familiar with the policy and knew what to do should they encounter an indicted war criminal (Major Boudreau 11 December 1996).

Where did it all go wrong?

There are many reasons why IFOR failed to detain any indicted war criminals. The very narrow way IFOR commanders chose to interpret IFOR's mandate in this regard meant that its soldiers were precluded from doing anything proactively to detain indicted war criminals. The IFOR soldiers did not search for or gather any intelligence about the wanted individuals. They also did not act on information they received about their whereabouts or increase patrols and checkpoints when they knew that the accused were in a specific area. However, as pointed out by Hooper, in addition to not doing anything proactive, IFOR did not even carry out actions sanctioned by the interpretation of its mandate (Hooper, undated). In accordance with IFOR's interpretation of its own mandate, its soldiers could have detained indicted war criminals if encountered in the course of their ordinary duties but on several occasions refrained from doing so (Major Boudreau 11 December 1996, Major Haselock 20 June 1996, 12 September 1996). IFOR soldiers apparently even avoided areas where the criminals were believed to operate and, if they accidentally encounter one, immediately left the area (Century Foundation 1998).

Many interlinked factors can potentially help explain IFOR's cautious approach to this task. First and foremost the political leaders in NATO bear a large part of the responsibility. The political leaders with most influence in NATO were also those who had negotiated the DPA without the participation of the ICTY or UN (Kalinauskas 2002). The objective had been to put an immediate end to the violence, with accountability for violations of international criminal law largely ignored (ibid.). Hence, the DPA did not provide a clear framework for cooperation between the ICTY and IFOR (ibid.). In addition, the political leaders of NATO failed to grant IFOR explicit powers to detain indicted war criminals which meant IFOR's actual authorisation remained a moot point (Kalinauskas 2002, Leurdijk 2001, Sliedregt 2001). It also meant that it was left to the military leadership of IFOR to decide whether the soldiers should be involved rather than it being a political decision (Kalinauskas 2002, United States Institute of Peace 1997). NATO's political leaders have also been blamed for failing to convince their citizens to support a long-term commitment to the peace process and that Bosnia was not another Somalia because the mission was simpler (United States Institute of Peace 1997). They have also been accused of misjudging the unity and strength of nationalist leaders in

Bosnia-Herzegovina and the negative impact the failure to detain wanted criminals had on the implementation on the rest of the DPA (ibid.). It has also been argued that the political leadership of NATO failed to realise that it was in the national interest of their states that IFOR soldiers detained indicted war criminals (ibid.). In addition, negative experiences from former peacekeeping missions can also help explain why both the political and military leadership of IFOR were reluctant to involve international soldiers in this activity. Experiences from Cyprus, where international peacekeepers had been deployed much longer than ever envisaged, meant that international politicians were too focused on keeping mission tasks to a minimum and bringing the international military operation to an end in order to avoid another never-ending deployment (ibid.). Negative experiences from Somalia, where eighteen American soldiers were killed while hunting a militia leader also meant that both political and military leaders feared similar fiasco and were thus also reluctant to allow international soldiers to become embroiled in detaining indicted war criminals (Leurdijk 2001, United States Institute of Peace 1997). Finally, it is likely that the failure of IFOR's predecessor UNPROFOR in preventing a great number of war crimes being committed in Bosnia-Herzegovina and the subsequent international criticism of UNPROFOR, especially in connection with the Srebrenica atrocities, meant that IFOR was very reluctant to tackle anything to do with war crimes and war criminals and thereby risk repeating the failures of UNPROFOR.

The assessment of high operational risks and fear of retaliation resulting in injured or killed peace enforcement soldiers are also highly likely to have influenced this decision not to get involved (Century Foundation 1998, Sliedregt 2001). In this connection it has also been argued that the political leaders' overestimation of Serb military capabilities contributed to the poor results concerning the detention of indicted war criminals (United States Institute of Peace 1997). It is also likely that the fear of losing support from vital partners might have influenced the decision to opt out of engagement. Richard Holbrooke, the chief American negotiator of the DPA, apparently thought that, since it was not in the interest of Slobodan Milosevic to detain indicted war criminals such as Radovan Karadžić and Ratko Mladić, and send them to The Hague because they might link Milosevic to the atrocities, having international soldiers detain Karadžić and Mladić was likely to lead to Milosevic withdrawing his support for the DPA (Rieff 1996). Both the military and political leadership of IFOR apparently feared that the detention of war criminals would lead the parties to the peace agreement and Russia to withdraw support for the implementation of the DPA (Sharp 1997, Century Foundation 1998).

Furthermore, it has been contended that IFOR understood the detention of the indicted individuals to be a civilian policing task that IFOR soldiers should not execute because involvement in civilian tasks could lead to mission creep, undermine the successful implementation of the military tasks and thereby threaten the peace process in Bosnia-Herzegovina (Kalinauskas 2002, Leurdijk 2001, Ruxton 2001, United States Institute of Peace 1997). A survey has also indicated that only 35 per cent of the ordinary IFOR soldiers believed in the feasibility of arresting war criminals and a significant 28 per cent thought that it was not desirable to arrest war criminals (Biermann and Ugland 1998: 115). Hence, among ordinary IFOR soldiers, there was considerable disagreement concerning whether or not it was realistic and whether or not it was desirable, to detain indicted war criminals. In addition and quite controversially, interviews with peace enforcement soldiers suggest that not all support the idea that warfare needs to be regulated by international laws (KFOR interview 2003). The recent numerous violations of international law regulating warfare by international soldiers in places such as Iraq and Afghanistan also support the assumption that there are soldiers who still think that the end justifies all means in a war situation. Hence, it is possible that these soldiers also do not support the prosecution of individuals who violate international law. This could especially have been the case with IFOR soldiers, since for them the international prosecution of these individuals was still a new phenomenon and the ICTY had not gained much legitimacy at the time of IFOR's deployment. Thus a potential lack of support for international prosecution of alleged war criminals among at least some IFOR soldiers can also help explain why they were not very committed to detaining indicted war criminals. Finally Sharp has also blamed IFOR's minimal involvement in the detention of indicted war criminals on the fact that the deterrence value and the positive influence on the enforcement of the rule of law of such detentions were not stressed in the public debate (Sharp 1997).

Conclusion: no commitment, no detentions

In conclusion, IFOR interpreted its mandate concerning the detention of indicted war criminals very narrowly and even its very restrictive interpretation was not backed by any measures to facilitate this duty. Subsequently, IFOR failed to detain any of the individuals indicted by the ICTY and wanted for trial in The Hague. A mixture of political and military concerns can help explain IFOR's cautious approach. Both the military and political concerns were partly based on negative experiences in Cyprus, Somalia and Bosnia-Herzegovina, where missions had turned out to be more complicated and lasted much longer than expected; where soldiers had been killed; and where failed promises had resulted in thousands of local casualties. Military concerns were also partly based on a lack of faith that IFOR soldiers could detain indicted war criminals successfully since they had no experience or training in this regard.

6   SFOR and the detention of indicted war criminals

Introduction

SFOR took over from IFOR at the end of 1996. Like IFOR, SFOR was mandated to implement the military aspects of the Dayton Peace Agreement under Chapter VII of the UN Charter in accordance with UNSC 1088 (1996). This included permission to detain indicted war criminals though the actual powers vested in SFOR concerning this were debatable. When SFOR was deployed, the ICTY was in the middle of trying the first war criminals Tadic and Erdemovic whom the ICTY had managed to secure transfer of (President of the ICTY 1997). However, the ICTY was still struggling to secure the transfer of numerous other individuals indicted by the Prosecutor. During the eight years of operation SFOR managed to successfully detain twenty-eight indicted war criminals. In addition, three more, Simo Drljaca, Dragan Gagovic and Janko Janjic died during the operations to apprehend them. These thirty-one individuals constitute about 20 per cent of those indicted by the ICTY.

This chapter outlines SFOR's failed and successful attempts to detain indicted war criminals. The chapter also discusses why SFOR succeeded in some cases but did not manage to detain many others, why SFOR changed its policy and expanded its practices concerning the detentions and why SFOR never became fully committed to this task.

A slow beginning

In 1997, its first year of operation, SFOR managed to detain three indicted war criminals and one person died during SFOR attempts to detain him. The first person detained was Milan Kovacevic on 10 July (Major Riley 11 July 1997). Kovacevic, who had been under a sealed indictment since 13 March 1997, was detained in his office in a hospital in Prijedor by SFOR soldiers from Multinational Division (MND) South-West (ICTY 10 July 1997, Major Riley 11 July 1997). As part of the same operation SFOR soldiers from the same division also attempted to apprehend Simo Drljaca on 11 July 1997 (Major Riley 11 July 1997). Drljaca, who was also under a sealed indictment, was shot dead by SFOR soldiers when he attempted to escape and shot at them (CNN 10 July 1997,

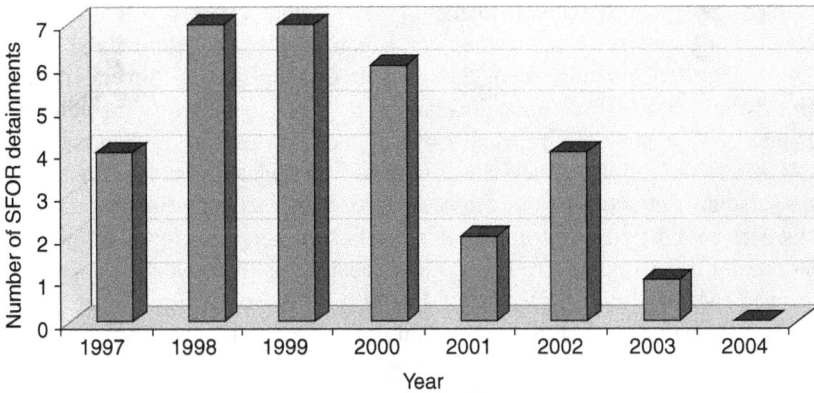

Figure 6.1 Overview of SFOR detentions 1997–2004.

Note
Detention operations that led to the death of the indicted war criminal are included. The figure is based on information from www.nato.int/sfor, www.un.org/icty and www.bbc.co.uk. (Figure taken from Majbritt Lyck, 'Peace Operations and Accountability for War Crimes', PhD thesis, Department of Peace Studies, University of Bradford, 2006).

Major Riley 14 July 1997). Finally, in December 1997, SFOR soldiers from MND South-West detained another two indicted war criminals. Anto Furundzija, who had been under a sealed indictment since November 1995, was detained in a car park outside his house and he did not resist (ICTY 18 December 1997, Major Clarke 18 December 1997). Vlatko Kupreskic, who had been under an open indictment for a couple of years, was detained in his house. He resisted and was subsequently hit three times by SFOR bullets only to survive and be sent to The Hague (BBC 18 December 1997, ICTY 18 December 1997, Major Clarke 18 December 1997).

Numerous interlinked factors contributed to SFOR's relatively low number of successful detentions. As had been the case with IFOR, SFOR had a vague mandate that did not explicitly authorise the soldiers to detain wanted individuals. Subsequently it was again left to the military leadership to interpret the mandate with a consequent negative impact on SFOR's willingness and ability to act in this regard (Kalinauskas 2002). Like IFOR, SFOR chose to interpret its mandate in this matter very restrictively. From the outset of its mission, various spokesmen from SFOR contended that SFOR soldiers were only authorised to detain indicted war criminals when they came across them while carrying out their ordinary duties and if the situation permitted (General Joulwan 7 July 1997, Major Riley 17 June 1997, 30 June 1997, 4 July 1997, Major White 29 January 1997). After the first successful detention, SFOR spokesmen contended that SFOR was mandated to carry out planned operations to detain any indicted war criminals if encountered when the situation did no permit an immediate detention (General Clark 18 July 1997, 13 August 1997, 12 September 1997, Major Clarke 18 December 1997, Major Riley 10 July 1997, 11 July 1997,

12 September 1997). Hence, like IFOR, SFOR's interpretation of its mandate precluded any proactive action to identify and detain indicted war criminals. Instead SFOR merely detained them or began to plan to detain them when SFOR soldiers encountered them during their ordinary duties. Several factors even indicate that SFOR commanders did not do much to enable their soldiers to encounter and identify the indicted war criminals. At least at the beginning of SFOR's mission, SFOR soldiers apparently had no updated photos or details of basic personal characteristics of those at large. This was underlined in an incident where an indicted war criminal voluntarily surrendered to SFOR soldiers at a checkpoint but was asked to leave again because his indictment could not be confirmed (Major Clarke 9 December 1997). It was also confirmed that SFOR was not informed about the individuals on the ICTY's list of secret indictments (ibid.). In addition, SFOR soldiers guarding roadblocks and checkpoints and on patrol were not actively looking out for these criminals. It even seemed like the soldiers purposely tried to avoid encountering them (Major Clarke 9 December 1997, Major Riley 23 July 1997). This was the case with Radovan Karadžić, who was reported to be moving freely around the areas where SFOR soldiers were on patrol without any action being taken (Major Riley 23 July 1997). SFOR defended this practice by arguing that its primary mission was not to hunt down indicted war criminals and that the tactical situation had to permit an immediate detention (ibid.).

The cooperation, coordination and information-sharing between SFOR and other international organisations were also far from optimal at the start of the mission (International Crisis Group 2000). Initially, SFOR did not always receive updated information about the individuals accused by the ICTY and any information that was passed on was sent to NATO rather than directly to SFOR (Major Clarke 9 December 1997). The ICTY's initial policy of publishing the indictments also made detentions more difficult for SFOR since it obviously meant that the indicted knew that SFOR had been instructed to detain them. An incident, where a supervisor from the OSCE, who was registering voters for elections, ran into Radovan Karadžić but did not pass on the information in time for SFOR to detain him, also exposed a lack of effective communication channels between OSCE and SFOR (Foley 1 July 1997). The International Police Task Force (IPTF) also did not always carry out adequate background checks on police officers, so that some indicted war criminals continued to work undisturbed as police officers (International Crisis Group 2000). The local population was also not very willing to help SFOR perform detentions. In contrast, the local population even demonstrated against SFOR's failed attempt to detain Simo Drljaca (SFOR soldiers killed Drljaca in self-defence) and against SFOR's detention of Vlatko Kupreskic. Civilians in the town of Vitez, where Kupreskic was detained, blocked the roads on both sides of the town so that SFOR had to stay put until the situation had calmed down (Major Clarke 18 December 1997, Major Riley 14 July 1997). Media campaigns initiated by the Office of the High Representative in Bosnia-Herzegovina aiming to convince people to provide SFOR with information about indicted war criminals did not seem to improve the local population's perception of SFOR (Lt Bullivant 14 July 1997). Hence, SFOR did not take any actions to locate indicted war criminals and apparently did not receive any timely information from other international organisations or from the local population concerning their location. Furthermore, considering SFOR's narrow interpretation of its mandate at this stage, it is not even likely that SFOR would have initiated an operation to detain someone even if they had received timely information about a sighting.

Though SFOR's passivity concerning these detentions overshadowed its first year of operation, SFOR did initiate some positive steps that contributed to its successful detention of three indicted individuals. SFOR did develop contingency plans on methods of detention and began to carry out planned operations to detain indicted war criminals (Ruxton 2001). It also asked for help from Special Forces from the national contingents when a detention operation was deemed too dangerous for ordinary SFOR soldiers to carry out (Major Clarke 18 December 1997). This was an essential improvement from not doing anything at all if a detention was so assessed. SFOR also adopted a case-by-case approach which meant that the fact that SFOR did not feel ready to detain high-level indicted war criminals such as Karadžić or Mladić did not prevent its efforts to detain lower-level criminals (Kalinauskas 2002).

In conclusion, during its first year of operation, SFOR began to carry out planned operations towards the detention of indicted war criminals that the soldiers encountered during normal duties but had not been able to detain immediately. However, SFOR soldiers still did not search for these individuals and did not receive timely information about their whereabouts from the local population or from the other international organisations working in Bosnia-Herzegovina at the time. Hence, there were no active searches for any of the many individuals the ICTY wanted to prosecute, which to a high degree explains why SFOR only managed to detain three of these individuals.

Getting better

SFOR made most of its detentions of indicted war criminals during the years 1998–2000 when its soldiers managed to detain seven, seven and six individuals respectively. SFOR soldiers from Multinational Division (MND) North's first successful detention was of Goran Jelisic, after encountering him on the streets of Bijeljina (ICTY 22 January 1998, Lt Cdr Garneau 22 January 1998). Jelisic had then been under an open indictment for more than two years (ibid.). In April and May SFOR soldiers from MND South-West added another three successful detentions to their achievements. In April the soldiers detained Miroslav Kvocka and Mladen Radic, who were both under open indictments in their homes in Prijedor, and neither man resisted (ICTY 9 April 1998, Lt Cdr Garneau 9 April 1998). In May the soldiers managed to detain Milojica Kos, who had been under an open indictment since February 1995 (ICTY 29 May 1998, NATO SG Solana 28 May 1998). In June SFOR soldiers from MND South-East had their first success with the detention of Milorad Krnojelac, who had been under a sealed indictment for about a year (ICTY 15 June 1998, Major Saint-Louis 16 June 1998). A month later SFOR soldiers from MND South-West believed that they had managed to detain Nenad and Predrag Banovic but, upon their arrival in the Hague, it became apparent that they were not the two indicted war criminals (NATO SG Solana 22 July 1998, Office of the High Representative 1 August 1998). The last two successful detention operations in 1998 were carried out by SFOR soldiers from MND North. In September and December the soldiers managed to detain Stevan Todorovic and Radislav Krstic (Lt Cdr Thomson 3 December 1998, NATO SG Solana 27 September 1998). The detention of Todorovic was controversial, since his defence later suggested that the SAS and the American Delta Unit had abducted him in the Former Republic of Yugoslavia (FRY) and thereby outside the territorial jurisdiction of SFOR (Vallières-Roland 2002).

SFOR began the year 1999 with a failed attempt to detain Dragan Gagovic, whom they ended up shooting dead when he tried to escape (Lt Cdr Chamberlain 10 January 1999, Lt Cdr Thomson 12 January 1999). This attempt created a lot of controversy as Dragan Gagovic, who was under an open indictment, had children in the car with him when he was shot (ibid.). Later that year SFOR soldiers from MND South-West successfully detained another four indicted war criminals. In June and July the soldiers first detained Dragan Kulundzija near Prijedor and later Radoslav Brdjanin in front of his flat in Banja Luka (CNN 7 July 1999, ICTY 23 September 2004, Lt Cdr Thomson 8 June 1999, Moore 8 June 1999, SFOR Peace Stabilisation Force 7 June 1999). In October and December Damir Dosen and Stanislav Galic were successfully transferred to The Hague (SFOR Peace Stabilisation Force 25 October 1999, 20 December 1999). SFOR soldiers from MND South-East also carried out two successful detention operations in 1999. Both took place in Foca, where first Radomir Kovac was detained in his home and later Zoran Vukovic was detained while walking along a street (BBC 4 August 1999, 24 December 1999, SFOR Peace Stabilisation Force 2 August 1999).

SFOR soldiers from MND South-East also achieved their first successful detention in 2000 with Mitar Vasiljevic, who was under a sealed indictment (Office of the High Representative 25 January 2000, SFOR Peace Stabilisation Force 25 January 2000). In March and April SFOR carried out three more successful detention operations. First, Dragoljub Prcac was detained near Prijedor, then Momcilo Krajisnik was detained in his home in Pale and finally Dragan Nikolic was also successfully detained by MND North (BBC 5 March 2000, 3 April 2000, NATO SG Lord Robertson 3 April 2000, SFOR Peace Stabilisation Force 5 March 2000, 22 April 2000). This detention was also very controversial since bounty hunters apparently abducted Nikolic in the FRY and handed him over to SFOR soldiers (Kalinauskas 2002, Supernor 2001). The last successful detention in 2000 came in June when SFOR soldiers detained Dusko Sikirica in his home in Prijedor (BBC 25 June 2000, SFOR Peace Stabilisation Force 25 June 2000). Finally, SFOR soldiers attempted to detain Janko Janjic in Eastern Bosnia in October 2000 but, when the soldiers confronted Janjic, he detonated a hand grenade that killed him (BBC 13 October 2000).

During 1998–2000 SFOR spokesmen maintained that the mission's mandate only allowed the immediate detention of indicted war criminals if encountered by SFOR soldiers and if the situation permitted it. Planned operations could be undertaken in cases where an immediate detention had not been possible (Lt Cdr Garneau 22 January 1998, 9 April 1998, SFOR Peace Stabilisation Force 7 June 1999, 2 August 1999, 25 October 1999, 20 December 1999, 25 January 2000, 5 March 2000, 3 April 2000, 22 April 2000, 25 June 2000). However, though SFOR maintained that it had not changed the interpretation of its mandate, this was now supported by some more effective measures towards facilitating these detentions.

To begin with, SFOR soldiers on patrol and at roadblocks became actively involved in identifying and detaining indicted war criminals. An example of this was the detention of Goran Jelisic at the start of 1998. He was detained after SFOR soldiers recognised him in the streets of Bijeljina (Lt Cdr Garneau 22 January 1998, 23 January 1998). Another example was the attempt to detain Dragan Gagovic in early 1999, when SFOR used a roadblock at a checkpoint as part of the detention operation (Lt Cdr Chamberlain 10 January 1999). In addition, SFOR seemingly also activated contingency plans more persistently when soldiers had encountered wanted individuals but been unable to detain them immediately (Lt Cdr Chamberlain 10 January 1999, Lt Cdr Thomson 3 December 1998). Furthermore, the ICTY also forwarded more and more sealed indictments to SFOR which meant that the alleged war criminals did not know that SFOR, was looking for them (Kalinauskas 2002, Ruxton 2001). The involvement of British SAS forces in the detention of Stanislav Galic also showed that SFOR still had recourse to Special Forces when operations were deemed too challenging for ordinary SFOR soldiers to carry out on their own (Captain Theriault 21 December 1999). The application of the case-by-case approach also meant that, even though not all national contingents were eager to participate in the detentions, other national contingents could still carry out these operations. This was the case in the French sector, where the French soldiers apparently remained reluctant to get involved in detentions, but where the German soldiers deployed in the same sector managed to detain a couple of indicted war criminals (International Crisis Group 2000). The war criminals rewards programme initiated by the US government in June 1999 apparently also helped SFOR detain Dragan Nikolic (Kalinauskas 2002, Supernor 2001, also Rewards for Justice).[23] Finally, it was also implied that SFOR was now willing to carry out detention operations despite the risk of negative responses from the local population that could potentially threaten the international presence in Bosnia-Herzegovina (Major Saint-Louis 16 June 1998).

However, despite these improved efforts and consequently also better results, SFOR's continued narrow interpretation of its mandate meant that the actions it was willing to take to secure detentions were still fairly restricted. Several statements from SFOR spokesmen underlined the fact that SFOR still did not see it as its unequivocal duty to initiate a detention operation if encountering an indicted war criminal (General Clark 25 April 2000, Lt Cdr Thomson 3 December 1998, Major Desjardins 15 August 2000). Hence, Ratko Mladić and Radovan Karadžić were reportedly sighted near SFOR troops without any attempt being made to detain the two individuals at the top of ICTY's list of wanted alleged war criminals (Lt Cdr Thomson 3 December 1998, Major Desjardins 15 August 2000). SFOR also continued to refuse to initiate detention operations based on information from non-SFOR sources (General Clark 25 April 2000). In addition, its detention policy was still not consistently applied, since SFOR apparently regularly received information about the whereabouts of Karadžić and apparently knew where he was but still did not attempt to detain him (International Crisis Group 2000, Kalinauskas 2002). The involvement of national contingents in the detention of indicted war criminals also continued to vary significantly (Kalinauskas 2002). Finally, SFOR also dismissed the idea of establishing a specialised NATO unit to focus solely on hunting indicted war criminals in accordance with Carla Del Ponte's suggestion (General Clark 25 April 2000).

Hence during 1998–2000 SFOR soldiers were still not taking proactive actions in order to detain indicted war criminals. Though apparently now looking out for them, the soldiers still did not perform specific searches for them. Furthermore, they were still not prepared to act on information from external sources about the whereabouts of indicted war criminals. SFOR's attempt to detain Dragan Gagovic also illustrates that SFOR continued to carry out some practices that had the effect of distancing the local population. When Gagovic tried to flee around the roadblock put up to stop his car (Lt Cdr Chamberlain 10 January 1999) SFOR soldiers shot at him even though he had several children with him (ibid.). After this unsuccessful attempt, about a hundred local people gathered outside the international police station. Some of the demonstrators assaulted officers and the police station was badly damaged (Seidel 10 January 1999). Finally, SFOR soldiers still did not receive any special training in effecting such detentions.

In conclusion, though improved efforts resulted in the detention of twenty indicted war criminals SFOR was still not proactively engaged in this task halfway through its mission.

Not keeping up

During its final four years of deployment, SFOR carried out numerous operations to detain indicted war criminals but the operations were only successful in seven cases. In 2001 SFOR successfully detained two individuals who were both under sealed indictments. Dragan Obrenovic was detained in April in Zvornik and Vidoje Blagojevic was taken into custody four months later in Banja Luka when he arrived at a meeting on mine clearance (BBC 15 April 2001, 10 August 2001, NATO SG Lord Robertson 15 April 2001, 10 August 2001). SFOR began the year 2002 with several failed detention efforts. First, an operation to detain Vinko Pandurevic failed in January 2002 and a month later two attempts to detain Radovan Karadžić in Celebici ended unsuccessfully (Major Odom 22 January 2002, NATO 28 February 2002, 1 March 2002). From April to July 2002 SFOR was more successful since the soldiers managed to detain four people. SFOR soldiers from MND North detained Momir Nikolic and Miroslav Deronjic in the area of Bratunac in April and July respectively (BBC 1 8 July 2000, April 2002, 2 April 2002, Major Lundy 2 April 2002, NATO SG Lord Robertson 7 July 2002). In addition SFOR soldiers from MND South-West detained Darko Mrdja in Prijedor and SFOR soldiers from MND South-East managed to detain Radovan Stankovic in his home in the village of Trebicina near Foca (BBC 13 June 2002, 9 July 2002, NATO SG Lord Robertson 13 June 2002, 9 July 2002). SFOR made its last successful detention attempt in April 2003 when SFOR soldiers from MND North detained Naser Oric, who was under a sealed indictment in Tuzla (BBC 11 April 2003, Captain MacEachern 11 April 2003, NATO SG Lord Robertson 11 April 2003). In addition to this successful detention, SFOR soldiers also carried out a couple of unsuccessful attempts at detaining indicted war criminals in 2003. In June the aim of the operation was the Croatian General Ante Gotovina. SFOR soldiers detained a man they thought was Gotovina but the formal identification by the ICTY revealed that he was not the wanted alleged war criminal (SFOR 9 June 2003). Two months later SFOR soldiers tried to detain Ratko Mladić in the home of his mother near Sarajevo the day after she had died but again the operation failed (SFOR 13 August 2003). Finally in 2004 SFOR did not manage to detain any indicted individuals but the soldiers did try in vain twice more to detain Radovan Karadžić in Pale in January and April (SFOR 10 January 2004, 1 April 2004, 2 April 2004). On at least three occasions, in July 2002, August 2003 and February 2004, SFOR soldiers also raided the homes of Karadžić family members (Human Rights Watch 2005a), with the aim to obtaining information about his support network and his whereabouts (ibid.). SFOR also carried out a large search operation in the areas of Celebici, Visegrad and Trebinje to gather information (Domin 2002).

Considering the number of indicted war criminals still at large during the last four years of SFOR's mission and the number who voluntarily surrendered during the same period, SFOR only managed to detain a disappointingly small proportion. This is somewhat surprising when one looks at how widely SFOR's interpretation of its own mandate expanded during its final years of operation. In 2001 SFOR tended the mandate to include operations to detain indicted war criminals based on reliable information from external sources about their whereabouts (General Ralston 22 May 2001, Lt Gen Dodson 4 September 2001). SFOR also no longer ruled out the establishment of special units solely focused on hunting and detaining indicted war criminals though such units were never established (Lt Gen Dodson 4 September 2001). Furthermore, in February 2002, SFOR argued that its mandate allowed it to use a broad range of means and capabilities to carry out detentions though no details about these means and capabilities were provided (NATO 28 February 2002). Two months later SFOR contended that its soldiers were authorised to hunt indicted war criminals rather than just detain them when encountered (Major Lundy 2 April 2002). In addition, in July 2002, SFOR also expanded its powers to include tracking down networks of individuals suspected of supporting those still at large and searching the properties belonging to these suspected supporters (Major Lundy 4 July 2002). Moreover, in 2003, SFOR's interpretation of its own mandate apparently also came to include actively obtaining information from the local population about the whereabouts of indicted war criminals (SFOR interview 2003). Finally, in 2004, SFOR also added detaining and questioning individuals from the alleged supported networks of the indicted war criminals to the tasks that the soldiers were allowed to carry out in accordance with SFOR's mandate (SFOR 28 January 2004a, 28 January 2004b, 12 February 2004, 17 February 2004, 3 March 2004, 14 May 2004, 31 July 2004, 31 August 2004a, 31 August 2004b). Hence the aim of SFOR's operations was now not merely the detention of the indicted war criminals but also the destruction of the support networks that enabled their continued escape from justice. Therefore, SFOR considerably broadened the interpretation of its own mandate concerning the detention of indicted war criminals.

In accordance with the broadened interpretation of its powers, SFOR also attempted to strengthen the practices the soldiers implemented in order to effect detentions. In 2002 all SFOR soldiers were allegedly provided with an updated booklet containing photos and basic information about all indicted war criminals still at large (SFOR interview 2003). Gradually, SFOR soldiers on patrol also became more involved in detaining indicted war criminals. Ground and helicopter patrols took part in operations to detain Radovan Karadžić and patrolling soldiers took part in the detention of members of the support networks and in searching properties belonging to indicted war criminals (Major Lundy 15 August 2002, SFOR 26 August 2003). SFOR soldiers also used roadblocks and checkpoints in their search for indicted war criminals and information about their support networks (Lt Bouysson 14 March 2002, Major Lundy 15 August 2002). In addition, SFOR soldiers gradually limited the freedom of movement of the wanted individuals and the soldiers began increasingly to involve the local police in both search and detention operations (Domin 2002, Lt Gen Dodson 4 September 2001, Major Lundy 4 July 2002, 15 August 2002, SFOR 15 October 2004, 21 October 2004, SFOR interviews 2003). SFOR also implemented media campaigns asking local people to come forward with information about the whereabouts of indicted war criminals (SFOR interview 2003). The US State Department also continued to offer large sums of money in exchange for information that would lead to detentions (Major Lundy 15 August 2002). Furthermore, SFOR soldiers on patrol questioned local people about the whereabouts of indicted war criminals (SFOR interview 2003). In addition, though SFOR never established a special unit solely focused on detaining indicted war criminals, the Multinational Specialised Unit (MSU) within SFOR became increasingly involved in this task (ibid.). The MSU comprised police forces with military status. An example of its involvement in detentions was its assistance of SFOR soldiers in their attempt to detain Radovan Karadžić in Pale (SFOR 1

April 2004). SFOR soldiers also began to receive special training in this type of detention. They received face recognition training and took part in training exercises that simulated detention operations (Second Lt Marin 9 January 2003, SFOR interview 2003, Staff Sgt Simpson 25 April 2002). SFOR soldiers also began to search for information in the private properties of indicted war criminals and members of their support networks (Captain MacEachern 11 March 2003, Major Lundy 4 July 2002, 15 August 2002, SFOR 13 January 2004, 28 January 2004a, 28 January 2004b, 19 February 2004, 7 October 2004, 8 October 2004, 14 October 2004, 15 October 2004, 21 October 2004). In addition SFOR soldiers searched both military and civilian properties in attempts to locate and detain indicted war criminals (Lt Bouysson 14 March 2002, NATO 28 February 2002, 1 March 2002, 6 March 2002, SFOR 10 January 2004, 1 April 2004, 2 April 2004). Finally, SFOR soldiers also detained and questioned members of the networks supporting indicted war criminals at large (SFOR 28 January 2004a, 28 January 2004b, 3 March 2004, 14 May 2004, 26 July 2004, 31 July 2004, 31 August 2004a, 31 August 2004b). Despite all these apparently improved efforts, SFOR managed to detain far fewer indicted war criminals during the last years of its mission than it had done during the middle stages.

Various factors can potentially help explain this relatively disappointing result. First, as more and more indicted war criminals were either detained or surrendered voluntarily, the number still at large was decreasing and accordingly the chances of SFOR making successful detentions were also falling. However, during the final four years of SFOR's mission, a significant number of indicted war criminals were still at large in SFOR's area of operation so that decreasing numbers cannot alone explain why SFOR's relative lack of success in these years (President of the ICTY 2001, 2002, 2003, 2004). In addition, though all SFOR soldiers were allegedly given information to help them identify indicted individuals, this information was apparently not updated very frequently. When asked how this information was updated, a senior member of SFOR's headquarter staff in Camp Butmir provided a year-old poster with photos of the wanted still at large with penned crosses over those who had meanwhile been detained (SFOR interview 2003). Other senior staff also admitted that they could not remember when such information had been given had last been updated (SFOR interviews 2003). Moreover, SFOR apparently sometimes warned the local population prior to carrying out search operations, which obviously meant that any indicted war criminals at large in the area had plenty of time to disappear before the SFOR soldiers arrived (Major Lundy 15 August 2002). SFOR defended this practice by arguing that the local population did not have to worry about what the aim of the operation was (ibid.). French soldiers were also continuously accused of warning indicted individuals ahead of detention operations (Baker 30 May 2004, Human Rights Watch 2005a). Furthermore, during this period, SFOR apparently never made any detentions on the grounds of information received from the local population. Even the large financial rewards offered by the US State Department for crucial information about the whereabouts of indicted war criminals apparently only led to one person being handed over to

SFOR. There are several possible reasons for this disappointing result. First, it might simply be that the local people still supported the indicted war criminals so much that they did not want to see them sent to The Hague. Second, the local population might have considered it dangerous to cooperate with SFOR on such a sensitive issue. The absence of a protection programme for informers might have dissuaded people from helping SFOR, if they perceived that doing so would endanger their lives. In addition, SFOR's behaviour towards the local population on certain occasions did not promote the local population's faith in SFOR. An example of this is SFOR's attempt to detain Radovan Karadžić in a house in Pale in 2004 (SFOR 1 April 2004, 2 April 2004). During this failed operation SFOR severely injured the Archpriest Stavrophore Jeremija and his son Aleksandar Starovlah (ibid.). Finally, it is also possible that the local population and other international organisations working in Bosnia-Herzegovina did provide SFOR with information but that SFOR soldiers did not act on the information (International Crisis Group 2000, Jelacic and Griffiths 2004).

Furthermore, the motive behind SFOR's searches for Radovan Karadžić has also been questioned (Baker 30 May 2004). Some were carried out in the Karadžić family home, arguably not the most obvious hideout for a man on the run from armies of international soldiers. It has therefore been argued that these searches amounted to nothing more than publicity stunts (ibid.). A final factor that can potentially help explain why SFOR was not more successful in detaining indicted war criminals is SFOR's reluctance to set up a specialist unit to do this (Lt Gen Dodson 4 September 2001, NATO SG Lord Robertson 21 December 2000). This meant that, rather than having a team of specialists focusing solely on detention operations, these remained just one of many tasks that ordinary SFOR soldiers were expected to carry out.

In conclusion, though SFOR broadened the interpretation of its mandate concerning the detention of indicted war criminals and improved its efforts in this regard, the results were still not completely satisfactory and lacked wholehearted commitment.

Explaining SFOR's ups and downs

Numerous factors can help explain SFOR's successes and failures concerning the detention of indicted war criminals.

In the beginning SFOR had many of the same concerns as IFOR had. The mandate did not explicitly authorise SFOR to detain indicted war criminals leaving military commanders on the ground without much political guidance as to how involved SFOR soldiers were supposed to be (Kalinauskas 2002). Hence, it was very much left to military commanders to interpret the mandate and they were very reluctant to involve their soldiers in these detentions (ibid.). American soldiers in particular were still marred by their experiences in Somalia, where an attempt to capture an alleged war criminal had gone horribly wrong (Lorenz 1997). It was apparently also perceived that time should be allowed for diplomatic and economic initiatives to convince the individual states to turn criminals over to the ICTY (ibid.). Concerns that involvement in such operations would be counterproductive to SFOR's main focus, the implementation of the military objectives of the DPA, and that these actions could threaten stability and undermine peace, also influenced the decision not to involve SFOR soldiers in detention operations at the start of the mission (Kalinauskas 2002, Lorenz 1997). Finally, fear that SFOR soldiers would get injured or killed either during the detention operations or as a result of retaliation from angry supporters of indicted war criminals also meant that SFOR commanders were very reluctant to commit troops to the task (ibid.). A part of this concern was also that some parts of SFOR were perceived to be more vulnerable to retaliation than others (Lorenz 1997). This meant that SFOR could face a situation where British soldiers' detention of an indicted war criminal could lead to retaliation against the French SFOR soldiers in charge of the area where Karadžić spent a lot of his time. Hence, unless all national contingent participating in SFOR agreed that the risk would be worth it, it was feared that the implementation of this new task could potentially splinter the coalition (ibid.). Considering all these concerns and fears preventing SFOR soldiers from detaining indicted war criminals at the start of the mission, what then made SFOR commanders change their mind and request their soldiers to get involved in detention operations in the middle of 1997?

What made SFOR decide to begin to detain indicted war criminals?

Several factors are likely to have influenced SFOR's decision to initiate its first detention operation. First, SFOR was under increasing external pressure from Western media and public opinion, the Prosecutor of the ICTY and human rights groups, who since the beginning of IFOR's deployment had been very critical of the peace enforcement missions' policy towards indicted war criminals (Kalinauskas 2002, Leurdijk 2001). Second, there was also a growing recognition outside and inside SFOR that SFOR was the only authority capable of detaining indicted war criminals in Bosnia-Herzegovina (Leurdijk 2001). Third, the American General Wesley Clark, who became the military leader of SFOR in 1997, and some of his colleagues in the US military began to recognise that the DPA could not be successfully implemented, which would mean that SFOR soldiers could be pulled out of Bosnia-Herzegovina, unless indicted war criminals were removed from the scene (Kalinauskas 2002). Fourth, in the Bosnian Serb part of Bosnia-Herzegovina less radical leaders such as President Biljana Plavsic and Prime Minister Milorad Dodik, whom NATO saw as potential allies against more uncompromising Bosnian Serbs, took power. This meant that, rather than viewing indicted war criminals as a threat to SFOR soldiers, NATO began to see them as obstacles towards Bosnian Serb reforms (Hooper undated). UNTAES's successful detention of Slavko Dokmanovic and the lack of serious reprisals are also likely to have influenced SFOR's decision to get actively involved (Ruxton 2001). Furthermore at the operational level it is also likely that the experience British troops had gained in Northern Ireland and the perception that Kovacevic and Drljaca were seen as considerable obstacles to peace-building in the British sector influenced the decision to initiate SFOR's first detention operation (Baker 30 May 2004, Lorenz 1997). Bearing in mind that SFOR soldiers were in danger when they attempted to detain Drljaca, and that one of the most considerable fears of SFOR commanders thereby materialised, what made SFOR continue to attempt to carry out detentions?

What made SFOR continue to detain indicted war criminals after the first detention attempts?

There are undoubtedly several reasons why SFOR decided to stay involved in the detention of indicted war criminals. First, though SFOR's initial efforts resulted in SFOR soldiers having to fire back at and consequently kill one of the indicted war criminals, the operations were still hailed as a success (Human Rights Watch 10 July 1997, President of the ICTY 1997). This was an indication to SFOR that its international soldiers were able to detain indicted war criminals successfully. The fact that no serious reprisal or civil unrest, with the potential to threaten the peace process, occurred after the first detentions also encouraged SFOR to initiate further operations (Kalinauskas 2002, Ruxton 2001, Sliedregt 2001). It has also been argued that NATO slowly realised that detaining indicted war criminals was one of the supporting tasks that SFOR had to carry out in order to help implement the DPA and thereby contribute to the peace process (Leurdijk 2001). Finally, the lack of any significant legal challenge to SFOR's right to detain is also likely to have influenced SFOR's decision to keep its involvement in the detention of indicted war criminals (International Crisis Group 2000).

Though SFOR continued to take part in these detentions until the end of its mission, this involvement never became consistent and effective with the result that only a relatively modest number were detained. Numerous interlinked factors can help explain this lack of firm commitment.

Why did SFOR never fully commit to detaining indicted war criminals?

First, an entrenched fear, that detaining indicted war criminals would lead to civil unrest and jeopardise the fragile peace in Bosnia-Herzegovina contributed to SFOR's reluctance to engage in this task (Human Rights Watch 2005a, International Crisis Group 2000, Supernor 2001). This fear apparently persisted despite the experience that operations provoked only relatively minor demonstrations and protests. Second, it was also feared that, if SFOR became involved in what was perceived as a civilian task, then it could threaten the implementation of its military tasks under the DPA and thereby undermine peace-building efforts in Bosnia-Herzegovina (Kalinauskas 2002). Within SFOR there was also a persistent perception that detaining war criminals was not a job that international soldiers had any experience in or were trained to carry out and that therefore it was better left to the local police (Human Rights Watch 2005a, International Crisis Group 2000, Kalinauskas 2002). Fear of SFOR soldiers being injured or killed during such an operation or in the aftermath of a detention as a result of reprisals also made SFOR reluctant to initiate detention operations (Human Rights Watch 2005a, International Crisis Group 2000, Kalinauskas 2002, Kampschror 2001). This was especially a concern for American troops, afraid that the scenario would be the same as it had been in Somalia and French troops, who had lost a lot of UNPROFOR soldiers and who were deployed in an area where Karadžić was reported to be residing some of the time (International Crisis Group 2000, Kampschror 2001, Lorenz 1997). Furthermore there were also rumours of casualties among SFOR soldiers who had taken part in detention operations (Leurdijk 2001). This fear of casualties was also linked to the perception that indicted war criminals remained strong despite the indictments. SFOR was faced with some indicted war criminals maintaining a relatively high profile which meant that, at least until the publication of their indictment and sometimes even also after that, the individuals met regularly with representatives from international organisations including SFOR (International Crisis Group 2000). Some of the indicted also retained strong links to the military and enjoyed wide public support in their communities (ibid.). Radovan Karadžić allegedly even had a network that included political, financial, military, police and legal powers (Baker 30 May 2004, Human Rights Watch 2005a). Factors within SFOR allegedly also influenced its decision not to commit fully to detaining indicted war criminals. Since some sections of SFOR were perceived to be more vulnerable to retaliation than others, it was also more difficult for the various national contingents in SFOR to agree on a common firm approach towards detentions, especially since the soldiers were unfamiliar with the task and its consequences (Lorenz 1997). There was allegedly also mutual mistrust among certain NATO members, especially between the French and the Americans, because the French were suspected of disclosing information ahead of detention operations, making US officers reluctant to share intelligence and conduct operations with the French soldiers in charge of the neighbouring section (Human Rights Watch 2005a). Finally and most controversially, SFOR's reluctant attitude to detaining indicted war criminals has also been explained by means of political reasons to do with the role of the states contributing to SFOR, in the violent conflict in Bosnia-Herzegovina that led to SFOR's deployment (International Crisis Group 2000, Kampschror 2001, Leurdijk 2001). Trials of Radovan Karadžić and Ratko Mladić in particular are expected to cause considerable embarrassment to high-ranking diplomats and political and military leaders since it is likely to reveal the flaws and failures of the Western approach to peacemaking in Bosnia-Herzegovina (ibid.). Hence, it was more in the interest of the states contributing to SFOR that Karadžić was allowed to move freely around than to detain him and send him to The Hague. Especially French soldiers in charge of MND South-East and American soldiers leading in MND North are said to have opposed detentions, fearing that the resultant trials would expose the soldiers' actions when part of UNPROFOR to criticism (International

Crisis Group 2000, Leurdijk 2001). French, American and Dutch soldiers met with Karadžić and Mladić at social functions during the violent conflict and praised Serb hospitality (Kampschror 2001). It has even been claimed that French soldiers shot indicted war criminal Dragan Gagovic to prevent him from surrendering voluntarily because French UNPROFOR soldiers had allegedly done business with him during the war (International Crisis Group 2000).

Conclusion: limited commitment, limited success in detentions

There is no doubt that the detentions that SFOR successfully carried out made a valuable contribution to the work of the ICTY at a time when the ICTY was close to failure due to a lack of indicted war criminals in its custody. However, it also has to be pointed out that, despite several good opportunities, SFOR failed to detain the two most wanted, Radovan Karadžić and Ratko Mladić and that the international SFOR soldiers only managed to detain about 30 indicted indi- viduals despite reliable reports that many more were roaming around SFOR's area of operation (President of the ICTY 1997, 1998, 1999, 2000, 2001, 2002, 2003, 2004, 2005). Despite a lot of criticism and many of the original fears con- cerning SFOR involvement, such as fatal injuries to its soldiers or mass demon- strations against SFOR never materialising, SFOR did not become fully committed to detaining indicted war criminals and this was clearly reflected in the results.

7 KFOR and the detention of indicted war criminals

Introduction

Not long after the violent conflict in Bosnia-Herzegovina had been brought to an end another violent conflict broke out in a different part of the former Yugoslavia. This time the fighting parties were military and paramilitary troops from the Federal Republic of Yugoslavia and the Kosovo Liberation Army over the territory of Kosovo in Serbia. After the initial Rambouillet negotiations had broken down because the Serb representatives withdrew their support for the process, NATO, without the consent of the UN, initiated a fierce bombing campaign against the Federal Republic of Yugoslavia (FRY) in the spring of 1999. A couple of months later the FRY reluctantly consented to the deployment of an international peace enforcement mission to help implement a peace process in Kosovo. Subsequently UNSC resolution 1244 authorised UNMIK to implement the civilian aspects of the peace process. The resolution also put NATO in charge of implementing the military aspects of the peace agreement as NATO soldiers had done in Bosnia-Herzegovina. Thus in the summer of 1999, NATO deployed Kosovo Force (KFOR) soldiers in order to establish and maintain security in Kosovo. This chapter examines KFOR efforts to detain indicted war criminals and it discusses KFOR response to becoming involved in these detentions and why KFOR chose a reactive rather than a proactive approach to the task.

Only one case

Unlike IFOR and SFOR, KFOR has not been faced with having to operate in an area where a lot of indicted war criminals have been reported being at large. The Prosecutor of the ICTY has only once requested KFOR to detain indicted war criminals. That was at the start of 2003 when the ICTY issued four sealed indictments against Fatmir Limaj, Haradin Bala, Isak Musliu and Agim Murtezi and forwarded arrests warrants to KFOR (Office of the Prosecutor 18 February 2003). On 17 February 2003 and hence, only a short while after having received the arrest warrants, KFOR initiated operations to detain the indicted (NATO 17 February 2003). The detention operations were carried out by ordinary Norwegian and British KFOR soldiers, British reconnaissance and intelligence specialists flown in specially to take part in the operations and Italian Carabinieri from the Multinational Specialised Unit (MSU) (Jennings 18 February 2003). Reportedly wearing balaclavas and heavily armed, the international soldiers managed to detain Haradin Bala in his house in a village outside Pristina (Abrashi 2003, Jennings 17 February 2003). The soldiers also successfully detained Isak Musliu and Agim Murtezi (KFOR 17 February 2003a). The fourth accused, Fatmir Limaj, was not in Kosovo at the time of the operations. He had left the province on a regular flight to Slovenia three days earlier (Office of the Prosecutor 18 February 2003). This raised fierce criticism from the Prosecutor of the ICTY, Del Ponte, who was outraged that Limaj, a public figure because of his seat in the Kosovo Assembly, had been allowed to pass through the KFOR-guarded Pristina airport two and a half weeks after the request to detain him (ibid.). However, since Fatmir Limaj was soon detained by the Slovenian authorities and transferred to The Hague, the criticism was not pursued any further (BBC 19 February 2003).

It was not until two years later in early 2005 that the Prosecutor of the ICTY announced three more indictments against individuals residing in Kosovo. This time the indicted were Idriz Balaj, Lahi Brahimaj and Ramush Haradinaj, who was the Prime Minister of Kosovo at the time the indictment was announced. However, arrest warrants were not served to KFOR on this occasion because the three indicted war criminals immediately surrendered voluntarily to the ICTY or were transferred to the ICTY by the local authorities in Kosovo (President of the ICTY 2005).

Only acting on request

Upon KFOR's successful detention of the indicted war criminals Bala, Musliu and Murtezi, KFOR, NATO's Supreme Allied Commander Europe, General Jones and NATO's Secretary General, Lord Robertson all contended that KFOR's mandate authorised KFOR soldiers to detain indicted war criminals (KFOR 17 February 2003a, KFOR 17 February 2003b, KFOR 17 February 2003c). NATO Secretary Lord Robertson also claimed that NATO was committed to such detentions throughout the region (KFOR 17 February 2003c). However, KFOR's commitment was apparently limited to only acting on request. After the successful detention operations, KFOR could not have known for sure whether the Prosecutor of the ICTY would decide to indict more individuals residing in Kosovo. Nonetheless, since only four individuals from the Kosovo-Albanian party to the violent conflict had been indicted, it was likely that the Prosecutor of the ICTY would indict more individuals from Kosovo and that KFOR would be requested to detain these individuals. As it happens, the Prosecutor of the ICTY did indict more individuals from Kosovo but they surrendered voluntarily before KFOR was asked to intervene. It was also not unlikely that persons from elsewhere in the former Yugoslavia, who had already been indicted by the ICTY but who were still at large, could have moved to

Kosovo and that therefore KFOR could have been requested to detain them. Hence, KFOR could have chosen to begin preparing for its response to such a request. However, KFOR apparently did not implement any practices that would prepare them for locating and detaining indicted war criminals at large in their area of operation (KFOR interview 2003). Half a year after KFOR had detained Bala, Musliu and Murtezi, interviews with senior KFOR soldiers revealed that even KFOR's headquarters had no list of indicted war criminals readily available (KFOR interview 2003). One interviewee had never heard about such a list of indicted war criminals and another had heard about one but did not know where it was (ibid.). Instead KFOR only took actions against indicted war criminals if UNMIK specifically requested KFOR to do so (ibid.).

Explaining KFOR's reactive approach

There are undoubtedly various reasons as to why KFOR did not take a more proactive approach towards indicted war criminals but merely acted when specifically asked to do so. First, officially there were no indicted war criminals at large in KFOR's area of operation and, though it was likely that more alleged war criminals from Kosovo would be indicted after the first indictments in 2003, there was no guarantee that this would happen. Hence, preparing a response to further indictments of individuals would have been preparing for a scenario that might never happen. Second, it is also likely that, KFOR's experience from the first operations, with three people relatively easily detained and one, though initially slipping through the net, also fairly swiftly transferred to The Hague, left KFOR with the impression that any further detentions would be easy. Hence, no further preparations were deemed necessary. Third, though KFOR was initially criticised for having let Limaj escape to Slovenia, there was no external pressure on KFOR to prepare for detaining indicted war criminals. Fourth, according to two of the KFOR interviewees, such detentions were considered as a job for the police and thus it should be UNMIK international police carrying out the detentions and KFOR only providing the necessary security backup (KFOR interviews 2003). Fifth, the detention of especially Fatmir Limaj was highly unpopular among Kosovo-Albanians and it led to mass demonstrations (UNMIK 26 February 2003). Thus, it is likely that KFOR did not wish to be seen in preparation for further detention operations, since this could potentially spark more demonstrations and negative feelings among the local population towards KFOR. Sixth, keeping in mind SFOR's limited success in detaining indicted war criminals, it is also likely that neither political nor military leaders in NATO were interested in getting KFOR soldiers further involved in locating and detaining indicted war criminals. Finally, it is also possible that especially UNMIK's but also KFOR's relationship with politicians such as Ramush Haradinaj, who was one of the individuals expected to be eventually indicted prevented KFOR from preparing for once again being involved in locating and detaining indicted war criminals.[24]

Conclusion

KFOR soldiers have only once been requested to detain indicted war criminals and on that occasion KFOR managed to secure the transfer of the individuals to The Hague, though with some considerable help from the Slovenian authorities. Since then KFOR has apparently done very little to prepare for further potential detention operations. This means that, at least in theory, indicted war criminals from other parts of the former Yugoslavia who are on the run from the ICTY could have lived or stayed over in Kosovo without KFOR knowing about it or doing anything to locate them. It also means that, if more individuals from Kosovo had been indicted and not immediately surrendered voluntarily, KFOR would most probably not have been better prepared for locating and detaining them than before the first detention operation. Hence, a situation such as when Fatmir Limaj slipped through a KFOR-guarded airport despite already being indicted, could easily have happened again.

Part IV

Preparing, authorising and ensuring the detention of indicted war criminals

8 Preparing peace enforcement soldiers for detaining indicted war criminals

Incorporating the detention of indicted war criminals into the military doctrines of peace enforcement missions

Introduction

The importance of military doctrines for the conduct of peace enforcement missions is often overlooked in the literature. All too often the analysis of successes and failures begins with the mandate the missions were given rather than the doctrine that influenced the way the mandate was interpreted and implemented.[25] This is unsatisfactory since a military doctrine helps determine how the military understands the nature of the conflict it is intervening in and the tasks required to make its intervention successful (Chief of the General Staff 1995). Hence, a military peace enforcement doctrine is the basis for the organisation, training, equipment and rules of engagement of the peace enforcement mission (Sewall 1994). Consequently, one of the fundamental prerequisites for detaining indicted war criminals becoming a responsibility of peace enforcement soldiers is that the task is included in the military doctrines that the peace enforcement mission is based on. If this is not the case, unless the detention of indicted war criminals is explicitly mentioned in the mandate, it is unlikely that the mission will include this in its interpretation of its mandate. In cases when such detention operations are explicitly mentioned in the mandate, it is still important that they are also addressed in the military doctrines since this will mean that the mission is more likely to have the required covered procedures in its preparation. Furthermore, if peace enforcement soldiers are to carry out successful detentions, it is important that this task is not just included in the doctrine but also properly incorporated into it.

Thus this chapter first examines how the peace enforcement doctrines of the states and international organisations that have dominated post-Cold War peace enforcement missions have responded to peace enforcers becoming involved in detaining indicted war criminals in Bosnia-Herzegovina and Kosovo. The question is whether the process of including and integrating the detention of indicted war criminals into the doctrines of peace enforcement missions has already begun and if so, how far the process has come. Based on this examination and the experience of IFOR, SFOR and KFOR, the chapter also discusses how the doctrines need to be further developed in order to fully incorporate the detention of indicted war criminals. This discussion is not only relevant for the further development of the doctrines included in this examination. It is also relevant for regional organisations such as the European Union (EU) and the African Union (AU) that are becoming increasingly involved in peace enforcement missions. The EU has already deployed one such mission, European Force (EUFOR), in Bosnia-Herzegovina, which is involved in detaining indicted war criminals and the EU is also likely to deploy another in Kosovo once the KFOR mission there comes to an end. So far the EU has adopted NATO's peace enforcement doctrine but it is not unlikely that the EU one day will develop one of its own. The AU is in the process of establishing a new African Standby Force and, given the International Criminal Court's involvement in Uganda, Sudan and the Democratic Republic of Congo, it is likely that soldiers from the African Union will be under pressure to get involved in detaining indicted war criminals. Hence, it is important that this task is also fully incorporated into the doctrine that will guide the AU's involvement in peace enforcement.

The following examination includes the military peace enforcement doctrines of the UK, the US and NATO. The UK has been included because Britain has a longstanding record of involvement in both peacekeeping and peace enforcement missions (Woodhouse and Ramsbotham 1999: 22–23). In addition British scholars have also dominated the development of recent peacekeeping and peace enforcement doctrines such as Wider Peacekeeping and Peace Support Operations (Fitz-Gerald 2003). The US has been included because it has been the dominant state in recent missions and highly influential in the decision to initiate an operation but also provides a lot of soldiers and other resources. Furthermore many of the commanders of the missions in the former Yugoslavia have either been from the UK or the US. NATO is not only interesting because it is the leading regional organisation involved in peacekeeping and peace enforcement but necessarily also because it is the organisation behind the deployment of IFOR, SFOR and KFOR.

British peace operation doctrines and the detention of indicted war criminals

When IFOR was deployed in the end of 1995 a new peace operation doctrine named Wider Peacekeeping had just been introduced.[26] The term 'wider peacekeeping' was used to describe the extended peacekeeping missions established in the early and mid-1990s. As these missions were deployed in ongoing violent conflicts, they were expected to carry out new tasks such as delivering humanitarian aid and establishing law and order (Chief of the General Staff 1995: page 2–2(paragraph 2d.), 3–9(25)). This new doctrine recognised that the environment where wider peacekeeping troops were deployed was characterised by gross violations of human rights (Chief of the General Staff 1995: 1–7(24)). However, the doctrine only contended that international soldiers should monitor and report on human rights abuses and not get actively involved in securing accountability for violations (Chief of the General Staff, 1995: 5–12(36d.)).

Thus, though international peacekeeping soldiers in especially Bosnia-Herzegovina and Rwanda had been fiercely criticised for not attempting to prevent or secure accountability for human rights atrocities, the Wider Peacekeeping doctrine did not anticipate that international peace missions would become involved in detaining indicted war criminals. Instead the doctrine was still to a high degree based on the basic principles of traditional peacekeeping. Upholding the principles of impartiality and consent of the parties to the conflict and using minimum force were seen as vital keys to a successful peace mission and thus becoming involved in detaining indicted war criminals, a task that would seriously challenge these three principles, appeared out of the question (Chief of the General Staff 1995: chapter 2, sections 3–6).[27]

In 1998, at a time when British soldiers had already detained several indicted war criminals in Bosnia-Herzegovina, the *Wider Peacekeeping* doctrine was replaced by a new doctrine named *Peace Support Operations*. This new doctrine acknowledged that reconciliation processes were taking place in the areas where peace enforcement soldiers were deployed (Chief of Joint Operations 1998: 2–4(207). It also contended the importance of peace support operations supporting the principles of not only the UN but also international humanitarian law (Chief of Joint Operations 1998: 3–1(303), 3–2). Based on the experience of UNPROFOR and UNAMIR, the doctrine also recognised the legal and ethical dilemmas that soldiers face when they encounter human rights abuses but their mandate and rules of engagement prevent them from actively responding (Chief of Joint Operations 1998: 2–8(217)). The doctrine called for these dilemmas to be taken into consideration when mandates are formulated and resources allocated (ibid.). *Peace Support Operations* also acknowledged the peace and justice dilemma.[28] On the one hand the doctrine contended that the active participation of the parties to the conflict in the negotiation and implementation of cease-fires and peace agreements is vital (Chief of Joint Operations 1998: 3–2(303), 4–2(404)). On the other hand it also argued that the local population needs to be protected from the fighting parties and that individuals who hinder the peace process need to be removed (Chief of Joint Operations 1998: 6–11(628)). The doctrine also pointed out that it should not only be the leaders of the fighting parties who dictate the peace settlement, since this can be perceived as rewarding individuals who have committed war crimes (Chief of Joint Operations 1998: 4–2(404)). This would ignore the victims of the atrocities' need for justice and therefore jeopardise the support of and consent to the peace process and it would not make use of all the people who are already working for peace (ibid.). The new doctrine explicitly recognised that the apprehension of indicted war criminals generally necessitated the deployment of peace enforcement soldiers (Chief of Joint Operations 1998: 6–8(619), 7–20(742b.)). However, the doctrine did emphasise that the soldiers should undertake this task in cooperation with military police units, CIVPOL, specialist war crimes investigators and other enforcement agencies (Chief of Joint Operations 1998: 5–11(528), 6–8(619)). Finally, the doctrine also reflected on the consequences of involving or not involving peace enforcement soldiers in the detentions. The doctrine argued that, if international soldiers failed to respond to violations of international law and human rights, then the credibility of their mission would be undermined internationally as well as locally (Chief of Joint Operations, 1998: 4–4(409)). In addition, if international soldiers become involved in detaining indicted war criminals, then it is likely that the parties to the conflict will no longer perceive the mission as impartial (Chief of Joint Operations 1998: 6–9(622)). However, the doctrine also argued that this should not deter the soldiers from taking the necessary actions (ibid.).

Hence the *Peace Support Operations* doctrine recognised that soldiers need to be involved in detaining indicted war criminals and it indicated that this task was slowly being incorporated into British peace operation doctrines. Nevertheless the doctrine also reflected the confusion SFOR soldiers faced regarding their role in detention operations on the ground in Bosnia-Herzegovina. The doctrine did not specify exactly what peace enforcement soldiers were expected to do to effect detentions. In addition, it failed to address how including the detention wanted individuals would influence the regulations on the use of force. Furthermore, the doctrine did not acknowledge that, in order for peace enforcement soldiers to carry out effective detentions, they require special training in, for example, detention procedures and practices.[29]

In SFOR's last year and KFOR's fifth year of operation the British military introduced an updated version of the *Peace Support Operations* doctrine, which is also the doctrine currently in use (Joint Doctrine and Concepts Centre 2004). The new version of the doctrine acknowledged that there are times when human rights should take priority over national sovereignty and therefore that international intervention to protect civilians is pivotal (Joint Doctrine and Concepts Centre 2004: 1–6(113)). It also acknowledged the significance of the establishment of the ICC though it did not comment on how this will influence future peace enforcement missions (Joint Doctrine and Concepts Centre 2004: B-20(B63)). Like the original *Peace Support Operations* doctrine, the new doctrine also acknowledged that, since it is often the perpetrators who set the terms for a peace settlement, victims of violent conflict are often left with unfulfilled expectations and the impression that the people who have committed war crimes are rewarded while their victims are left powerless (Joint Doctrine and Concepts Centre 2004: 5–4(506), 5–5). The doctrine also recognised that in such cases accountability for war crimes is a prerequisite for a successful peace enforcement mission, since impunity for the perpetrators and the consequent lack of justice for the victims is likely to lead to a return to violent conflict (ibid.). The new doctrine explicitly mentioned the detention of indicted war criminals as one of the tasks peace enforcement missions need to undertake (Joint Doctrine and Concepts Centre 2004: 5–26(560)). However, like its predecessor, the new doctrine did not specify the exact role international soldiers should play in detentions, though it underlined the fact that detentions should be undertaken in cooperation with other enforcement agencies (Joint Doctrine and Concepts Centre 2004: 5–24(554), 5–26 (560)). Furthermore, the new doctrine also recognised the role NATO peace enforcers have played in the detention of indicted war criminals in the former Yugoslavia and it acknowledged that the peace enforcement forces have so far not been able to detain all of the accused (Joint Doctrine and Concepts Centre 2004: B-21(B64)). Though the new doctrine did not address impartiality and the use of force in the context of detaining indicted war criminals, it acknowledged that missions need to be prepared for the parties to the violent conflict not perceiving it as impartial and to accept risks and casualties in order to implement the mandate successfully (Joint Doctrine and Concepts Centre 2004: 1–8(121), 4–6(411d.), B-5(B15b.)). Finally, in contrast to the first version of *Peace Support Operations*, the second version recommended that soldiers taking part in peace enforcement missions are given legal advice regarding war crimes and war criminals as part of their training (Joint Doctrine and Concepts Centre 2004: 4–13(435b.2)).

In conclusion and reflecting the experience of British soldiers taking part in IFOR, SFOR and KFOR, the detention of indicted war criminals has been included in the British military doctrine on peace operations. The current British peace enforcement doctrine acknowledges that the detention and prosecution of indicted war criminals is a prerequisite for long-term peace and that peace enforcers therefore need to participate in this matter. However, and also reflecting the situation in the field, the role of peace enforcers in detentions is not well defined. The doctrine recognises that peace enforcers need to cooperate with the national and/or international police when detaining indicted war criminals but it is not clear who is responsible for detentions. Though the doctrine acknowledges that peace enforcers need to be prepared to lose the consent of the parties to the violent conflict and to risk being injured or killed in order to carry out their mission successfully, the latest doctrinal publication does not deal with impartiality and the use of force in the context of these detentions. In addition, though the doctrine acknowledges that peace enforcement soldiers need training in international law, it does not recognise that other components, such as detention procedures and practices, also need to be included in training if soldiers are to successfully detain indicted war criminals. Finally, the doctrine acknowledges the peace or justice dilemma but it does not determine how the dilemma should be addressed in connection with the detention and prosecution of indicted war criminals. Hence, such detentions have been included in the British military doctrine on peace operations and steps have also been taken towards integrating the task in the doctrine. However, the incorporation is still far from complete since important points such as the exact role of peace enforcement soldiers and the consequences of the inclusion have not been adequately addressed.

US peace operation doctrines and the detention of indicted war criminals

In the year before IFOR's deployment the US military published two documents, *Peace Operations* and *Joint Doctrine for Military Operations Other than War* respectively, on military doctrines for peace operations (Headquarters Department of the Army 1994, Joint Chiefs of Staff 1995). *Peace Operations* recognised that peace missions could be deployed in areas where human rights were endangered, that encouraging respect for human rights was important and that protecting human rights should be included in soldiers' training (Headquarters Department of the Army 1994: 7, 28, 87). *Joint Doctrine for Military Operations Other than War* only mentioned human rights in connection with the use of exclusion zones in areas where international legislation on human rights were breached (Joint Chiefs of Staff 1995: III-4). Hence the doctrines only contended that peace enforcement soldiers should be involved in promoting human rights and preventing violations and it did not envisage that international soldiers would become involved in securing accountability for human rights atrocities.

In 1999, on the brink of KFOR's deployment, three years into SFOR's mission and a year after US soldiers became involved in detaining indicted war criminals in Bosnia-Herzegovina, these doctrines were followed up by another publication, *Joint Tactics Techniques and Procedures for Peace Operations* (Chairman of the Joint Chiefs of Staff 1999). Like its British counterpart this doctrine recognised that the environment peace operations were deployed in was characterised by human rights violations (Chairman of the Joint Chiefs of Staff 1999: I-15). The doctrine also recommended that military support should be given to other agencies investigating human rights violations (Chairman of the Joint Chiefs of Staff 1999: I-8). However, although American troops had already participated in the detention of indicted war criminals and probably reflecting US reluctance to engage in these operations, the doctrine did not acknowledge the need for peace enforcement soldiers to be actively involved in war criminal detentions or the importance of accountability for war crimes for long-term peace-building.

Two years later when four indicted war criminals had been detained in the American-led zone in Bosnia-Herzegovina, the US military released the *Joint Doctrine for Civil-Military Operations* (Joint Chiefs of Staff 2001). This doctrinal publication recognised the difficulty of integrating the protection of human rights in military operations (ibid.: I-7(2f.)). It emphasised that soldiers need to monitor and report violations of human rights and be trained in recognising such abuses (ibid.: I-13(3c.), III-15(9a.), III-16)). It also underlined the fact that all members of foreign military forces trained by US forces should be vetted for human rights atrocities (ibid.: III-7(4k.)). Finally and more importantly the doctrine also identified the apprehension of individuals indicted for crimes against humanity as a potential military task (ibid.: B-A-5(IVC1e.)). However, few attempts were made to incorporate the detention of these individuals in the doctrine, reflecting a continued US reluctance to allow peace enforcement soldiers to become actively involved in such operations.

Another two years later in 2003, when eight indicted war criminals had been apprehended in the American sector of Bosnia-Herzegovina and when KFOR soldiers had also been involved in detentions, the doctrine *Peace OPS Multi-Service Tactics, Techniques and Procedures for Conducting Peace Operations* was introduced (Army, Marine Corps, Navy Corps, Navy and Air Force 2003).

Though this doctrine underlined the importance of respecting human rights and establishing the rule of law, it did not link these with the detention of indicted war criminals (ibid.: VI-8(a.)). However, it did mention these detentions and the fact that the military might provide backup for high-risk detentions for the police (ibid.: VI-12(h.1, 4)). Hence, like its predecessor, the new doctrine included the detention of indicted war criminals but failed to incorporate it, thus indicating the continued reluctance of the US military to get involved in this task.

In conclusion the detention of indicted war criminals has been included in the American peace enforcement doctrine but, in contrary to its British counterpart, the process of integrating the matter is still in its infancy. The doctrine does not specify the role of peace enforcement soldiers in detaining indicted war criminals; it does not address the impact on impartiality and use of force; and it does not address the extra training peace enforcement soldiers would need to perform this task effectively. This mirrors the US opposition to enforcing international accountability for violations of international criminal law, also manifest in the US withdrawal of support for the International Criminal Court (ICC) and the coercion on some states to sign agreements that prevent the states from handing over US citizens to the ICC.[30]

NATO's peace enforcement doctrines and the detention of indicted war criminals

NATO did not take part in peace missions during the Cold War because of the tense relationship between, on the one hand, the US and its partners in NATO and, on the other hand, the USSR and its partners in the Warsaw Pact. NATO's first involvement in peace missions was UNPROFOR's mission in Bosnia-Herzegovina, where it provided, for example, multinational HQ staff and infra-structure. In 1995 NATO was granted leadership of IFOR and later also led SFOR and KFOR. Recently NATO soldiers have also been deployed in Bosnia-Herzegovina as part of NATO Headquarters Sarajevo and in Afghanistan as part of ISAF.

From July 2001 NATO's doctrinal publication *Peace Support Operations* recognised the need for linking the short-term military goal of security with long-term aims such as reconciliation to be carried out by civilian agencies in order to establish a self-sustaining peace (NATO Standardization Agency 2001a: 2–2(0207), 2–7(0224), 3–6(0324)). The doctrine also acknowledged that accountability for human rights atrocities should be included in the reconciliation process in order for the peace process to be accepted and widely supported and for local people to gain or regain confidence in the defence and security sectors (ibid.: 3–3(0311), 6–11(0631f.)). The doctrine also recognised that peace enforcement missions should actively support and take part in international criminal tribunals' attempts to hold individuals accountable for war crimes and that such issues need to be considered at the planning stage of the operations (ibid.: 4B-2(4B7)). Furthermore, it accepted that soldiers taking part in such a mission might need to assist civilian enforcement agencies in detaining indicted war criminals (ibid.: 6–7(0625e.), 6–14(0634)). In addition, the doctrine also emphasised that military police taking part in a peace enforcement mission might need to become involved in the prosecution of war criminals (ibid.: 5–8(0530)). It argued that the missions need to take part in accountability processes even though it might jeopardise the impartiality of the mission as perceived by the local population (ibid.: 4B-2(4B7)). Finally, the doctrine also recognised that the missions should be willing to use force despite the increased risk of casualties to the mission in cases concerning widespread human rights atrocities (ibid.: 3–5(0321), 3–6(0322)).

In August 2001 *Peace Support Operations* was supplemented by *Peace Support Operations: Techniques and Procedures* (NATO Standardization Agency 2001b). This publication contended that war crimes investigations are politically sensitive activities that demand specialist investigating teams (ibid.: 2–8(0212)). It also stated that international soldiers have a legal and moral responsibility to prevent violations and to systematically and accurately gather details and evidence and hand it over to the official investigators (ibid.: 2–8(0212)). The doctrine also contended that, if peace troops fail to prevent violations, it undermines the credibility of the mission (ibid.: 2–9(0214)). Thus the doctrine argued that it is important that peace enforcement soldiers address all breaches of the peace agreement and international humanitarian law effectively in accordance with the mission mandate (ibid.: 2–9(0214)). The doctrine also mentioned the search for and arrest of indicted war criminals and pointed out that peace enforcement soldiers' right to search for and arrest civilians will depend on the powers granted in the mandate (ibid.: 2–11(0218)). Finally, the doctrine also underlined that peace enforcement soldiers are supposed to create an environment in which human rights atrocities are limited (ibid.: 1–7(0116)).

Hence, the detention of indicted war criminals is included in NATO doctrine on peace operations and steps have also been taken to incorporate the task into the doctrine. These two publications recognised that peace troops need to take part in such detentions since justice is an important part of reconciliation and the establishment of a self-sustainable peace and therefore also important for gaining local support for the peace process and the work of the mission in other areas such as defence and security. *Peace Support Operations* recognised that missions need to be willing to use force in order to counter abuses of human rights without specifying whether this included detaining indicted war criminals, even though such actions might jeopardise the impartiality of the mission in the eyes of the local population and increase the risk of casualties among the soldiers involved. It also argued that war crimes issues need to be considered when peace enforcement missions are planned. However, none of the two publications specified the role of peace enforcement soldiers in the detention of indicted war criminals and they did not acknowledge the need for special training in this matter.

A couple of other publications have also illustrated NATO's peace enforcement doctrine. NATO's handbook from 2001 recognised that SFOR soldiers were authorised to detain indicted war criminals when they came into contact with them and that the soldiers had already carried out such detentions (NATO 2001: 119, 123). However, though the publication acknowledged that such detentions constituted a security cooperation activity, it was maintained that national authorities were responsible for them (ibid.: 123). In addition, the *Allied Joint Operations* publication only pointed out that international law on war crimes institutes limitations on the conduct of military operations (NATO Standardization Agency 2002: 1–4(1011)). Finally the NATO handbook from 2006 acknowledged that NATO Headquarters Sarajevo, the small NATO peace enforcement mission that remained in Bosnia-Herzegovina when EUFOR took over from SFOR, should support the ICTY with detaining indicted war criminals within its means and capabilities (NATO 2006: 148).

In conclusion, the detention of indicted war criminals has been included in NATO's doctrine on peace operations but the task is still not fully integrated into the doctrine. It is also worth noting that the British military doctrine has significantly influenced NATO's doctrine (compare for example paragraph 0212, pp. 2–8 and paragraph 214, pp. 2–9 in NATO Standardization Agency 2001b with paragraph 735, pp. 7–16 in Chief of Joint Operations 1998). The doctrine does not detail the exact role and responsibilities of peace enforcement soldiers in detaining indicted war criminals and, though it addresses the impact on perceived impartiality, it does not address the impact on the use of force. NATO's doctrine also does not recognise the need for any special training to enable peace troops to perform detention operations effectively. Hence, though NATO soldiers in Bosnia-Herzegovina and Kosovo have been already been involved in such operations, the task is still not fully integrated into NATO doctrine, mirroring the situation on the ground where IFOR, SFOR and KFOR efforts towards detentions have been equivocal.

British, American and NATO peace enforcement doctrines and the detention of indicted war criminals

In conclusion the American, British and NATO military doctrines all recognise that their soldiers need to be involved to some extent in detaining indicted war criminals. The British and NATO doctrines also acknowledge the importance of addressing human rights violations in order to achieve reconciliation and sustainable peace. However, though all three doctrines explicitly mention the detention of wanted war criminals as a possible task for peace enforcement soldiers, none is very detailed about the exact role soldiers should play in this regard. All three doctrines also stipulate that their soldiers should cooperate with civilian enforcement agencies over such operations and they imply that these civilian agencies should bear the main responsibility for and play the leading role in the detention process. Hence, the doctrines do not account for cases such that of Bosnia-Herzegovina, where there are no civilian enforcement agencies willing or able to take on this task. The doctrines also imply that peace troops should only be involved in the actual detention of the indicted rather than also in the process of identifying and locating individuals concerned. Again, on the grounds of the experience in Bosnia-Herzegovina, this is problematic when no other agencies are willing or able to carry out these tasks, which represent necessary preconditions for successful detentions. In addition none of the doctrines comments on the use of force in connection with detentions and only the British and NATO ones address the impact that authorising peace enforcement soldiers to detain indicted war criminals is likely to have on the perceived impartiality of the mission. Furthermore, although one of the US doctrines acknowledges that foreign military forces need to be vetted for human rights violations before they are trained; NATO's doctrine recognises that prosecuting indicted war criminals is politically sensitive, and the British doctrine points out the risk of war criminals being rewarded in the peace process, none fully acknowledges the impact of peace troops' involvement in detentions on the wider peacemaking and peacebuilding processes. Finally, the British doctrine alone recognises that the soldiers will need extra training but it only covers legal advice, without mentioning any methods and skills the soldiers may need to acquire to carry out effective and legitimate detentions.

Hence, though the detentions have been included in the dominating doctrines on peace enforcement missions, the task is still far from being fully integrated into them, despite the fact that the missions have already been heavily involved in such operations. Thus a discussion of what steps the various militaries need to take in order to improve the incorporation of detentions into their military doctrines on peace enforcement missions is highly relevant.

Recommendations on the incorporation of the detention of indicted war criminals into peace enforcement doctrines

Based solely on the experience of IFOR, SFOR and KFOR, it is obviously not possible to develop a definite and detailed list of recommendations on incorporating the detention of indicted war criminals into peace enforcement doctrines. However, certain recommendations for the officers who develop military doctrines to seriously consider can be identified.

Recognising the importance of accountability

A primary step towards making the detention of these wanted individuals a task for peace enforcement soldiers to become seriously involved in is necessarily acknowledging the importance of accountability for gross violations of international humanitarian and human rights law. Thus, it is essential that the doctrines acknowledge that reconciliation and sustainable peace, often at least officially the ultimate aims of the missions, cannot be obtained without accountability.

Accepting primary responsibility

The examination of the British, American and NATO military doctrines on peace operations revealed that all three imply that their soldiers should not bear the main responsibility for detentions but rather only assist other national and international agencies. In cases where a national or international police force is authorised, able and willing to carry out the detentions, a role restricted to assistance seems reasonable. Detaining indicted war criminals is ultimately a policing task and it is important that police forces bear the main responsibility for it as soon as they are willing and able. However, experience from Bosnia-Herzegovina has shown that there are not always other agencies willing or able to take on this responsibility. Hence it is essential that the doctrines specify that, in cases where other agencies have not taken on the task, peace enforcement soldiers need to be ready to bear the main responsibility for detaining indicted war criminals.

Specifying the roles of peace enforcement soldiers

The examination of the British, American and NATO military doctrines on peace operations also revealed that none is very detailed concerning the role their troops should play in the detention of indicted war criminals. In cases where the international or national police are authorised, able and willing to identify and locate these individuals, it is reasonable that peace soldiers only assist with the actual detention, if this is assessed as too dangerous or complicated for the police authorities to execute on their own. This does not mean that the soldiers should not still assist the police by looking out for and reporting sightings of indicted war criminals in the same way that ordinary citizens are required to do, but it does mean that it is not primarily their responsibility. However, as in Bosnia-Herzegovina, there is not always an international or national police force able and willing to identify and locate indicted war criminals. Thus it is vital that the doctrine accommodate for these cases by specifying that, in these cases peace troops should be involved in all aspects of the process from the moment the international arrest warrant is presented to the mission to the moment the criminal is transferred to the prison facilities of the international criminal tribunal. Hence peace troops need to be ready to get involved in activities such as gathering intelligence about the whereabouts of the indicted and actively looking out for them.

Recognising the need for special training

Since these detentions were originally a policing task that soldiers are not normally trained to carry out, it is essential that the doctrines recognise that peace enforcement soldiers need special training in order to carry out detentions effectively and legally. Of the doctrines included in this examination it is only the British one that recognises the need for special training and in its case only demands lessons on how to detain people in accordance with international law. This is important because if all legal rules are not adhered to, this could create serious problems for the Prosecutor and, in the worst case scenario, might mean that the accused walks free thanks to a legal technicality. Experience from

SFOR, where indicted war criminals Stevan Todorovic and Dragan Nikolic both challenged the legality of their detention, underlines the need for these legal lessons (ICTY 9 October 2002, 22 June 2004). It is especially important that the training includes information on the rights of the accused.

In addition, experience from IFOR and SFOR indicates that peace enforcement soldiers also need training in other areas. First, experience from IFOR showed that even when soldiers have received photos and basic personal characteristics of the indicted, they still find it difficult to recognise them (Major Haselock 1 July 1996). On at least one occasion SFOR soldiers also sent individuals, with the indicted war criminals when they were detained, to The Hague for confirmation that they were not wanted for war crimes as well (Major Riley 11 July 1997). These experiences indicate a need for training in face recognition to help the soldiers to recognise indicted war criminals whom they encounter and clearly identify them for detention (SFOR interview 2003). Second, since detaining criminals is not a normal task, it is imperative that the soldiers are trained in the same way as police officers in making successful detentions. In order to prevent situations where the soldiers are unsure of how much force they are allowed to use, the training should include discussions of how rules of engagement regarding the level of force authorised are applied to various situations. Third, experience from SFOR shows that indicted war criminals do not always surrender voluntarily during detention operations (Lt Cdr Chamberlain 10 January 1999, Major Clarke 18 December 1997, Major Riley 14 July 1997). On several occasions, such as when SFOR soldiers shot dead indicted war criminals and endangered children in detention operations or when SFOR injured an Archpriest and his son while attempting to detain Radovan Karadžić, the local people also protested against SFOR actions (Lt Cdr Chamberlain 10 January 1999, Major Riley 11 July 1997, SFOR 1 April 2004, 2 April 2004). These situations indicate that if not already a part of the doctrine, training in communication and mediation needs to be included to help the soldiers tackle situations involving resistance or local protest. It is obviously important that this training is adapted to the cultural setting where the soldiers are to be deployed, since successful communication and mediation are obviously closely linked to cultural awareness and adaptation. In addition, experience from SFOR shows that inevitably cases will arise where demonstrations escalate into riots (Lt Cdr Chamberlain 10 January 1999, Major Clarke 18 December 1997, Major Riley 11 July 1997, SFOR 1 April 2004, 2 April 2004). Thus if riot control techniques are not already part of the training recommended by the doctrine, then these should now be added. Finally, interviews with senior officers from KFOR indicate a need for military doctrines to recognise that soldiers require classes in the importance of transitional justice processes for the development of sustainable peace in order to understand that detaining indicted war criminals is a vital task for the success of the mission (KFOR interviews 2003).

Consequently, in order to enable peace enforcement soldiers to detain indicted war criminals legally and effectively, it is important that the doctrines recognise the need for special training in international law, identification techniques, detention, mediation and communication, riot control and transitional justice processes and peace-building. This list is not exclusive and experience from future missions is likely to indicate further areas where special training is needed.

Recognising the impact on approaches to peacemaking and peace-building

So far the approaches to peacemaking and peace-building have depended on the support of individuals who have also been responsible for or even committed mass atrocities during the violent conflict. Hence, there has often been a considerable overlap between the military and political leaders taking part in the conflict and the subsequent peace negotiations and the war criminals the international criminal tribunals have indicted and attempted to prosecute. If peace enforcement soldiers become involved in detaining indicted war criminals, this has some significant consequences for peacemaking and peace-building processes.

First, as acknowledged by the British doctrine, the current dominant international approach to peacemaking is based on negotiations with individuals who are also often responsible for many of the atrocities. This is obviously problematic because it is less likely that these individuals will take part in the peacemaking process if they know that they may be detained as part of the peace-building process after signing the peace agreement. Hence it is not sustainable to depend on the cooperation of these individuals when making and building peace and this necessarily needs to be reflected in the doctrine. Second, and as partly acknowledged by the US doctrine, if peace enforcement soldiers are to detain indicted war criminals, then these indicted individuals should be excluded from all the activities of the mission. Thus the doctrine needs to underline that alleged war criminals should not be allowed to take part in any activity, from reconstruction to de-mining, that the peace enforcement soldiers are involved in. Third, as NATO's doctrine points out, it is also important that doctrines acknowledge that indicting, detaining and prosecuting war criminals are politically sensitive processes, which, regardless of how they are carried out, are likely to stir up controversy and resentment among politicians as well as local citizens.

Accordingly, the involvement of peace troops in the detention of indicted war criminals necessitates a rethinking of approaches to peacemaking and peace-building and this should be acknowledged in the doctrines guiding the missions.

Recognising the impact on perceived impartiality

The examination of the doctrines also revealed that, though it is generally recognised that the local people in the mission's area of deployment do not always perceive the mission impartial, the NATO doctrine alone recognises that authorising the soldiers to detain indicted war criminals is likely to increase these perceptions among the local population and local politicians. Experience from

Bosnia-Herzegovina, Croatia and Kosovo shows that the local people's support of indicted war criminals often continues long after the official end of the violent conflict and that they find it difficult to accept that individuals they consider war heroes are being indicted and prosecuted. In the case of Radovan Karadžić, posters praising him were still displayed in Republika Srpska long into SFOR's mission (CBC News 20 January 2004, Larson 2004). In the cases of Croatia and Kosovo mass demonstrations against the prosecution of alleged local war criminals have been staged on several occasions (Simons 12 December 2005, Traynor 12 February 2001, UNMIK 26 February 2003). Serbs and Bosnian Serbs especially have also felt that a disproportionate number of individuals from their respective ethnic groups have been indicted and prosecuted, indicating unfair targeting. Hence, regardless of whether the peace troops detain indicted war criminals irrespective of their ethnic origin and religious and political affiliation, it is likely that the local population will perceive the mission as biased when the soldiers detain someone from their ethnic group. Therefore it is important that the doctrines reflect actions the soldiers can take if the local population stop perceiving them as impartial, for example, more force and campaigns to regain trust in the local area might be needed.

Recognising the impact on the use of force

Finally, the analysis of the dominating peace enforcement doctrines also revealed that it is only some that explicitly recognise that missions need to be ready to use force even if this increases the risk of casualties among the troops involved. Experience from especially SFOR showed that even if everything possible is done to minimise the risks, soldiers might still come under fire during detention operations (Lt Cdr Chamberlain 10 January 1999, Major Clarke 18 December 1997, Major Riley 14 July 1997). Consequently, it is important that doctrines recognise that including the war criminal detentions in the task expected of peace enforcers means that the peace enforcers need to be prepared to use force and to risk their lives for the sake of implementing their mandate.

Integrating the detention of indicted war criminals into the doctrines of peace enforcement missions

In conclusion it is imperative that military doctrines that form the basis of peace enforcement missions do not merely add the detention of indicted war criminals to the tasks that the soldiers are expected to carry out. The doctrines also need to fully incorporate the detentions if soldiers are to carry out detention operations effectively and in accordance with international law. This chapter has suggested some areas that doctrines need to address to incorporate such detentions but the list is by no means definite. The examination of more case studies is needed in order to identify more ways to incorporate detentions into the doctrines.

This incorporation is by no means an uncontroversial process. Experience from Bosnia-Herzegovina shows that the detention of indicted war criminals is a task that military contingents undertake only reluctantly. Therefore attempts to include and incorporate the task into peace enforcement doctrines are likely to meet opposition. The fact that peace troops need to be ready to take part in detention operations that could endanger their lives is especially likely to be used as an argument against incorporation. In addition, to include and incorporate the task into the doctrines will mean that peace enforcement soldiers will always be expected to take part and the expectations of successful detentions will be high. Hence, there will be very little space for the soldiers to opt out of such operations even when the circumstances are very difficult. On the other hand, experience from IFOR especially indicates that the risk of failure is considerable if the soldiers are not well prepared for the tasks. Peace enforcement soldiers on the ground have already been significantly involved in detaining indicted war criminals and it is likely that there will be a pressure on future missions to participate actively as well. Hence, the soldiers need to be prepared to take on this task and an important precondition for success is that the task is included and properly incorporated in the doctrines. Finally, experience from SFOR, where the national contingents adopted divergent approaches to detaining indicted war criminals, underlines the importance of all national contingents within a mission following the same military doctrine or at least agreeing on a common approach to incorporating detentions into their respective doctrines in order to ensure that all troops adhere to the same doctrinal recommendations regarding such operations.[31] With the development of a common military doctrine within regional organisations such as NATO, important steps towards a shared approach to peace enforcement have been taken. Still national contingents too often follow their own national doctrines and this is a dilemma that organisations responsible for peace enforcement missions need to address if they want their missions to be more successful.

9 Authorising peace enforcement soldiers to detain indicted war criminals

Incorporating the detention of indicted war criminals into the mandate and rules of engagement

Introduction

A vital prerequisite for having peace enforcement soldiers detain indicted war criminals is necessarily that the mandates authorise the soldiers to do so and that the rules of engagement enable the soldiers to carry out the detentions successfully. Unsurprisingly, experience from IFOR and SFOR shows that the way the mandate is formulated seriously influences the mission's ability to detain the indicted. In IFOR's case, because the authorisation was not explicit, the mandate allowed for a wide variety of interpretations.[32] This endorsed IFOR to apply a very flexible and ineffective approach to the task, which meant that IFOR failed to detain any indicted war criminals. Similarly, SFOR commanders also spent a lot of time discussing actions allowed by the mandate, which meant that SFOR only detained a relatively limited number of indicted war criminals. In KFOR's case, the failure to mention the task in the mandate meant that KFOR seemingly did nothing to detain indicted war criminals on its own initiative but rather only responded to the requests of UNMIK (KFOR interview 2003). Hence, the experiences of IFOR, SFOR and KFOR call for a discussion about what should be included in the mandates of missions if peace enforcement soldiers are to successfully carry out detention operations.

In addition, experience from IFOR, SFOR and KFOR has shown that a mandate that implicitly authorises peace enforcement soldiers to detain indicted war criminals does not necessarily lead to the development of rules of engagement that enable effective detentions. Thus this chapter also discusses what rules of engagement future missions should be given for the soldiers to achieve successful detentions.

Incorporating the detention of indicted war criminals into the mandates of peace enforcement missions

As in the case of the doctrines of peace enforcement missions, it is important that the detention of indicted war criminals is not merely included in the mandates of missions but also properly incorporated. Based on the experience of

IFOR, SFOR and KFOR, the following points should be considered when the mandates are formulated.

Explicit authorisation to detain indicted war criminals

The bewilderment over whether IFOR and SFOR were authorised to detain indicted war criminals and the resulting time and resources wasted on discussing the powers of the missions call for a discussion as to whether such authorisation should be explicitly given in the mandate.[33] This lack of an explicit authorisation also meant that KFOR did not initiate any actions to detain indicted war criminals but merely responded to specific requests from UNMIK and this also indicates the need for debating the usefulness of an explicit authorisation (KFOR interview 2003).

On the one hand it can be argued that an explicit authorisation would necessarily place these detention operations on the peace enforcement mission's agenda of tasks. If this had been the case for KFOR, IFOR and SFOR, the missions would probably have been more inclined to take a proactive approach to detentions since defending a passive approach would have been much more difficult. An explicit authorisation would also prevent wasting a lot of time and resources on discussing actions allowed by the mandate, as was the case for IFOR and SFOR. Explicitly including the detention of indicted war criminals in the mandate would also mean that the missions could take that into consideration at the planning and preparation stage. Hence, in contrast to IFOR and SFOR, a mission explicitly authorised to detain indicted war criminals will hopefully be ready to take such action from its very beginning. The likelihood of mission creep will also be reduced because such operations will not be a new task that is introduced in the middle of the mission. An explicit authorisation would also underline the fact that the decision to involve peace soldiers in these operations has been taken by politicians rather than military commander, such as was the case for IFOR, SFOR and KFOR. In addition, explicitly including the task in the mandate would also signal that the international institutions behind the missions acknowledge that accountability for gross violations of international criminal law constitutes a vital part of creating long-term peace. Explicitly authorisation would also help prevent situations where some national contingents within a mission actively attempt detentions while others refrain from them, as was the case at the start of SFOR's missions, when British forces detained indicted war criminals but their American and French colleagues refused to take any action in this regard. Finally, inclusion in the mandate would also warn the indicted that the soldiers will be looking for them and perhaps lead them to surrender voluntarily.

However, there are also several arguments against such explicit authorisation. First, it has to be kept in mind that any peace agreement is a compromise between warring parties that often find it difficult to consent on even basic parts of the peace accord. One of the ways contentious issues are addressed is by making the formulation of the agreement so weak that various interpretations can be applied. Since the prosecution of war criminals is a highly contentious issues, especially given that the individuals taking part in the peace negotiations were often also responsible for atrocities during the conflict, an explicit authorisation to detain indicted war criminals is likely to make the peace negotiations more difficult. Second, it might also be more difficult for states to agree on deploying a peace enforcement mission if such detentions are explicitly included in the mandate. Third, an explicit authorisation would not leave any room for the military commanders of the missions to argue that they are not allowed to detain indicted war criminals. This argument is potentially useful at the start of a mission, when commanders assess that it is not in the immediate interest of the mission to get involved in such operations, as was apparently the case with IFOR. In addition, an explicit authorisation could induce indicted war criminals to flee the peace enforcement mission's area of operation.

Based on the experience of especially IFOR and SFOR, which were criticised for not doing enough to detain indicted war criminals, the arguments against an explicit authorisation seem short-sighted (Human Rights Watch 2005a, International Crisis Group 2000, Century Foundation 1998, United States Institute of Peace 1997). Since accountability for war crimes is increasingly seen as a precondition for sustainable peace, it is highly likely that peace missions will sooner or later have to address the atrocities that were committed during the violent conflict in their area of operation. Based on the experience of especially SFOR, where the detention of indicted war criminals was closely linked with the final assessment of the mission, it is unlikely that missions can operate in an area where such criminals are at large without getting involved in their detention. Hence, unless it is absolutely indisputable that the mandate does include an explicit authorisation it is likely that military commanders who claim that their soldiers are not authorised to detain wanted individuals will later have to retract their comments and acknowledge this, as was the case with IFOR and SFOR. Furthermore, as soon as the first detention has been made, the indicted will know that the international troops are looking out for them. Thus there are strong arguments for the mandate to include the explicit authorisation of peace enforcement soldiers to detain indicted war criminals.

Obligation to detain indicted war criminals?

Whereas it is difficult to argue convincingly against the mandate including such an explicit authorisation, the issue of whether the mission should be obliged or merely authorised to detain indicted war criminals is more contentious.

On the one hand, if the politicians include this obligation in the mandates of missions, it would underline the fact that the decision has been taken by the politicians rather than the military commanders. Experience from IFOR and KFOR shows that the consequences of leaving the interpretation of a vague mandate to military commanders can lead to inaction. A comparison of statements from political and military leaders of IFOR also exposes a noteworthy discrepancy in the way IFOR's mandate was interpreted at the political and military levels respectively (Col Kirkwood 13 February 1996, Lt Col Rayner 12 February 1996, Major Haselock 20 June 1996, North Atlantic Council 14 February 1996, Supreme Headquarters Allied Powers Europe 9 May 1996). While there was disagreement at the military level as to whether IFOR was authorised or obliged to detain indicted war criminals if encountered during the course of ordinary duties, the message at the political level was seemingly that IFOR soldiers were indeed obliged rather than just authorised to detain them (ibid.). Hence there are indications that the politicians behind IFOR's deployment were possibly more committed to detention operations than the military leadership of IFOR in Bosnia-Herzegovina. Thus the lack of an obligation in this regard potentially allows for a discrepancy in the way the military commanders interpret the mandate and the way the politicians envisaged its implementation. In the cases both of IFOR and SFOR this lack of an explicit obligation also led to a lot of uncertainty and confusion about actions the mandate authorised the mission to take in order to detain indicted war criminals.

The inclusion of this task as an obligation, however, would not prevent disagreement over what measures the mission is allowed to undertake to achieve it. For example, it will always be debatable how much force a peace mission is allowed to use. Yet it is likely that an obligation to detain will prevent disagreement over, for example, whether international soldiers on patrol and at checkpoints should be involved in the detentions. An obligation would also help ensure that all national contingents within the mission are equally committed to the task, which was not always the case for the national contingents in SFOR. If the peace enforcement mission is obliged to detain indicted war criminals, it is also more likely that the soldiers will be more inclined to implement a broader range of measures aimed at securing detentions. In addition, if a mission knows that its soldiers are going to be involved in such detentions, this task can be included in the planning and preparation of the mission, therefore hopefully rendering the soldiers ready to fulfil this obligation from the start of the mission. Furthermore, obliging peace enforcement soldiers to detain indicted war criminals would send a firm message to the indicted and other individuals, who have either committed atrocities or who intend to do so, that the mission is committed to bringing such individuals to justice.

On the other hand there are also some substantial arguments against making detentions an obligation. Though accountability for war crimes is increasingly seen as an important step towards sustainable peace, many states are still opposed to trying individuals in international criminal tribunals and involving international soldiers in detentions. Thus, if a mandate obliges the soldiers to carry out these detentions, it is likely that certain states will refuse to let their soldiers participate in the mission. It is also possible that the UNSC will not be able to agree on the deployment of the mission in the first place if it is implied that the international soldiers will be obliged to detain indicted war criminals. Furthermore, it is also important that the mandate recognises that there are situations where it is either dangerous or unethical for peace enforcement soldiers to detain indicted war criminals. For example, on a couple of occasions SFOR soldiers continued to carry out planned detention operations despite seriously endangering the lives of children (Lt Cdr Chamberlain 10 January 1999, Major Riley 11 July 1997, 14 July 1997, Seidel 10 January 1999, SFOR 1 April 2004, 2 April 2004). Thus the mission mandates need to accommodate such situations and acknowledge that there are circumstances where international soldiers should not attempt detentions. Hence, a possible compromise could be to oblige peace enforcement soldiers to detain indicted war criminals if the situation permits it. However, as experience from especially IFOR but also SFOR and KFOR shows, such a compromise runs the risk of giving the mission an excuse not to act, since they could always just argue that the situation was not conducive for a detention operation. Thus it is debatable how explicit the mandate needs to be concerning individual situations. On the one hand, the experience of IFOR and SFOR, when a lot of time and resources went into discussing what measures the missions were allowed to take supports the notion that the mandate should be fairly explicit concerning these points. A fairly explicit mandate will mean that missions will know what is expected of them and be unable to justify significant changes to its interpretation. On the other hand, the mandate also has to accommodate the fact that all detention situations are different. For example, the level of force that the soldiers are authorised to use should depend on the security situation on the ground and how much resistance is expected. Looking at SFOR's experience, the means used to identify and detain indicted war criminals also changed substantially during its eight years of operation. A mandate that is too detailed about what situations allow for an immediate detention will not be able to accommodate this diversity and development. Furthermore, a mandate that is too specific about what actions are allowed will hinder the use of new innovative means to detain indicted war criminals. Therefore there needs to be room for flexibility. Hence, a mandate that is most likely to lead to successful detentions will convey the importance of peace soldiers taking their responsibility in this regard seriously and implementing a wide range of measures in order to do so, while also acknowledging that situations will arise where a detention may not be possible.

Acknowledging the consequences

As was the case with doctrines, it is also essential that peace enforcement mandates recognise the consequences of authorising international soldiers to detain indicted war criminals. Based on the experience of especially IFOR and SFOR that were relatively lightly armed but still expected to detain heavily guarded wanted criminals, it is important that the mandate authorises use of a suitable amount of force (Lorenz 1997). This is especially important in cases where the indicted individual is expected to be armed and surrounded by supporters willing to help him resist. It is also vital that the mandates, just like the doctrines, recognise that detentions might jeopardise the perceived impartiality of the mission and that the soldiers therefore need to be ready to deal with the consequences of the local population and politicians' possible change in perception.

Finally, as was also argued in connection with military doctrines, one of the most important consequences of requesting peace troops to detain indicted war criminals is the exclusion of the indicted persons from all activities, both civilian and military, that the peace mission undertakes to help develop sustainable peace. Otherwise, the peace enforcers risk being in a situation where they have to cooperate with the indicted war criminals on one day and detain them on the next. This was the case when SFOR soldiers detained indicted war criminal General Krstic from the Republika Srpska Army, with whom the mission had cooperated until his detention in connection with the army's de-mining operations (Lt Cdr Thomson 3 December 1998).[34]

Coherent approach to transitional justice and sustainable peace

Another important lesson that can be learned from the experience of IFOR, SFOR and KFOR is that if peace missions are to make a significant contribution to sustainable peace, it is essential that their mandates recognise that detaining indicted war criminals is just one component in a coherent approach to transitional justice and sustainable peace-building. In the case of the ICTY the tribunal was only ever meant to prosecute the individuals who had committed or were responsible for the worst atrocities. This did not mean that all other individuals should be granted amnesty but rather that they should be prosecuted in national courts once effective and fair legal systems had been re-established. Hence, in Bosnia-Herzegovina IFOR and SFOR were deployed together with a civilian component, UNMIBH, which was requested to assist in the establishment of the rule of law by evaluating the functioning of the judicial system, helping restructure and reform the local police and monitor agencies participating in maintaining law and order.[35] KFOR was also deployed with a civilian component, UNMIK, mandated to promote human rights and uphold law and order.[36] However, as argued in chapter 4, neither UNMIBH nor UNMIK have managed to ensure accountability for atrocities committed during the violent conflicts.

Detaining and prosecuting indicted war criminals is only going to contribute to long-term peace-building if it is part of a process that also focuses on holding individuals accountable for the atrocities that they committed through either national retributive or restorative processes and on building institutions that aim to prevent recurrence of the violence and establish a society ruled by law and order. Thus peace enforcement missions also need to be supportive of, and if necessary actively involved in, other activities such as judicial reforms and effective policing to establish justice and accountability for mass atrocities.

Incorporating the detention of indicted war criminals into the mandates of peace enforcement missions

As was the case with doctrines, the inclusion and incorporation of the detention of indicted war criminals into the mandates of peace enforcement missions is by no means uncontroversial and straightforward. It is actually likely to cause more controversy because it requires the support of all members of the UNSC and because it contributes to the dilemma between immediate negative peace (and the need to convince war criminals to lay down their arms and thereby prevent more human suffering) and justice (and the need to indict and prosecute war criminals regardless of their status during and after the violent conflict). However, the support for peace troops taking part in these detentions is slowly but steadily increasing and so peace missions may as well be provided with a mandate that enables them to carry out these operations successfully. This chapter has argued that it is important that the mandate explicitly authorises the soldiers to detain indicted war criminals and that it also obliges the soldiers to do so if the situation permits. It has also been argued that it is vital that the mandate acknowledges the consequences of including the detentions and that it recognises that they represent only one component of a successful approach to transitional justice and long-term peace-building.

Two UNSC resolutions, namely no. 1468 (2003), which attempted to exclude individuals who had committed mass atrocities during the violent conflict from the peace process, and no. 1638 (2005), which explicitly authorised UNMIL soldiers to detain Charles Taylor, represent possible points of departure for the development of peace enforcement mandates that include and incorporate the detention of indicted war criminals.

Rules of engagement and the detention of indicted war criminals

The case of IFOR in particular, but also those of SFOR and KFOR, show that it is not enough for mission mandates to authorise their soldiers to detain indicted war criminals. Such authorisation is worth little and no action will be taken, unless it is turned into robust rules of engagement for the involvement of the soldiers in the detentions.

Though the rules of engagement of IFOR, SFOR and KFOR are not publicly available, it is still possible to gain an insight into them through an examination of comments from mission spokesmen at press conferences and interviews with some of the senior officials of SFOR and KFOR. Based on the experience of IFOR, SFOR and KFOR, some important lessons can be learnt concerning what rules of engagement would enable peace enforcement soldiers to detain indicted war criminals.

Rules of engagement concerning the detention of indicted war criminals

First and foremost, experience from KFOR especially, which for a long time seemingly had no proactive rules of engagement concerning these detentions of, underlines the need for the development of such rules.

How detailed should the rules of engagement be?

Experience from IFOR especially, where vague rules of engagement meant that no detentions took place, raises the question as to how detailed the rules need to be. Two of IFOR's spokesmen argued against detailed rules of engagement, contending that the military commander on the ground should make the decisions based on his own assessment of the situation with no specific guidance (Lt Col Rayner 29 February 1996, Major Haselock 29 February 1996). Nevertheless, experience from KFOR, IFOR and SFOR points to a need for international soldiers to be provided with some rules of engagement in this area. First, experiences from all three missions have shown that, if fairly vague rules apply and it is left to commanders on the ground to decide whether to attempt a detention, then often no action is taken. For example, in the beginning IFOR's rules of engagement were allegedly limited to a general instruction that the soldiers should apprehend any indicted individual encountered in the course of normal duties, if the situation permitted (Lt Col Rayner 11 February 1996, Lt Col Reddin 13 February 1996). However, IFOR soldiers never took any action, despite alleged encounters with war criminals on numerous occasions. This indicates that vague rules of engagement do not work. Second, experience from the missions also indicates that, unless given fairly detailed rules of engagement, international soldiers do not know what their role in the detentions is and what they are expected to do in different situations. Third, experience from SFOR has also shown considerable variation in what actions the regional sections within SFOR carried out in order to detain indicted war criminals. Though exact information about how many indicted war criminals were at large in SFOR's three areas of deployment is not available, it is noticeable that soldiers from the

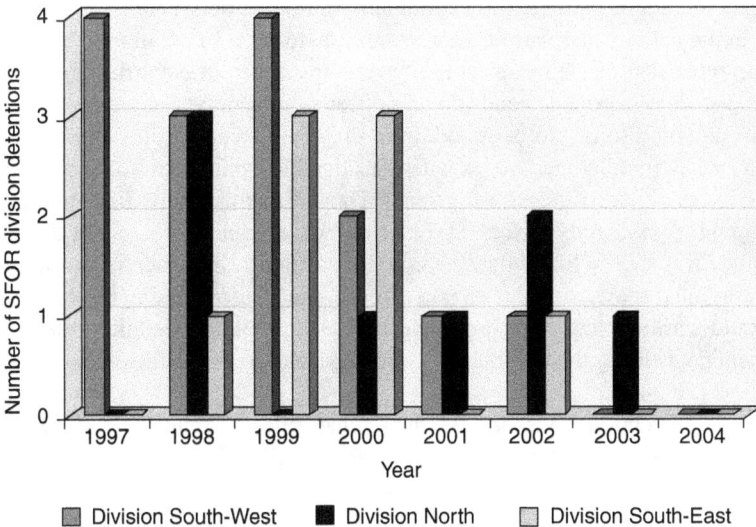

Figure 9.1 Overview of SFOR division detentions 1997–2004.

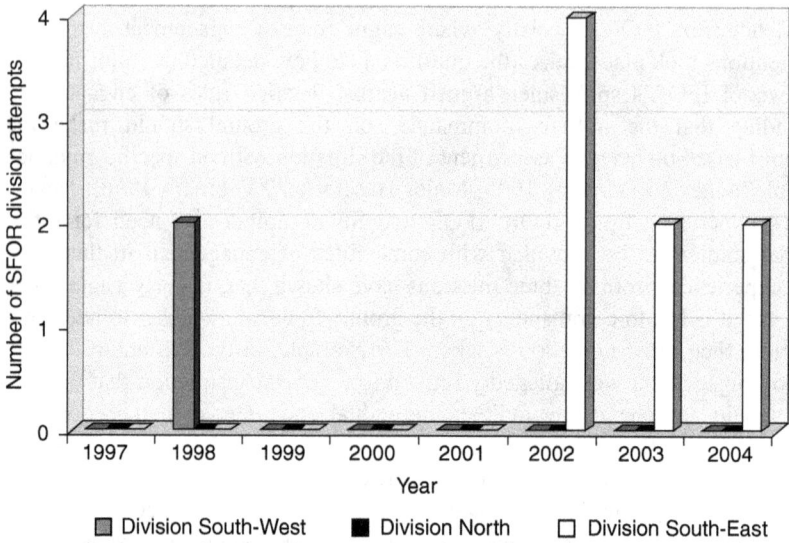

Figure 9.2 Overview of SFOR division failed detention attempts 1997–2004.

MND South-West detained almost as many indicted individuals as their colleagues from MND South-East and North put together. It is also worth noting that international soldiers from MND South-East carried out the vast majority of reportedly failed detention attempts.

Detailed rules of engagement concerning international soldiers' responsibilities in the detention of indicted war criminals would probably prevent such differences in the actions that various sections decide to take. In addition, it should not be forgotten that peace troops come from many different countries and cultures and that their experience and training differ significantly. For example, the degree of 'common sense' to be relied on in the case of vague rules of engagement of a British middle-aged major with considerable experience from Iraq and Afghanistan, as opposed to that of a young Danish recruit on his first mission abroad might significantly differ. If the rules of engagement are not fairly detailed then it is highly likely that there will be a significant difference in what actions individual soldiers decide to take. Hence, the military leadership of missions should seriously consider providing soldiers with fairly detailed rules of engagement concerning the role that they are expected to play in the detention of indicted war criminals.

The next contentious question is then what rules of engagement peace enforcement soldiers should to be given.

Rules of engagement on what peace enforcement soldiers are expected to do if they recognise indicted war criminals

All through the missions of KFOR and at the start of IFOR's and SFOR's, soldiers were apparently not given detailed rules of engagement on what action to take if encountering an indicted war criminal. In KFOR's case international soldiers apparently only carried out detention operations on request from UNMIK and took no active part in locating such individuals (KFOR interview 2003). Since KFOR soldiers were not provided with any means to, or any rules of engagement on identifying and locating them, any indicted war criminals could in theory have been living freely in Kosovo without fear that KFOR soldiers might recognise and detain them. In the cases of IFOR and SFOR, the lack of detailed rules of engagement meant, that though the military commanders of IFOR and SFOR dictated that soldiers should detain indicted individuals if encountered while carrying out their ordinary duties, the soldiers often took no action.[37] Hence, during IFOR's mission and at the start of SFOR's mission, indicted war criminals were allowed to move freely around areas where international soldiers were patrolling (Col Kirkwood 17 February 1996, Lt Col Rayner 29 February 1996, Major Haselock 29 February 1996, Major Riley 23 July 1997). IFOR soldiers never managed to detain any immediately after encountering them and SFOR soldiers only managed to do so on one reported occasion, when Goran Jelisic was apprehended in the streets of Bijeljina (Lt Cdr Garneau 22 January 1998, 23 January 1998). However, there were numerous reports that both IFOR and SFOR soldiers had been seen near the accused persons and it is unlikely that these situations never permitted an immediate detention (Lt Cdr Thomson 3 December 1998, Major Desjardins 15 August 2000, Major Haselock 20 June 1996, 12 September 1996, Major Riley 23 July 1997). In addition, within IFOR there was apparent disagreement over what criterion should be used to assess whether a situation allowed for an instant detention. One IFOR spokesman argued that the criterion should be whether the operation would endanger the lives of international soldiers or civilians, whereas another contended that IFOR should never rule out taking action in any circumstances, even if action endangered the lives of international soldiers (Lt Col Rayner 29 February 1996, Major Haselock 16 May 1996). All these points seem to indicate that fairly detailed rules of engagement are necessary to guide soldiers in encounters with indicted war criminals. The rules should include guidelines on which scenarios allow for an immediate detention and address dilemmas such as the risk of endangering civilians and the soldiers and the risk of resistance, which may include the subjects even harming themselves. In addition, experience from IFOR and SFOR on several occasions when immediate detentions were not possible and the subjects escaped also indicates that soldiers need rules of engagement on what to do if the situation does not permit an instantaneous detention (Lt Cdr Thomson 3 December 1998, Major Desjardins 15 August 2000, Major Haselock 20 June 1996, 12 September 1996, Major Riley 23 July 1997). This might include a call for reinforcement or an attempt to shadow the subjects, such as police officers would have done in a similar situation.

Rules of engagement on carrying out a detention operation

It is obviously also important that international soldiers are given clear rules of engagement on how to carry out a detention operation and when to abandon one. Experience from SFOR shows that international soldiers on a couple of occasions continued with planned detention operations despite serious risk to the lives of children (Lt Cdr Chamberlain 10 January 1999, Major Riley 11 July 1997, 14 July 1997, Seidel 10 January 1999, SFOR 1 April 2004, 2 April 2004). In addition, soldiers are normally trained to reach the target irrespective of the level of threat with retreat not seen as an option (Hendrickx 2001). Hence, this calls for rules of engagement on when a planned operation should be abandoned.

First and foremost, it is morally questionable for peace enforcers to endanger the lives of children during detention operations. Such behaviour in the past has led to local demonstrations against SFOR (Lt Cdr Chamberlain 10 January 1999, Major Riley 11 July 1997, 14 July 1997, Seidel 10 January 1999, SFOR 1 April 2004, 2 April 2004). It is also questionable whether SFOR should have halted the operation and shadowed the subject in order to detain him when he was alone.

One of the most contentious aspects of involving peace troops in these detentions is undoubtedly that international soldiers might be injured or killed during such operations. This risk of injury or death has long served as a powerful argument against involvement (Leurdijk 2001, Sliedregt 2001, Century Foundation 1998, United States Institute of Peace 1997). In the cases of IFOR, SFOR and KFOR, no international soldiers have been reported seriously injured or killed during such operations. Experience from SFOR and KFOR also shows that international soldiers have taken part in numerous detention operations where they have risked being seriously injured or killed (Abrashi 2003, Jennings 17 February 2003, Lt Cdr Chamberlain 10 January 1999, Major Clarke 18 December 1997, Major Riley 11 July 1997, SFOR 1 April 2004). Hence, the risk of injury or death has not prevented the peace enforcement missions from carrying out detention operations. Still, it is important that the rules of engagement address what risks are acceptable and which so severe as to demand termination of the operation. Thus, when the rules of engagement are written, serious consideration should be given to how detention operations should be stopped if they risk endangering the lives of either the suspect, the soldiers or the local population (Reenen 2001).

The guidelines also need to stipulate what the soldiers are to do once an operation has been halted.

Rules of engagement on the use of force

When developing rules of engagement on the detention of indicted war criminals, it should also be kept in mind that such an operation puts the peace enforcement soldiers in an often unfamiliar role, closer to that of a police officer than that of a typical military officer. The rules governing when police are allowed to use force are necessarily very different from those governing when the military can. Hence, it is important that the rules are as explicit as possible regarding the use of force. They should address the level of force allowed if the subject resists and the level permitted towards any civilians and military personnel with the indicted war criminal or protesting the detention.

Applying the rules of engagement

If peace enforcement soldiers are to be able to apply the rules of engagement, it is important that they know what they are. Experience from IFOR indicates that it should not be taken for granted that all will be familiar with these rules. In IFOR's case a lot of uncertainty surrounded the rules of engagement and hence, until the end of the mission not all soldiers were aware of what action to take when encountering an indicted war criminal (Major Boudreau 11 December 1996). Thus it is important that the mission ensures from its very start that all soldiers are familiar with the rules of engagement.

As mentioned earlier, there was a significant variation in the number of indicted war criminals the various sections of SFOR managed to detain. It is suspected that the difference was mainly due to an unequal application of the rules of engagement (International Crisis Group 2000, Kalinauskas 2002). In order to avoid a similar situation where parts of the mission are accused of not carrying out the actions prescribed by the rules of engagement, it is important that future missions apply the rules of engagement equally across their various divisions.

Adapting the rules of engagement

SFOR significantly expanded its range of measures during deployment, which emphasises the need for missions to continuously adapt their rules of engagement. For example, at the start of the mission, SFOR soldiers did not actively search for indicted war criminals but merely detained them in planned operations once they encountered them, towards the end, soldiers became actively involved in such searches (Lt Cdr Chamberlain 10 January 1999, Lt Cdr Garneau 22 January 1998, 9 April 1998, Lt Cdr Thomson 3 December 1998, SFOR 1 April 2004, 2 April 2004). In addition, initially SFOR troops only targeted the actual indicted individuals but, towards the end of the mission, the soldiers also targeted members of the support network (SFOR 28 January 2004a, 28 January 2004b). Furthermore, whereas some of the indicted aggressively defended themselves, others did not resist detention. Some had supporters who also protested detention whereas other detentions were seemingly relatively peacefully accepted by the local population. Hence, it is important that the rules of engagement are continuously reviewed and adapted to the various situations peace enforcement soldiers face during detention operations. Experience from IFOR and SFOR has also underlined the need to avoid ruling out using measures early in the mission that can be used later on when the situation on the ground has improved. For example, at the start of the mission, IFOR commanders contended that measures such as distributing photos of indicted war criminals to IFOR troops and looking out for them at checkpoints were outside the mission mandate (Lt Col Rayner 11 February 1996). However, by the end of the mission both these measures were in use (Major Haselock 30 October 1996). Similarly, at the beginning of SFOR's mission, its commanders argued that soldiers on patrol should not be involved in detaining indicted war criminals (Major Riley 23 July 1997). Nevertheless towards the end of its mission, soldiers on patrol were used in searches not only for indicted war criminals but also for members of their support network, tracking of information about Radovan Karadžić's support network and searches of properties belonging to the criminals (Domin 2002, Lt Gen Dodson 4 September 2001, Major Lundy 15 August 2002, Major Mell 21 January 2003, SFOR 26 August 2003). It is obviously not very credible if measures first ruled outside the mandate are later deployed. Since, for example, peace enforcement missions are often deployed in the immediate aftermath of the signing of a peace agreement when the security situation is still critical, the measures at soldiers' disposal will necessarily be limited at least initially. However, it is important that the justification for not using certain measures is not that their use is outside the mission mandate, if the measures might be used productively at a later date. The justification should rather be that the situation does not allow these measures to be implemented but that they can be implemented when the situation is more favourable.

Rules of engagement and the detention of indicted war criminals

In conclusion, future peace enforcement missions can learn some important lessons from the experiences of IFOR, SFOR and KFOR. First of all, it is obviously important that all the rules of engagement are in accordance with international humane law. It is vital that the soldiers are provided with clear rules of engagement on what they are expected to do regarding the detention of indicted war criminals. It is also important that these rules are developed from the start of the mission and that they are continuously adapted to the situation on the ground. Furthermore, it is imperative that measures that can be implemented once the situation on the ground has changed are not deemed as outside the mission mandate at the start. Finally, it is also essential that the rules of engagement are applied equally across the various sections of the mission.

If international soldiers are authorised or even obliged to detain indicted war criminals, the inclusion of this task in the rules of engagement is likely to be less controversial than including and incorporating it into the mandates and doctrines of missions. However, some difficulties should still be anticipated. Based on the experience of IFOR, SFOR and KFOR, which have all been criticised for not doing enough to detain indicted war criminals, it is likely that peace missions will face continuous pressure to strengthen their rules of engagement concerning such detentions. Especially in cases where soldiers or civilians are killed or seriously injured during detention operations, such as was the case when SFOR soldiers attempted to detain Radovan Karadžić in Pale in April 2004, it is also likely that the rules of engagement will encounter fierce scrutiny (SFOR 1 April 2004, 2 April 2004). If one or more sections of a mission are less able or willing to detain indicted war criminals, as was the case with SFOR it is also expected that they will face accusations of unequal application of the rules of engagement. It is also likely that it will be difficult for the various national contingents within the missions to agree on common content and application of rules of engagement. However, as experience from IFOR, SFOR and KFOR has constantly underlined, proper content and application of rules of engagement are vital keys to successful detention operations and hence the missions need to find ways to address these obstacles if they are to be successful in detaining indicted war criminals. A possible point of departure would be for the national contingents taking part in the peace enforcement mission to agree on a common peace enforcement doctrine, thereby laying the foundation for a common approach to addressing the obstacles to firm content and application of rules of engagement on the detention of indicted war criminals.

10   Ensuring the detention of indicted war criminals

Improving the practices of peace enforcement missions aiming at detaining indicted war criminals

Introduction

It is not enough that peace enforcement missions have doctrines, mandates and rules of engagement intended to enable them to detain indicted war criminals; these also need to be turned into proper actions to ensure successful detentions. Based on the experience of IFOR, SFOR and KFOR, it is not possible to develop a definitive list of actions likely to secure detentions in all possible circumstances. Even within the same peace enforcement mission every detention operation is unique and there are even more significant differences between one mission to another. However, disseminating recommendable practices on the basis of lessons learned from past missions is still a widely recognised method within international organisations such as the UN and NATO (Lightburn 2001, Lt Gen Silva 1998, NATO 17th February 2003).[38] Hence, based on lessons learned from IFOR, SFOR and KFOR, this chapter identifies and discusses some of the actions that peace missions should seriously consider implementing if they want to detain indicted war criminals successfully.

Develop and activate contingency plans

Thoroughly developed contingency plans are important foundations for all operations and hence both SFOR and KFOR developed contingency plans on how to carry out detention operations. These plans help to ensure that every soldier knows his role in the operation thereby enhancing the chances of success. They are especially important if the mission does not conduct many detention operations, since it is then likely that the international soldiers taking part will not have done so before because they are often only deployed for a relatively short period of time. In SFOR's case contingency plans were activated when indicted war criminals had been located and a time and a place chosen for the operation, designed to minimise the risk to both the soldiers and local people (Lt Cdr Garneau 22 January 1998, 9 April 1998). In order to continuously improve the contingency plans, it is also important that missions evaluate every operation, derive lessons from any mistakes made and adapt the contingency plans in accordance with the lessons learnt, as SFOR did (SFOR interview 2003).

Experience from IFOR and SFOR in Bosnia-Herzegovina indicates that the peace enforcers came across indicted war criminals much more often in the early stages of the mission than in the latter stages (Col Kirkwood 13 February 1996, Major Haselock 20 June 1996, 12 September 1996, Major Riley 23 July 1997, SFOR interview 2003). Several of the SFOR interviewees also argued that it would have been much easier for SFOR to perform detentions at this stage before the indicted individuals developed wide support networks that enabled them to stay at large (SFOR interview 2003). It should be taken into account that detaining indicted war criminals might be more dangerous at the beginning of the mission when the negative peace is still fragile and in cases where the indicted war criminals are still in possession of weapons and enjoy support from their former fellow combatants and local supporters. However, experience from SFOR indicates that if peace troops are well prepared, they are able to handle some resistance from a subject's supporters and still successfully detain him (Major Clarke 18 December 1997, Major Riley 11 July 1997, Seidel 10 January 1999, SFOR 1 April 2004, 2 April 2004). Hence, it is important that peace enforcement missions develop contingency plans for detaining indicted war criminals from the outset of the mission.

Experience from SFOR also shows that it is important that the missions select the right time to detain indicted war criminals (SFOR interview 2003). Hence, if the soldiers encounter an indicted person, it might sometimes be better to keep him under surveillance until a well-prepared detention operation can be carried out at a favourable time, when he for example is not surrounded by a lot of supporters or other civilians. Therefore it is important that there are no tight limits on the time-frame for detention operations and that the soldiers remain patient until the conditions are favourable (Col Wiggen 2001).

It is debatable whether the missions should activate contingency plans for detention operations in cases where the indicted have announced that they intend to surrender voluntarily prior to their indictment. SFOR chose to activate contingency plans and carry out detention operations irrespective of whether the subject had already promised to surrender voluntarily. This was the case when SFOR initiated an operation to detain Naser Oric, who had already given testimony to the ICTY investigators on several occasions and who had announced that he would hand himself over to the ICTY if indicted (Captain MacEachern 11 April 2003). However, KFOR allowed Ramush Haradinaj to surrender voluntarily when the ICTY indicted him in 2005 while he was serving as Prime Minister for Kosovo. SFOR defended its decision to proceed with the detention operation by arguing that its unbiased approach dictated that its contingency plans should always be put into effect irrespective of circumstances (ibid.). It can also be argued that, just because an alleged war criminal has announced that he wants to surrender voluntarily, this does not mean that he will do so once officially indicted. Nevertheless, it can also be argued that initiating a large military operation against someone who has already publicly pledged to surrender voluntarily could upset the local population unnecessarily, such as was the case when SFOR detained Oric (Stephen 2003). In addition, a large group of Kosovo-Albanians also protested when Fatmir Limaj was not allowed to surrender voluntarily but instead arrested by the Slovenian authorities in 2003 (ibid.). A peace enforcement mission is also more likely to come under criticism if soldiers or civilians are injured or killed during efforts to detain those who have already announced their willingness to surrender voluntarily. Thus contingency plans should not necessarily be activated without due consideration of the individual circumstances.

Helping soldiers recognise indicted war criminals

Experience from IFOR, SFOR and KFOR, where international soldiers on several occasions were not able to recognise indicted individuals indicates that troops need means to help them make identifications (Col Kirkwood 17 February 1996, Major Clarke 9 December 1997, Major Haselock 1 July 1996). In IFOR's case it took a while before photos and basic personal characteristics of indicted persons were circulated to the soldiers and in SFOR's case the information was apparently not updated regularly (Ivanko 12 December 1996, Lt Col Rayner 11 February 1996, Major Clarke 9 December 1997, Major Moyer 12 February 1996, SFOR interview 2003). In KFOR's case, indicted criminal Fatmir Limaj managed to pass through the KFOR-guided airport in Pristina on his way to Slovenia (BBC 19 February 2003). It is likely that future peace enforcement missions will face similar problems with the collection and distribution of information to enable international soldiers to recognise wanted persons. It is especially likely that it will be difficult to obtain information and photos of subjects who have acted as military commanders in the field and therefore have not been exposed in the international press. Thus it is important to explore ways and practices of how collecting and distributing information about indicted war criminals can be improved. First, IFOR especially found that details of indicted persons were not swiftly passed on from the international criminal tribunal to the mission (Lt Col Rayner 12 February 1996, 14 February 1996). Hence, closer cooperation between the tribunal and the mission is needed. It is also possible that other sources, such as the international and local press will be able to provide photos of indicted individuals and thus it is important that the mission air a broad-ranging appeal for help in identification. Second, once these photos and basic personal characteristics have been collected, it is vital that it is widely distributed among soldiers as soon as possible. This was not the case with IFOR, where it took a long time before all soldiers received the information, leaving them unable to identify indicted war criminals. It was also not the case for KFOR, where the international soldiers apparently had not been given the information they needed in order to identify and detain people, allowing Fatmir Limaj to escape Kosovo. It is important that the details are made available in a form that the soldiers can consult at all times. In SFOR's case, the soldiers were eventually given posters and a small booklet containing photos and personal characteristics of the indicted at large in their area of operation, allowing them to consult and confer if they thought they had seen an indicted war criminal. Another method of distributing the information would be to make it available on a homepage but this is only a good idea if the peace enforcers have regular internet access, which may not always be the case if they are deployed in areas with poor infrastructure. However, it is anticipated that in the future computer and satellite technology will ensure that internet access will be significantly expanded all over the world so that the vast majority of peace troops will have access. Third, it is also essential that any information provided is regularly updated. Thus the booklet format should facilitate updating. The homepage should also be updated regularly not only with details about newly indicted persons but also with the latest information about the whereabouts of all indicted individuals. These updates should not only be based on the intelligence collected by the missions but also on the information gleaned by the investigators of the international criminal court. One way to ensure effective exchange of updated information is by allowing the court investigators to place information on the homepage accessed by the peace enforcers. Finally experience from SFOR has also indicated a need for soldiers to receive face recognition training (SFOR interview 2003). If not received prior to their deployment, this should be provided as soon as possible after soldiers join the mission.

Involve soldiers patrolling and guarding roadblocks and checkpoints

Throughout IFOR's mission and at the start of SFOR's, international soldiers patrolling and guarding roadblocks and checkpoints were not actively involved in identifying and detaining indicted war criminals (Col Kirkwood 13 February 1996, Lt Col Rayner 11 February 1996, 12 February 1996, Major Moyer 12 February 1996, Major Riley 23 July 1997). Though IFOR soldiers made regular patrols in Pale, the village where Radovan Karadžić was living, the soldiers did not attempt to detain him (Ivanko 11 December 1996, Major Boudreau 11 December 1996). Radovan Karadžić was also reported to have driven unhindered through several IFOR checkpoints in his large Mercedes between Pale and Banja Luka and was reportedly seen 100 metres from a US checkpoint (Anonymous questioner 11 February 1996, Major Haselock 20 June 1996). While the international soldiers had been instructed to detain indicted persons when encountered, those on patrol and at checkpoints and roadblocks were not given information enabling them to identify indicted war criminals (Lt Col Rayner 11 February 1996, 12 February 1996). Among senior IFOR officials there was also confusion as to what actions IFOR's mandate sanctioned these soldiers to take (Captain Van Dyke 6 June 1996, Col Kirkwood 13 February 1996, Lt Col Rayner 11 February 1996, 12 February 1996, Major Haselock 27 May 1996, Major Moyer 12 February 1996). KFOR soldiers patrolling Pristina Airport had apparently also not been instructed to look out for indicted war criminals at a time when four indicted war criminals were at large. In addition at the beginning of SFOR's mission it seemed that SFOR soldiers patrolling the streets of Bosnia-Herzegovina deliberately avoided encountering indicted war criminals.

Individuals such as Radovan Karadžić were reported to be moving freely around in SFOR-patrolled areas (Major Riley 23 July 1997). Like IFOR, SFOR defended this practice by arguing that the primary mission of its soldiers on patrol and at checkpoints and roadblocks was not to hunt down indicted persons (ibid.). Later on in SFOR's mission experience showed that soldiers on patrol and guarding checkpoints and roadblocks can play significant roles in the detention of indicted war criminals (Domin 2002, Lt Bouysson 14 March 2002, Lt Cdr Chamberlain 10 January 1999, Lt Cdr Garneau 22 January 1998, 23 January 1998, Lt Gen Dodson 4 September 2001, Major Desjardins 15 August 2000, Major Lundy 15 August 2002, SFOR 26 August 2003). SFOR soldiers on patrol looked out and searched for indicted war criminals and ground and helicopter patrols also became involved in tracking information about Radovan Karadžić's support network and about the methods of transportation, routes and locations enabling him to remain at large (Lt Gen Dodson 4 September 2001, Major Lundy 15 August 2002, Major Mell 21 January 2003, SFOR 26 August 2003). Patrolling soldiers were also expected to apprehend members of the support networks of the indicted if encountering them (Domin 2002, Major Lundy 15 August 2002). Finally, patrolling soldiers also began to take part in searches of the properties belonging to indicted war criminals (Major Lundy 15 August 2002).

Hence, experience from the latter part of SFOR's mission underscores that soldiers on patrol and guarding roadblocks and checkpoints can potentially play a variety of important roles in the pursuit of indicted war criminals. First, experience from IFOR and SFOR indicates that, especially in the immediate aftermath of the violent conflict, peace troops on patrol and guarding checkpoints and roadblocks often encounter indicted individuals (President of the ICTY 1997, 1998). Therefore, unless these soldiers are equipped and ready to look out for and detain such individuals from the outset of the mission, vital opportunities to do so will be missed. The case of Radovan Karadžić, whom peace enforcement soldiers often encountered throughout IFOR's mission and at the start of SFOR's mission, but who is still at large twelve years after his indictment illustrates this. Second, experience from IFOR showed that promising opportunities to detain people were missed because IFOR did not send soldiers on patrols on occasions when it knew that indicted war criminals would appear in public e.g. at a military parade in Zepa and at the general elections (Anonymous questioner 12 September 1996, Eick 4 June 1996, Major Haselock 4 June 1996, 12 September 1996). Hence, in the future, the soldiers should carry out extra patrols and set up special roadblocks and checkpoints in areas where the indicted are residing or expected to appear in public. Third, and in contrast to IFOR's practice, peace soldiers on patrol and guarding checkpoints and roadblocks can also help limit the freedom of movement of indicted persons. Finally, experience from SFOR also indicates that these soldiers can play important roles in planned operations to detain indicted war criminals and in obtaining information about their whereabouts. The soldiers can participate in searches and provide vital assistance to those carrying out the actual detention.

Involving peace enforcement soldiers on patrol and guarding roadblocks and checkpoints in the detention of indicted war criminals is unlikely to be free of risks. The subjects may still carry heavy weapons and may be surrounded by supporters willing to risk their own lives to protect the life of the indicted war criminal. The situation might not always allow for an immediate detention but at least the subject will have been located so that soldiers can shadow him until detention is possible.

Collecting intelligence and maintaining surveillance

IFOR apparently neither collected intelligence about indicted war criminals nor maintained any kind of surveillance of them (Col Kirkwood 17 February 1996, Major Boudreau 13 August 1996). One result of this inaction was that three indicted war criminals were allowed to hold positions within the police force in Prijedor while IFOR was trying to detect minefields in the area (Anonymous questioner 29 October 1996). Instead of collecting its own intelligence on the whereabouts of indicted war criminals, IFOR relied on intelligence collected by the ICTY (Major Boudreau 29 November 1996). Not maintaining intelligence and keeping surveillance was defended on the grounds of a limited mandate (Major Boudreau 11 December 1996). Likewise, at the beginning of its mission, SFOR relied on the Office of the High Representative (OHR) to organise media campaigns to convince local people to inform SFOR about the whereabouts of indicted war criminals (Bullivant 14 July 1997). Later on SFOR initiated its own campaigns, asking people to come forward with information (SFOR interview 2003). In addition, in the latter stages of the mission numerous SFOR press releases were concluded by encouraging local people to pass on information to SFOR (SFOR 28 January 2004a, SFOR 7 October 2004, 8 October 2004, 14 October 2004, 15 October 2004, 21 October 2004). Furthermore, in an attempt to gather information, a reward programme was established by the US' State Department (Major Lundy 15 August 2002). Some $5 million were promised in exchange for information leading to the detention of the indicted war criminals Radovan Karadžić and Ratko Mladić (General Clark 25 April 2000, Major Lundy 15 August 2002). SFOR distributed posters and leaflets publicising the reward (Major Lundy 15 August 2002). However, SFOR was not directly linked to the reward programme and any information gleaned did not go directly to SFOR but to the US State Department (ibid.). Apparently, the information was supposed to be passed on to SFOR via its American contingent on the ground to SFOR's command structure (ibid.). SFOR soldiers also contacted local people when on patrol to ask if any had information about the indicted still at large (SFOR interview 2003). However, the information retrieved was apparently very limited since it has never been reported that it led to SFOR carrying out any detention operations.

The experience from Bosnia-Herzegovina underlines some of the problems peace enforcement soldiers encounter when they attempt to gather intelligence. The passing of information retrieved through the reward programme to

American soldiers rather than directly to SFOR illustrates that each national contingent involved in a peace enforcement mission may often only reluctantly share its intelligence with other contingents (Hendrickx 2001). This limited success in obtaining reliable information from the local population also empha-sises that building a network of local informants is a slow and difficult process (Col Wiggen 2001, Hendrickx 2001). Differences in language, appearance and culture between the international soldiers and the local population make effect-ive surveillance operations difficult (Hendrickx 2001).

Still several of the interviewees from SFOR identified inadequate intelligence gathering as the most important reason behind SFOR's failure to detain all indicted war criminals (SFOR interview 2003). Furthermore, these experiences expose a need to seriously strengthen the peace enforcement missions' intelligence and sur-veillance capabilities (ibid.). Possible solutions include relying on national teams or using more technical means in surveillance operations (Hendrickx 2001). In addi-tion, the amount and quality of intelligence the missions receive will necessarily also be dependent on the kind of relationship and cooperation the mission enjoys with the various actors also operating in its area of operation. This is further addressed in chapter 12. Better cooperation and trust between the national contin-gents taking part in operations are also needed in order to increase the likelihood of the national contingents that they will pool intelligence.

Ensuring institutional memory

Interviews with senior officials from SFOR indicate that the mission suffered from a failure of institutional memory concerning which actions had previously been taken to detain indicted war criminals (SFOR interview 2003). For example, when asked about previous media campaigns aimed at locals to pass on information, interviewees answered that the campaigns had been successful but knew nothing about how the campaigns had been conducted and did not think that any records of the campaigns were available any more (ibid.). A pre-vious study focusing on the control of small arms has also confirmed that SFOR suffered from a failure of institutional memory (Wille and Pietz 2006). Hence, experience from SFOR shows that in a peace operation setting, where there is a high turnover of personnel, it is vital to develop institutional memory. If this does not happen then experiences and lessons learnt are not carried over from one year to the other and each new group of soldiers deployed risks repeating the mistakes of previous groups and has to come to its own understanding. In order to establish institutional memory concerning actions implemented, it is essential that detailed records of all actions taken are developed and made accessible to succeeding personnel.

Unannounced detention operations

Considering that experience has shown that local people often continue to support indicted war criminals long after the violent conflict has ended, it seems needless to point out that detention operations against these subjects or intelligence-gathering about their whereabouts should not be announced in advance, since this will give them a chance to escape and destroy incriminating evidence. However, on at least one occasion IFOR announced in advance that the objective of its operation was not to detain Ratko Mladić but rather to search some premises in order to collect information (Major Boudreau 13 August 1996). Furthermore, SFOR's policy on at least one occasion was to announce its search operations beforehand (Major Lundy 2 April 2002, 15 August 2002). The main reason for announcing such operations in advance seemed to be to cause less upset to local people and supporters of the indicted (Major Boudreau 13 August 1996, Major Lundy 15 August 2002). Unsurprisingly, on both these occasions the operations were unsuccessful (ibid.). Hence, though unannounced operations might upset the local population more, the benefits of prior warning need to be weighed against the often significant disadvantages, such as the targets escaping or important evidence being destroyed. A possible alternative way to address the dilemma could involve the peace enforcement mission warning the locals in its area of deployment that operations to detain indicted war criminals or collect information might be carried out at any time without prior notice but that the mission will do all it can to minimise the disruption to the lives of the local citizens.

Training

Preferably, international soldiers should receive training before deployment but, if this is not possible, it is important that they are trained once deployed. In addition to basic training in, for example, the application of humane law and mediation and communication, experience from SFOR also indicates that international soldiers can benefit from taking part in simulation exercises. On several occasions SFOR carried out training exercises that simulated an operation to detain an indicted war criminal. On one occasion the Multinational Special Unit (MSU) simulated a situation where a targeted individual was hiding in a house (Staff Sgt Simpson 25 April 2002). During the detention attempt the men protecting him began to riot. After a failed attempt to negotiate with the rioters, SFOR troops entered the village and got the riot under control so that other SFOR soldiers could successfully detain the subject. The exercise also included training in riot control with and without weapons and how to cooperate with a SWAT team. Romanian and Slovenian SFOR soldiers that were about to join the Italian Carabinieri in MSU took part in the exercise (ibid.). The Spanish and French contingents of SFOR also held an exercise called *Operation Hilton*, aiming to detain an indicted war criminal who had the support of the local population. Intelligence units provided the soldiers with information about the identification and location of the subject and some details about his local support. All groups were assigned their own tasks such as providing security, blockading escape routes and identifying the indicted war criminal (Second Lt Marin 9 January 2003). The platoons first practised the various activities and then carried out the actual detention (ibid.).

Though some countries now carry out training exercises together, many of the international soldiers taking part in peace enforcement missions will not have been trained together prior to their deployment.[39] The often rapid turnover of personnel in peace enforcement missions also means that soldiers do not always know their colleagues very well. In addition, many of them will have no or very little experience in detaining indicted war criminals. Hence, it is recommended that training and exercises aimed at familiarising all soldiers with procedures for detention operations and strengthening the cooperation between soldiers are carried out regularly after deployment. Special training and exercises are especially important if the mission lacks experience in detention operations or if the detention operations are very different from each other.

Targeting the indicted war criminals' support network

Experience from Bosnia-Herzegovina shows that networks of people who continue to support alleged war criminals help them stay at large. Hence, in order to be able to detain the indicted, it might be necessary to target these support networks. SFOR began doing this towards the end of its mission (Major Lundy 15 August 2002, NATO 28 February 2002, 1 March 2002). Its soldiers conducted operations aimed at disrupting the activities of the support networks (SFOR 26 August 2003).[40] The soldiers also searched the private and business properties of people in the support network in order to glean information about the networks and the whereabouts of indicted war criminals (Captain MacEachern 11 March 2003, Major Lundy 15 August 2002, NATO 28 February 2002, 1 March 2002, SFOR 13 January 2004, 28 January 2004a, 19 February 2004, 1 April 2004, 7 October 2004, 14 October 2004, 21 October 2004). The operations included at least three searches of properties belonging to the family of indicted war criminal Radovan Karadžić, in July 2002, August 2003 and February 2004 respectively, where documents were seized that assisted SFOR in its search for Karadžić though they did not lead to a successful detention (Human Rights Watch 2005a, Major Lundy 4 July 2002). Finally, SFOR also detained and questioned members of support networks (SFOR 28 January 2004a, 3 March 2004, 14 May 2004, 26 July 2004, 31 July 2004, 31 August 2004a, 31 August 2004b).

Keeping in mind that SFOR's attempts to target these support networks have not led to any successful detentions, it still seems recommendable that future peace enforcement missions target the network of people who help indicted war criminals stay at large. By searching their properties and by detaining and questioning them, the missions can hopefully obtain important information about the whereabouts of the indicted. This targeting can hopefully also prevent these people from continuing to assist the indicted to stay at large by providing financial assistance and shelter. Finally, by targeting especially the family members of the indicted war criminals, it is also likely that the indicted individuals will feel under pressure and therefore may be more likely to surrender voluntarily in order to avoid further aggravations for themselves and their families.

Conclusion

The identification of the above practices constitutes the first cautious step towards the development of a set of best practices to aid future peace enforcement missions in detaining indicted war criminals more successfully. Every detention operation will always entail its own unique features. The indicted war criminals' access to weapons and their determination to resist detention will vary considerably. The level of support the indicted war criminals enjoy and the opposition to their detention will also differ significantly. The terrain and infrastructure surrounding each detention operation are also likely to vary a lot. The political support, resources and soldiers granted to each peace enforcement mission and the security situation will also differ and this affects what practices peace troops will be able to carry out in order to detain indicted war criminals. Therefore it will never be possible to develop a model of best practices to ensure that all detention attempts are successful. However, it is still important that missions learn from each other's mistakes and successes. Hence, thorough studies of more missions and their actions in this regard are needed. Further debates within the sphere of both academic and military scholarship about which practices lead to the desired results are also needed. Finally, it is important that reports of valuable lessons derived from the experiences of various peace enforcement missions are not just archived but fed back into the planning and implementation of future missions. In the light of more regional organisation such as the EU, NATO and AU becoming more involved in peace enforcement missions, it is especially vital that lessons learnt are shared across not only peace enforcement missions but also sponsoring organisations.

Part V
Peace missions and politics

11 Peace missions

Peace, justice and politics

Introduction

Whereas KFOR responded fairly quickly and effectively to the request from Del Ponte, the Prosecutor of the ICTY, to detain indicted war criminals residing in KFOR's area of deployment,[41] their colleagues from IFOR and SFOR in Bosnia-Herzegovina were much less successful in fulfilling ICTY expectations. Chapters 5 and 6 showed that it was not only factors such as an inadequate mandate that hindered the peace enforcers in this task. In the case of IFOR, the soldiers often encountered indicted war criminals while carrying out their ordinary duties and hence, detaining them would have been within the powers granted by their mandate, but they still did not attempt to detain them. Similarly, though SFOR began to carry out detention operations and managed to complete many successfully, the mission never became fully committed to the task. Thus the experiences of IFOR and SFOR indicates that the involvement of peace enforcement soldiers in such detentions is also influenced by political considerations. This chapter identifies some of the most important of these in Bosnia-Herzegovina. The chapter also discusses the considerations in their temporal and territorial context.

Political considerations influencing the involvement of IFOR and SFOR in the detention of indicted war criminals

The fear that pursuing justice would threaten peace

One of the most considerable political concerns undoubtedly influencing the support for peace enforcement missions' involvement in detentions was the fear that these actions would threaten the fragile peace. The Dayton Peace Agreement had not been very firm on the importance of implementing a transitional justice process. The negotiations leading to the DPA had focused on an immediate end to the violent conflict rather than on securing accountability for atrocities committed during the conflict and neither the UN nor the ICTY had taken part in the NATO-led peace negotiations (Kalinauskas 2002). Hence, the DPA only stated that all parties were obliged to cooperate in the investigation and prosecution of war crimes and that all authorities in Bosnia-Herzegovina were obliged to provide unrestricted access to personnel from the ICTY and to cooperate with the tribunal, especially concerning the detention of indicted war criminals (Office of the High Representative 14 December 1995: Article IX, Annex 4(II.8)). However, the DPA did not declare what the consequences for not fulfilling these obligations would be. Neither did it address what the role of the peace enforcement missions would be. An article in the DPA also stated that:

> No person who is serving a sentence imposed by the International Tribunal for the Former Yugoslavia, and no person who is under indictment by the Tribunal and who has failed to comply with an order to appear before the Tribunal, may stand as a candidate or hold any appointive, elective, or other public office in the territory of Bosnia and Herzegovina.
>
> (Office of the High Representative 14 December 1995: Annex 4 (IX.1))

Nevertheless, this article did not prevent alleged war criminals such as Radovan Karadžić from remaining influential members of political parties and from retaining substantial political and financial power (Baker 2004, Human Rights Watch 2005a). It also did not prevent alleged war criminals such as Ratko Mladić from remaining influential figures in the local military. Hence, since some indicted war criminals stayed very powerful, the peace missions feared that attempting to detain them could potentially encourage them and their supporters to take up arms again. The fear was apparently so considerable that the American chief negotiator of the DPA, Richard Holbrooke, after the initial negotiations had failed, allegedly ended up promising Karadžić that he would not be sent to The Hague if he gave up his political career and disappeared from the public eye (Adnkronos International 22 March 2007, BBC 26 October 2007, Perlez 1996, Associated Press 19 September 2007, Vulliamy 2 December 2007). The peace missions also feared that the three parties to the conflict represented by Alija Izetbegovic, Franjo Tudjman and Slobodan Milosevic, who had all been very influential political leaders throughout, would withdraw their support for the implementation of the DPA if the peace enforcement missions began to detain indicted war criminals (Rieff 1996, Sharp 1997, Century Foundation 1998). Finally, the missions were apparently also afraid that the considerable proportion of the local population who still supported the indicted war criminals would withdraw support for the DPA and maybe even begin to demonstrate against the missions should they become involved in such detentions (Human Rights Watch 2005a, International Crisis Group 2000, Supernor 2001). If the local population and the parties to the DPA withdrew their support like this, the implementation process would most certainly fail. Similarly, if the local people were to stage large demonstrations against the mission or if the indicted war criminals and their supporters were to take up arms against the peace troops, the mission would fail. Hence, in both cases the consequences of becoming involved in detentions might prevent successful implementation of the DPA. Finally, the consent of the parties to the conflict was also still seen as an essential precondition for a successful peace mission and hence, the prospect of losing this was viewed as a danger to one of the fundamental pillars of a contemporary peace mission and thus something to be avoided by all means.

The fear of mission creep

Another factor that is likely to have influenced the involvement of peace enforcers in the detention of indicted war criminals is the political consequences of mission creep. Mission creep occurs when the tasks a military operation is expected to carry out are gradually expanded, diverting personnel and resources away from the original aims and in the worst case scenario, resulting in the complete failure of the operation. In the cases of IFOR and SFOR, detention of war criminals was not a task explicitly included in their mandates and it had not been an explicit part of previous peace mission mandates. Therefore detentions were not a task that the soldiers were trained to and experienced in and the task had not been taken into consideration when the missions were planned and resources allocated. Accordingly, it was feared that involvement in this new task would divert attention and resources away from the original aim of the missions, which was to implement the military objectives of the Dayton Peace Agreement (Human Rights Watch 2005a, International Crisis Group 2000, Kalinauskas 2002, Leurdijk 2001, Lorenz 1997, Ruxton 2001, United States Institute of Peace 1997). In the worst case scenario the missions would then not only fail to detain indicted war criminals but also fail to achieve their original aims and therefore be considered a complete failure.

Protecting the lives and well-being of peace enforcement soldiers

Another political consideration influencing IFOR's decision not to get involved in these detentions and SFOR's decision to take a cautious approach to them was the wish to protect the lives and well-being of the peace soldiers (Century Foundation 1998, Human Rights Watch 2005a, International Crisis Group 2000, Kalinauskas 2002, Kampschror 2001, Sliedregt 2001). It was not only feared that the soldiers might get injured or killed during operations but also that detentions could provoke retaliation from the supporters of the alleged war criminals that could threaten the lives of the peace enforcement soldiers (ibid.).

Fear of the testimonies of indicted war criminals

Yet another political consideration likely to have influenced the involvement of peace troops in the detention of indicted war criminals in Bosnia-Herzegovina was the fear of what some of these subjects might say when on trial in The Hague. The situation in Bosnia-Herzegovina was special because many of the states participating in IFOR's and SFOR's missions had also participated in UNPROFOR and played important roles in the negotiation process leading to the DPA. During UNPROFOR's mission international soldiers had on several occasions been involved in embarrassing situations with individuals now indicted for war crimes. American, Dutch and French UNPROFOR soldiers apparently praised Serb hospitality during social events with Karadžić and Mladić (Kampschror 2001). The British General Sir Michael Rose and the French General Bernard Janvier also met with Ratko Mladić; and the American Lieutenant General Wesley Clark was photographed after receiving a bottle of brandy and a pistol from Ratko Mladić and exchanged hats with him (Novak 2003, Vulliamy 2007). Janvier even had dinner with Mladić a short while before the Srebrenica massacre, which Janvier could have prevented if he had ordered timely air strikes. The French General also allegedly considered Mladić a good military officer who was only attempting to defend his people to the best of his abilities (Vulliamy 2007). In addition, Dutch soldiers trying to protect civilians in Srebrenica had been heavily criticised for not doing enough to stop Ratko Mladić and his forces' attempt to ethnically cleanse Srebrenica. Western diplomats' and politicians' attempts to end the violence in Bosnia-Herzegovina had also been marred by considerable flaws and a lack of commitment (International Crisis Group 2000, Kampschror 2001, Leurdijk 2001). During the hostilities Karadžić had negotiated with leading Western diplomats like Malcolm Rifkind, Cyrus Vance, Douglas Hurd, David Owen and Lord Carrington (Vulliamy 2007). Western diplomats had also considered to accept Karadžić and his allies' promises of cease-fires and other guarantees even though the agreements were broken all the time (ibid.). Western negotiators were also accused of rewarding Karadžić and his allies for their military advancements obtained through horrendous violence in the various peace maps and plans (ibid.). Hence, if Karadžić and Mladić were detained and sent to The Hague, it was considered likely that their testimonies would include some embarrassing stories about leading Western diplomats and expose Western negotiators and politicians' lack of will and ability to end the violent conflict in Bosnia-Herzegovina.

No support for the prosecution of indicted war criminals

Finally, another political consideration likely to have influenced the reluctance and lack of full commitment of peace enforcement soldiers to be involved in the detention of indicted war criminals is a general lack of support for the ICTY's prosecution of individuals who had committed atrocities during the violent conflict. This lack of support was also manifested in the ICTY's struggle to secure adequate funding and support (Blakesley 1997). There are several potential reasons why the political leaders behind the deployment of IFOR and SFOR were not very supportive of the ICTY work. First, some may have assessed that attempts to prosecute these individuals was simply not worthwhile from a financial point of view. Second, it is also likely that the political leaders feared that if the ICTY succeeded in bringing justice to the victims in the former Yugoslavia, then victims of other conflicts around the world would also call for justice and the establishment of further costly international criminal tribunals. Finally, it is also likely that some leaders worried that a successful ICTY would mean that they themselves might also be held accountable for atrocities they bore political responsibility for. This would not only mean that the leaders risked being put on trial for their role in conflicts in the past but also that their involvement in future conflicts would be restrained.

The political considerations in their contemporary context

The political considerations influencing the involvement of IFOR and SFOR in the detention of indicted war criminals necessarily need to be seen in the context of the period in which they were deployed.

The considerations regarding a general lack of support for securing account-ability for atrocities and the fear that pursuing accountability could threaten peace were probably linked to the fact that, up until the establishment of the ICTY, the vast majority of peace agreements had been based on amnesty rather than accountability. Thus the importance of securing accountability was still not widely acknowledged. In addition, the ICTY was the first international criminal tribunal set up after a violent conflict had ended with a peace agreement based on compromise rather than clear victory by one party such as after the Second World War. Hence, there was no prior experience in how detention of indicted war criminals and their prosecution by an international criminal tribunal would affect the implementation of a peace agreement.

These fears that the mission would fail and jeopardise the fragile peace, experience mission creep or lead to injury or death to soldiers also needs to be seen in the context of NATO's ambition to strengthen its position among inter-national organisations. The deployments of IFOR and SFOR were among NATO's first attempts to enter the group of international organisations that assist states recovering from internal violent conflict implement a peace agree-ment. If these first attempts had ended in failure, it could have meant that NATO's ability in this regard would have been seriously questioned, obviously very embarrassing for an organisation trying to manifest itself as a powerful player on the international scene. Moreover, IFOR's predecessor in Bosnia-Herzegovina, UNPROFOR had been heavily criticised for failing to put an end to the brutal violence and to protect the local civilian population from becoming victims and hence, international organisations could hardly afford to fail to help bring peace to Bosnia-Herzegovina once again. This heavy criticism and the failure to protect civilians from violence are also factors likely to have enhanced the fear that the indicted war criminals might incriminate Western political leaders in their testimonies about what went on during the violent conflict.

The importance of fear of potential mission creep also needs to be seen in the context of the experience of missions in the years before IFOR's deployment. As shown in Chapters 3 and 4, many additional tasks were assigned to peace-keeping missions in the aftermath of the Cold War. The majority of these mis-sions, such as those in Somalia and Rwanda, failed miserably in carrying out these new tasks and thereby failed to prevent the death and injury of millions of civilians. The same was the case with UNPROFOR, deployed in the former

Yugoslavia prior to IFOR and SFOR. UNPROFOR's mandate was expanded numerous times and tasks were added that the soldiers were not trained or equipped to carry out (DPKO Bosnia-Herzegovina – UNPROFOR: Background, Office of the Historian undated). This contributed to UNPROFOR failing to carry out its mission successfully and caused a lot of suffering for the civilian population in Bosnia-Herzegovina. Hence, both at the political and military level there was a reluctance to involve peace missions in new tasks because experience had shown that this could lead to the missions failing to reach their original aims and therefore becoming complete failures.

Finally, the fear that the detention of indicted war criminals could result in dead or injured soldiers is also related to the experience of peacekeeping missions in the beginning of the 1990s. Prior to IFOR and SFOR's deployment, UN peacekeepers in other parts of the world had encountered very violent deaths that had challenged the general support of UN peacekeeping missions. In Somalia twenty-five Pakistani peacekeepers from UNOSOM II were brutally murdered and mutilated on 5 June 1993 (DPKO Somalia – UNOSOM II: Background). Three months later eighteen US soldiers were also murdered and their bodies subjected to degrading treatment on public television when US troops attempted to arrest individuals thought to be responsible for the massacre carried out three months earlier (ibid.). Ten Belgian UNAMIR soldiers were also brutally killed at the beginning of the genocide in Rwanda in the spring of 1994 (DPKO Rwanda – UNAMIR: Background). In addition the predecessor to IFOR, UNPROFOR had also suffered more than 200 fatalities during its three years of operation (DPKO Bosnia-Herzegovina – UNPROFOR: Profile). Hence, around the time when IFOR and SFOR were deployed a significant number of peacekeepers had not only recently lost their lives but under degrading and horrifying circumstances. It was feared that, if television stations kept on showing soldiers coming home in body-bags, local populations in the states that contributed soldiers to the missions would stop supporting deployment abroad making it unviable for politicians to support overseas missions as well. Thus there was a reluctance to involve peace missions in tasks that would endanger the lives of the soldiers.

Hence, the context of the deployment can help explain the importance of some of the political considerations impacting the involvement of peacekeepers in the detention of indicted war criminals. An interesting question is then whether these political considerations are also likely to influence the involvement of contemporary peace enforcement soldiers in such detentions.

The political considerations in a current perspective

It is questionable whether politicians and military leaders still see the detentions as a potential cause of mission creep and that thus prefer enforcers not to get involved. On the one hand NATO peace troops have now already been involved in such operations in Bosnia-Herzegovina and Kosovo and UN soldiers from UNTAES and UNMIL have been involved in detaining one indicted war criminal in Croatia and Liberia respectively. Hence, rather than representing a totally new task, such operations constitute a task that missions have been both implicitly and explicitly mandated to carry out. Such operations are also slowly but steadily becoming part of the doctrines of peace missions. On the other hand missions are still not routinely involved in them. Much will also depend on whether the mandate explicitly authorises the soldiers to detain indicted war criminals or whether this task is added after deployment. If it is included in the mandate, then peacekeepers are hopefully also prepared for the task and hence will not perceive it as a factor leading to mission creep. If on the other hand the detentions are added to the expected tasks in the middle of the mission, then it is likely that it will still be seen as a potential contributor to mission creep. Whether it will be seen as a potential reason for mission creep will probably also depend on whether or not politicians and military leaders perceive that it will be relatively easy to detain the indicted war criminals. Thus, though the fear of mission creep will probably be less influential due to more preparedness and experience in carrying out detention operations, it is still likely to influence the involvement of peace enforcement soldiers in detention operations in some cases.

It is also debatable whether the fear of injuries and fatalities to peace troops will prevent missions' involvement in detaining indicted war criminals. Based on the experience in Bosnia-Herzegovina it is difficult to determine whether the perceived dangers are well founded. On the one hand a couple of the indicted war criminals whom SFOR eventually tried to detain used weapons against SFOR soldiers and, though not officially confirmed, there were also rumours stating that SFOR troops had been injured during some operations (Leurdijk 2001). High-profile alleged war criminals such as Radovan Karadžić and Ratko Mladić were apparently also constantly surrounded by heavily armed body-guards. On several occasions local people also demonstrated after SFOR had detained an indicted individual (Major Clarke 18 December 1997, Major Riley 14 July 1997, Seidel 10 January 1999). On the other hand, at least officially, no SFOR soldiers were ever seriously injured or killed while taking part in a deten-tion operation or as a result of retaliation for a detention operation. In addition, it can be argued that some of the main states contributing to peace missions have become more used to their soldiers getting injured or killed while on inter-national military missions. Since the turn of the millennium, many soldiers from the US, UK, Canada, Denmark, Germany, Spain, France and Italy have lost their lives or been seriously injured in the invasions of Iraq and Afghanistan and hence, these states and their populations are steadily becoming used to soldiers taking part in military operations abroad and paying the ultimate price. In recent years UN workers have also been killed in Iraq, Lebanon and Algeria and, though this has obviously had an impact on the work of the missions, resulting for example in the mission in Iraq mainly working out of Jordan, it has not led to the missions being untimely terminated or deemed complete failures (Howard 2007). Hence, there are indications that the fear of injuries and fatalities to peacekeepers is no longer a factor that prevents them from carrying out tasks and missions, at least to the same degree. On the other hand it is also likely that the context in which the individual mission is deployed could affect whether the fear of killed or injured soldiers would influence their involvement in the detention of indicted war criminals. If, for example, a considerable number of soldiers in a mission had already been killed and injured or if the indicted were thought to be heavily armed and prepared to fight back, it is more likely that the fear of injury or death of soldiers would prevent them from becoming involved in detention operations. Thus, though the impact of the fear of injury or death to troop on the decision of which tasks to undertake is probably not so prevalent today as it was in the mid-1990s, it is still likely to influence the peace soldiers' involvement in some cases.

Furthermore, as argued previously, the call for accountability for past atrocities as an important part of post-conflict peace-building has also steadily grown over the years and is on the way to becoming a part of the UN's approach to peace-building. Many states also now support the involvement of peace missions in the implementation of transitional justice processes. However, this support for accountability through a trial process is still not so prevalent that it is routinely included in the mandates of all peace missions. In, for example, Liberia focus has so far only been on setting up a truth and reconciliation commission rather than a trial process to ensure criminal accountability for at least the worst atrocities. Support for the new International Criminal Court is also not unanimous, since important states in the UNSC such as China, Russia and the US and significant contributors to peace missions such as India and Pakistan have still not ratified the Rome Statute. Thus it is very likely that a lack of full support for the accountability issue will still influence the involvement of peace missions in war criminal detentions.

Whether or not the fear of incriminating testimonies from indicted war criminals will still prevent peace enforcement missions from becoming involved in detaining them is likely to depend on what role the states participating in the mission have played in the peace negotiation process. In cases where the states have not been much involved in the process they obviously do not have much to fear from the testimonies. In addition, in cases where the role of the states has been fairly uncontroversial and where they have been able to successfully facilitate the peace negotiation, it is also likely that they will not fear what may be said in court. However, if the states or international organisations behind the peace mission have been heavily involved in the peace negotiation process and their involvement has been controversial such as was the case with UNPROFOR in Bosnia-Herzegovina, then it is likely that the fear of such testimony will still influence the involvement of missions in detentions. The dominating international approach to reaching a peace agreement is still very much based on negotiations with the individuals who are also directly or indirectly responsible for some of the worst atrocities committed during the violent conflict. Thus, it is still very likely that missions will be requested to detain individuals after the peace agreement has been signed, despite having been in close contact with them during the negotiation process. In addition, cases such as Sudan and the

Democratic Republic of Congo indicate that the international approach to building peace is still often incoherent and flawed and that states and international organisations are still often not fully committed to help bring an immediate end to the violent conflict, resulting in prolonged civilian suffering and destruction. Hence, it is likely that the fear of revealing testimony from the indicted will continue to influence the involvement of missions in detention operations in some cases.

Finally, the fear that detaining indicted war criminals threatens the often fragile peace that peace missions are trying to uphold is also likely to continue to influence whether contemporary missions become involved in such detentions. Peace agreements still often fail to ensure that the individuals responsible for mass atrocities are held accountable and prevented from playing influential roles in the peace process. Alleged war criminals are still often allowed to play important parts in the peace process by, for example, transforming themselves into influential politicians such as in the case of ICTY-indicted Ramush Haradinaj in Kosovo and one of the ministers in the Sudanese government, who has been indicted by the ICC, or otherwise maintaining their position in the military such as is the case with some alleged war criminals in the Democratic Republic of Congo (Action Aid 2006a). Even in cases like the Democratic Republic of Congo, where attempts have been made to exclude alleged war criminals from the peace agreement, a lack of firm implementation of the provisions mean that these individuals are still allowed to participate in the peace process (ibid.). In the case of Kosovo the constitution also only excludes individuals who are serving a sentence imposed by the ICTY or who refuse to cooperate with the ICTY from becoming politicians, which means that Ramush Haradinaj has been able to continue his political career despite his indictment because he is assessed as cooperating with the ICTY. Thus, as long as alleged war criminals are allowed to take a significant part in the peace process and thereby stay powerful, the fear that detaining them poses a threat to peace will continue to influence the involvement of peace missions in their detention.

Conclusion

Political considerations concerning mission creep, dead or injured soldiers, a lack of support for accountability, testimonies of indicted war criminals and threats to peace significantly influenced the involvement of IFOR and SFOR soldiers in the detention of indicted war criminals. All these factors are still likely to be influential although the impact of some, such as the fear of mission creep and possibility of death or injury, is likely to have reduced with peace missions' increased experience and preparedness in this regard and the involvement of key states in recent international interventions in, for example, Afghanistan and Iraq. The prospects for peace troops being involved in detaining indicted war criminals in contemporary and future missions are further discussed in the conclusion to this book.

Part VI

Assisting peace enforcement missions in the apprehension of indicted war criminals

12 Peace enforcement soldiers cannot do it alone

Involving international institutions and organisations and the local population in locating indicted war criminals

Introduction

Just like an ordinary national police force needs help from various actors in order to locate and arrest criminals, peace enforcement missions also need assistance from international and local actors. On numerous occasions both IFOR and SFOR complained that not knowing the whereabouts of the indicted war criminals was the main reason why they did not detain them (Lt Cdr Thomson 3 December 1998, Major Boudreau 29 November 1996, 11 December 2006, Major Desjardins 15 August 2000, Major Haselock 30 October 1996, Major Riley 23 July 1997). Hence, this chapter focuses on the international and local actors that are not part of the international civilian administration or the international military presence and not involved in the actual detention of indicted war criminals but who can still provide the peace missions with vital assistance in locating the subjects. In the light of the experience of the missions in Bosnia-Herzegovina, the chapter discusses which actors can potentially help with location aspects as well as some of the obstacles that missions need to overcome to ensure the cooperation of these actors.

Involving the international criminal tribunal

If missions are to successfully detain indicted war criminals it is obviously paramount that they establish a good working relationship with the international criminal tribunal responsible for the indictments. Experience from IFOR and especially SFOR has underlined that some actions by the tribunal significantly influence the peace mission's ability to locate and detain indicted war criminals. For example, during IFOR's mission and at the start of SFOR's ICTY indictments were available to the public (President of the ICTY 1996, 1997). This apprised the indicted individuals of their wanted status and the fact that the international peacekeepers were probably looking for them, which made their apprehension more difficult. Later, the ICTY changed this practice by issuing sealed indictments, meaning that no one was forewarned in this manner (President of the ICTY 1998). The fact that SFOR's first detention attempts were based on sealed indictments underlines the impact that this change of practice had on

SFOR efforts in this regard (CNN 10 July 1997, ICTY 10 July 1997). In addition, at the start of SFOR's mission, communication and exchange of information between the ICTY and SFOR were apparently less than optimal. On at least one occasion during its first year of operation, SFOR had not received details from the ICTY of an indicted war criminal at large in its area of operation, so that when that individual wanted to hand himself in voluntarily to SFOR troops, they would not detain him (Major Clarke 9 December 1997). Furthermore, SFOR's enquiries as to whether or not this person was really wanted for war crimes came back negative (ibid.). It appears that at that time SFOR was not informed about all the persons on the ICTY's list of sealed indictments (ibid.). Initially the ICTY also only handed over the indictments on a case-by-case basis and, rather than passing on details directly to SFOR, it passed the information to NATO (Major Clarke 9 December 1997, Major Riley 23 July 1997). Later practice saw the ICTY inform SFOR whenever a new alleged war criminal was indicted (Captain MacEachern 11 April 2003, Hodzic 11 April 2003). The ICTY also perceived SFOR to have a legal obligation to detain indicted war criminals and thus the tribunal had far greater expectations concerning SFOR involvement in such detentions than had the mission itself (Leurdijk 2001). Hence, on numerous occasions the Chief Prosecutor of the ICTY, Del Ponte criticised KFOR and SFOR for not doing enough to detain indicted war criminals (BBC 11 April 2001, 23 November 2004, Office of the Prosecutor 18 February 2003). Del Ponte also disapproved of SFOR's approach to detentions and contended that it would be better if SFOR set up a special taskforce focusing solely on the detentions (Lt Gen Dodson 4 September 2001, NATO SG Lord Robertson 21 December 2000). Del Ponte and SFOR also disagreed on which indicted individuals were actually at large in the mission's area of operation (Lt Gen Dodson 4 September 2001).

Important lessons can be learnt from the often troublesome relationship between ICTY and SFOR. First, the international criminal tribunal needs to seriously consider keeping its indictments sealed. The disadvantage of this is that it does not give the indicted person the chance to surrender voluntarily, so that peace missions or other authorities will have to actively detain him. Furthermore, experience from Kosovo has also shown that in some situations voluntary surrender is preferable because the reaction of the local people is likely to be less negative if the individual has been able to surrender voluntarily with dignity. This was the case with Ramush Haradinaj, who was the Prime Minister of Kosovo and involved in the peace process at the time of his indictment and who surrendered voluntarily when it was announced in March 2005. On the other hand one advantage of keeping the indictments sealed is that the indicted war criminals will not know that the peace enforcement soldiers are trying to detain them. Experience from Bosnia-Herzegovina where Milan Lukic and Dragan Zelenovic, whose indictments had both been published, escaped SFOR detention by fleeing to Argentina[42] and Russia,[43] respectively also underlines the advantages of keeping the indictments sealed. Hence, in most cases it is recommended that the indictments are kept sealed if the indicted person is expected to be residing within the mission's area of deployment. Exceptions should be seriously considered and it should be remembered that, even if an individual has promised to surrender voluntarily, this does not necessarily mean that he really will do that once the indictment has been announced.

Second, the experience of SFOR and ICTY underlines the need for effective exchange of information between the tribunal and the peace mission. It is important that the tribunal hands over the arrest warrants to the mission as soon as they have been issued. If the missions are explicitly authorised to carry out the detentions, it should also be more politically acceptable that they receive warrants directly rather than the political body behind the mission receiving them first.

Third, in cases where many indicted war criminals are at large in a peace enforcement operation's area of deployment, it might also help the mission if the tribunal provides it with a priority list of such individuals, as the ICTY did for SFOR (Ruxton 2001).

Finally, the relationship between the peace mission and the international criminal tribunal is likely to benefit from the tribunal acknowledging that these detentions are not necessarily easy tasks, so that constructive criticism rather than condemnation is advised when indicted war criminals remain at large despite requests for their detention.

Thus, international criminal tribunals can potentially play an important role in assisting peace enforcement missions locate and detain indicted war criminals and therefore it is important that the two establish an effective working relationship.

Involving international non-governmental human rights organisations

Whenever a peace enforcement mission is deployed, the international civilian and military presence is always joined by a considerable number of Non-governmental organisations (NGOs). Some of these NGOs focus on promoting and implementing human rights and hence also often have an interest in the successful prosecution of individuals responsible for gross violations of human rights. A vital part of a successful prosecution is necessarily that the indicted war criminals are located, detained and transferred to the prosecuting body and thus these human rights NGOs have an interest in successful detentions. Therefore they may potentially be able and willing to assist peace troops in locating alleged war criminals.

In Bosnia-Herzegovina, some of these international human rights NGOs such as Human Rights Watch (HRW), Amnesty International (AI) and the International Crisis Group (ICG) became engaged in campaigning for the transfer of indicted war criminals from the former Yugoslavia to the ICTY. On numerous occasions the three organisations heavily criticised first IFOR and later SFOR for not doing enough to effect detentions.[44] Most of these reports and press releases merely pointed out the failures of IFOR and SFOR and urged the missions to do more. However, a couple of the publications also offered the missions assistance in locating indicted individuals. In November 1997 HRW published a report including a map that allegedly pointed out the location of forty-one indicted war criminals living within SFOR's deployment area (Human Rights Watch 18 November 1997). Twenty three were reported to live in the British sector, eight in the French-controlled area and a further eight in the American sector (ibid.). The map also showed the location of major SFOR military bases and claimed that in at least eight cases indicted war criminals were living close to these bases (ibid.). Three years later in November 2000 the ICG published a report that supposedly established the location of more than sixty individuals who had allegedly committed atrocities falling under the jurisdiction of the ICTY, making these individuals potentially indictable (International Crisis Group 2000). The report also claimed that the ICG was in possession of significant detailed information about the whereabouts of indicted war criminal Radovan Karadžić (ibid.). In addition and quite controversially, the ICG report stated that some of the individuals mentioned in the report were already on the ICTY's list of secret indictments (ibid.). For example, the report mentioned Miroslav Deronjic, who was not indicted until July 2002. SFOR soldiers managed to detain Deronjic a couple of days after he was indicted but the mention of his name in the ICG report two years earlier could have given him the opportunity to flee SFOR's area of operation and thereby potentially escape justice (NATO SG Lord Robertson 7 July 2002). The report also mentioned Milan and Sredoje Lukic whose indictment had only been unsealed a couple of days before its publication (International Crisis Group 2000) Furthermore the report also contested that the sources providing this information has also passed it on to SFOR but that SFOR had not responded to it (ibid.).

In contrast to peace enforcement missions, international human rights organisations focus solely on human rights issues and hence often have better research facilities and contact networks than the missions when it comes to investigating human rights violations and establishing the location of alleged perpetrators. Thus, in addition to putting pressure on missions to effect detentions, international human rights organisations can also provide vital information about the whereabouts of those indicted. However, the experience from Bosnia-Herzegovina also indicates that the relations between these organisations and the missions are often troublesome, which can negatively affect matters. First, the organisations are often fierce in their criticism of the missions' efforts showing limited understanding of and consideration for the difficult dilemmas the missions encounter when involved in those operations. For example, unlike international human rights organisations, it is the peace enforcement missions that face the consequences of detaining indicted war criminals. Hence, if international soldiers or local citizens are injured or killed during detention, it is the missions that have to face the families left behind and the upset politicians calling for withdrawal. Similarly, it is also the peacekeepers who could be the target for violent reprisals from supporters of the indicted war criminals. Experience from Bosnia has also shown that international human rights organisations readily publish information about alleged war criminals that both the international criminal tribunal and the peace enforcement mission would prefer was kept secret. Hence, there is a fine line between when this publication of information can potentially assist in mission attempts to detain indicted war criminals and when it can actually hinder them. Therefore these organisations need to consider when publication only serves their own interest and when it actually assists the missions and the international criminal tribunals' efforts to hold individuals accountable for mass atrocities. They should also consider providing peace missions with any relevant information straight away rather than waiting until the research is published. Finally, it is also important that international human rights organisations acknowledge that, just like national police forces, peace enforcers receive many tip-offs that turn out to be untrue or out of date and that therefore the mere provision of information does not necessarily always result in a successful detention.

Likewise, it is also important that peace missions consider how they can form constructive relationships with international human rights organisations and make such organisations feel that they have a positive role to play in locating indicted war criminals. The missions should undoubtedly make it clear whether or not they interpret their mandate to include carrying out detention operations based on information obtained from international human rights organisations. If this is the case, it is clearly also imperative that the missions react swiftly on such information. If no successful detention follows, the mission should report back to the international human rights organisation about what went wrong. Finally, it is also essential that missions keep their sources confidential if the international organisations do not want their involvement known, especially since it is likely that the supporters of the detained indicted war criminal will turn against the international human rights organisation in question.

Thus, international human rights organisations can potentially be vital allies for peace enforcement missions. They can in many cases help missions locate indicted war criminals but this requires that the information is handed over as soon as it is obtained and that the missions take immediate action. Hence, good relations and communication between international human rights organisations and peace enforcement missions are considerable preconditions for the organisations being able to assist missions in locating indicted persons. If in contrast, for example, international human rights organisations report the whereabouts of alleged war criminals without first handing this information to the missions and giving them the chance to react or if missions refuse to react to such information then the two bodies who should be working towards the same aim will instead impair each other's work.

Involving other international non-governmental organisations

In addition to international human rights NGOs, many other international NGOs also operate in the areas where peace enforcement missions are deployed. These organisations also engage with the local population and through their work could potentially come across information about the whereabouts of indicted war criminals. Though these NGOs, like their colleagues in the human rights organisations could undoubtedly assist peace missions with such information, their involvement is much more controversial than that of the human rights bodies. For international non-governmental organisations involved, for example, in delivering humanitarian aid and providing medical care such as Oxfam, Médicin Sans Frontières and the International Red Cross, being seen as impartial organisations that help all individuals and groups regardless of their involvement in the violent conflict is vital for their work. In the context of international criminal justice, this for example means that, in accordance with rule 73 of the Rules of Procedure and Evidence of the ICC, employees of the International Committee of the Red Cross do not have to disclose information to the ICC against their will (Jeannet 2000). Just as handing over information to the ICC can be against the interest of these organisations, becoming involved in the location of indicted war criminals can also have detrimental consequences for their work. If such NGOs report the sighting of an indicted war criminal and it becomes known that this information has led to his detention, it is likely that his local supporters will no longer perceive the organisation as impartial and perhaps even alienate themselves from it. Hence, though these organisations are likely to support the detention of indicted war criminals, it is not necessarily always in their interest to assist peace missions by providing information in this way. However, the missions could benefit from an agreement similar to that the International Committee of the Red Cross has with the ICC, which, for example, would mean that the organisations would hand over information to the mission in cases where such information would be published at a latter stage anyway (ibid.).

Hence, other international NGOs can potentially provide peace enforcement missions with vital information about the whereabouts of indicted war criminals enabling detentions. However, these organisations might not always be willing to hand over information because that action might potentially damage their relationship with the local population.

Involving the local population

Neither IFOR nor KFOR apparently attempted to involve the local population in locating indicted war criminals. IFOR's main reason for this was that it's interpretation of its mandate only allowed its troops to take action if encountering indicted individuals while carrying out their ordinary duties (Col Kirkwood 13 February 1996, Lt Col Rayner 11 February 1996, Major Haselock 16 May 1996, 12 September 1996). Thus reacting to tip-offs from the local population was not seen as within IFOR's mandate. It is not known how the indicted war criminals whom KFOR detained were located but interviews with senior officers suggest that KFOR was not involved in their location but merely asked to detain them once UNMIK had established where they were (KFOR interview 2003). At the start of its mission SFOR took over IFOR's interpretation of its mandate, which meant that local people were not meant to be involved in locating indicted war criminals (Major Riley 4 July 1997, Major White 29 January 1997). From 2001 SFOR expanded the interpretation of its mandate to include acting on reliable information about the whereabouts of indicted war criminals without SFOR soldiers necessarily having encountered them (General Ralston 22 May 2001, Lt Gen Dodson 4 September 2001). Hence, SFOR now in various ways actively encouraged the local people to come forward with any information about the whereabouts of the indicted. For example, SFOR promoted the US State Department's reward programme and SFOR soldiers on patrol also directly encouraged the local population to hand over information about the whereabouts of indicted war criminals (General Clark 25 April 2000, SFOR interview 2003). It is not fully known whether SFOR ever received any information from the local population in Bosnia-Herzegovina that led to the successful detention of an indicted war criminal. SFOR did on a couple of occasions carry out searches for Radovan Karadžić after tip-offs from the local population but on all occasions Karadžić was nowhere to be found (Lt Bouysson 14 March 2002, NATO 28 February 2002, 1 March 2002, 6 March 2002, SFOR 10 January 2004, 1 April 2004, 2 April 2004). Keeping in mind that police officers normally rely considerably on help from the general public when trying to locate criminals, it is of considerable concern that SFOR did not receive more useful information about the whereabouts of indicted war criminals at large.

There are numerous possible reasons as to why the local population was not very eager to provide SFOR with information about possible sightings of indicted war criminals. First, parts of the local population maintained their support for the indicted war criminals and did not want to see them sent to The Hague. It is also possible that the local population questioned SFOR's commitment to detaining indicted war criminals because of various past experiences. Throughout IFOR's mission and in the beginning of SFOR's mission the peace enforcement missions argued that it was not their job to detain indicted war criminals. In addition senior military personnel from one of SFOR's predecessors, UNPROFOR on numerous occasions had openly met and been seen on local media with the same individuals who were now indicted war criminals (International Crisis Group 2000, Kampschror 2001, Leurdijk 2001, Novak 2003). IFOR and SFOR soldiers had also on numerous occasions been seen near indicted war criminals without doing anything to detain them (Major Haselock 12 September 1996, Major Riley 23 July 1997, President of the ICTY 1997). Furthermore, it was not until towards the end of its mission that SFOR began to ask the local population to report on sightings of indicted war criminals to SFOR and it is likely that the local population thought that, if SFOR had been committed to detaining indicted war criminals, then the local population would have been involved much earlier in the mission. It is also likely that local people did report sightings of indicted war criminals to SFOR but that SFOR did not react on the received information (International Crisis Group 2000). Moreover, it is also possible that the local population did not dare to report on the whereabouts of indicted war criminals because they were afraid of revenge from supporters of the indicted war criminals. In parts of Bosnia-Herzegovina lower-level alleged war criminals stayed in powerful positions long after the violent conflict had ended (ibid.). Reports from Kosovo in particular where individuals who had cooperated with the ICTY later died under suspicious circumstances might also have deterred local people from informing SFOR about sightings of indicted war criminals (International Crisis Group 2005). The way SFOR tried to convince local people to hand over information might also not have been very fruitful. When asked how SFOR encouraged people to come forward with useful information, a senior SFOR interviewee replied that:

> I can point to examples where their local communities have been hurt by the fact that these people are still at large. And that is true at a very local level where money has been filtered out of PTT organisations, is being filtered out of local councils and out of entity governments that should have gone to roads and hospitals and infrastructure or to put their bills down all of that is true.
>
> (SFOR interview 2003)

In a community where full confidence in the local police and the prevalence of law and order has yet to be fully restored, arguing that, by handing over information, local people take away money away from often very powerful people who might then seek revenge is hardly the best incentive, especially considering that handing over information does not mean being included in a witness protection programme. The senior SFOR officer also responded that:

> I can point on a slightly greater scale that if you do not cooperate with the ICTY, if your government does not cooperate with the ICTY, the ICTY is going to say bad things to Javier Solana and bad things to George Robertson about your entry into PFP (Partnership for Peace) and PFP is not a great example because that is still not well understood here but the EU is, it will mean a real economical reduction. So both membership of the PFP and NATO and membership of the European Union ... you will have heard in the paper this week some key opinion makers in the country talking about this, saying that, I think it was Mr Ivanic the foreign minister, that cooperation with the ICTY is going to be our biggest stumble block on the road to Europe and the road to NATO and he did not go on to say that we must then do something about it but it was an indication and it is being made all the time. Certainly when we are talking, whether it is me talking to press conferences or talking to people on the street, we make that point all the time. I am not making this up – it is absolutely the case.
>
> (SFOR interview 2003)

As the senior official admitted, possible membership of international organisations that local people might not have heard of or fully comprehend is not likely to convince them to come forward with sensitive information about the where-

abouts of indicted war criminals. Finally, it is also likely that the local population did not have a positive relationship with SFOR in general and thus was
not willing to help SFOR regardless of what this help consisted. Hence, it is
imperative to see the attempts to convince the local population to hand over
information about the whereabouts of the indicted war criminals in the broader
context of the general relations between the local population and the peace
enforcement mission.

Though one would think that the relationship between the peace enforcement
mission and the local population that the soldiers are sent to help is a vital key to
the success of any peace enforcement mission, relatively few studies have so far
focused on how the local population perceive peace enforcement missions.
However, some factors that make it difficult for peace enforcement missions to
establish a positive relationship with the local population have been identified.
First, as was also the case with IFOR, SFOR and KFOR, peace enforcement
missions often have a rapid turnover of staff that makes it hard for the soldiers to
form personal relationships with the local population because they are not
deployed in any one place long enough for this to happen (Pouligny 2006). In
addition, in most cases, peace enforcement soldiers do not share the same language, culture and customs as the local population, which makes it complex for
the international soldiers to communicate and form relationships with the local
population (ibid.). Often international peace enforcement soldiers do not have an
adequate number of interpreters or the interpreters are not sufficiently trained
and skilled to carry out their jobs properly (ibid.). Communication is also further
complicated in the cases where the peace enforcement soldiers are not sufficiently familiar with the official language of the peace enforcement mission.
Often the local population is also unsure about the content of the mandate of the
peace enforcement mission or they interpret the mandate differently from the
peace enforcement mission and therefore the local population form expectations
that the peace enforcement mission does not meet (ibid.). These unmet expectations then have a negative impact on the local population's relationship with the
peace enforcement mission (ibid.). In some cases previous peace enforcement or
peacekeeping missions deployed in the same area can also have a damaging
effect on the reputation of the peace enforcement mission in the eyes of the local
population (ibid.). In SFOR's case it is not unlikely that some of UNPROFOR's
actions or rather inactions, such as the passive Dutch UNPROFOR soldiers, who
witnessed but did not attempt to prevent the Srebrenica massacre, negatively
impacted the local population's view of SFOR.

A lot of research still needs to be carried out before the relationship between
the local population and a peace enforcement mission is sufficiently understood
and before the factors that positively and negatively affect the relationship are
identified. Taking into consideration that each community peace enforcement
missions are deployed to has its own history, culture and customs, preconcep-
tions of peace enforcement missions, ideas about what peace is and how it can
be restored, this will be a long and challenging process. However, based on
especially SFOR's actions and experiences, some lessons can be drawn that can

form the first tentative steps towards improving peace enforcement soldiers' ability to establish more positive relationships with the local population and to convince the local population of the importance of reporting on the whereabouts of indicted war criminals.

First, peace enforcement missions need to realise that the individuals whom they perceive as war criminals are still seen, at least by some of the local people, as war heroes who defended them against the enemy. Here it might be helpful if the peace enforcement mission attempts to convey to the local population that defending one's own community against the enemy is praiseworthy but that using any means available is not. Hence, the action that the indicted war criminal is held accountable for is not that he defended his local community but that he used unlawful means and methods to do so. It is also important that the peace enforcement mission understands that for the local population the issue of accountability is highly sensitive and turning in an indicted war criminal from one's own community is not necessarily an easy step to take.

The lack of cooperation from the local population also needs to be seen in the context of the relationship between the local population and the international criminal tribunal. For the people in the former Yugoslavia the ICTY's location in The Hague meant that the tribunal was seated far away from the communities affected by the atrocities. The lack of information filtering through to the local people also meant that they did not know much about what was going on in The Hague (Askin 2003, Ratner and Abrams 2001, Schvey 2003). It is also likely that the local population perceived the ICTY and its accountability process as something that had been imposed on them and that it was not a part of (ibid.). The lack of perceived ownership of, and participation in, the accountability process is likely to have contributed to the local population's lack of commitment to assisting the peace enforcement missions in locating indicted war criminals.

It is also possible that, due to the continued power of some of the indicted war criminals, local people also feared that handing over information about the whereabouts of indicted war criminals might come at considerable personal cost for the informer in the form of threats from, or actual assaults by, the supporters of the indicted war criminals. Hence offering a financial reward for information and arguing that the state will be denied the opportunity to join influential regional organisations as long as indicted war criminals are at large might not be the best inducements. A financial reward might convince local people to hand over information about indicted war criminals who no longer hold powerful positions in their community and widespread support since it will then be relatively safe for local people to assist the peace enforcement missions. However, when this is not the case and where therefore the informant and his or her family are likely to be in danger if it becomes known that they have cooperated with the peace enforcement mission, a financial reward in itself is unlikely to be enough to convince anyone to hand over sensitive information. Likewise, linking the handover of information with financial assistance to the local community like SFOR did is also not necessarily the best way to convince the local population to report sightings of indicted war criminals (SFOR interview 2003). If indicted war criminals still have so much power that they are able to draw money out of the funds of the local communities, then they are also likely to be able to threaten individuals who inform peace enforcement soldiers of their where-abouts. In addition the states that used to be a part of the former Yugoslavia are in a unique position in that both the peace enforcement operations and inter-national NGOs have invested a lot of money in rebuilding the local communities which means that local communities have a lot to lose. Other peace enforcement missions might not be deployed in areas where a lot of money is being invested in rebuilding the local communities and where therefore the local communities have a lot to lose financially if the indicted war criminals are not detained. Linking the handover of information to the state's potential membership of influential regional or international organisations is also not a sustainable prac-tice. In addition, unlike the states in the former Yugoslavia, the majority of states where peace enforcement missions are deployed are not in a situation where membership of influential international organisations is around the corner and, even if that were the case, then local people have not necessarily heard about the organisations or understood what membership of one would mean for their own life. Rather than focusing on financial gains at the micro- and macro-economic levels, it is important that the handing over of sensitive information about indicted war criminals in cases where the indicted war criminals still remain powerful is linked to some sort of protection programme that can ensure the safety of the informer and his or her family. Such a programme could poten-tially be linked to the international criminal tribunal's victim and witness protec-tion programme. In cases where the risk of handing over information is relatively low, it is important that the reporting of sightings of indicted war criminals is linked to the need for accountability for atrocities committed during the violent conflict in order to reconcile the former warring parties.

It is also important that peace enforcement missions acknowledge that, if they are to convince the local population to assist them in locating indicted war crim-inals, it is paramount that they treat the local population with respect during the detention operations. This includes recognising the inconveniences local people suffer when search or detention operations are carried out in their area. It also includes a full commitment to protecting the local population from any kind of physical or psychological harm when operations are implemented. If search or detention operations cause damages to private people's property or if local people are wrongly detained, it is important that the peace enforcement mission promptly accepts responsibility and pays out compensation.

Conclusion

Experience from IFOR and SFOR shows that merely relying on peace enforce-ment soldiers recognising indicted war criminals while they carry out their ordinary duties is not adequate if peace missions are to successfully locate and detain indicted war criminals. Like national police forces, peace enforcement missions also need other actors to look out for indicted war criminals and to report any sightings or other relevant information about the whereabouts of indicted war criminals back to the peace enforcement mission. Several different actors can potentially help peace enforcement missions locate indicted war criminals. Two of the most obvious allies in the process of locating indicted war criminals are the international criminal tribunal that indicted the war criminals and the international human rights NGOs that are deployed in the peace enforcement mission's area of operation, as they share an interest in the indicted war criminals being located, detained and held accountable. Both actors are involved in investigating the atrocities that have been committed and both actors are likely to have a lot of contact with the local population and therefore also likely to come across information that if it is passed on and in a timely manner, could assist the peace enforcement soldiers in locating indicted war criminals. However, experience from Bosnia-Herzegovina has also shown that the relationship between the peace enforcement mission and the international criminal tribunal and international human rights NGOs is not always straightforward and cooperative. A lack of appreciation of each others' interests and resources can negatively influence the relationship between the different parties. In the case of SFOR and the ICTY and the international human rights NGOs operating in Bosnia-Herzegovina, the international organisations failed to fully appreciate that, whereas the international criminal tribunal and international human rights NGOs can relentlessly pursue justice, the peace enforcement mission also needs to consider the consequences of pursuing justice and it is also responsible for carrying out numerous other tasks. Peace enforcement missions are often deployed in order to help implement a peace agreement and unless this peace agreement clearly excludes all alleged war criminals from the peace process, the peace enforcement mission is likely to have to tolerate the fact that alleged war criminals play significant roles in the peace process at least until the moment when they are indicted. Hence, if alleged war criminals are located, detained and held accountable, it might at least in the short term negatively impact the peace enforcement mission's attempt to implement the peace agreement. Supporters of alleged war criminals are also likely to vent their anger about the detention of indicted war criminals on the peace enforcement mission. Thus, in contrast to the case with the international criminal tribunal and the international human rights NGOs, locating and detaining indicted war criminals might have negative consequences for the peace enforcement missions and therefore make them hesitant to locate and detain indicted war criminals. If international criminal tribunals and international human rights NGOs are to develop a positive working relationship with the peace enforcement mission, it is important that the organisations consider this when they assess the performance of the peace enforcement mission. International criminal tribunals and human rights NGOs also need to recognise that other factors, such as a lack of resources and political support, might negatively impact the peace enforcement mission's ability to detain indicted war criminals. On the other hand peace enforcement missions also need to realise that, if they want to receive help from the international criminal tribunal and human rights NGOs, then they need to show the international organisations that they act on the information the organisations have provided and that they appreciate the help the organisations are offering them. Hence, though these organisations can provide significant assistance to the peace enforcement missions in their quest to locate indicted war criminals, effective assistance and relations between the peace enforcement mission and the international criminal tribunal and human rights NGOs cannot be taken for granted but require efforts from all the involved parties.

Peace enforcement missions can also benefit from the assistance of other international NGOs and from the local population who are likely to come across essential information about the whereabouts of indicted war criminals. However, whereas it is in the immediate interest of international criminal tribunals and human rights NGOs to assist peace enforcement missions, this is not necessarily the case for other international NGOs and for the local population in general. The successful outcome of the work of other international NGOs might depend on the organisations being seen as impartial and this might be jeopardised if the organisations begin to assist peace enforcement missions in locating indicted war criminals. The local population might also not be interested in assisting the peace missions in locating indicted war criminals for reasons such as the continued support of the indicted war criminals or fear of reprisal if the assistance became publicly known. If peace enforcement missions want to receive the assistance of these parties, they need to find ways of overcoming these obstacles. Peace enforcement missions need to accept that these international organisations might not always be able to share all information about indicted war criminals with the peace enforcement missions. On the other hand international NGOs also need to acknowledge that peace enforcement missions need information from third parties if they are to successfully detain indicted war criminals and hence, if it does not harm the international NGOs, then any information they obtain about indicted war criminals should be swiftly passed on to the peace enforcement mission. Concerning the cooperation from the local population the implementation of a solid reliable witness protection programme that also covers informants and a guarantee of absolute anonymity might help convince the local population, to pass on information about the whereabouts of indicted war criminals to the peace enforcement mission. Involving the local population in, and securing local ownership of, the transitional justice process might also make the local population more inclined to help peace enforcement missions locate indicted war criminals.

13 Peace enforcement soldiers cannot do it alone

Involving international and local agencies in apprehending indicted war criminals

Introduction

Since the ICTY began indicting war criminals it has been widely debated who should be involved in detaining the individuals the tribunal wanted to prosecute in addition to or instead of ordinary peace enforcement soldiers.[45] Many suggestions, some more controversial than others, have been considered and discussed. At the extreme end of the spectrum of possible alternatives to letting peace enforcement soldiers detain indicted war criminals lies the research editor of the *Columbia Journal of Law and Social Problems* Beverly Izes's proposition of authorising state-sanctioned abductions of indicted war criminals and Major Christopher M. Supernor's proposal to legalise international bounty hunters (Izes 1997, Supernor 2001). More plausible alternatives or supplements include using external Special Forces such as SFOR and KFOR, have done, setting up an international tracking or arresting team such as Del Ponte has proposed, setting up a special unit within the peace enforcement mission or involving the international or the local police. Mainly based on the experience of IFOR, SFOR and KFOR this chapter discusses the viability of including these various actors in the process of apprehending indicted war criminals and it initiates the development of a framework for including them.

External special forces

Both SFOR and KFOR have used external Special Forces in some of their detention operations. Already in 1996 NATO established a special team consisting of special military forces from Germany, Holland, France, the US and UK, which was requested to coordinate operations aimed at detaining indicted war criminals (Kalinauskas 2002). SFOR initiated the use of Special Forces in July 1997 when British SAS soldiers were flown into Bosnia-Herzegovina and helped SFOR detain its first indicted war criminals Milan Kovacevic and Simo Drljaca (Sharp 1997). Six months later a special Dutch army unit helped SFOR detain indicted war criminals Anto Furundzija and Vlatko Kupreskic (Major Clarke 18 December 1997). The special Dutch army unit was apparently placed under SFOR control for this operation only (ibid.). Two years later British SAS forces detained indicted war criminal Stanislav Galic (Captain Theriault 21 December 1999). British Special Forces apparently also assisted KFOR in the detention of Haradin Bala, Isak Musliu and Agim Murtezi in February 2003 (Jennings 17 February 2003). Hence experience from both SFOR and KFOR indicates that external Special Forces can contribute positively to the process of detaining indicted war criminals.

However, it is still debatable whether or not future peace enforcement missions should rely on external Special Forces carrying out challenging detention operations. Arguments supporting the use of Special Forces include:

1   Especially in the immediate aftermath of the violent conflict some detention operations might be deemed too dangerous for ordinary peace enforcement soldiers to carry out (Col Eiting 2001). Thus, rather than not attempting to detain the indicted war criminals, a plausible alternative is to call on Special Forces, who have received special training in carrying out dangerous operations, to carry out dangerous operations aiming at detaining indicted war criminals.

2   When indicted war criminals might be hiding in places where it is difficult to detain them, as has been the case on several occasions in Bosnia-Herzegovina (NATO 28 February 2002, 1 March 2002), it might be easier for Special Forces with training and experience in operating in strenuous terrain to detain the indicted war criminals.

3   In contrast to peace enforcers, soldiers in Special Forces have been trained together and are used to working together and thus may be better equipped to carry out detention operations.

Arguments against peace enforcement missions relying on the assistance of Special Forces in carrying out detention operations include:

1   It takes time to have Special Forces flown in to detain the indicted war criminals and therefore valuable time might be lost since the indicted war criminals will have more time to escape from the location where the peace enforcement missions expect to find them.

2   Letting Special Forces detain indicted war criminals might send the signal that the peace enforcement mission is unable to carry out its mandate on its own.

3   Special Forces are accustomed to utilising considerable force in their operations, which is prone to increase the likelihood of injuries to the indicted war criminal and local citizens who happen to be around the subject at the time of the detention operation.

4   For future peace enforcement missions it might not be possible to receive assistance from Special Forces outside the peace enforcement mission either because of a lack of military will or because the infrastructure makes external assistance difficult to attain.

In conclusion, especially in the immediate aftermath of violent conflict where the security situation is still very fragile and in cases where indicted war criminals can be expected to be heavily armed and maintain considerable support, there might be situations where Special Forces represent the most suitable option. However, it is vital that peace enforcement missions do not become dependent upon assistance from Special Forces since they may not always be the most desirable and feasible solution.

The peace enforcement mission's international military police

In addition to soldiers some peace missions now also include international military police officers. The peace enforcement missions in both Bosnia-Herzegovina and Kosovo included a military police unit called the Multinational Specialised Unit (MSU).

In Bosnia-Herzegovina the MSU was deployed in August 1998 before the first elections (SFOR August 2004). The unit was established in order to fill the public order security gap between the peace enforcement soldiers and the civilian police and it was requested that it support the activities of the peace enforcement soldiers, local police, Office of the High Representative and the ICTY (ibid.). This included collecting special information, monitoring compliance with the DPA and handling civil disturbances (ibid.). The MSU comprised police forces with military status, which meant that it was capable of executing a wide range of military and police tasks (ibid.). The MSU used minimum force, focused on the civilian population and often divided into smaller units to carry out different operations (ibid.). Though not officially requested to detain indicted war criminals, the MSU became increasing involved in these operations over the years (SFOR interview 2003). The MSU apparently did not carry out any detention operations on their own but did assist SFOR's peace enforcement soldiers in detaining indicted war criminals. An example of this assistance took place in the beginning of April 2004 when MSU assisted SFOR soldiers from the UK and the US in their attempt to detain Radovan Karadžić in Pale (SFOR 1 April 2004).

Like their colleagues in Bosnia-Herzegovina the MSU in Kosovo is a police force with military status (KFOR 11 October 2007). The unit in the main consists of Italian Carabinieris and French Gendarmers who perform a wide variety of tasks including gathering information, assisting UNMIK in enforcing the rule of law, carrying out special police operations, countering terrorism, tackling organised crime, handling civil disturbances and helping KFOR peace enforcement soldiers to maintain a secure environment (KFOR interview 2003, KFOR 11 October 2007). The MSU get in contact with the local communities through their many patrol activities (KFOR 11 October 2007). Though not a part of the MSU's explicit tasks, it was military police officers from the unit who assisted Special Forces from Britain in the detention of the indicted war criminals Haradin Bala, Isak Musliu and Agim Murtezi in February 2003 (KFOR interview 2003).

Hence experience from both Bosnia-Herzegovina and Kosovo indicate that military police officers can play a constructive role in the detention of indicted war criminals. This has already been recognised in NATO's military peace enforcement doctrine, which emphasises that military police taking part in a peace enforcement mission might need to be involved in the prosecution of war criminals (NATO Standardization Agency 2001a: 5–8(0530)). One of the advantages of including military police officers in the detention of indicted war criminals is that they are trained and have experience in police activities such as investigating crimes and detaining criminals (Hendrickx 2001). Therefore it is likely that they will be better at gathering the intelligence that is a prerequisite for successful detention of indicted war criminals. Based on the experience of the MSU in Kosovo, where military police officers, through their frequent patrols interacted with the local population, it would seem that they are likely to be better at gathering intelligence from the local population concerning the whereabouts of indicted war criminals than peace enforcement soldiers (KFOR 11 October 2007). Since military police officers are used to detaining indicted criminals, it is also more likely that they will be able to carry out the detention of indicted war criminals in accordance with international standards, which is one of the preconditions for a successful conviction. They are also used to applying less force than peace enforcement soldiers and hence it is less likely that the indicted war criminals or bystanders would be injured or killed during the detention operation. In cases where a detention operation requires cooperation between different actors, military police officers also have the advantage that they are used to cooperating with military units (Hendrickx 2001). Finally, experience from Bosnia-Herzegovina and Kosovo also shows that military police officers are often drawn from the Italian Carabineri or the French Gendarmerie, which means that the officers have trained together and that they have prior experience in working together.

However, there are also some disadvantages of using military police officers in the detention of indicted war criminals. In cases where, for example, the indicted war criminal is heavily armed or surrounded by supporters willing to defend him, it might be too dangerous for military police officers to carry out the detention. In addition, some peace enforcement missions still do not include military police officers which obviously excludes the option of always leaving it to military police officers to detain indicted war criminals as it is unlikely that military police officers would be included in a peace enforcement mission solely to detain indicted war criminals. Furthermore in all peace enforcement missions so far the number of military police officers has been significantly lower than the number of peace enforcement soldiers. Hence, if detentions are left exclusively to military police officers, a significantly lower number of people will be involved in the search for and detention of indicted war criminals than would be the case if the task was left to peace enforcement soldiers to carry out.

In conclusion, though it should not be left solely to military police officers to detain indicted war criminals, they can potentially play a significant role in such detentions in conjunction with other actors. This will be further discussed below.

The peace enforcement mission's international police

Many peace enforcement missions today include an international police force that could potentially become involved in detaining indicted war criminals.

The peace enforcement missions in Bosnia-Herzegovina and Kosovo both included an international police force but the role of the international police was very different in the two missions. In Bosnia-Herzegovina the International Police Task Force (IPTF)[46] was mainly expected to monitor and inspect law enforcement activities and advise and train law enforcement personnel.[47] The IPTF was not authorised to take active part in the law enforcement.[48] In contrast, in Kosovo, the UNMIK police were authorised to temporarily enforce the law and to establish and develop a national police force.[49] Hence, the potential role of the IPTF in the process of detaining indicted war criminals was very different from that of the UNMIK police. The IPTF was not mandated to take active part in the detention of indicted war criminals. Instead, the IPTF was expected to report to IFOR when the international police officers came across indicted war criminals (Ivanko 13 February 1996). Several incidents indicated that the communication and cooperation between IPTF and IFOR was far from optimal. In August 1996 indicted war criminal Radovan Stankovic entered an IPTF office to file a report of harassment against the local police in Bosnia-Herzegovina who had attempted to arrest him (President of the ICTY 1997). Following this incident an IPTF spokesman stated that IPTF was not obliged to inform IFOR that an indicted war criminal was present in their offices (ibid.). This incident and other difficulties encountered with the local police force in Republika Srpska led to IPTF tightening their procedures to ensure that UN personnel did not come into contact with indicted war criminals (ibid.). Another incident was uncovered in the end of October 1996, when it became apparent that the IPTF had not swiftly reported to IFOR that several indicted war criminals were still working as police officers in the police stations in Prijedor and Omarska (Anonymous questioner 29 October 1996, Murphy 30 October 1996). On that occasion Commissioner Fitzgerald from the IPTF contended that, if the IPTF came across indicted war criminals, they should report this to IFOR (Commissioner Fitzgerald 31 October 1996). However, he also admitted that they would not immediately call IFOR but rather inform them about it at presumably a later stage (ibid.). Finally, in the middle of December some IPTF officers spotted Karadzic driving around in a police-guarded convoy of cars but it took the IPTF a couple of hours to report the sighting to IFOR (Major Boudreau 11 December 1996). According to IPTF spokesman Ivanko, it took such a long time because the IPTF officers were surprised to see Karadžić driving around in the open and because the officers' radios were only able to report back to the IPTF station and not directly to IFOR (Ivanko 11 December 1996). Ivanko also admitted that the communication had been too slow and that this had to be looked into (Ivanko 12 December 1996). He also acknowledged that IPTF had received posters of the indicted war criminals but he was not sure how widely they had been distributed and how many of them had actually been put up (ibid.). A review of documents, press releases and press conferences relating to SFOR's operations aimed at detaining indicted war criminals also reveals that the IPTF and its predecessor, the European Union Police Mission, (EUPM) which it took over from in 2003, did not play a significant role in the detention of indicted war criminals in Bosnia-Herzegovina. In contrast to the IPTF, UNMIK police were authorised to take active part in the law enforcement in Kosovo and therefore could potentially have participated actively in the detention of indicted war criminals. However, on the occasions where KFOR detained indicted war criminals, UNMIK police were not included in the operations (UNMIK interview 2003).

Hence, international police were not involved in the detention of indicted war criminals in any of the peace enforcement missions. However, there are some potential advantages of involving the international police in the detention of indicted war criminals. First, involving the civilian international police force is a solution favoured by the British, American and NATO peace enforcement doctrines (Army, Marine Corps, Navy and Air Force 2003: VI-12(h.1, h.4), NATO Standardization Agency 2001a: 6–7(0625e.), 6–14(0634), Joint Doctrine and Concepts Centre 2004: 5–24(554), 5–26(560)). Using international police officers is also recommended because these operations are usually considered to be a police job, that it takes police training and experience to carry out successfully (Hendrickx 2001, KFOR interviews 2003, Reenen 2001). It has also been contended that, whereas the military forces are trained to never retreat, police officers are accustomed to deferring an arrest if the circumstances do not allow for a successful arrest in accordance with police standards (Hendrickx 2001). Thus the chance of injury to the civilian population, the indicted war criminal or the individuals carrying out the detention is less when using police forces compared to military forces (ibid.). Also the police generally also have clearer and more basic rules for using firearms, making it less likely that people would be injured during the detention operations (Reenen 2001). In 2003 a senior officer from UNMIK police also argued that UNMIK police had the capacity, expertise and special units needed to carry out detention operations (UNMIK interview 2003). The same police officer also pointed out that UNMIK police had already successfully arrested very dangerous terrorist suspects (ibid.). Another senior UNMIK police officer supported this view and contended that UNMIK was able to carry out the detention operations even if the detention would lead to demonstrations and create negative feelings among the local population towards UNMIK police (UNMIK interview 2003). The first senior UNMIK police officer also reasoned that:

> In a sense it does enforce it, does enhance the image of the rule of law when civilian police are seen to do these things. One of the messages that we have consistently been giving to people is that no one is above the law and I believe that when you use civilian police to make such arrests as these it is sending the strong message to the public that it does not matter whether you are a war criminal or a car thief, you are a criminal and the police will deal with you. So perhaps calling on the military sends the wrong message,

calling them, by effectively creating a special class of criminals if you send helicopters and special forces and whisk them out at midnight in black military aircraft, it creates a climate of secrecy and it dramatises and romanticises them. Whereas if the ordinary police arrest these people and take them out in handcuffs as ordinary criminals, it demystifies them and it builds support among the general population although undoubtedly it would cause some reaction.

(UNMIK interview 2003)

Against the use of international police detaining indicted war criminals it has been argued that indicted war criminals might be willing and able to use considerable force in order to avoid being detained and that consequently the international police would not be able to handle the detention operation (Reenen 2001). The level of resistance from the local population and the danger they may pose to the international police have also been used as arguments against involving international police in the detention of indicted war criminals (ibid.). It has also been argued that in contrast to military police officers, ordinary international police officers are not used to communicating with soldiers (Hendrickx 2001). Finally, a senior police officer from UNMIK has also argued that, in situations where the indicted war criminal has a large public following, the detention of the indicted war criminal by the international police, might result in public reactions against the international police which would negatively impact on the population's relationship with not only the international police but also the international civilian administration that the international police is a part of (UNMIK interview 2003). Hence, by leaving the detention of indicted war criminals to the peace enforcement soldiers, the international police is kept away from the unpopular detention operations (ibid.).

In conclusion, though international police officers have yet to become involved in detaining indicted war criminals, they could potentially play a significant role in the process of bringing indicted war criminals to justice. The arguments against involving them in the detention of indicted war criminals indicate that their role might be limited in cases where the indicted war criminals are likely to be armed and to resist the detention and where the local population might also fiercely protest against the detention. However, this does not mean that international police officers should not participate in the detention of indicted war criminals in other cases. The question that future peace enforcement missions need to address is thus not necessarily whether or not the international police should be involved but rather when the international police should become involved in the detention of indicted war criminals. This will be further addressed below.

Special detention unit within peace enforcement mission

Neither the peace enforcement missions in Bosnia-Herzegovina nor the one in Kosovo set up a special unit solely aimed at detaining indicted war criminals and hence there is no experience from the field concerning the advantages and disadvantages of having such a unit.

It is debatable whether or not peace enforcement missions should establish a unit that only focuses on detaining indicted war criminals. NATO SG Lord Robertson has already argued against the establishment of a special unit, since he contended that it is better that all peace enforcement soldiers are committed to detaining indicted war criminals rather than just relying on a small, specialised unit (NATO SG Lord Robertson 21 December 2000). It can also be argued that, especially in the immediate phase after their deployment, peace enforcement missions are expected to carry out a lot of challenging tasks with often relatively limited resources. Hence, it is not feasible for the peace enforcement mission to form a group of soldiers solely to the tasks of locating and detaining indicted war criminals. Especially in the immediate aftermath of the violent conflict, it might also be politically contentious if such a unit was established, since this would place a lot of focus on the issue of accountability at a time when the negative peace is still fragile.

However, there are also several plausible arguments to support the setting up of a specialised unit. First, if a specialised unit was set up it would ensure that at least some members of the peace enforcement mission were engaged in locating and detaining indicted war criminals. The establishment of a permanent unit would also mean that its members could build up a lot of knowledge and experience in locating and detaining indicted war criminals. The setting up of a dedicated unit also does not preclude that other peace enforcement soldiers from helping the unit locate and detain the indicted war criminals. Compared with members of an international tracking or arresting team that will be further discussed below, a special unit within the peace enforcement mission would hopefully also know more about the situation on the ground and the culture, customs and people of the community they are deployed in, which would enhance their chances of detaining indicted war criminals successfully. It is most definitely also easier to gain international political support for the establishment of specialised unit within the specific peace enforcement mission rather than an international tracking or arresting team that can potentially be deployed anywhere in the world. The establishment of a specialised unit would also open up new ways of cooperation on the issue of locating and detaining indicted war criminals, since such a unit could potentially include not only peace enforcement soldiers but also military police officers, international police officers and ultimately also local police officers and representatives from local authorities. Such a cooperation could potentially also smoothes the process of transferring the responsibility of locating and detaining indicted war criminals from initially the peace enforcement soldiers to ultimately the local police within the broader framework of the transferral of powers from international to national agencies.

In conclusion, the establishment of a unit specialising in locating and detaining indicted war criminals has some potential that is yet to be fully explored.

The local authorities and the local police

Throughout IFOR's mission the local authorities in Republika Srpksa did nothing to help IFOR and the ICTY detain indicted war criminals (President of the ICTY 1996, 1997). The local authorities in the Federation of Bosnia-Herzegovina advertised the indictments they received from the ICTY on TV and radio and in newspapers and in many cases claimed that the indicted war criminals were not living in areas under their control (ibid.). During SFOR's mission the assistance of the local authorities in Republika Srpska in the pursuit of indicted war criminals did not improve much and the local authorities were on numerous occasions criticised for not attempting to detain indicted war criminals in their area (President of the ICTY 1997, 1998, 1999, 2000, 2001, 2002, 2003, 2004, 2005). In contrast, except on a few occasions, the local authorities in the Federation of Bosnia-Herzegovina were praised for their cooperation with the ICTY (ibid.). However, it has to be kept in mind that most of the time during SFOR's deployment many fewer indicted war criminals were at large in the territory of the Federation of Bosnia-Herzegovina and thus the local authorities were not much involved in the detention of indicted war criminals (ibid.).

In Kosovo the local authorities were not involved in detaining indicted war criminals.

Experience from Bosnia-Herzegovina underlines some of the disadvantages of involving local authorities in the detention of indicted war criminals. In Bosnia-Herzegovina the local authorities had been heavily involved in the violent conflict and therefore the ICTY could not rely on local authorities to detain and hand over indicted war criminals (Hendrickx 2001, Leurdijk 2001). Experience from Bosnia-Herzegovina even showed that, unless the local authorities were only told about the detention operations shortly before they were carried out, the detention operations were doomed to fail because the indicted war criminal could be warned and given an opportunity to escape (Ruxton 2001).

However, there are also several reasons as to why local authorities need to be kept on board in the process of locating and detaining indicted war criminals. At least ideally peace enforcement missions are deployed to help local authorities and communities recover from violent conflict and not to take over power of the territory and carry out all tasks on their own. Hence, it is important that local authorities continue to participate in all activities aimed at developing sustainable peace. It is also highly likely that it is easier for local authorities than for any international agency to locate and detain indicted war criminals. Furthermore, it is not unlikely that the peace enforcement soldiers will end their mission before all indicted war criminals are detained and hence, ultimately it will be up to the local authorities to detain the indicted war criminals remaining at large.

During IFOR's deployment the development of a democratic local civilian police force in Bosnia-Herzegovina was still in its infancy. This was underlined towards the end of IFOR's mission when it was reported that several indicted war criminals were still working as police officers in Prijedor and Omarska (Anonymous questioner 29 October 1996, Murphy 30 October 1996, President of the ICTY 1997). Hence, IFOR did not involve local police forces in their scarce activities to detain indicted war criminals. However, in the Federation of Bosnia-Herzegovina the local police on their own detained Hazim Delic and

Esad Landzo in May 1996 (President of the ICTY 1996). The local police in Republika Srpska did not take any actions to detain the indicted war criminals who were apparently living in their area (President of the ICTY 1996, 1997).

Up until the end of SFOR's mission the local police in Republika Srpska did not attempt to detain any indicted war criminals allegedly at large within their territory (President of the ICTY 1997, 1998, 1999, 2000, 2001, 2002, 2003). In 2004 the local police in Republika Srpska attempted a couple of times to detain lower-level indicted war criminals but none of the attempts was successful (President of the ICTY 2004). During SFOR's mission there were hardly any indicted war criminals at large within the territory of the Federation of Bosnia-Herzegovina (President of the ICTY 1997, 1998, 1999, 2000, 2001, 2002, 2003, 2004, 2005). On one occasion the local police did not respond to the handover of the arrest warrant against Dragan Gagovic and his seven fellow indictees (President of the ICTY 1998). In contrast on another occasion in 2001, the local police detained Enver Hadzihasanovic, Mehmed Alagic and Amir Kubura (Office of the Prosecutor 3 August 2001). All in all the local police in both the Federation of Bosnia- Herzegovina and Republika Srpska were not much involved in independently detaining indicted war criminals.

At the start of SFOR's mission the local police were also not involved in SFOR's activities to detain indicted war criminals. SFOR only informed the local police about their planned operations right before they were carried out (SFOR interview 2003). However, in the latter years of its mission SFOR began to request assistance from the local police when carrying out detention operations. This was the case in SFOR's operation to detain Radovan Karadžić in the Celebici area on 28 February and 1 March 2002 when SFOR cooperated with the Ministry of Interior Police from Republika Srpska (Domin 2002). In June 2002 the local police in Republika Srpska helped the Office of the Prosecutor and SFOR search different locations in order to obtain evidence in Republika Srpska (President of the ICTY 2002). In connection with the searches the local police also responded to a protest from the public (ibid.). In addition, during SFOR's search operations in southern Republika Srpska in August 2002, the local police also assisted SFOR by upholding law and order while the SFOR soldiers searched the buildings (Major Lundy 15 August 2002). Finally, the local police in Republika Srpska also provided operational support to SFOR's search operations in Banja Luka and Pale (SFOR 15 October 2004, 21 October 2004).

In contrast to their colleagues in Bosnia-Herzegovina, the local police in Kosovo were not involved at all in detaining indicted war criminals (UNMIK interviews2003).

If the local police in Bosnia-Herzegovina and Kosovo had been heavily involved in detaining indicted war criminals, then obviously there would have been no need for the peace enforcement missions to get involved and therefore also no need to write this book. Hence, it is hardly surprising that a review of the local police's involvement in detaining indicted war criminals reveals that they played only a very marginal role. There are several reasons why the local police did not become more involved in detaining indicted war criminals. First, some indicted war criminals managed to keep their positions within the local police force, which indicates that at least parts of the local police did not support attempts to hold individuals accountable for the violations they had committed during the violent conflict (President of the ICTY 1997). It is also likely that other members of the local police forces than those indicted had also been involved in the conflict and would therefore not be interested in taking part in the detention of indicted war criminals. In addition, in contrast to the powers of UNMIK police in Kosovo, the IPTF was not authorised to compel the local police forces to implement certain policies or get involved in activities such as detaining indicted war criminals (Hendrickx 2001). Furthermore, the continued support for indicted war criminals, especially among the local population in Republika Srpska, might also have deterred the local police in Republika Srpska from getting involved in detaining indicted war criminals. In Kosovo the detention operations were deemed too dangerous and too unpopular for the local police to be involved in (UNMIK interview 2003). Thus, based on the experience of the local police in Bosnia-Herzegovina and Kosovo, there are many plausible reasons as to why the local police were not involved in detaining indicted war criminals. However, there are also some good reasons as to why the local police should not be left out of the process of detaining indicted war criminals. First, the idea behind developing a democratic and effective local police force is necessarily that it should ultimately be in charge of enforcing the rule of law in its area of operation. Since detaining indicted war criminals is an important part of enforcing the rule of law in a post-conflict society, it would undermine the credibility of the local police force if they were totally excluded from taking part in detaining indicted war criminals. In addition the local police are likely to be better at locating and detaining indicted war criminals because they know their area and its people better than their international counterparts. Furthermore, if all indicted war criminals are not arrested by the time the peace enforcement soldiers and international police officers finish their mission, it will inevitably be up to the local police to detain the remaining indicted war criminals. Hence the question is not whether the local authorities and the local police should be involved in detaining indicted war criminals but rather at what time they need to become involved in detaining indicted war criminals.

An international tracking team

In 2001 in frustration over the many unexecuted arrest warrants on grounds of claims that the location of the indicted war criminals was unknown, ICTY Prosecutor Del Ponte suggested the establishment of an international tracking team able to establish the whereabouts of indicted war criminals (Del Ponte 15 December 2005, Joris 2 May 2001). At the time such a team had already been set up to track down individuals on the ICTR's list of wanted indicted war criminals. Del Ponte discussed the plan with NATO officials and Western governments, who were apparently not too supportive of the idea, since the outcome was the establishment of a very small unit consisting of four investigators working under the Office of the Prosecutor (Del Ponte 15 December 2005, Joris 2 May 2001, Leurdijk 2001). Due to a lack of the human and technical resources necessary for initiating advanced intelligence operations, the tracking team focused on coordinating the collection of information about the whereabouts of the indicted war criminals carried out by the involved states and international organisations and analysing it (Del Ponte 15 December 2005, Nikiforov 2006). The tracking team managed to establish the location of several indicted war criminals and passed on information to national and international authorities responsible for apprehending the indicted war criminals. However, this information was only occasionally responded to (Del Ponte 15 December 2005). For example, the tracking team provided the Russian authorities with information about the location of two indicted war criminals, Vlastimir Djordjevic and Dragan Zelenovic who were residing in Russia but the Russian authorities only managed to detain Zelenovic (ibid.). On another occasion the tracking team located indicted war criminal Goran Hadzic and informed the Serbian authorities about his location (Tolbert 2006). The tracking team even photographed someone from the Serbian authorities giving Hadzic a tip-off call (ibid.). Consequently Hadzic managed to flee and he remains at large.

Hence, based on the experience of the ICTY, there are some significant advantages to the creation of an international tracking team able to track down indicted war criminals. First, in cases where the national authorities and the peace enforcement mission are reluctant to locate the indicted war criminals, the international tracking team might be the only unit actively trying to do this. In addition an international tracking team can collect information from various sources that would not otherwise share their information and establish patterns of intelligence that could ultimately lead to the team being able to locate the indicted war criminal (Ruxton 2001). Furthermore, in cases where the international tracking team manages to locate the indicted war criminal and passes the information on to the authorities responsible for the detention, these authorities can also no longer claim that the reason why they have not detained the indicted war criminal is that they do not know their location (Del Ponte 15 December 2005, Leurdijk 2001).

However, relying on an international tracking team to establish the whereabouts of indicted war criminals also has some considerable shortfalls. First, as the experience of the ICTY's tracking team illustrated, the fact that an international tracking team locates indicted war criminals and passes the information on to the detaining authority does not automatically mean that the indicted war criminals are also successfully apprehended (Lopez-Terres 2006). It was also difficult for the tracking team to collect information on its own so the team still relies on obtaining information from uncooperative states and international organisations that may be very reluctant to share their intelligence (ibid.). In some cases valuable time was also lost from when the tracking team had established a location to when this information reached those expected to those carry out the detention (Leurdijk 2001). If an international tracking team is established, then it might also lead to the peace enforcement mission and the local authorities, for whom collecting intelligence is likely to be easier than for the international tracking team, feeling that they can scale down their own tracking activities. It is also likely that it will be more difficult for an international tracking team than for peace enforcement missions and local authorities to establish a network of intelligence sources that is often vital for locating indicted war criminals.

The ICTY's international tracking team was set up as a last resort because no other authorities were able or willing to persistently track down indicted war criminals. The experience of the ICTY and SFOR and keeping in mind that the main problem of detaining indicted war criminals still persisted after the creation of the international tracking team, indicates that a tracking team should only be engaged if no other national or international agency has been able or willing to locate indicted war criminals. Hence, at least initially, it should be left to the detaining authority to locate indicted war criminals.

An international arresting team

The creation of an international arresting team able to arrest indicted war criminals has only ever been discussed and never implemented. Hence there is no experience to base an assessment of the usefulness of such a team on.

The use of an international arresting team would necessarily have certain advantages. First, it has been argued that the main components for an international arresting team, such as international military police officers, are already available and hence such a team could be established relatively quickly (Leurdijk 2001). An international arresting team that solely focuses on arresting indicted war criminals regardless of where they are residing would also significantly increase the likelihood of detentions. Such a team would be able to gain a lot of experience in locating and detaining indicted war criminals and they would be able to develop their own techniques, methods and expertise that would hopefully in the longer term enable them to locate them to do this effectively. An international arresting team can also be tailored to specific time-frames and scenarios (Col Wiggen 2001).

However, there are also plenty of arguments against reliance on an international arresting team to carry out the detention of indicted war criminals. First, the existence of an international arresting team is likely to render national authorities and international peace enforcement missions less inclined to do the job themselves (Unknown Participant in Workshop 1 2001). There is also a danger of revenge against international forces on the ground if an international arresting team detains indicted war criminals who still enjoy a lot of local support (Col Wiggen 2001). Within an international arresting team the participating nations might also have divergent operational and political points of view that might impair its work (ibid.). An international arresting team, as opposed to local authorities, will also be disadvantaged concerning factors such as language skills, knowledge of local customs and culture, ethnicity, appearance and the ability to gain trust locally (ibid.). If an external international arresting team is relied upon, then the transfer of the responsibility for detaining indicted war criminals to local police forces once the control of the area has been handed back to local authorities will also be more difficult, since the arresting team is not likely to have established cooperation with the local police. The hostile environment that indicted war criminals often hide in, which will be unfamiliar to an international arresting team, also counts against reliance on such a team (Lt Col Hardenbol 2001). It is probable that controversies over rules of engagement for the arresting team and the risk of its actions escalating the conflict also speak against the proposal (ibid.). However, the most powerful argument against an international arresting team is that, despite the possible desirability of such a team, the proposal is very unlikely to muster the necessary political support (Lt Col Hardenbol 2001, Leurdijk 2001, Ruxton 2001). First, it is unlikely that states will agree to allow an international arresting team to enter any national territory and arrest a citizen without the consent of the national authorities (Ruxton 2001). Second, due to a dearth of immediate political support, a lengthy political decision process before a possible compromise can be agreed upon is inevitable, which would mean that, in any event, the setting up of an arresting team is still many years away and hence cannot be relied upon by contemporary international criminal tribunals (Lt Col Hardenbol 2001). Finally, at the moment it is also unlikely that states would permit their soldiers or military police officers to participate in dangerous operations not under their own national command without being fully informed about the operation in advance and given an opportunity to opt out if the risks are considered too high (Unknown Participant in Workshop 1 2001).

Hence at least for the foreseeable future an international arresting team is not a viable solution to the problem of detaining indicted war criminals.

Who should be involved in the detention of indicted war criminals?

In conclusion, peace enforcement soldiers, international military police officers, international police officers, a special unit focusing on detaining indicted war criminals, local police officers and local authorities all have potentially significant roles to play in the process of detaining indicted war criminals. How and when these different agencies should be involved in this process will be discussed below.

Major Hendrickx's framework for detaining indicted war criminals

The Dutch Major Hendrickx has already suggested a framework for detaining indicted war criminals (Hendrickx 2001). Called a 'Blue Box', this framework is based on the assumption that detentions have to be carried out by persons trained in policing (ibid.). Hence, in Hendrickx's framework Special Forces and peace enforcement soldiers do not carry out the actual detentions they only provide security control of the surroundings (ibid.). The actual detentions are predominantly carried out by international military police officers because they are police trained, used to working together with military personnel and experienced in carrying out operations in difficult circumstances (ibid.). When the general security situation improves and the detention operations become less challenging, the international police and ultimately the local police would begin to perform the detention operations (ibid.). Keeping in mind that the interviews were conducted four years into the international peace enforcement mission in Kosovo, when the security situation on the ground had already improved significantly, Hendrickx's model mirrors the points of view of the interviewees from KFOR and UNMIK, who all argued that actual detentions should be carried out by international police officers (KFOR interview 2003, UNMIK interview 2003). The role that Hendrickx envisaged for peace enforcement soldiers in the detentions is also in accordance with one KFOR interviewee's views, since this person argued that:

> So really our role is in support when asked to go in and secure the area and possibly to secure premises and possibly even to secure a whole area. You might need to secure several houses we might need to secure half a town.
>
> (KFOR interview 2003)

Furthermore Hendrickx's model also echoes the opinion of some of the interviewees in Kosovo that the decision as to who should carry out the detention operation is based on a tactical assessment of the dangers involved (KFOR interview 2003, UNMIK interview 2003).

Hendrickx's model also has some considerable weaknesses. First, it assumes that the peace enforcement mission includes international military police and international police units with enforcement rather than solely monitoring powers. This has not always been the case and it cannot be taken for granted that future missions will necessarily comprise such personnel, with the authority to carry out detention operations. Second, the model only includes who should be involved in the detention operation itself and does not consider the process of locating indicted war criminals, though that is a vital precondition for a successful detention as experience from Bosnia-Herzegovina especially has shown that locations are often difficult to ascertain. Third, the model argues against detention operations in the immediate aftermath of the deployment of the peace enforcement mission, though experience from Bosnia-Herzegovina indicates that it would have been much easier to detain indicted war criminals early in the mission because they were much more visible and had yet to develop networks of supporters enabling them to stay at large (SFOR interview 2003). Fourth, the model ignores experience from both SFOR and KFOR that shows both Special Forces and peace enforcement soldiers can carry out detention operations successfully. Fifth, Hendrickx seems to assume that there is a linear connection between the improvement of the general security situation and a reduction in the dangers of carrying out a detention operation. Hence, when the general security situation improves, then the detention operations also become less dangerous and can therefore be left to the international and local police. However, experience from Bosnia-Herzegovina indicates that, even though the security situation on the ground significantly improved, some indicted war criminals, most notably Radovan Karadžić, had developed networks of supporters who were seemingly willing to defend the indicted war criminals during detention attempts, and hence such attempts remained dangerous. Experience from Bosnia-Herzegovina also showed that the dangers involved in detention operations carried out at the same time varied considerably. One of the SFOR soldiers' first attempts at detaining an indicted war criminal concerned Milan Kovacevic, who was detained in his office in a hospital in Prijedor, did not resist of pose any danger (Major Riley 11 July 1997). In contrast, at the same time, other SFOR troops tried to apprehend suspect Simo Drljaca, who resisted shooting and injuring a SFOR soldier before being killed himself when SFOR returned fire (Major Riley 11 July 1997, 14 July 1997). Experience from Kosovo, where the detentions of indicted war criminals Haradin Bala, Isak Musliu and Agim Murtezi went fairly unnoticed but where the simultaneous arrest of Fatmir Limaj led to mass demonstrations also indicates that some indicted war criminals are more popular among the local population than others and hence they may be more difficult to carry out (UNMIK 26 February 2003). Furthermore, Hendrickx's model ignores that the actions of peace enforcement missions are seldom solely based on tactical considerations. Instead political considerations often dictate the division of labour within a peace enforcement mission and the activities it carries out. For example, in Kosovo, when asked whether UNMIK police were involved in detaining indicted war criminals, one senior UNMIK police officer explained that:

We can be. We have the capacity to effect these arrests. Who actually does it, is actually a political decision not a tactical decision. We have arrested terrorist suspects that were extremely dangerous. We have the capacity, we have the expertise, we have the people, we have the specialist units to make these arrests. However, it is a political decision as to whether or not UNMIK wants its police to be involved in arresting people, who have a high local profile or whether it is better to distance UNMIK from that and have the military do it. Obviously some names of the people that are suggested as possible indictees are people who have a large public following and, if they were to be arrested by the civilian police that we are a part of UNMIK, it might well result in public demonstrations or reactions against UNMIK. So in effect by using KFOR to do it, it puts UNMIK at an arm's length since the enforcement agency being the military. In that sense it is a political decision. We have got the capacity to do it. And that KFOR is given the responsibility, we can serve it with them. The last time it was exclusively a military functioning and we were not involved at all.

(UNMIK interview 2003)

Finally, Hendrickx's model also only envisaged a very limited role for the local authorities and the local police. Considering that peace enforcement missions are deployed to help local authorities rebuild their state institutions and assist the local police in enforcing the rule of law and that, if any indicted war criminals are still at large once the peace enforcement mission leaves, it will be up to local authorities and local police to detain them, it is important to acknowledge that local authorities and police officers need to become actively involved in the detention of indicted war criminals at some point after the violent conflict has ended.

A new framework for apprehending indicted war criminals

Assessing each detention operation individually

Experience from SFOR and KFOR has shown that the circumstances characterising each detention operation are very different. Some operations are significantly more dangerous than others and, when the indicted war criminal has remained popular, some can provoke widespread violent demonstrations and protests whereas others are peacefully accepted. Hence, rather than building on the highly questionable assumption that detention operations automatically become less challenging as the general security situation improves and that the responsibility for detaining indicted war criminals can therefore be linearly transferred from highly armed special forces to lightly armed police officers, it is important that each detention operation is assessed individually. This will take into account cases such as Radovan Karadžić who, until the end of SFOR's mission, eight years after its hunt for him began, maintained a network of supporters apparently willing to defend him and so, though the general security situation in Bosnia-Herzegovina significantly improved, the challenges involved in detaining Karadzic remained relatively unchanged. It will also allow military police officers or even international police officers, possibly backed up by peace enforcement soldiers, to detain indicted war criminals who have, for example, publicly expressed a willingness to surrender voluntarily once indicted, early in the mission when the general security situation is still relatively unstable. Thus it is important that a framework for locating and detaining indicted war criminals allows for each detention operation to be assessed individually.

Dividing the apprehension of indicted war criminals into three tasks: locating, securing surrounding area and detaining

The debates about detaining indicted war criminals indicate that the process of apprehending them can be meaningfully split up into several separate yet interlinked tasks. The discussions on the feasibility of setting up an international tracking team indicate that locating subjects can be a separate task, carried out by people who do not necessarily have to take part in the rest of the process towards apprehension (Del Ponte 15 December 2005, Joris 2 May 2001, Leurdijk 2001). The dialogues on the role of Special Forces, peace enforcement soldiers, international military police officers and international police officers also indicate that the people who secure the area surrounding the detention do not necessarily have to take part in the actual detention (Hendrickx 2001, Leurdijk 2001, Ruxton 2001). Thus, the process of apprehending indicted war criminals can be split up into three tasks namely, locating the indicted war criminal, securing the area surrounding the detention operation, and carrying out the actual detention. Locating indicted war criminals entails looking out for them, collecting intelligence about their whereabouts, patrolling areas and setting up roadblocks and checkpoints where they are thought to be staying and keeping them under temporary surveillance if the encounter does not permit immediate detention. It also includes establishing good relationships with and collecting information from the local and international actors who can provide vital assistance in locating indicted persons. Securing the area surrounding the detention operation includes setting up roadblocks and checkpoints in the area to temporarily control who gets in and out, keeping civilians away from the detention operations so that they are not injured and mediating with or, if the situation escalates, controlling local citizens who oppose the detention. The next stage is planning and carrying out the actual detention operation.

There are obviously many ways in which these tasks are interlinked. The people who are mainly tasked with locating indicted war criminals should be in close contact with those carrying out the actual detention operations so that, for example, any reported sightings can be promptly acted upon. The people who are mainly tasked with locating indicted war criminals also need to cooperate with those responsible for securing the surrounding area in cases where, for example, an indicted war criminal has been kept under surveillance due to the fear that the local population would readily defend him in the event of an immediate detention. Finally, there also needs to be close cooperation between those in charge of securing the area surrounding the detention operation and those carrying out the detention operation itself.

Hence, the framework should reflect that the apprehension of indicted war criminals can be divided into three separate but correlated tasks that could potentially be carried out by three different groups of people.

A special coordinating unit focusing on apprehending indicted war criminals

Experiences from, for example, Bosnia-Herzegovina, where the international police did not always swiftly report sightings of indicted war criminals to the peace enforcement soldiers and from Kosovo where, against their wishes, the international police were not involved in the detention of indicted war criminals, indicate a need for the establishment of a special unit within the peace mission to focus solely on apprehending indicted war criminals. This will help ensure that the efforts are coordinated and that the responsibility of carrying out the various tasks is smoothly moved from one agency to another in due course.

Since experience from Bosnia-Herzegovina shows that it is likely to be easier to detain indicted war criminals in the early stages of the mission and that it is especially in these that the efforts to detain indicted war criminals are uncoordinated, it is important that the coordinating unit is established from the start of the mission. Initially, it is likely that the coordinating unit will only consist of peace enforcement soldiers since they are usually the first deployed. However, it is also important that specialist advisors are included in the unit from the outset. The group of specialist advisers should preferably include representatives from the international criminal tribunal who can liaise between the tribunal and the peace enforcement mission, to help ensure a swift exchange of information between the two institutions and provide legal advice on how to carry out detention operations in accordance with international standards. It might also be necessary to include political advisors to help the mission assess the consequences of the various detention operations and advise on who should be involved. Media specialists to liaise with the local and international press and individuals to intercede with local and international actors should also preferably be included. In cases where international military police officers are not included in the peace mission at its start, it is also important that individuals with police training and experience in locating and detaining criminals are added to the coordinating unit from its beginning. As international military police officers and ordinary international police officers are added to the peace missions, representatives from these agencies should be added to the unit as well. In cases where international police officers are not granted executive powers but merely given monitoring and advising roles, it is still important that they be included since they can still help locate indicted war criminals. Finally, as local authorities and local police forces are established, representatives from these agencies should be included in due course as well. Experience especially from Bosnia-Herzegovina shows that some individuals within both the local authorities and the local police forces remain close to alleged war criminals and thus, to avoid the coordinating unit being infiltrated by individuals who will pass information on to the subjects, it is important that any of these representatives are properly vetted before inclusion in the unit. It is obviously also important that the vetting excludes individuals who have themselves been involved in committing atrocities during the violent conflict. The addition of representatives from local authorities and local police forces is likely to be the most controversial inclusion, since it might be difficult to ensure that only individuals committed to detaining indicted war criminals participate. Peace missions are likely to have to find ways of dealing with difficult situations such as local authorities and local police forces nominating candidates to the coordinating unit who are known to have links to the alleged war criminals. It is also likely that, if alleged war criminals manage to escape the peace enforcement mission's attempt to detain them after representatives from the local police and local authorities have been included in the unit, then these people will be accused of having passed information on to the indicted war criminals. On the other hand it is vital that local authorities and local police forces take part in the task of detaining indicted war criminals as early as possible as they will have to take sole responsibility when the peace mission leaves and because their contacts and assistance can help ensure a successful detention.

It is preferable that the coordinating unit is given authority to decide on who should be involved in detentions without needing the decision to be approved by the political institution behind the deployment of the peace mission or the leaders of the various national contingents within the mission. However, if this is not possible, then the peace mission should seriously consider including representatives from the political institution and the national contingents in the coordinating unit in order to ensure that plans are approved swiftly and smoothly.

Locating indicted war criminals

Ideally all members of a peace enforcement mission should be involved in locating indicted war criminals as they could all come across indicted war criminals while involved in their ordinary duties. Nevertheless, it is also important that other activities, such as gathering intelligence, are initiated from the start of the mission. In the beginning it is likely that only peace enforcement soldiers will be deployed and able to take an active part in locating indicted war criminals. However, as soon as international military police officers and international police forces are added to the mission, they should also be involved in location tasks since, in contrast to most peace enforcement soldiers, they are trained and have experience in gathering intelligence about alleged criminals. International military police officers and international police officers are also likely to be in closer contact with the local population through their patrols and hence more likely to come across useful intelligence. A precondition for an involvement in gathering intelligence about indicted war criminals is necessarily that they have executive powers rather than merely monitoring and advising roles. If the latter is the case, then they can only be involved in looking out for indicted war criminals.

Though participating in the process of locating indicted war criminals is likely to be seen as being less controversial and challenging than being involved in the actual detention operations, both tactical and political considerations might sometimes prevent international police officers especially from being involved in gathering intelligence in particular cases. If, for example, a particular indicted war criminal is known to be fiercely opposed to being transferred to the international criminal tribunal and if he has a network of armed supporters, even gathering intelligence about this particular individual might be considered dangerous. Thus the task should be carried out by trained peace enforcement soldiers rather than lightly armed international police officers. In addition, particularly initially, when the local population and authorities in many cases may still be sceptical concerning the desirability of having international police officers present in their communities, involving these officers in locating indicted war criminals who still enjoy considerable local support might negatively impact the local population's support for the presence of international police. So, in cases where the indicted war criminal still enjoys a lot of support, it is possible that political considerations will result in only peace enforcement soldiers and international military police officers being involved in locating him. However, in order to ensure that as many individuals as possible take part in locating indicted war criminals, it is important that the assessment of who should be involved is decided on a case-by- case basis so that, even if it is decided that international police officers should not take part in locating a particular individual, they can still be fully involved in locating other less controversial suspects. Though both international military police officers and international police officers are likely to be better trained and experienced in locating criminals than peace enforcement soldiers, a range of factors still means that international military and ordinary police officers do not represent the ideal solution to the problem of locating indicted war criminals. Experience from peace missions around the world has shown that international military police officers as well as ordinary international police officers often do not speak the local language and know only little about local cultures and customs and hence may find it difficult to gather intelligence effectively. Even their appearance might prevent them from, for example, being able to shadow individuals who are thought to be in contact with indicted war criminals because they will stand out from the local people. Hence, the involvement of local police officers as soon as possible is preferable. Local police officers are likely to have a better network of local contacts and are therefore also more likely to succeed in gleaning information about the whereabouts of indicted war criminals. In addition, such officers will eventually have to take over the responsibility for locating indicted war criminals, making it imperative that they are included as early as possible. However, as with the inclusion of local police officers in the coordination unit, a thorough vetting procedure and often also basic and specialised training are preconditions for the beneficial involvement of local police officers in locating indicted war criminals. The timing of their involvement will necessarily depend on how successful the establishment of an independent national police force is. If, as in the Kosovan case, a national police force is established relatively fast and the vetting procedure manages to ensure that individuals with links to indicted war criminals are excluded, then national police officers can be included relatively quickly in locating indicted war criminals. If on the other hand, progress towards establishing a national police force is as slow as it has been in Haiti, then it is likely national police officers may not become involved in locating indicted war criminals at all. This would obviously be very unfortunate since, once the peace enforcement mission has left, it will be up to the local police to locate and detain the indicted war criminals still at large and since local police officers are undoubtedly better at locating indicted war criminals if they are committed to the task. On the other hand, though it is likely that it will be more difficult for the peace mission to locate indicted war criminals without the help of the local police, excluding the local force from taking part could be preferable to situations where they constantly pass information on to the indicted war criminals about the activities of the peace enforcers.

Factors influencing who should be involved in securing surrounding area and detaining indicted war criminals

Many factors are likely to influence the decision about who should be involved in securing the area surrounding the detention operation and in the operation itself. Based on the experience in Bosnia-Herzegovina and Kosovo, it is recommendable that the following factors are taken into consideration: the characteristics of the indicted war criminal, the characteristics of the local people and the area surrounding the location of the subject and the characteristics of the political climate in which the detention operation is to take place. The assessment of the characteristics of the indicted individual should at least include an evaluation of the available intelligence on issues such as his temper, his attitude towards the international criminal tribunal, the likelihood of him having and using weapons and the likelihood of him being surrounded by people who are willing to use weapons to protect him. It should also feature an assessment of the area of the arrest and the risk of his escape. The assessment of the characteristics of the local people and the area in question should encompass an evaluation of how much support the indicted war criminal still enjoys in his neighbourhood and the likelihood that local people will defend him or protest violently against his detention. An assessment of the political climate should at least involve an evaluation of the national level of support for the international criminal tribunal in general and the specific indicted war criminal in particular, the continued political influence of indicted war criminals and the likelihood of national widespread demonstrations and violent responses to the detention operation.

Securing the surrounding area of the detention operation and carrying out the actual detention

Many different factors will necessarily influence the decisions on who should participate in securing the area surrounding the detention operation and in the actual operation. In cases where the indicted war criminal is known to be aggressive and willing and able to fight any attempts to detain him, it is obviously important that the detention operation is carried out by equally armed peace enforcement soldiers or international military police officers. The same is the case if the indicted war criminal is known to be surrounded by armed bodyguards or supporters ready to defend him. In contrast, if the indicted war criminals has expressed a willingness to surrender voluntarily, if he were to be indicted and is known to be unarmed and not surrounded by armed supporters, then international military officers or international police officers can carry out the detention operation. The involvement of peace enforcement soldiers or armed international military police officers in the actual detention operation does not necessarily mean that securing the surrounding area also has to be handled by either soldiers or military police officers. If, for example, the indicted war criminal is known to be heavily armed and aggressive but is not supported by the local population, peace enforcement soldiers or international military police officers should carry out the detention operation, whereas securing the surrounding area can be left to international police officers or even the local police if they are ready to be included. Similarly, there might be situations where an indicted war criminal has indicated that he will not resist detention but where he still enjoys a lot of support in the local population such as was the case with, for example, Ramush Haradinaj. In such cases the actual detention can be carried out by international or national police officers but peace enforcement soldiers or international military police officers might need to assist in securing the surrounding area. In cases where the prosecution process is generally supported both by local authorities and local people and where the indicted war criminal has no political influence, political considerations are not likely to have much impact on the decision as to who should be involved in the detention or securing the surrounding area. In contrast, if both the local authorities and local people oppose the prosecution of indicted war criminals so that the detention of an indicted war criminal is likely to lead to mass demonstrations, then peace enforcement soldiers might need to carry out the detention operation even if the risk involved is considered to be low. This might be preferable to involving the international and local police in the unpopular operation and exposing them to the anger and condemnation of the local population and authorities.

As in the case of whether to involve the local police in locating indicted war criminals, the timing of their involvement in securing the area and carrying out the actual detention will depend on factors such as the successful establishment, vetting and training of a new police force and the support of the local population and local authorities for detaining indicted war criminals. If the prosecution process is generally supported by the local population and the local authorities and the local police have been properly trained and vetted, then they can become involved in detentions at a relatively early stage. If, on the other hand, the local police have not been properly vetted and perhaps are even known to have close ties with a particular indicted war criminal or if they generally do not support the prosecution process, then it will take longer before they can become involved in detaining indicted war criminals. Since it should still primarily be the responsibility of the local police to detain indicted war criminals, it is obviously desirable that they become involved at an early stage. However, experience from Bosnia-Herzegovina, where the involvement of the local police led to the indicted war criminals being tipped off, indicates that involving them too early could jeopardise effective detention operations and should be avoided. One possible way of attempting to involve the police earlier in the process of apprehending indicted war criminals could be to include lectures on the workings of the international criminal tribunal and the importance of ensuring accountability for atrocities committed during the violent conflict in their training. That would possibly at least convince some police officers of the importance of supporting the prosecution of indicted war criminals. Another possible though more controversial solution could also be, at least in the beginning, not to notify local police officers about the details of the detention operation until immediately before it is carried out, in order to help ensure that information about the operation is not passed on to the indicted war criminals. This is controversial since it is likely that the local police will interpret the lack of prior information to signify a lack of trust, which will obviously negatively influence the relations between the local police and the peace mission.

Conclusion

If indicted war criminals are to be successfully detained, it is important that not only peace enforcement soldiers but also international military police officers, international police officers and the local police become involved in the process of their apprehension. In order to ensure that the activities of these various actors are coordinated, it is recommendable that the peace missions establish a coordinating unit to focus solely on the task of apprehending indicted war criminals. It is also essential that the peace missions ensure that all individuals involved in the detention of indicted war criminals are familiar with the relevant international regulations, for example, in relation to arrests. The apprehension of indicted war criminals can be meaningfully divided into three separate tasks, namely, locating the indicted war criminals, securing the area surrounding the detention operation and carrying out the actual detention operation. This means that whichever actor is most suitable to carry out a particular task can do so. Concerning locating indicted war criminals, local police officers are most likely to be successful because of their knowledge of, for example, the language, culture and ways of behaving. If local police cannot take part in locating indicted war criminals, then international military police officers and international police officers are preferable to peace enforcement soldiers because they have been trained and have experience in collecting intelligence and locating criminals. In cases where, for example, the dangers involved in detaining an indicted war criminal are considered low, the job is best carried out by international military police officers or international police officers since they have been trained and have experience in carrying out arrest orders. However, if the dangers of being involved are considered high or if involvement is considered unpopular among the local population and authorities, peace enforcement soldiers are a better option. Concerning securing the surrounding area, international military police officers or international police officers are also preferable in cases where, for example, the local population is not expected to react very violently to the detention of the indicted war criminal since they are more used to dealing with smaller incidents of public demonstrations than their military colleagues. If, on the other hand, a violent reaction is expected, then peace enforcement soldiers may represent the preferable option. Regarding the local police, it is preferable that they are included in the process of apprehending indicted war criminals as early as possible though it is obviously important to ensure that they have been properly vetted and trained before they are allowed to take part.

Conclusion

This book set out to explore the involvement of peace enforcement missions in the detention of indicted war criminals. An argument has been made for their involvement to help international criminal tribunals ensure accountability for violations of humane law committed during violent conflicts in cases where national authorities are either unwilling or unable to do so, and thereby to assist in making the current global order more cosmopolitan. It has also been argued that their involvement is important because peace missions need to support and be involved in implementing transitional justice processes in order to help societies recover from violent conflict. Hence the book concludes with a discussion of the prospects for peace missions supporting a more cosmopolitan global order, becoming more involved in transitional justice activities and in detaining indicted war criminals. The possible lessons that future peace enforcement missions can learn from the experience of IFOR, SFOR and KFOR are also discussed.

The prospects for peace missions supporting a more cosmopolitan global order

The degree to which future peace missions are likely to be involved in assisting in transforming the current global order into a more cosmopolitan one is still unclear.

On the one hand there are some indications that future peace missions are likely to support a more cosmopolitan global order. For example, at the World Summit meeting in 2005, world leaders agreed on the so-called *Responsibility to Protect* project, which aims to protect civilians around the world from war crimes, crimes against humanity, ethnic cleansing and genocide (Institute for Global Policy 4 January 2008). The participants agreed that, though the main responsibility to protect civilians from these atrocities should remain with national authorities, the international community has a responsibility to take action in cases where national authorities fail to protect their citizens from becoming victims of such crimes (ibid.). So far one of the UN's most favoured responses to mass atrocities committed against civilians has been the deployment of a peace mission. Hence, it can be inferred from the *Responsibility to*

Protect project that the world leaders implied that peace missions should be used to uphold humane law in cases where national authorities prove unable or unwilling to do so, and thereby to assist in making the implementation of humane law more cosmopolitan. Another indication for peace missions supporting a more cosmopolitan application of humane law is that the mandates of recent peace missions in, for example, the Democratic Republic of Congo, Côte d'Ivoire and Sudan, have all included relatively extensive roles in protecting civilians from becoming victims of violations of humane law (DPKO Democratic Republic of Congo – MONUC: Mandate, DPKO Côte d'Ivoire – UNOCI: Mandate, DPKO Sudan – UNMIS: Mandate). Another way that peace missions could support a more cosmopolitan global order, namely by the establishment of a permanent UN force as envisaged in the UN Charter, where soldiers are placed solely under UN command and deployed in order to protect civilians from mass atrocities, is also being more and more widely debated (Woodhouse and Ramsbotham 2005). Furthermore, an increasing number of states are also cooperating on the formation of multinational contingents that can be deployed as parts of UN-supported peace missions.[50] Hence, there are some indications of a growing willingness to allow peace missions to assist in the formation of a more cosmopolitan global order where the upholding of humane law and the prosecution of violations become a global, rather than a national, responsibility.

On the other hand, there are also many indications that peace missions are not committed to promoting a more cosmopolitan global order. Concerning the *Responsibility to Protect* project, only the parts of humane law that deal with the worst atrocities have been included. In addition, though the UNSC has reaffirmed its responsibility to protect civilians from becoming victims of certain violations, the UN has still not addressed how this extended responsibility should influence its actions (Institute for Global Policy 4 January 2008). Moreover, it has taken the UN a very long time to respond to the alleged genocide in Darfur and the UN is still not routinely deploying peace missions in areas where mass atrocities are committed on a daily basis. Furthermore, though their mandates included provisions aimed at protecting human rights, the peace missions in Liberia, Côte d'Ivoire, the Democratic Republic of Congo and Sudan have been unable to prevent mass atrocities being committed against civilians. Finally, the UNSC is also yet to oblige its peace missions to fully cooperate with the ICC in order to assist the court in ensuring accountability for violations of humane law. Thus, though there are some signs of a growing willingness to commit peace missions to the support of a more cosmopolitan global order, the consolidation of the commitment is still in its infancy and it remains to be seen how rooted it will become.

The prospects for peace missions becoming increasingly involved in implementing transitional justice processes

In this book, a second argument has been presented for the involvement of peace missions in detaining indicted war criminals and that is to help ensure transitional justice. Transitional justice has already been introduced in the UN's approach to peace-building but it is still far from being fully integrated and the likelihood of this happening in the foreseeable future is debatable.

On the one hand the importance of transitional justice for the development of sustainable peace is increasingly being recognised in UN publications and debates. Peace missions have also become increasingly involved in a wide variety of transitional justice activities such as investigating atrocities committed during the violent conflict, supporting national and international attempts to ensure individual accountability for mass atrocities and establishing courts aiming to ensure accountability for violations committed during the violent conflict. Hence important initial steps towards integrating transitional justice in the UN's approach to peace-building have already been taken.

On the other hand all UN peace missions are still not routinely granted mandates that include provisions on transitional justice. In addition the transitional justice-related tasks allocated to peace missions in their mandates have significantly varied, from hardly any involvement in cases such as Haiti, to fairly extensive involvement in cases such as Sierra Leone. Moreover with a few exceptions such as that of Sierra Leone, peace missions have so far only been involved in fairly autonomous transitional justice activities rather than in attempting to implement a coherent and comprehensive transitional justice programme. The peace missions' transitional justice activities have also suffered from a lack of funding and adequately trained and experienced staff. Thus there is still a considerable disparity between the commitment expressed in various UN reports and debates and the will to authorise peace missions to engage in transitional justice processes and provide them with the resources and powers necessary to carry out their transitional justice activities effectively.

Whether this disparity will persist or diminish is obviously difficult to predict. First, the likelihood of peace missions becoming more involved in transitional justice processes ties in closely with the debate as to how much the UN can legally and legitimately interfere in what happens inside a state. Traditionally, respect for state sovereignty has, for example, meant that state leaders have been able to treat the civilian population in the way that they saw fit without international actors trying to stop any atrocities being committed or attempting to hold the leaders accountable for the mistreatment. Hence transitional justice processes that aim to hold especially political and military leaders accountable for atrocities committed during violent conflicts challenge one of the fundamental pillars of state sovereignty. Thus the remaining supporters of a global order based on the upholding of state sovereignty such as China are likely to oppose UN involvement in transitional justice processes unless a state specifically requests UN involvement. In addition, though there is a general agreement that the UN's involvement in transitional justice processes should be based on national needs and ensure that the ownership of the process remains local, there are still many unanswered questions as how this should be carried out in practice. UN involvement is fairly uncontroversial in cases where the national authorities and the local population generally support the implementation of a comprehensive transitional justice process such as has been the case in Sierra Leone. However, it is highly controversial in cases where, for example, national authorities see amnesty as a necessary concession in order to end the violent conflict and so are not interested in, for example, attempting to hold individuals responsible for atrocities committed during the conflict accountable in a trial process, as has been the case in East Timor. If there are many more cases like that of East Timor, where the UN peace mission seemingly imposes its own transitional justice approach irrespective of what the national leaders consider to be national needs and therefore also without ensuring local ownership of the process, then it is likely that the supporters of state sovereignty will fiercely oppose UN involvement in transitional justice processes. If, on the other hand, the UN and its peace missions find ways of cooperating with national authorities and the local population concerning the development of a transitional justice process that is based on national needs and that ensures that the ownership of the process remains local, then it is also more likely that the national authorities and local population will support UN involvement. Hence, UN involvement will not to the same degree be seen as an infringement on state sovereignty and it is also more likely that even supporters of upholding state sovereignty will actively support the involvement of UN peace missions in implementing transitional justice processes. The involvement of future UN peace missions in transitional justice activities is also likely to depend on how successful current transitional justice institutions will be in contributing to the development of long-term sustainable peace. If the ICC and the national truth commissions and criminal tribunals that UN peace missions support successfully address atrocities committed during the violent conflict and are seen to be contributing to societies recovering from internal violent conflict in coming to terms with their past, and moving towards a more peaceful future, then it is also more likely that UN peace missions will be involved in transitional justice activities in the future. However, there are some considerable factors that make such an evaluation difficult to judge. Since there is no agreement on how to assess when sustainable peace has been obtained, it is for example also difficult to measure the impact of the activities of transitional justice institutions on the development of long-term peace and the impact might not become apparent until years after the transitional justice process began. Hence, it is also difficult to determine the positive impact of the involvement of UN peace missions in the implementation of transitional justice processes on long-term peace-building. This is likely to negatively impact the support for peace missions becoming involved in transitional justice activities since peace missions' are often assessed by their impact on the situation on the ground while they are still deployed rather than on their long-term effects.

In addition, even if members of the UN generally agree that UN peace missions need to be involved in transitional justice processes, the incorporation of transitional justice in the tasks UN peace missions are expected to carry out is likely to be a fairly long-term process. A recent study has for example contended that the UN, like any other organisation, has certain ways of addressing specific problems such as developing peace in societies recovering from internal violent conflict that are seen as the most suitable solutions and hence there is an inherent resistance towards adding new tasks to their approach to peace-building (Paris 2003).

Transitional justice also rocks the foundation of the UN's approach to peace-making, which has long been built on the idea that an end to the conflict is best obtained through negotiations with the individuals and groups mostly respons-ible for the violence. Thus there is a considerable inconsistency between the UN's current approach to peacemaking, which allows alleged war criminals to play significant roles in the peacemaking process and accommodates alleged war criminals who turn into politicians after the signing of the peace agreement, and the inclusion of transitional justice, which dictates that individuals responsible for atrocities committed during the conflict should somehow be held account-able. If transitional justice becomes an integrated part of peace-building, then individuals and groups responsible for mass atrocities are likely to refuse to take part in peace negotiations because they will be afraid of being held accountable for their actions during the violent conflict. Hence the full incorporation of tran-sitional justice in the tasks UN peace missions are expected to carry out necessitates a radical rethink of how to bring an end to a violent conflict and these changes are therefore longer-term projects.

On the other hand, there are also some factors that indicate a possible reduc-tion in the gap between the commitment to involve peace missions in transi-tional justice activities expressed in UN debates and publications and the lack of will to include provisions on transitional justice in the peace mission mandates. First, experience from, for example, the UN's involvement in ensuring justice for crimes committed after violent conflict has underlined that it takes a long time to introduce and incorporate a new set of tasks in UN peace missions. Hence, the current lack of provisions for transitional justice in mandates granted to contemporary peace missions and the inconsistent involvement of peace mis-sions in transitional justice processes is far from unique to the process of incor-porating transitional justice and thus not necessarily just a sign of a lack of commitment. Attempts to significantly reform the UN are also already taking place, which include the establishment of a new Peacebuilding Commission and a Human Rights Council and therefore imply an increased focus on human rights issues. In addition, the influence of international human rights organisa-tions such as Amnesty International and Human Rights Watch and national actors such as victims of mass atrocities who lobby for accountability for atroci-ties committed during violent conflicts should not be underestimated. For example, in the case of the Srebrenica massacre, international human rights organisations and national victims groups such as the Mothers of Srebrenica continue to lobby for the individuals responsible for the atrocities to be held accountable and to put pressure on the UN to ensure that this happens.[51] Further-more, international media now ensure that people are made aware of not only mass atrocities committed during violent conflicts around the world but also attempts to hold these individuals accountable. For example, in the case of

Darfur, people from around the world have voiced their discontent with the inaction of the UN in preventing further atrocities and called for the individuals responsible for the genocide to be held accountable.[52] Hence it is increasingly unlikely that political leaders from around the world in the future will be able to get away with not responding to mass atrocities. Thus it is also likely that peace missions will become more involved in addressing these mass atrocities once the violent conflict has been brought to an end and thereby become increasingly involved in transitional justice activities.

The prospects for peace missions becoming increasingly involved in detaining indicted war criminals

This book has also called for routinely including the detention of indicted war criminals in the tasks peace enforcement missions are expected to carry out in cases where indicted war criminals are at large in the peace missions' areas of deployment.

Several factors support the assumption that the detention of indicted war criminals is indeed a task that peace enforcement missions are becoming more and more involved in. First, the detention of indicted war criminals is increasingly being included and incorporated into dominant military doctrines guiding peace missions. In addition, the UN peace missions have already successfully detained indicted war criminals when UNTAES in Croatia helped to detain Slavko Dokmanovic and UNMIL in Liberia arrested Charles Taylor. Also IFOR, SFOR and KFOR, though led by NATO, were also supported by the UN, and have all been involved in detaining indicted war criminals. The detention of an indicted war criminal has now been explicitly mentioned in the mandate granted to a peace enforcement mission since UNMIL was explicitly authorised to detain Charles Taylor. There is also an increasing acceptance that soldiers taking part in operations abroad may be injured or killed in their attempts to implement their mandate. Many states also support the work of the ICC and, since the detention of indicted war criminals is a problem that the ICC is already facing and is likely to face again in the future the parties to the ICC, who want the court to succeed, need to help the ICC secure custody over indicted war criminals. In addition, even states that are not members of the ICC have supported calls for UNSC to refer the situation in Darfur to the ICC and hence, if these states want the ICC to succeed in prosecuting cases from Darfur, they might need to agree to the peace missions in Sudan becoming involved in detaining the indicted war criminals. Furthermore, in the future the ICC will hopefully also be able to identify which individuals should be held accountable for their deeds while the violent conflict is still ongoing and thereby help the peace missions deployed during violent conflicts avoid becoming involved with alleged war criminals whom the ICC wants to prosecute. It is also noteworthy that even now, twelve years after they were indicted, the failure to detain indicted war criminals Radovan Karadžić and Ratko Mladić is still covered in the media and still represents an important obstacle to a positive relationship between Serbia and the US,

EU and NATO. International human rights groups are also still lobbying for international organisations to ensure that the indicted war criminals are brought to justice.

However, there are also some indications that future peace missions will not be increasingly involved in detaining indicted war criminals. First, though the ICC has indicted alleged war criminals from Sudan and the Democratic Republic of Congo, the peace missions in these countries are not involved in detaining indicted war criminals. In addition, three of the permanent members of the UNSC, whose support for the involvement of peace missions in detaining indicted war criminals is obviously vital, are still not members of the ICC. Furthermore, though the populations in states which normally provide many soldiers to peace missions such as the US and the UK, have become more used to their soldiers being injured or killed abroad, soldiers coming back in coffins still make these populations question whether or not the aim is justifiable given the cost in terms of human life. Hence, it is still questionable whether the citizens of the major contributing countries will support the involvement of peace missions in the detention of indicted war criminals if the consequences are that the soldiers get injured or killed in the process. Soldiers taking part in missions abroad also continue to be involved in unlawful actions, which obviously make it morally difficult for them to engage in detaining indicted war criminals. Finally, alleged war criminals are also still allowed to play significant roles in the peace negotiations and the peace processes and hence the fear persists that detaining indicted war criminals might threaten the peace.

However, the likelihood of peace missions becoming increasingly involved in detaining indicted war criminals is also likely to depend on factors yet to be fully addressed in the debates. It is, for example, remarkable that politicians have so far focused on the fear that detaining indicted war criminals might threaten the peace rather than focusing on the consequences of indicted war criminals not being detained. Experience from Bosnia-Herzegovina has, for example, shown that if, allegedly, war criminals such as Radovan Karadžić are allowed to stay powerful in their local communities, they could seriously obstruct the implementation of the peace agreement and the activities of the peace mission. Hence, unless peace missions become involved in detaining indicted war criminals, they risk having the indicted war criminals obstruct their activities and maybe even attack their personnel in an attempt to force the peace mission to withdraw. It is also highly unlikely that the peace mission will manage to develop sustainable peace if the indicted war criminals are allowed to stay at large and the victims' demands for justice thereby go unheard. Thus, if peace missions are to succeed in reaching their ultimate aim, namely, the establishment of a sustainable peace that prevents the recurrence of violence and further UN involvement, then increased involvement of peace missions in the detention of indicted war criminals is unavoidable, a prospect politicians behind the deployment of UN peace missions will have to acknowledge sooner rather than later.

Lessons learnt from IFOR, SFOR and KFOR

Future peace missions can learn several important lessons from IFOR, SFOR and KFOR. First, it is recommendable that all peace enforcement soldiers follow the same military doctrine and that the detention of indicted war criminals has been fully integrated into this military doctrine. If peace enforcement soldiers continue to follow different military doctrines, then it is important that these doctrines include similar provisions on the involvement of peace missions in the detention of indicted war criminals. It is also important that the mandates of peace missions explicitly authorise the missions to become involved in detaining indicted war criminals, that they acknowledge the consequences of involving the mission in the detention of indicted war criminals and that this task is only one component of a coherent transitional justice approach. It is also important that the rules of engagement include provisions on the involvement of peace enforcement soldiers in the detention of indicted war criminals, including guidelines on what the soldiers are expected to do when they encounter an indicted war criminal, how to carry out detention operations, when to abandon an operation and how much force the peace enforcement soldiers are allowed to use in a given situation. It is also important that the rules of engagement are applied equally across the mission and that they are adapted regularly. It is also imperative that future peace enforcement missions establish contingency plans aimed at detaining indicted war criminals from the beginning of the mission and that they provide all peace enforcement soldiers with information about the personal characteristics and whereabouts of the indicted war criminals so that they are able to identify and locate the indicted war criminals. Soldiers on patrol, at checkpoints and roadblocks should also be involved in detaining indicted war criminals from the beginning of the mission and soldiers should initiate gathering intelligence and surveillance operations. It is also important that future peace enforcement missions ensure institutional memory on activities aimed at detaining indicted war criminals and that peace enforcement soldiers receive training and take part in simulation exercises in order to enable them to carry out detention operations effectively and in accordance with international standards. It is also recommendable that the detention operations remain unannounced and that they do not only target the indicted war criminals but also their supporters. Peace enforcement missions should also seek to establish positive relationships with the international criminal tribunal, international human rights organisations operating in their area of deployment and the local population, since these actors can potentially help peace enforcement soldiers locate indicted war criminals. Finally, it is also recommendable that peace missions involve not only soldiers but also international military police officers, international police officers and local police and authorities in the process of apprehending indicted war criminals.

Some of these lessons learnt, such as explicitly including the detention of indicted war criminals in the mandates granted to peace missions and developing rules of engagement on the role of peace enforcement soldiers in the detention of indicted war criminals, are easily applicable to future peace missions. Other lessons learnt, such as the importance of gathering intelligence and swiftly responding to sightings of indicted war criminals might be more difficult to implement in cases like the Democratic Republic of Congo and Sudan where the peace missions for example cover an enormous geographical area with limited infrastructure. In some cases it might also be really difficult to establish a positive relationship with the local population because their cultural background is significantly different from that of the peace enforcement soldiers. The amount of personnel and resources allocated to peace missions also differs considerably and hence some peace missions might only be able to allocate limited resources and personnel to the task of detaining indicted war criminals. Furthermore, not all peace missions include, for example, international military police officers and in some cases the peace missions might not manage to help establish a national police force able to assist them in the detention of indicted war criminals. In these cases it will be paramount for the peace missions to develop their own strategies for detaining indicted war criminals and it will be important for the peace missions to seek out possible windows of opportunity to detain indicted war criminals. Experience from Bosnia-Herzegovina, for example, shows that, especially in the immediate aftermath of the violent conflict, some indicted war criminals still take part in public events and, though it might not be possible to detain them while the event is still ongoing, they will at least have been located and can therefore be shadowed until a planned detention operation can be carried out. Finally, it is also important that future peace missions develop their own lessons learnt, for the success of all future peace missions.

Notes

1 See Century Foundation 1998, Dijk and Hovens 2001, Gaeta 1998, International Crisis Group 2000, Kalinauskas 2002, Lamb 2000, United States Institute of Peace 1997, Vallières-Roland 2002.

2 Some of the noteworthy exceptions to this general observation are Michael Pugh, Tom Woodhouse and Oliver Ramsbotham, and Mary Kaldor, who all argue in favour of a more cosmopolitan world order but who only briefly discuss the role of peace missions in the development of this alternative order (Kaldor 2001, Pugh 2004, Woodhouse and Ramsbotham 2005).

3 Lustrations mean that perpetrators are removed from their official positions. See Schwartz 1995.

4 See Boven et al. 1995.

5 These are official indictments. The number of secret indictments is not known.

6 Representing the following countries: Bolivia, Brazil, Canada, Costa Rica, Cyprus, Finland, France, Germany, Ghana, Ireland, Italy, Korea (South), Latvia, Mali, Samoa, South Africa, Trinidad and Tobago and the UK.

7 For more information see: www.icc-cpi.int/cases.html (accessed 27 December 2007).

8 For more information see: www.globalpolicy.org/intljustice/sierraindx.htm and www.sc-sl.org (accessed 27 December 2007).

9 For more information see: www.globalpolicy.org/intljustice/etimorindx.htm (accessed 27 December 2007).

10 For more information see: www.globalpolicy.org/intljustice/camindx.htm and www.krtrial.info (accessed 27 December 2007).

11 See chapter 4.

12 UNMIBH was first deployed together with the NATO-led IFOR and later with SFOR, which were mandated to help implement the military parts of the Dayton Peace Agreement (see Chapters 5 and 6).

13 See UNSC resolutions 1088 (1996), 1103 (1997), 1107 (1997), 1144 (1997), 1168 (1998) and 1184 (1998).

14 Also known under the acronym ONUCI.

15 Simultaneously with the deployment of UNMIBH, NATO troops were also deployed and put in charge of implementing the military parts of the DPA. Chapters 5 and 6 examine the efforts of these troops to detain indicted war criminals and thereby contribute to securing accountability for atrocities committed during the violent conflict.

16 Simultaneously with the deployment of UNMIK, NATO troops were also deployed in Kosovo in order to help implement the military parts of the peace agreement. Chapter 7 examines the efforts of the Kosovo Force to detain indicted war criminals and thereby contribute to securing accountability for atrocities committed during the violent conflict.

17 Since UNMIBH's international police officers were only authorised to monitor the

national police carrying out policing tasks rather than execute the policing tasks them-selves, it was mainly left to IFOR and SFOR to help the ICTY through providing security for ICTY investigators and detaining individuals indicted by the ICTY (President of the ICTY 1997, 1998, 1999).

18 Initially the ICTY had issued a secret indictment against Slavko Dokmanovic on 3 April 1996 and requested UNTAES to detain him (Arbour 30 June 1997). However, since Dokmanovic was not residing within its area of operation, UNTAES was not able to detain him. In June 1997 a representative from the ICTY, Kevin Curtis, went to visit Dokmanovic in his house in the Former Republic of Yugoslavia. Curtis claimed that he could help Dokmanovic get his property in Croatia back. Curtis con-vinced Dokmanovic to come to Vukovar in UNTAES's area of operation to meet the head of UNTAES, Jacques Klein. Representatives from the ICTY and UNTAES picked up Dokmanovic on the Serbian side of the border and brought him across the border to UNTAES's headquarters in Vukovar. Here Dokmanovic was detained and sent to The Hague (Dokmanovic 8 September 1997).

19 See Wilson 1997.

20 The resolution also demanded that all parties to the violent conflict in the Democratic Republic of Congo cooperate in the process of bringing perpetrators to justice (DPKO Democratic Republic of Congo – MONUC: Mandate)

21 See Lyck 2007.

22 For legal analyses of whether or not IFOR was authorised or obliged to detain indicted war criminals, see Gaeta 1998, Kalinauskas 2002, Lamb 2000, Vallières-Roland 2002.

23 For further information see: www.rewardsforjustice.net/english/index.cfm?page=wci (accessed 28 December 2007).

24 See Lyck 2007.

25 See for example Bratt 1996, Diehl 1993, Jett 1999.

26 See Chief of the General Staff 1995.

27 For further analyses and criticism of *Wider Peacekeeping*, see Bellamy 1996, Bellamy *et al.* 2004, Cassidy 2004, Connaughton 2001.

28 For an analysis of the peace and justice dilemma in the context of Kosovo, see Lyck 2007.

29 For analyses and criticism of peace support operations, see Bellamy *et al.* 2004, Cassidy 2004, Connaughton 2001, Frantzen 2005, Wilkinson 2000.

30 The US opposition to the ICC has already been examined and discussed elsewhere. See AMICC 2006, Fanton 29 March 2005, Kahn 2003, Kristof 16 October 2005, Kyl 2004, Rozenberg 12 January 2006.

31 See also Pouligny 2006, pp. 96–123 for different views of what is expected from a peace enforcement mission.

32 For a discussion of what IFOR's and SFOR's mandates authorised the peace enforce-ment missions to do concerning the detention of indicted war criminals, see Gaeta 1998, Lamb 2000, Kalinauskas 2002, Vallières-Roland 2002.

33 See also Pouligny 2006, pp. 96–141 on the problems caused by vaguely formulated mandates.

34 See also Lyck 2007 for an analysis of the relationship between indicted war criminal Ramush Haradinaj and UNMIK.

35 See DPKO Bosnia-Herzegovina – UNMIBH: Background. For analyses of inter-national efforts aiming at re-establishing the rule of law in Bosnia-Herzegovina, see Bailey 2006, International Crisis Group 2002c, Okuizumi 2002, Rausch 2006.

36 See UNMIKonline – At a Glance: Introduction, www.unmikonline.org/intro.htm (accessed 5 January 2008).

37 See President of the ICTY 1996, 1997, 1998 for accounts of when SFOR soldiers could have detained indicted war criminals.

38 See for example www.un.org/Depts/dpko/lessons/ (accessed 5 January 2008).

39 For example, the cooperation between Estonia, Latvia and Lithuania in the Baltic Battalion, see www.mil.ee/index_eng.php?s=kooseesm (accessed 5 January 2008) and the cooperation between Denmark, Finland, Iceland, Norway and Sweden in NORD-CAPS, see: www.nordcaps.org/ (accessed 5 January 2008).

40 NATO Headquarters Sarajevo and EUFOR conducted similar operations after the departure of SFOR, see Chappell 8 March 2005, Lt Cdr Percival 25 January 2005, Major General Leakey 16 December 2004, Ryall 9 August 2005, Thomas 11 October 2005.

41 Though KFOR supported the work of the ICTY through detaining three indicted war criminals, the support the peace enforcement mission has offered the ICTY has not been unanimous. The civilian part of the peace enforcement mission, UNMIK, has lately been criticised by the ICTY for its role in supporting and ensuring the provisional release of the former President of Kosovo, Ramush Haradinaj, who is currently on trial in The Hague. See Lyck 2007.

42 See www.un.org/icty/cases-e/cis/lukic/cis-lukiclukic.pdf (accessed 5 January 2008).

43 See www.un.org/icty/cases-e/cis/zelenovic/cis-zelenovic.pdf (accessed 5 January 2008).

44 See for example Amnesty International 2003b, Human Rights Watch 1996b, 18 November 1997, 2005a, International Crisis Group 1996, 1997, 2000.

45 See Hendrickx 2001, Izes 1997, Kalinauskas 2002, Leurdijk 2001, Reenen 2001, Ruxton 2001, Supernor 2001.

46 The IPTF was replaced by the European Union Police Mission (EUPM) in Bosnia-Herzegovina in January 2003. The EUPM was given the same mandate as the IPTF. See www.consilium.europa.eu/cms3_fo/showPage.asp?id=585&lang=EN (accessed 5 January 2008).

47 See Article III of Annex 11 of the General Framework Agreement www.nato.int/ifor/gfa/gfa-an11.htm (accessed 5 January 2008).

48 See Article III of Annex 11 of the General Framework Agreement www.nato.int/ifor/gfa/gfa-an11.htm (accessed 5 January 2008).

49 See www.unmikonline.org/civpol/mandate.htm (accessed 5 January 2008).

50 For example, the cooperation between Estonia, Latvia and Lithuania in the Baltic Battalion. See: www.mil.ee/index_eng.php?s=kooseesm (accessed 5 January 2008) and the cooperation between Denmark, Finland, Iceland, Norway and Sweden in NORD-CAPS, see: www.nordcaps.org/ (accessed 5 January 2008).

51 See www.srebrenica.ba/index.en.php? (accessed 5 January 2008).

52 See www.genocideindarfur.net/?gclid=CMSa-oGh7pACFQlIMAod8G-zqw and www.darfurgenocide.org/ (accessed 5 January 2008).

Bibliography

Abrashi, F. (2003) 'NATO Detain Three Ethnic Albanians on War Crimes', 17 February, Associated Press.

Action Aid (2006a) 'MONUC: DDRRR, DDR, Military and Rule of Law Reform – Reducing Violence against Women'. Online. Available at: www.actionaidusa.org/pdf/-MONUC-DRC.pdf (accessed 2 January 2008).

Action Aid (2006b) 'MINUSTAH: DDR and Police, Judicial and Correctional Reform in Haiti – Recommendations for Change'. Action Aid, July 2006

Adnkronos International (22 March 2007) 'Karadzic Made Secret Deal with US to Spare Him from Prosecution, Paper Claims'. Online. Available at: globalpolicy.igc.org/intljustice/wanted/2007/0322usdeal.htm (accessed 5 January 2008).

Akhavan, P. (2001) 'Beyond Impunity: Can International Criminal Justice Prevent Future Atrocities?', *American Journal of International Law*, 95(1): 7–32.

AMICC (American Non-Governmental Organisations Coalition for the International Criminal Court) (2006) 'Chronology: From "Signature Suspension" to Impunity Agreements to Darfur', 23 October. Online. Available at: www.iccnow.org/documents/FS_AMICC_US_ChronologyOct2006.pdf (accessed 5 January 2008).

Amnesty International (1996) 'Chile Impunity in the Making – Justice Defeated by Amnesty Law', 11 June. Online. Available at: web.amnesty.org/library/Index/ENGAMR220041996?open&of=ENG-CHL (accessed 28 December 2007).

Amnesty International (1998) 'Mozambique: Human Rights and the Police', April. Online. Available at: web.amnesty.org/library/index/ENGAFR410011998 (accessed 7 January 2008).

Amnesty International (2001) 'East Timor: Justice Past, Present and Future'. Online. Available at: www.amnesty.org/en/report/info/ASA57/001/2001 (accessed 3 January 2008).

Amnesty International (2002) 'Kingdom of Cambodia: Urgent Need for Judicial Reform'. Online. Available at: www.amnesty.org/en/report/info/ASA23/004/2002 (accessed 1 January 2008).

Amnesty International (2003a) 'Argentina, Legal Memorandum, the Full Stop and Due Obedience Laws', December. Online. Available at: news.amnesty.org/library/pdf/AMR130182003ENGLISH/$File/AMR1301803.pdf (accessed 28 December 2007).

Amnesty International (2003b) 'Bosnia-Herzegovina: Shelving Justice – War Crimes Prosecutions in Paralysis'. Online. Available at: www.amnesty.org/en/alfresco_asset/56988dc6-a4e0–11dc-a92d-271514ed133d/eur630182003en.pdf (accessed 7 January 2008).

Amnesty International (2004) 'Sierra Leone', Amnesty International Report 2004. Online. Available at: www.web.amnesty.org/report2004 (accessed 7 January 2008).

Amnesty International (2005) 'Sierra Leone', Amnesty International Report 2005. Online. Available at: www.web.amnesty.org/report2005 (accessed 7 January 2008).

Amnesty International (2006a) 'Sierra Leone', Amnesty International Report 2006. Online. Available at: www.amnesty.org/en/alfresco_asset/da6b6b57-a5c7–11dc-bc7d-3fb9ac69fcbb/pol100012006en.pdf (accessed 7 January 2008).

Amnesty International (2006b) 'Democratic Republic of Congo', Amnesty International Report 2006. Online. Available at: www.amnesty.org/en/alfresco_asset/da6b6b57-a5c7–11dc-bc7d-3fb9ac69fcbb/pol100012006en.pdf (accessed 7 January 2008).

Amnesty International (2006c) 'Haiti', Amnesty International Report 2006. Online. Available at: www.amnesty.org/en/alfresco_asset/da6b6b57-a5c7–11dc-bc7d-3fb9ac 69fcbb/pol100012006en.pdf (accessed 7 January 2008).

Amnesty International (2006d) 'Liberia', Amnesty International Report 2006. Online. Available at: www.amnesty.org/en/alfresco_asset/da6b6b57-a5c7–11dc-bc7d-3fb9ac 69fcbb/pol100012006en.pdf (accessed 7 January 2008).

Amnesty International (2007a) 'Serbia', Amnesty International Report 2007. Online. Available at: thereport.amnesty.org/document/15 (accessed 1 January 2008).

Amnesty International (2007b) 'Democratic Republic of Congo', Amnesty International Report 2007. Online. Available at: thereport.amnesty.org/document/15 (accessed 1 January 2008).

Amnesty International (2007c) 'Côte d'Ivoire', Amnesty International Report 2007. Online. Available at: thereport.amnesty.org/document/15 (accessed 1 January 2008).

Amnesty International (2007d) 'Sudan', Amnesty International Report 2007. Online. Available at: thereport.amnesty.org/document/15 (accessed 1 January 2008).

Amnesty International (2007e) 'Liberia: Time for Truth, Justice and Reparation for Liberia's Victims'. Online. Available at: www.amnesty.org/en/report/info/AFR34/001/2007 (accessed 3 January 2008).

Amnesty International (2007f) 'Sierra Leone', Amnesty International Report 2007. Online. Available at: thereport.amnesty.org/document/15 (accessed 1 January 2008).

Aning, E.K. (2000) 'War to Peace: Dilemmas of Multilateral Intervention in Civil Wars', *African Security Review*, 9(3).

Anonymous questioner (11 February 1996) Transcript of the Press Briefing, Sarajevo: Coalition Press Information Centre. Online. Available at: www.nato.int/ifor/trans/t960211a.htm (accessed 27 December 2007).

Anonymous questioner (12 September 1996) Transcript of the Press Briefing, Sarajevo: Coalition Press Information Centre. Online. Available at: www.nato.int/ifor/trans/t960912a.htm (accessed 2 January 2008).

Anonymous questioner (29 October 1996) Transcript of the Press Briefing, Sarajevo: Coalition Press Information Centre. Online. Available at: www.nato.int/ifor/trans/t961029a.htm (accessed 27 December 2007).

Anonymous questioner (5 December 1996) Transcript of the Press Briefing, Sarajevo: Coalition Press Information Centre. Online. Available at: www.nato.int/ifor/trans/t961205a.htm (accessed 27 December 2007).

Arbour, L. (30 June 1997) Press Statement by the Prosecutor, Justice Louise Arbour. Online. Available at: www.un.org/icty/pressreal/STA970630.htm (accessed 2 January 2008).

Army, Marine Corps, Navy and Air Force (2003) *Peace OPS Multi-Service Tactics, Techniques and Procedures for Conducting Peace Operations*, FM3–07.31, MCWP3–33.8, AFTTP(I)3–2.40, Air Land Sea Application Center. Online. Available at: www.doctrine.usmc.mil/signpubs/w3338.pdf (accessed 29 December 2007).

Askin, K.D. (2003) 'Reflections on Some of the Most Significant Achievements of the International Criminal Tribunal for the Former Yugoslavia', *New England Law Review*, 37(4): 903–914.

Associated Press (19 September 2007) 'Serbia Investigating Whether US had Secret Deal with War Crimes Fugitive Karadzic', *International Herald Tribune*. Online. Available at: www.iht.com/articles/ap/2007/09/19/europe/EU-GEN-Serbia-US-Karadzic.php (accessed 6 January 2008).

Aucoin, L. (2007) 'Building the Rule of Law and Establishing Accountability for Atrocities in the Aftermath of Conflict', *Whitehead Journal of Diplomacy & International Relations*, 8(1). Online. Available at: diplomacy.shu.edu/academics/journal/current_issue.html (accessed 5 January 2008).

Babo-Soares, D. (2001) 'Comparing Experiences with State Building in Asia and Europe: The Cases of East Timor, Bosnia and Kosovo, Successes, Weaknesses and Challenges: A Critical Overview of the Political Transition in East Timor', Conference report: Council for Asia Europe Co-operation (CAEC). Online. Available at: www.caec-asiaeurope.org/Conference/Publications/soares.PDF (accessed 1 January 2008).

Bailey, D.H. (2006) *Changing the Guard, Developing Democratic Police Abroad*, Oxford: Oxford University Press.

Bailey, M., Maguire, R. and Pouliot, J.O.G. (2002) 'Haiti: Military-Police Partnership for Public Security', in R.B. Oakley, M.J. Dziedzic and E.M. Goldberg (eds) *Policing the New World Disorder: Peace Operations and Public Security*, Washington, DC: National Defense University Press.

Baker, R. (30 May 2004) 'Where's Radovan? A Bosnian Serb Leader Indicated on Genocide Charges Remains at Large – and Few Seem to Care', *San Francisco Chronical*. Online. Available at: www.globalpolicy.org/intljustice/wanted/2004/0530where.htm (accessed 29 December 2007).

Bald, S.H. (2002) 'Searching for a Lost Childhood: Will the Special Court of Sierra Leone Find Justice for Its Children?', *American University International Law Review*, 18(2): 537.

Baroni, F. (2000) 'The International Criminal Tribunal for the Former Yugoslavia and Its Mission to Restore Peace', *Pace International Law Review*, 12(2): 233–252.

Barsalou, J. (2005) 'Trauma and Transitional Justice in Divided Societies', Special Report No. 135 (April), New York: United States Institute of Peace.

Bass, G.J. (2000) *Stay the Hand of Vengeance: The Politics of War Crimes Tribunals*, Princeton, NJ: Princeton University Press.

BBC (18 December 1997) 'NATO Nabs Two Alleged War Criminals in Bosnia'. Online. Available at: news.bbc.co.uk/1/hi/world/europe/40585.stm (accessed 27 December 2007).

BBC (4 August 1999) 'Croatia Hands over War Crimes Suspect'. Online. Available at: news.bbc.co.uk/1/hi/world/europe/412114.stm (accessed 28 December 2007).

BBC (24 December 1999) 'War Crimes Suspect Arrested'. Online. Available at: news.bbc.co.uk/1/hi/world/europe/577251.stm (accessed 28 December 2007).

BBC (5 March 2000) 'Omarska Commander Arrested'. Online. Available at: news.bbc.co.uk/1/hi/world/europe/667021.stm (accessed 28 December 2007).

BBC (3 April 2000) 'Nato Swoops on Karadzic Aide'. Online. Available at: news.bbc.co.uk/1/hi/world/europe/700012.stm (accessed 28 December 2007).

BBC (25 June 2000) 'Bosnian Serb War Crimes Suspect Arrested'. Online. Available at: news.bbc.co.uk/1/hi/world/europe/805316.stm (accessed 28 December 2007).

BBC (8 July 2000) 'Bosnia Massacre Suspect Held'. Online. Available at:

news.bbc.co.uk/1/hi/world/europe/2114140.stm (accessed 28 December 2007).

BBC (13 October 2000) 'War Crime Suspect Killed'. Online. Available at: news.bbc.co.uk/1/hi/world/europe/970207.stm (accessed 28 December 2007).

BBC (11 April 2001) 'Indicted War Criminals Still at Large'. Online. Available at: news.bbc.co.uk/1/hi/programmes/pm/1271580.stm (accessed 5 January 2008).

BBC (15 April 2001) 'Bosnian Genocide Suspect Arrested'. Online. Available at: news.bbc.co.uk/1/hi/world/1279356.stm (accessed 28 December 2007).

BBC (10 August 2001) 'Bosnian Serb Colonel Arrested'. Online. Available at: news.bbc.co.uk/1/hi/world/europe/1484166.stm (accessed 28 December 2007).

BBC (1 April 2002) 'Bosnia Genocide Suspect Arrested'. Online. Available at: news.bbc.co.uk/1/hi/world/europe/1905737.stm (accessed 28 December 2007).

BBC (2 April 2002) 'Bosnian Genocide Suspect Extradited'. Online. Available at: news.bbc.co.uk/1/hi/world/europe/1907122.stm (accessed 28 December 2007).

BBC (13 June 2002) 'Bosnian Serb War Crimes Suspect Seized'. Online. Available at: news.bbc.co.uk/1/hi/world/europe/2043368.stm (accessed 28 December 2007).

BBC (9 July 2002) 'Nato Troops Seize War Crimes Suspect'. Online. Available at: news.bbc.co.uk/1/hi/world/europe/2118373.stm (accessed 28 December 2007).

BBC (19 February 2003) 'Prominent Kosovo Suspect Held'. Online. Available at: news.bbc.co.uk/go/pr/fr/1/hi/world/europe/2778079.stm (accessed 28 December 2007).

BBC (11 April 2003) 'Nato Warns Karadzic and Mladic'. Online. Available at: news.bbc.co.uk/1/hi/world/europe/2938715.stm (accessed 28 December 2007).

BBC (23 November 2004) 'SFOR Defends Pursuit of Karadzic'. Online. Available at: news.bbc.co.uk/1/hi/world/europe/4036359.stm (accessed 5 January 2008).

BBC (20 February 2007) 'Afghan War Crimes Amnesty Passed'. Online. Available at: news.bbc.co.uk/1/hi/world/south_asia/6379587.stm (accessed 28 December 2007).

BBC (26 October 2007) 'Hague Probes Karadzic "Deal" Claim'. Online. Available at: news.bbc.co.uk/1/hi/world/europe/7062288.stm (accessed 5 January 2008).

Beigbeder, Y. (1999) *Judging War Criminals: The Politics of International Justice*, London/Basingstoke: Palgrave Macmillan.

Bellamy, A.J., Williams, P. and Griffin, S. (2004) *Understanding Peacekeeping*, Cambridge: Polity Press.

Bellamy, C. (1996) *Knights in White Armour*, London: Random House.

Beruto, G.L. (ed.) (2006) 'Justice and Reconciliation: An Integrated Approach', Proceedings, the 29th Round Table on Current Problems of International Humanitarian Law, 7–9 September 2006, Sanremo: International Institute of Humanitarian Law.

Biermann, W. and Ugland, O.F. (1998) 'Lessons Learned in the Field: A Survey of UNPROFOR Officers', in W. Biermann and M. Vadset (eds) *UN Peacekeeping in Trouble: Lessons Learned from the Former Yugoslavia*, Aldershot: Ashgate Publishing Limited.

Blakesley, C.L. (1997) 'Atrocities and Its Prosecution: The Ad Hoc Tribunals for the Former Yugoslavia and Rwanda', in T.H.L. McCormack and G.J. Simpson (eds) *The Law of War Crimes: National and International Approaches*, The Hague: Kluwer Law International.

Bourgon, S. (2002) 'Jurisdiction Ratione Temporis', in A. Cassese, P. Gaeta and J.R.W.D. Jones (eds) *The Rome Statute of the International Criminal Court: A Commentary*, vol. 1, Oxford: Oxford University Press.

Boven, T.v., Flinterman, C., Grünfeld, F. and Westendorp, I. (1995) 'Seminar on the Right to Restitution, Compensation and Rehabilitation for Victims of Gross Violations of Human Rights and Fundamental Freedoms: Summary and Conclusions', in N.J.

Kritz (ed.) *Transitional Justice: How Emerging Democracies Reckon with Former Regimes. Volume 1: General Considerations*, Washington, DC: United States Institute of Peace Press.

Bratt, D. (1996) 'Assessing the Success of UN Peacekeeping', *International Peacekeeping*, 3(4): 64–81.

Brito, A.B. d. (2001) *The Politics of Memory and Democratization: Transitional Justice in Democratizing Societies*, Oxford: Oxford University Press.

Broer, H. and Emery, M. (1998) 'Civilian Police in UN Peacekeeping Operations', in R.B. Oakley, M.J. Dziedzic and E.M. Goldberg (eds) *Policing the New World Disorder: Peace Operations and Public Security*, Washington, DC: National Defense University Press.

Bullivant, D. (14 July 1997) Transcript of Joint Press Conference, Sarajevo: Coalition Press Information Centre. Online. Available at: www.nato.int/sfor/trans/1997/t970714a.htm (accessed 28 December 2007).

Captain MacEachern, D. (11 March 2003) Transcript of Press Conference, Sarajevo: Coalition Press Information Centre. Online. Available at: www.nato.int/sfor/trans/2003/t030311a.htm (accessed 28 December 2007).

Captain MacEachern, D. (11 April 2003) Transcript of Press Conference, Sarajevo: Coalition Press Information Centre. Online. Available at: www.nato.int/sfor/trans/2003/t030411a.htm (accessed 28 December 2007).

Captain Theriault, M. (21 December 1999) Transcript of Joint Press Conference, Sarajevo: Coalition Press Information Centre. Online. Available at: www.nato.int/sfor/trans/1999/t991221a.htm (accessed 28 December 2007).

Captain Van Dyke, M.A. (6 June 1996) Transcript of the Press Briefing, Sarajevo: Coalition Press Information Centre. Online. Available at: www.nato.int/ifor/trans/t960606a.htm (accessed 27 December 2007).

Cassidy, R.M. (2003) *Peacekeeping in the Abyss: British and American Peacekeeping Doctrine and Practice after the Cold War*, Westport, CT: Greenwood Press.

CBC News (20 January 2004) 'Posters of Karadzic Taunt NATO Troops'. Online. Available at: www.cbc.ca/world/story/2004/01/19/karadzic040119.html (accessed 5 January 2008).

Century Foundation (1998) *Making Justice Work: The Report of the Century Foundation/ Twentieth Century Fund Task Force on Apprehending Indicted War Criminals*, New York: Century Foundation Press.

Chairman of the Joint Chiefs of Staff (1999) *Joint Tactics Techniques and Procedures for Peace Operations*, Joint Publication 3–07.3, 12 February. Online. Available at: www.dtic.mil/doctrine/jel/new_pubs/jp3_07_3.pdf (accessed 29 December 2007).

Chandler, D. (2004) 'The Responsibility to Protect? Imposing the "Liberal Peace"', *International Peacekeeping*, 11(1): 59–81.

Chappell, D. (8 March 2005) Transcript of the International Agency's Joint Press Conference, Sarajevo: OHR. Online. Available at: www.ohr.int/ohr-dept/presso/pressb/default.asp?content_id=34146 (accessed 2 January 2008).

Chief of the General Staff (1995) *Wider Peacekeeping, Army Field Manual Volume 5, Operations Other than War, Part 2, Army Code 71359(A)*. London: HMSO.

Chief of Joint Operations (1998) *Peace Support Operations: Joint Warfare Publication 3–50*, London: HMSO.

Chris, P.M. (1997) 'The International Criminal Tribunal of Rwanda: Bringing the Killers to Book', *International Review of the Red Cross*, 321: 695–704.

Chuter, D. (2003) *War Crimes: Confronting Atrocity in the Modern World*, London: Lynne Rienner Publishers.

CNN (10 July 1997) 'NATO Roundup Signals Tougher Stand on Bosnian War Criminals'. Online. Available at: www.cnn.com/WORLD/9707/10/bosnia (accessed 27 December 2007).

CNN (7 July 1999) 'Top Bosnian Serb Politician Arrested for War Crimes'. Online. Available at: edition.cnn.com/WORLD/europe/9907/07/bosnia.war.crimes.arrest.01/ index.html (accessed 28 December 2007).

Cogan, J.K. (2000) 'The Problem of Obtaining Evidence for International Criminal Courts', *Human Rights Quarterly*, 22(2): 404–427.

Col Eiting, R.M. (2001) 'Workshop 2: The Need for Police Capacities and Skills when Arresting War Criminals; Aspects of Proportionality, Subsidiarity and Human Rights', in v.W.A.M. Dijk and J.I. Hovens (eds) *Arresting War Criminals: Special Publication by the Royal Dutch Constabulary*. Nijmegen: Wolf Legal Productions.

Col Kirkwood, J. (13 February 1996) Transcript of the Press Briefing, Sarajevo: Coalition Press Information Centre. Online. Available at: www.nato.int/ifor/trans/t960213a.htm (accessed 27 December 2007).

Col Kirkwood, J. (17 February 1996) Transcript of the Press Briefing, Sarajevo: Coalition Press Information Centre. Online. Available at: www.nato.int/ifor/trans/t960217a.htm (accessed 27 December 2007).

Col Wiggen, v.O.P. (2001) 'Workshop 3: Requirements, Conditions, Supplies and Feasibility of an Operational International Arrest Team', in v.W.A.M. Dijk and J.I. Hovens (eds) *Arresting War Criminals: Special Publication by the Royal Dutch Constabulary*. Nijmegen: Wolf Legal Productions.

Commissioner Fitzgerald (31 October 1996) Transcript of the Press Briefing, Sarajevo: Coalition Press Information Centre. Online. Available at: www.nato.int/ifor/trans/ t961031a.htm (accessed 27 December 2007).

Connaughton, R. (2001) *Military Intervention and Peacekeeping: The Reality*, Aldershot: Ashgate Publishing Group.

Del Ponte, C. (15 December 2005) 'Address by Carla Del Ponte, Prosecutor of the International Criminal Tribunal for the former Yugoslavia to the Security Council'. Online. Available at: www.un.org/icty/pressreal/2005/speech/delponte-sc-051215.htm (accessed 7 January 2008).

Del Ponte, C. (10 December 2007) 'Statement by Carla Del Ponte, Prosecutor, International Criminal Tribunal for the Former Yugoslavia to the Security Council 10 December 2007'. Online. Available at: www.un.org/icty/pressreal/2007/pr1202e-annex.htm (accessed 7 January 2008).

Diehl, P.F. (1993) *International Peacekeeping*, Baltimore, MD and London: Johns Hopkins University Press.

Dijk, W.A.M. and Hovens, J.J. (2001) *Arresting War Criminals: Special Publication by the Royal Dutch Constabulary*, Nijmegen: Wolf Legal Productions.

Dodson, M. and Jackson, D. (2004) 'Horizontal Accountability in Transitional Democracies: The Human Rights Ombudsman in El Salvador and Guatemala', *Latin American Politics and Societies*, 46(4): 1–27.

Doggett, M. and Kircher, I. (2005) El Salvador, Paper for Review Meeting on 'Role of Human Rights in Peace Agreements', International Council on Human Rights Policy, Belfast, 7–8 March 2005.

Dokmanovic, S. (8 September 1997) Transcript of Trial Hearing, Case number IT-95–13a-PT, Prosecutor v Slavko Dokmanovic. Online. Available at: www.Un.org/icty/transe13a/970908IT.html (accessed 3 January 2008).

Domin, T. (2002) 'The Noose Is Tightening around Karadzic', *SFOR Informer Edition*,

146. Online. Available at: www.nato.int/sfor/indexinf/146/p11a/t02p11a.htm (accessed 28 December 2007).

Dorn, W., Matloff, J. and Matthews, J. (2000) 'Preventing the Bloodbath: Could the UN Have Predicted and Prevented the Rwanda Genocide?' Online. Available at: www.rmc.ca/academic/gradrech/dorn4_e.html (accessed 1 January 2008).

Dougherty, B.K. (2004) 'Searching for Answers: Sierra Leone's Truth and Reconciliation Commission', *African Studies Quarterly*, 8(1). Online. Available at: www.africa.ufl.edu/asq/v8/v8i1a3.htm (accessed 3 January 2008).

Dziedzic, M.J. and Barr, A. (2002) 'Bosnia and the International Police Task Force', in R.B. Oakley, M.J. Dziedzic and E.M. Goldberg (eds) *Policing the New World Disorder: Peace Operations and Public Security*, Washington, DC: National Defense University Press.

Eick, M. (4 June 1996) Transcript of the Press Briefing, Sarajevo: Coalition Press Information Centre. Online. Available at: www.nato.int/ifor/trans/t960604a.htm (accessed 5 January 2008).

Fanton, J.F. (29 March 2005) 'US Obstructs Global Justice', *Los Angeles Times*. Online. Available at: www.globalpolicy.org/intljustice/icc/2005/0329usobstructs.htm (accessed 5 January 2008).

Fatic, A. (2000) *Reconciliation via the War Crimes Tribunal?*, Aldershot: Ashgate Publishing Ltd.

Feil, S.R. (1998) 'Preventing Genocide: How the Early Use of Force Might Have Succeeded in Rwanda', A Report to the Carnegie Commission on Preventing Deadly Conflict, Carnegie Corporation of New York. Online. Available at: www.wilsoncenter.org/subsites/ccpdc/pubs/rwanda/frame.htm (accessed 1 January 2008).

Ferencz, B.B. (1980) *An International Criminal Court: A Step towards World Peace*, London/Rome/New York: Oceana Publications Inc.

Fitz-Gerald, A.M. (2003) 'Implications for American, British and Other Allied Force Planning and for Postconflict Iraq', *Journal of Security Sector Management*, 1(2): 1–21. Online. Available at: www.ssronline.org/jofssm/issues/jofssm_0102_fitzgeralda_iraq.pdf?CFID=421646&CFTOKEN=73751898 (accessed 1 January 2008).

Foley, D. (1 July 1997) Transcript of Joint Press Conference, Sarajevo: Coalition Press Information Centre. Online. Available at: www.nato.int/sfor/trans/1997/t970701a.htm (accessed 28 December 2007).

Forsythe, D.P. (2002) 'The United States and International Criminal Justice', *Human Rights Quarterly*, 24(4): 974–991.

Frantzen, H.A. (2005) *Nato and Peace Support Operations, 1991–1999: Policies and Doctrines*, Abingdon: Taylor & Francis.

Gaeta, P. (1998) 'Is NATO Authorized or Obliged to Arrest Persons Indicted by the International Criminal Tribunal for the Former Yugoslavia?' *European Journal of Law*, 9(1): 174–181.

Gantz, P.H. (2004) 'No Peace without Justice: Lessons from Haiti for Afghanistan', *Refugees International*, 28 January. Online. Available at: www.refintl.org/content/article/detail/935/ (accessed 1 January 2008).

General Clark, W.K. (18 July 1997) Transcript of SACEUR Press Conference, Sarajevo: Coalition Press Information Centre. Online. Available at: www.nato.int/sfor/trans/1997/t970718b.htm (accessed 28 December 2007).

General Clark, W.K. (13 August 1997) Transcript of Joint Press Conference, Sarajevo: Coalition Press Information Centre. Online. Available at: www.nato.int/sfor/trans/1997/t970813b.htm (accessed 28 December 2007).

General Clark, W.K. (12 September 1997) Transcript of Joint Press Conference, Sarajevo: Coalition Press Information Centre. Online. Available at: www.nato.int/sfor/trans/1997/t970912b.htm (accessed 28 December 2007).

General Clark, W.K. (25 April 2000) Transcript of SACEUR Press Conference, Sarajevo: Coalition Press Information Centre. Online. Available at: www.nato.int/sfor/trans/2000/t000425a.htm (accessed 28 December 2007).

General Joulwan, G. (7 July 1997) Transcript of Joint Press Conference, Sarajevo: Coalition Press Information Centre. Online. Available at: www.nato.int/ifor/trans/t970707b.htm (accessed 28 December 2007).

General Ralston, J.W. (22 May 2001) Remarks at the Atlantic Treaty Association, the Eisenhower Centre, SHAPE Headquarters. Online. Available at: www.nato.int/shape/opinions/2001/s010522a.htm (accessed 28 December 2007).

General Walker, M. (22 May 1996) Transcript of the Press Briefing, Sarajevo: Coalition Press Information Centre. Online. Available at: www.nato.int/ifor/trans/t960522a.htm (accessed 27 December 2007).

Gray, T. (2003) 'To Keep You Is No Gain, to Kill You Is No Loss – Securing Justice through the ICC', *Arizona Journal of International Comparative Law*, 20: 645–688.

Hagan, J. (2003) *Justice in the Balkans: Prosecuting War Crimes in the Hague Tribunal*, Chicago, IL: University of Chicago Press.

Haines, A.D. (2003) 'Accountability in Sierra Leone: The Role of the Special Court', in J.E. Stromseth (ed.) *Accountability for Atrocities: National and International Responses*, Ardsley, NY: Transnational Publishers Inc.

Harris, P. and Reilly, B. (1998) *Democracy and Deep-rooted Conflict: Options for Negotiators*, Stockholm: International Institute for Democracy and Electoral Assistance.

Harston, J. (2000) Statement by Mr Julien Harston, Deputy Special Representative of the Secretary-General UNMIBH, 'Responding to International Crises: Are Current Policies and Practices the Answer?' The Institute for Research on Public Policy, Montreal, 18 November. Online. Available at: www.irpp.org/events/archive/nov00/harston.pdf (accessed 1 January 2008).

Hayner, P.B. (1994) 'Fifteen Truth Commissions – 1974–1994: A Comparative Study', *Human Rights Quarterly*, 16(4): 597–655.

Hayner, P.B. (2001) *Unspeakable Truths: Facing the Challenges of Truth Commissions*, London: Taylor & Francis.

Headquarters Department of the Army (1994) *Peace Operations*, FM 100–23, December, Washington, DC: Headquarters Department of the Army.

Held, D. (1993) 'Democracy: From City-states to a Cosmopolitan Order?', in D. Held (ed.) *Prospects for Democracy: North, South, East, West*, Cambridge: Polity Press.

Held, D. (1995) 'Democracy and the New International Order', in D. Archiburgi and D. Held (eds) *Cosmopolitan Democracy*, Cambridge: Polity Press.

Held, D. (1996) *Democracy and the Global Order: From the Modern State to Cosmopolitan Governance*, Cambridge: Polity Press.

Held, D. (2001) 'Violence, Law and Justice in a Global Age'. Online. Available at: www.ssrc.org/sept11/essays/held.htm (accessed 22 December 2007).

Held, D. and McGrew, A. (eds) (2000) *The Globalisation Transformations Reader: An Introduction to the Globalisation Debate*, Cambridge: Polity Press.

Held, D., McGrew, A., Goldblatt, D. and Perraton, J. (1999) *Global Transformations: Politics, Economics and Culture*, Oxford: Blackwell Publishers.

Hendrickx, M.M.L.A. (2001) 'An Operational Blueprint for Arresting War Criminals: A Low Risk and a High Risk Scenario', in v.W.A.M. Dijk and J.I. Hovens (eds) *Arrest-*

ing *War Criminals*: *Special Publication by the Royal Dutch Constabulary*, Nijmegen: Wolf Legal Productions.

Henry L. Stimson Centre (2007) *UNMIL*, Peace Operations Fact Sheet Series. Online. Available at: www.stimson.org/fopo/pdf/UNMIL_Fact_Sheet_Jul_07.pdf (accessed 1 January 2008).

Hodzic, R. (11 April 2003) Transcript of Press Conference, Sarajevo: Coalition Press Information Centre. Online. Available at: www.nato.int/sfor/trans/2003/t030411a.htm (accessed 28 December 2007).

Hooper, J. (undated) 'Dayton's Mandate for Apprehending War Criminals', *Frontline Online*. Available at: www.pbs.org/wgbh/pages/frontline/shows/karadzic/trial/hooper. html (accessed 27 December 2007).

Howard, M. (2007) 'Four Years after Its Compound Was Bombed, UN Renews Mission to Bring Peace to Iraq', *Guardian*, 10 December. Online. Available at: www.guardian.co.uk/international/story/0,,2224864,00.html (accessed 5 January 2008).

Human Rights Watch (1996a) 'Rwanda'. Online. Available at: www.hrw.org/reports/1996/WR96/Africa-08.htm (accessed 1 January 2008).

Human Rights Watch (1996b) 'Human Rights in Bosnia and Herzegovina Post Dayton: Challenges for the Field', 8(2) March 1996. Online. Available at: www.hrw.org/summaries/s.bosnia963.html (accessed 7 January 2008).

Human Rights Watch (10 July 1997) 'Human Rights Watch Applauds NATO Efforts to Apprehend War Criminals'. Online. Available at: hrw.org/english/docs/1997/07/10/yugosl8842.htm (accessed 29 December 2007).

Human Rights Watch (18 November 1997) 'Good Neighbours? NATO and Indicted War Crimes Suspects in Bosnia and Herzegovina', Human Rights News. Online. Available at: hrw.org/english/docs/1997/11/18/bosher1510.htm (accessed 5 January 2008).

Human Rights Watch (1998) 'Liberia', *World Report*. Online. Available at: www.hrw.org/worldreport/Africa-07.htm (accessed 1 January 2008).

Human Rights Watch (1999a) 'Angola Unravels'. Online. Available at: www.hrw.org/reports/1999/angola/Angl998–10.htm (accessed 1 January 2008).

Human Rights Watch (1999b) 'Croatia', *World Report*. Online. Available at: www.hrw.org/worldreport99/europe/croatia.html (accessed 2 January 2008).

Human Rights Watch (1999c) 'Guatemala', *World Report*. Online. Available at: www.hrw.org/worldreport99/americas/guatemala.html (accessed 1 January 2008).

Human Rights Watch (1999d) 'Sierra Leone', *World Report*. Online. Available at: www.hrw.org/worldreport99/africa/sierraleone.html (accessed 2 January 2008).

Human Rights Watch (2001) 'East Timor', *World Report*. Online. Available at: www.hrw.org/wr2k1/asia/etimor.html (accessed 1 January 2008).

Human Rights Watch (2002) 'East Timor', *World Report*. Online. Available at: hrw.org/wr2k2/asia5.html (accessed 1 January 2008).

Human Rights Watch (2003) 'East Timor', *World Report*. Online. Available at: hrw.org/wr2k3/asia5.html (accessed 1 January 2008).

Human Rights Watch (2004) 'Bringing Justice: The Special Court for Sierra Leone Accomplishments, Shortcomings, and Needed Support', (8 September), New York: Human Rights Watch.

Human Rights Watch (2005a) '"Safe Areas" for Srebrenica's Most Wanted: A Decade of Failure to Apprehend Karadzic and Mladic', *A Human Rights Watch Briefing Paper*, (29 June). Online. Available at: hrw.org/backgrounder/eca/srebrenica0605/ (accessed 29 December 2007).

Human Rights Watch (2005b) 'Essential Background: Overview of Human Rights Issues in East Timor', *World Report*. Online. Available at: hrw.org/english/docs/2005/01/13/eastti9825.htm (accessed 1 January 2008).

Human Rights Watch (2006a) 'Argentina: "Disappearances" Trial Break Years of Impunity', *Human Rights News*, 19, June. Online. Available at: hrw.org/english/docs/2006/06/19/argent13580.htm (accessed 27 December 2007).

Human Rights Watch (2006b) 'Chile: Pinochet's Legacy May End Up Aiding Victims'. *Human Rights News*, 10, December. Online. Available at: hrw.org/english/docs/2006/12/10/chile14805.htm (accessed 27 December 2007).

Human Rights Watch (2006c) 'Not on the Agenda: The Continuing Failure to Address Accountability in Kosovo Post-March 2004'. Online. Available at: hrw.org/reports/2006/kosovo0506/ (accessed 2 January 2008).

Human Rights Watch (2006d) 'Tortured Beginnings: Police Violence and the Beginnings of Impunity in East Timor'. Online. Available at: hrw.org/reports/2006/eastti-mor0406/5.htm (accessed 1 January 2008).

Human Rights Watch (2006e) 'Liberia', *World Report*. Online. Available at: hrw.org/english/docs/2006/01/18/liberi12315.htm (accessed 1 January 2008).

Human Rights Watch (2006f) 'Haiti', *World Report*. Online. Available at: hrw.org/english/docs/2006/01/18/haiti12210.htm (accessed 1 January 2008).

Human Rights Watch (2006g) 'Democratic Republic of Congo', *World Report*. Online. Available at: hrw.org/english/docs/2006/01/18/congo12237.htm (accessed 3 January 2008).

Human Rights Watch (2006h) 'Côte d'Ivoire', *World Report*. Online. Available at: hrw.org/english/docs/2006/01/18/cotedi12314.htm (accessed 3 January 2008).

Human Rights Watch (2007a) 'Congo', *World Report*. Online. Available at: hrw.org/eng-lishwr2k7/docs/2007/01/11/congo14780.htm (accessed 1 January 2008).

Human Rights Watch (2007b) 'Liberia', *World Report*. Online. Available at: hrw.org/englishwr2k7/docs/2007/01/11/liberi14716.htm (accessed 1 January 2008).

Human Rights Watch (2007c) 'Côte d'Ivoire', *World Report*. Online. Available at: hrw.org/englishwr2k7/docs/2007/01/11/cotedi14956.htm (accessed 1 January 2008).

Human Rights Watch (2007d) 'Sudan', *World Report*. Online. Available at: hrw.org/eng-lishwr2k7/docs/2007/01/11/sudan14715.htm (accessed 1 January 2008).

Human Rights Watch (2007e) 'Haiti', *World Report*. Online. Available at: hrw.org/eng-lishwr2k7/docs/2007/01/11/haiti14862.htm (accessed 1 January 2008).

Huyse, L. (1995) 'Justice after Transition: On the Choices Successor Elites Make in Dealing with the Past', *Law & Social Inquiry*, 20(1): 51–78.

ICTR (2007) 'The Tribunal at a Glance'. Online. Available at: 69.94.11.53/default.htm (accessed 27 December 2007).

ICTY (10 July 1997) 'Accused Kovacevic Transferred to the Hague', Press release CC/PIO/225-E. Online. Available at: www.un.org/icty/latest/index.htm (accessed 27 December 2007).

ICTY (18 December 1997) 'Anto Furundzija to Enter a Plea on Friday 19 December 1997', Press release CC/PIO/277-E. Online. Available at: www.un.org/icty/latest/index.htm (accessed 27 December 2007).

ICTY (22 January 1998) 'Initial Appearance of Goran Jelisic on Monday 26 January', Press release CC/PIO/285-E. Online. Available at: www.un.org/icty/latest/index.htm (accessed 28 December 2007).

ICTY (9 April 1998) 'Initial Appearance of Miroslav Kvocka and Mladen Radic on Tuesday 14 April', Press release CC/PIU/308-E. Online. Available at: www.un.org/icty/latest/index.htm (accessed 28 December 2007).

ICTY (29 May 1998) 'Initial Appearance of Milojica Kos Scheduled on Tuesday 2 June 1998 at 5 pm', Press release CC/PIU/320-E. Online. Available at: www.un.org/icty/latest/index.htm (accessed 28 December 2007).

ICTY (15 June 1998) 'Milorad Krnojelac Detained under a Sealed Indictment and Transferred to the International Tribunal', Press release CC/PIU/324-E. Online. Available at: www.un.org/icty/latest/index.htm (accessed 28 December 2007).

ICTY (9 October 2002) 'The Prosecutor v. Dragan Nikolic – Case no. IT-94-2-PT; Decision on Defense Motion Challenging the Exercise of Jurisdiction by the Tribunal, Trial Chamber II', *Judicial Supplement*, 37.

ICTY (22 June 2004) Todorovic (IT-95-9/1), Case Information Sheet. Online. Available at: www.un.org/icty/latest-e/index.htm (accessed 29 December 2007).

ICTY (23 September 2004) Brdjanin (IT-99-36), Case Information Sheet. Online. Available at: www.un.org/icty/glance/brdjanin.htm (accessed 28 December 2007).

ICTY (28 September 2007) 'Key Figures of ICTY Cases'. Online. Available at: www.un.org/icty/cases-e/factsheets/profact-e.html (accessed 27 December 2007).

ICTY Chambers (20 October 2000) 'Decision on Todorovic's Motion for Judicial Assistance', Press release XT/P.I.S./536-e. The Hague.

ICTY Registry (1998) 'The Omarska and Keraterm Cases: Further Initial Appearance of 10 December 1998 of Defendants Radic, Kvocka, Zigic and Kos', Press release CC/PIU/366-E, The Hague, 30 November.

Institute for Global Policy (4 January 2008) 'Responsibility to Protect Engaging Civil Society'. Online. Available at: www.responsibilitytoprotect.org/ (accessed 4 January 2008).

International Centre for Transitional Justice (2004) 'Bosnia and Herzegovina: Selected Developments in Transitional Justice', Case Studies Series, October. Online. Available at: www.ictj.org/images/content/1/1/113.pdf (accessed 6 January 2008).

International Centre for Transitional Justice (2006) 'The Price of Healing', *All Africa*, 4 August. Online. Available at: www.ictj.org/en/news/coverage/article/990.html (accessed 7 January 2008).

International Centre for Transitional Justice (2007) 'Timor-Leste'. Online. Available at: www.ictj.org/en/where/region3/628.html (accessed 7 January 2008).

International Crisis Group (1996) 'Why the Bosnian Elections Must Be Postponed', *Bosnia Report*, 14, 14 August. Online. Available at: www.crisisgroup.org/home/index.cfm?id=1504&l=1 (accessed 6 January 2008).

International Crisis Group (1997) 'Dayton: Two Years O: A Review of Progress in Implementing the Dayton Peace Accords in Bosnia, *Bosnia Project – Report*, 27, 19 November. Online. Available at: www.crisisgroup.org/library/documents/report_archive/A400154_19111997.pdf (accessed 6 January 2008).

International Crisis Group (1999) 'Starting from Scratch in Kosovo: The Honeymoon Is Over', *Balkans Report*, 83, Prishtinë/Pri_tina, 10 December 1999. Online. Available at: www.crisisgroup.org/library/documents/report_archive/A400022_10121999.pdf (accessed 3 January 2008).

International Crisis Group (2000) 'War Criminals in Bosnia's Republika Srpska: Who Are the People in Your Neighbourhood?' *ICG Balkans Report No. 103*, 2 November.

International Crisis Group (2002a) 'Policing the Police in Bosnia: A Further Reform Agenda, *Europe Report*, 130, 10 May. Online. Available at: www.crisisgroup.org/home/index.cfm?id=1500&l=1 (accessed 1 January 2008).

International Crisis Group (2002b) 'Finding the Balance the Scales of Justice in Kosovo', *Balkans Report*, 134, 12 September, Pristina/Brussels. Online. Available at: www.crisisgroup.org/home/index.cfm?id=1609&l=1 (accessed 1 January 2008).

International Crisis Group (2002c) 'Courting Disaster: The Misrule of Law in Bosnia and Herzegovina', *Europe Report*, 127, 25 March. Online. Available at: www.crisisgroup.org/home/index.cfm?id=1497&l=1 (accessed 5 January 2008).

International Crisis Group (2002d) 'Sierra Leone's Truth and Reconciliation Commission: A Fresh Start?', *Africa Briefing*, 12, 20 December. Online. Available at: www.crisisgroup.org/home/index.cfm?id=1801&l=1 (accessed 6 January 2008).

International Crisis Group (2003a) 'The Special Court for Sierra Leone: Promises and Pitfalls of a "New Model"', *Africa Briefing*, 16, 4 August. Online. Available at: www.crisisgroup.org/home/index.cfm?l=1&id=1803 (accessed 27 December 2007).

International Crisis Group (2003b) 'The International Criminal Tribunal for Rwanda: Time for Pragmatism', *Africa Report*, 69, 26 September. Online. Available at: www.crisisgroup.org/home/index.cfm?l=1&id=2303 (accessed 27 December 2007).

International Crisis Group (2004) 'Liberia and Sierra Leone: Rebuilding Failed States', *Africa Report*, 87, 8 December. Online. Available at: www.crisisgroup.org/home/ index.cfm?id=3157&CFID=26191110&CFTOKEN=48139809 (accessed 1 January 2008).

International Crisis Group (2005) 'Kosovo after Haradinaj', *Europe Report*, 163, 26 May. Online. Available at: www.crisisgroup.org/home/index.cfm?id=3474 (accessed 6 January 2008).

International Crisis Group (2006a) 'Kosovo: The Challenge of Transition'. Online. Available at: www.crisisgroup.org/home/index.cfm?id=3955&CFID=26191110& CFTOKEN=48139809 (accessed 1 January 2008).

International Crisis Group (2006b) 'Liberia: Resurrecting the Justice System', *Africa Report*, 107, 6 April 2006. Online. Available at: www.crisisgroup.org/ home/index.cfm?id=4061&l=1 (accessed 1 January 2008).

International Crisis Group (2006c) 'Haiti: Security and the Reintegration of the State', *Latin America/Caribbean Briefing*, 12, Port-au-Prince/Brussels, 30 October. Online. Available at: www.crisisgroup.org/home/index.cfm?id=4475&l=1 (accessed 3 January 2008).

International Crisis Group (2007) 'Haiti: Justice Reform and the Security Crisis', *Latin America/Caribbean Briefing*, 14, Port-au-Prince/Brussels, 31 January. Online. Available at: www.crisisgroup.org/home/index.cfm?id=4639&l=1 (accessed 1 January 2008).

Ivanko, A. (13 February 1996) Transcript of the Press Briefing, Sarajevo: Coalition Press Information Centre. Online. Available at: www.nato.int/ifor/trans/t960213a.htm (accessed 5 January 2008).

Ivanko, A. (11 December 1996) Transcript of the Press Briefing, Sarajevo: Coalition Press Information Centre. Online. Available at: www.nato.int/ifor/trans/t961211a.htm (accessed 27 December 2007).

Ivanko, A. (12 December 1996) Transcript of the Press Briefing, Sarajevo: Coalition Press Information Centre. Online. Available at: www.nato.int/ifor/trans/t961212a.htm (accessed 27 December 2007).

Izes, B. (1997) 'Drawing Lines in the Sand: When State-Sanctioned Abductions of War Criminals Should Be Permitted', *Columbia Journal of Law and Social Problems*, 31(1): 1–37.

Järvinen, T. (2004) 'Human Rights and Post-Conflict Transitional Justice in East Timor', *UPI Working Papers*, 47. Helsinki: Finnish Institute of International Affairs.

Jeannet, S. (2000) 'Testimony of ICRC Delegates before the International Criminal Court', *International Review of the Red Cross*, 840: 993–1000.

Jelacic, N. and Griffiths, H. (2004) 'Why Can't NATO Catch Radovan Karadzic, Europe's Most Wanted Man?' *Balkan Crisis Report*, 490, 2 April, Institute for War and Peace Reporting. Online. Available at: iwpr.net/index.php?apc_state=hen&s=o&o=p=bcr&s=f&o=157412 (accessed 1 January 2008).

Jennings, C. (17 February 2003) 'British Special Forces in Albanian Arrest Mission', *The Telegraph*. Online. Available at: www.telegraph.co.uk/news/main.jhtml?xml=/news/2003/02/18/wkos18.xml (accessed 28 December 2007).

Jennings, C. (18 February 2003) 'British Troops Hunt Down Former KLA Men', *The Scotsman*. Online. Available at: http://news.scotsman.com/latestnews/British-troops-hunt-down-former.2403394.jp (accessed 28 December 2007)

Jett, D.C. (1999) *Why Peacekeeping Fails*, Basingstoke: Palgrave.

Joint Doctrine and Concepts Centre (2004) *The Military Contribution to Peace Support Operations, Joint War Publication 3–50*, 2nd edn, Shrivenham: Ministry of Defence. Online. Available at: coe-dmha.org/PKO/USA04/images/references/jwp3_50.pdf (accessed 29 December 2007).

Joint Chiefs of Staff (1995) *Joint Doctrine for Military Operations other Than War*, Joint Pub 3–07, June. Online. Available at: www.bits.de/NRANEU/others/jp-doctrine/jp3_07.pdf (accessed 1 January 2008).

Joint Chiefs of Staff (2001) *Joint Doctrine for Civil-Military Operations*, Joint Pub 3–57, February. Online. Available at: www.dtic.mil/doctrine/jel/new_pubs/jp3_57.pdf (accessed 1 January 2008).

Joris, J.J. (2 May 2001) 'ICTY Weekly Press Briefing'. Online. Available at: www.un.org/icty/briefing/PB020501.htm (accessed 7 January 2008).

Juma, L. (2002) 'The Human Rights Approach to Peace in Sierra Leone: The Analysis of the Peace Process and Human Rights Enforcement in a Civil War', *Denver Journal of International Law and Policy*, 30(3): 81–138.

Kahn, P.W. (2003) 'Why the United States Is So Opposed', the International Criminal Court: An End to Impunity, *Crimes of War Project*, December 2003. Online. Available at: www.crimesofwar.org/icc_magazine/icc-kahn.html (accessed 5 January 2008).

Kaldor, M. (2001) *New and Old Wars: Organised Violence in a Global Era*, Cambridge: Polity Press.

Kalinauskas, M. (2002) 'The Use of International Military Force in Arresting War Criminals: The Lessons of the International Criminal Tribunal for the Former Yugoslavia', *Kansas Law Review*, 50: 383–429.

Kamatali, J.M. (2003) 'The Challenge of Linking International Criminal Justice and National Reconciliation: The Case of ICTR', *Leiden Journal of International Law*, 16(1): 115–133.

Kampschror, B. (2001) 'A Bit Suspect: What Is the Real Reason So Many War Criminals Still Walk Free in Bosnia', *Central Europe Review*, 3(3), 22 January. Online. Available at: www.ce-review.org/01/3/kampschror3.html (accessed 5 January 2008).

Kauffman, C. (2005) 'Transitional Justice in Guatemala: Linking the Past and the Future', Prepared for the ISA-South Conference, Miami, Florida, 3–5 November.

Kaye, M. (1997) 'The Role of Truth Commissions in the Search for Justice, Reconciliation and Democratization: The Salvadorian and Honduran Cases', *Journal of Latin American Studies*, 29(3): 693–717.

Keohane, R.O. and Nye, J.S. (1972) *Transnational Relations and World Politics*, Cambridge, MA: Harvard University Press.

Keohane, R.O. and Nye, J.S. (1974) 'Transgovernmental Relations and International Organizations', *World Politics*, 27 (1): 39–62.

Keohane, R.O. and Nye, J.S. (1977) *Power and Interdependence: World Politics in Transition*, Boston, MA: Little, Brown.

KFOR interview (2003) Interviews with senior military officers from KFOR conducted by the author in Kosovo.

KFOR (17 February 2003a) 'KFOR's Detention of Indicted War Criminals', Press release. Online. Available at: www.nato.int/docu/pr/2003/p03–010e.htm (accessed 28 December 2007).

KFOR (17 February 2003b) 'KFOR's Detention of Indicted War Criminals Haradin Bala (aka Shala), Isak Musliu (aka Qerqiz) and Agim Murtezi (aka Murrizi)', Press release. Online. Available at: www.nato.int/docu/pr/2003/p03–011e.htm (accessed 28 December 2007).

KFOR (17 February 2003c) 'SACEUR "Well Done KFOR"', Press release, *SHAPE News*. Online. Available at: www.nato.int/shape/news/2003/02/i030219a.htm (accessed 28 December 2007).

KFOR (11 October 2007) 'Multinational Specialised Unit'. Online. Available at: www.nato.int/kfor/structur/units/msu.html (accessed 7 January 2008).

Khouri-Padova, L. (2004) 'Haiti: Lessons Learned', United Nations Peacekeeping in the Name of Peace Discussion Paper, March. New York: UN Department of Peacekeeping Operations, Peacekeeping Best Practices Unit.

Kolodkin, R. (1996) 'Ad Hoc International Tribunal for the Prosecution of Serious Violations of International Humanitarian Law in the Former Yugoslavia', in R.S. Clark and M. Sann (eds) *The Prosecution of International Crimes: A Critical Study of the International Tribunal for the Former Yugoslavia*, New Brunswick, NJ and London: Transaction Publishers.

Kristof, N.D. (16 October 2005) 'Schoolyard Bully Diplomacy', *New York Times*. Online. Available at: www.globalpolicy.org/intljustice/icc/2005/1016schoolyard.htm (accessed 5 January 2008).

Kritz, N.J. (1995) *Transitional Justice: How Emerging Democracies Reckon with Former Regimes, Volume 1: General Considerations*, Washington, DC: United States Institute of Peace Press.

Kyl, J. (2004) 'Senator Calls on Congress and White House to Protect Troops from the International Criminal Court', *Human Events*, 10 December. Online. Available at: www.globalpolicy.org/intljustice/icc/2004/1210kyl.htm (accessed 5 January 2008).

Lamb, S. (2000) 'The Powers of Arrest of the International Criminal Tribunal for the Former Yugoslavia', in J. Crawford and V. Lowe (eds) *The British Yearbook of International Law*, Oxford: Clarendon Press.

Larson, E. (2004) 'Comment: Karadzic's Protective Ring', 26 January. Online. Available at: www.globalpolicy.org/intljustice/wanted/2004/0126ring.htm (accessed 3 January 2008).

Lederach, J P. (1998) *Building Peace: Sustainable Reconciliation in Divided Societies*, Washington, DC: United States Institute of Peace.

Leurdijk, D.A. (2001) 'Arresting War Criminals: The Establishment of an International Arresting Team: Fiction, Reality or Both?', in v.W.A.M. Dijk and J.I. Hovens (eds) *Arresting War Criminals: Special Publication by the Royal Dutch Constabulary*. Nijmegen: Wolf Legal Productions.

Lightburn, D. (2001) 'Lessons Learned', *NATO Review*, 49(2): 12–15. Online. Available at: www.nato.int/docu/review/2001/0102–03.htm (accessed 29 December 2007).

Linklater, A. (1998) *The Transformation of Political Community: Ethical Foundations of the Post-Westphalian Era*, Oxford: Blackwell Publishers.

Lopez-Terres, P. (2006) 'Arrest and Transfer of Indictees: The Experience of the ICTY', 15 December. Online. Available at: www.icln.net/htm/Annual%20conference%202006/Presentation_Lopez-Terres.pdf (accessed 7 January 2008).

Lorenz, F.M. (1997) 'War Criminals – Testing the Limits of Military Force: Commentary', *Joint Force Quarterly*, 16: 59–65.

Lt Bouysson, E. (14 March 2002) 'Searching for Doctor Karadzic', *SFOR Informer Edition*, 134. Online. Available at: www.nato.int/sfor/indexinf/134/p03a/t02p03a.htm (accessed 28 December 2007).

Lt Cdr Chamberlain, G. (10 January 1999) Transcript of Joint Press Conference, Sarajevo: Coalition Press Information Centre. Online. Available at: www.nato.int/sfor/trans/1999/t990110a.htm (accessed 28 December 2007).

Lt Cdr Garneau, L. (22 January 1998) Transcript of Joint Press Conference, Sarajevo: Coalition Press Information Centre. Online. Available at: www.nato.int/sfor/trans/1998/t980122a.htm (accessed 28 December 2007).

Lt Cdr Garneau, L. (23 January 1998) Transcript of Joint Press Conference, Sarajevo: Coalition Press Information Centre. Online. Available at: www.nato.int/sfor/trans/1998/t980123a.htm (accessed 28 December 2007).

Lt Cdr Garneau, L. (9 April 1998) Transcript of Joint Press Conference, Sarajevo: Coalition Press Information Centre. Online. Available at: www.nato.int/sfor/trans/1998/t980409a.htm (accessed 28 December 2007).

Lt Cdr Percival, C. (25 January 2005) Transcript of the International Agency's Joint Press Conference, Sarajevo: OHR. Online. Available at: www.ohr.int/ohr-dept/presso/pressb/default.asp?content_id=33955 (accessed 2 January 2008).

Lt Cdr Thomson, S. (3 December 1998) Transcript of Joint Press Conference, Sarajevo: Coalition Press Information Centre. Online. Available at: www.nato.int/sfor/trans/1998/t981203a.htm (accessed 28 December 2007).

Lt Cdr Thomson, S. (12 January 1999) Transcript of Joint Press Conference, Sarajevo: Coalition Press Information Centre. Online. Available at: www.nato.int/sfor/trans/1999/t990112a.htm (accessed 28 December 2007).

Lt Cdr Thomson, S. (8 June 1999) Transcript of Joint Press Conference, Sarajevo: Coalition Press Information Centre. Online. Available at: www.nato.int/sfor/trans/1999/t990608a.htm (accessed 28 December 2007).

Lt Col Hardenbol, R.A. (2001) 'Workshop 3: Requirements, Conditions, Supplies and Feasibility of an Operational International Arrest Team', in v.W.A.M. Dijk and J.I. Hovens (eds) *Arresting War Criminals: Special Publication by the Royal Dutch Constabulary*. Nijmegen: Wolf Legal Productions.

Lt Col Rayner, M. (11 February 1996) Transcript of the Press Briefing, Sarajevo: Coalition Press Information Centre. Online. Available at: www.nato.int/ifor/trans/t960211a.htm (accessed 27 December 2007).

Lt Col Rayner, M. (12 February 1996) Transcript of the Press Briefing, Sarajevo: Coalition Press Information Centre. Online. Available at: www.nato.int/ifor/trans/t960212a.htm (accessed 27 December 2007).

Lt Col Rayner, M. (14 February 1996) Transcript of the Press Briefing, Sarajevo: Coalition Press Information Centre. Online. Available at: www.nato.int/ifor/trans/t960214a.htm (accessed 27 December 2007).

Lt Col Rayner, M. (29 February 1996) Transcript of the Press Briefing, Sarajevo: Coalition Press Information Centre. Online. Available at: www.nato.int/ifor/trans/t960229a.htm (accessed 27 December 2007).

Lt Col Reddin, D. (13 February 1996) Transcript of the Press Briefing, Sarajevo: Coalition Press Information Centre. Online. Available at: www.nato.int/ifor/trans/t960213a .htm (accessed 27 December 2007).

Lt Gen Dodson, M. (4 September 2001) Transcript of Joint Press Conference, Sarajevo: Coalition Press Information Centre. Online. Available at: www.nato.int/sfor/trans/ 2001/t010904b.htm (accessed 28 December 2007).

Lt Gen Silva, M. d. (1998) 'Implementing the Combined Joint Task Force Concept', *NATO Review*, 46(4): 16–19.

Lyck, M. (2006) 'Peace Operations and Accountability for War Crimes', PhD thesis, Department of Peace Studies, University of Bradford, June.

Lyck, M. (2007) 'International Peace Enforcers and Indicted War Criminals: The Case of Ramush Haradinaj', *International Peacekeeping*, 14(3): 418–432.

Mackinlay, J. and Alao, A. (1995) 'Liberia 1994: ECOMOG and UNOMIL Response to a Complex Emergency', Occasional Papers Series 2: UNU Press. Online. Available at: www.unu.edu/unupress/ops2.html#Fundamental (accessed 1 January 2008).

Major Boudreau, B. (3 July 1996) Transcript of the Press Briefing, Sarajevo: Coalition Press Information Centre. Online. Available at: www.nato.int/ifor/trans/t960703a.htm (accessed 27 December 2007).

Major Boudreau, B. (13 August 1996) Transcript of the Press Briefing, Sarajevo: Coalition Press Information Centre. Online. Available at: www.nato.int/ifor/trans/t960813a. htm (accessed 27 December 2007).

Major Boudreau, B. (29 November 1996) Transcript of the Press Briefing, Sarajevo: Coalition Press Information Centre. Online. Available at: www.nato.int/ifor/trans/ t961129a.htm (accessed 27 December 2007).

Major Boudreau, B. (11 December 1996) Transcript of the Press Briefing, Sarajevo: Coalition Press Information Centre. Online. Available at: www.nato.int/ifor/trans/ t961211a.htm (accessed 27 December 2007).

Major Clarke, P. (9 December 1997) Transcript of Joint Press Conference, Sarajevo: Coalition Press Information Centre. Online. Available at: www.nato.int/sfor/trans/ 1997/t971209a.htm (accessed 28 December 2007).

Major Clarke, P. (18 December 1997) Transcript of Joint Press Conference, Sarajevo, Tito Barracks: Coalition Press Information Centre. Online. Available at: www.nato.int/ sfor/trans/1997/t971218a.htm (accessed 27 December 2007).

Major Desjardins, Y. (15 August 2000) Transcript of Joint Press Conference, Sarajevo: Coalition Press Information Centre. Online. Available at: www.nato.int/sfor/trans/ 2000/t000815a.htm (accessed 28 December 2007).

Major General Leakey, D. (16 December 2004) COM EUFOR Press Statement, Press Release. Online. Available at: www.euforbih.org/press/p041216b.htm (accessed 2 January 2008).

Major Haselock, S. (29 February 1996) Transcript of the Press Briefing, Sarajevo: Coalition Press Information Centre. Online. Available at: www.nato.int/ifor/trans/t960229a. htm (accessed 29 December 2007).

Major Haselock, S. (16 May 1996) Transcript of the Press Briefing, Sarajevo: Coalition Press Information Centre. Online. Available at: www.nato.int/ifor/trans/t960516a.htm (accessed 27 December 2007).

Major Haselock, S. (27 May 1996) Transcript of the Press Briefing, Sarajevo: Coalition Press Information Centre. Online. Available at: www.nato.int/ifor/trans/t960527a.htm (accessed 27 December 2007).

Major Haselock, S. (4 June 1996) Transcript of the Press Briefing, Sarajevo: Coalition Press Information Centre. Online. Available at: www.nato.int/ifor/trans/t960604a.htm (accessed 27 December 2007).

Major Haselock, S. (20 June 1996) Transcript of the Press Briefing, Sarajevo: Coalition Press Information Centre. Online. Available at: www.nato.int/ifor/trans/t960620a.htm (accessed 27 December 2007).

Major Haselock, S. (1 July 1996) Transcript of the Press Briefing, Sarajevo: Coalition Press Information Centre. Online. Available at: www.nato.int/ifor/trans/t960701a.htm (accessed 27 December 2007).

Major Haselock, S. (12 September 1996) Transcript of the Press Briefing, Sarajevo: Coalition Press Information Centre. Online. Available at: www.nato.int/ifor/trans/t960912a.htm (accessed 27 December 2007).

Major Haselock, S. (30 October 1996) Transcript of the Press Briefing, Sarajevo: Coalition Press Information Centre. Online. Available at: www.nato.int/ifor/trans/t961030a.htm (accessed 27 December 2007).

Major Lundy, S. (2 April 2002) Transcript of Press Conference, Sarajevo: Coalition Press Information Centre. Online. Available at: www.nato.int/sfor/trans/2002/t020402a.htm (accessed 28 December 2007).

Major Lundy, S. (4 July 2002) Transcript of Press Conference, Sarajevo: Coalition Press Information Centre. Online. Available at: www.nato.int/sfor/trans/2002/t020704a.htm (accessed 28 December 2007).

Major Lundy, S. (15 August 2002) Transcript of Press Conference, Sarajevo: Coalition Press Information Centre. Online. Available at: www.nato.int/sfor/trans/2002/t020815a.htm (accessed 28 December 2007).

Major Mell, S. (21 January 2003) Transcript – Press Conference, Sarajevo: Coalition Press Information Centre. Online. Available at: www.nato.int/sfor/trans/2003/t030121a.htm (accessed 29 December 2007).

Major Moyer, T. (12 February 1996) Transcript of the Press Briefing, Sarajevo: Coalition Press Information Centre. Online. Available at: www.nato.int/ifor/trans/t960212a.htm (accessed 27 December 2007).

Major Odom, M. (22 January 2002) Transcript of Joint Press Conference, Sarajevo: Coalition Press Information Centre. Online. Available at: www.nato.int/sfor/trans/2002/t020122a.htm (accessed 28 December 2007).

Major Riley, C. (17 June 1997) Transcript of Joint Press Conference, Sarajevo: Coalition Press Information Centre. Online. Available at: www.nato.int/sfor/trans/1997/t970617a.htm (accessed 28 December 2007).

Major Riley, C. (30 June 1997) Transcript of Joint Press Conference, Sarajevo: Coalition Press Information Centre. Online. Available at: www.nato.int/sfor/trans/1997/t970630a.htm (accessed 28 December 2007).

Major Riley, C. (4 July 1997) Transcript of Joint Press Conference, Sarajevo: Coalition Press Information Centre. Online. Available at: www.nato.int/sfor/trans/1997/t970704a.htm (accessed 28 December 2007).

Major Riley, C. (10 July 1997) Transcript of Joint Press Conference, Sarajevo: Coalition Press Information Centre. Online. Available at: www.nato.int/sfor/trans/1997/t970710a.htm (accessed 28 December 2007).

Major Riley, C. (11 July 1997) Transcript of Joint Press Conference, Sarajevo: Coalition Press Information Centre. Online. Available at: www.nato.int/sfor/trans/1997/t970711a.htm (accessed 27 December 2007).

Major Riley, C. (14 July 1997) Transcript of Joint Press Conference, Sarajevo: Coalition Press Information Centre. Online. Available at: www.nato.int/sfor/trans/1997/t970714a.htm (accessed 27 December 2007).

Major Riley, C. (23 July 1997) Transcript of Joint Press Conference, Pale. Online.

Available at: www.nato.int/sfor/trans/1997/t970723a.htm (accessed 28 December 2007).

Major Riley, C. (12 September 1997) Transcript of Joint Press Conference, Sarajevo: Coalition Press Information Centre. Online. Available at: www.nato.int/sfor/trans/1997/t970912a.htm (accessed 28 December 2007).

Major Saint-Louis, R. (16 June 1998) Transcript of Joint Press Conference, Sarajevo: Coalition Press Information Centre. Online. Available at: www.nato.int/sfor/trans/1997/t970616a.htm (accessed 28 December 2007).

Major White, T. (29 January 1997) Transcript of Press Briefing, Pale. Online. Available at: www.nato.int/sfor/trans/1997/t970129a.htm (accessed 28 December 2007).

Malan, M., Rakate, P. and McIntyre, A. (2002) *Peacekeeping in Sierra Leone: UNAMSIL Hits the Home Straight*, Pretoria, South Africa: Institute for Security Studies.

Mani, R. (1998) 'Conflict Resolution, Justice and Law; Rebuilding the Rule of Law in the Aftermath of Complex Political Emergencies', *International Peacekeeping*, 5(3): 1–25.

Maogoto, J.N. (2004) *War Crimes and Realpolitik: International Justice from World War I to the 21st Century*, London: Lynne Rienner Publishers.

McAdams, A.J. (1997) *Transitional Justice and the Rule of Law in New Democracies*, Notre Dame and London: University of Notre Dame Press.

McConnell, T. (16 March 2007) 'Liberia in Transition', 16 March 2007. Online. Available at: www.globalpolicy.org/security/issues/liberia/2007/0316transition.htm (accessed 3 January 2008).

McCormack, T.L.H. (1997) 'From Sun Tzu to the Sixth Committee: The Evolution of an International Criminal Law Regime', in T.H.L. McCormack and G.J. Simpson (eds) *The Law of War Crimes: National and International Approaches*, The Hague: Kluwer Law International.

McDonald, A. (2002) 'Sierra Leone's Shoestring Special Court', *International Review of the Red Cross*, 84(854): 121–143.

McGrew, A. (2000) 'Democracy beyond Borders?', in D. Held and A. McGrew (eds) *The Global Transformation Reader: An Introduction to the Globalization Debate*, Cambridge: Polity Press.

Meernik, J. (2003) 'Victor's Justice or the Law? Judging and Punishing at the International Criminal Tribunal for the Former Yugoslavia', *Journal of Conflict Resolution*, 47(2): 140–162.

Minow, M. (1998) *Between Vengeance and Forgiveness: Facing History after Genocide and Mass Violence*, Boston, MA: Beacon Press.

Miraldi, M. (2003) 'U.N. Report: Overcoming Obstacles to Justice: The Special Court for Sierra Leone', *New York Law School Journal of Human Rights*, 19(3): 849–858.

Miskowiak, K. (2000) *The International Criminal Court*. Copenhagen: DJØF Publishing.

Montgomery, T.S. (1995) 'Getting to Peace in El Salvador: The Roles of the United Nations Secretariat and UNOSAL', *Journal of Interamerican Studies and World Affairs*, 37(4): 139–172.

Moore, K. (8 June 1999) Transcript of Joint Press Conference, Sarajevo: Coalition Press Information Centre. Online. Available at: www.nato.int/sfor/trans/1999/t990608a.htm (accessed 28 December 2007).

Murphy, C. (30 October 1996) Transcript of the Press Briefing, Sarajevo: Coalition Press Information Centre. Online. Available at: www.nato.int/ifor/trans/t961030a.htm (accessed 27 December 2007).

NATO (2001) *NATO Handbook*. Online. Available at: www.nato.int/docu/handbook/2001/index.htm (accessed 29 December 2007).

NATO (28 February 2002) 'Operation in Bosnia-Herzegovina', *NATO Update*. Online. Available at: www.nato.int/docu/update/2002/02-february/e0228a.htm (accessed 28 December 2007).

NATO (1 March 2002) 'SFOR News Release', *NATO Update*. Online. Available at: www.nato.int/docu/update/2002/03-march/e0301b.htm (accessed 28 December 2007).

NATO (6 March 2002) 'Bosnia Snatch Operations', *NATO Update*. Online. Available at: www.nato.int/docu/update/2002/02-february/e0228b.htm (accessed 28 December 2007).

NATO (17 February 2003) 'KFOR's Detention of Indicted War Criminals Haradin Bala (aka Shala), Isak Musliu (aka Qerqiz) and Agim Murtezi (aka Murrizi)', Press Release (2003)011. Online. Available at: www.nato.int/docu/pr/2003/p03-011e.htm (accessed 28 December 2007).

NATO (2006) *Nato Handbook*. Brussels: NATO, Public Diplomacy Division.

NATO Secretary General Lord Robertson (3 April 2000) Statement by NATO Secretary General Lord Robertson, on Actions by SFOR to Detain Persons Indicted for War Crimes, Press Release (2000) 036. Online. Available at: www.nato.int/docu/pr/2000/p00-036e.htm (accessed 28 December 2007).

NATO Secretary General Lord Robertson (21 December 2000) Statement by Lord George Robertson, Sarajevo: Coalition Press Information Centre. Online. Available at: www.nato.int/sfor/trans/2000/t001221a.htm (accessed 28 December 2007).

NATO Secretary General Lord Robertson (15 April 2001) Statement by the Secretary General, Press Release (2001) 049. Online. Available at: www.nato.int/docu/pr/2001/p01-049e.htm (accessed 28 December 2007).

NATO Secretary General Lord Robertson (10 August 2001) Statement by the Secretary General of NATO, the Right Hon. Lord Robertson of Port Ellen, Press Release (2001) 111. Online. Available at: www.nato.int/docu/pr/2001/p01-111e.htm (accessed 28 December 2007).

NATO Secretary General Lord Robertson (13 June 2002) Statement by the Secretary General of NATO on SFOR's Detention of Indicted War Criminal Darko Mrda 13 June 2002, Press Release (2002) 082. Online. Available at: www.nato.int/docu/pr/2002/p02-082e.htm (accessed 28 December 2007).

NATO Secretary General Lord Robertson (7 July 2002) Statement by NATO Secretary General, Lord Robertson, Press Release (2002) 091. Online. Available at: www.nato.int/docu/pr/2002/p02-091e.htm (accessed 28 December 2007).

NATO Secretary General Lord Robertson (9 July 2002) 'SFOR's Detention of Indicted War Criminal Radovan Stankovic', Press Release (2002) 093. Online. Available at: www.nato.int/docu/pr/2002/p02-093e.htm (accessed 28 December 2007).

NATO Secretary General Lord Robertson (11 April 2003) 'SFOR'S Detention of Indicted War Criminal Naser Oric', Press Release (2003) 039. Online. Available at: www.nato.int/docu/pr/2003/p03-039e.htm (accessed 28 December 2007).

NATO Secretary General Solana, J. (28 May 1998) Statement by the Secretary General of NATO Dr. Javier Solana on SFOR's Action against an Indicted War Criminal, Press Release (98) 68. Online. Available at: www.nato.int/docu/pr/1998/p98-068e.htm (accessed 28 December 2007).

NATO Secretary General Solana, J. (22 July 1998) Statement by the Secretary General of NATO Dr. Javier Solana on SFOR's Action against an Indicted War Criminal, Press Release (98) 93. Online. Available at: www.nato.int/docu/pr/1998/p98-093e.htm (accessed 28 December 2007).

NATO Secretary General Solana, J. (27 September 1998) Statement by the Secretary

General of NATO Dr. Javier Solana on SFOR's Action against an Indicted War Criminal, Press Release (98) 106. Online. Available at: www.nato.int/docu/pr/1998/ p98–106e.htm (accessed 28 December 2007).

NATO Standardization Agency (2001a) *Peace Support Operations*, AJP-3.4.1, July, Brussels: NATO. Online. Available at: www.pronato.com/peacekeeping/AJP-3.4.1 (accessed 29 December 2007).

NATO Standardization Agency (2001b) *Peace Support Operations: Techniques and Procedures*, AJP-3.4.1.1, August, Brussels: NATO.

NATO Standardization Agency (2002) *Allied Joint Operations*, AJP-3, September, Brussels: NATO.

Neou, K. and Gallup, J.C. (1997) 'Human Rights and the Cambodian Past: In Defence of Peace before Justice', 5 March. Online. Available at: www.cceia.org/resources/ publications/dialogue/1_08/articles/554.html (accessed 28 December 2007).

Nikiforov, A. (4 October 2006) 'ICTY Weekly Press Briefing'. Online. Available at: www.un.org/icty/briefing/2006/PB061004.htm (accessed 7 January 2008).

Nino, C.S. (1995) 'Response: The Duty to Punish Past Abuses of Human Rights in Context – The Case of Afghanistan', in N.J. Kritz (ed.) *Transitional Justice: How Emerging Democracies Reckon with Former Regimes. Volume 1: General Considerations*, Washington, DC: United States Institute of Peace Press.

Nizich, I. (2001) 'International Tribunals and Their Ability to Provide Adequate Justice: Lessons from the Yugoslav Tribunal', *ILSA Journal of International & Comparative Law*, 7(2): 353–368.

North Atlantic Council (14 February 1996) 'IFOR Assistance to the International Tribunal', Press Release (96) 26. Online. Available at: www.nato.int/docu/pr/ 1996/p96–026e.htm (accessed 29 December 2007).

Novak, R.D. (2003) 'The Trouble with Wes'. Online. Available at: www.townhall.com/ columnists/RobertDNovak/2003/09/22/the_trouble_with_wes (accessed 5 January 2008).

Nullis, C. (2006) 'Apartheid Era Victims Want Justice in South Africa', *The Boston Banner*, 41(37), 27 April.

Office of the High Representative (14 December 1995) *The General Framework Agreement for Peace in Bosnia and Herzegovina*. Online. Available at: www.ohr.int/dpa/ default.asp?content_id=380 (accessed 5 January 2008).

Office of the High Representative (1 August 1998) *OHR Bulletin 1 August 1998*, 73(1). Online. Available at: www.ohr.int/ohr-dept/presso/chronology/bulletins/default.asp? content_id=4999 (accessed 28 December 2007).

Office of the High Representative (25 January 2000) OHR BiH TV News Summary. Online. Available at: www.ohr.int/ohr-dept/presso/bh-media-rep/summaries-tv/bhtv/default.asp?content_id=577 (accessed 28 December 2007).

Office of the Historian (undated) 'History of the Department of State during the Clinton Presidency (1993–2001)', Bureau of Public Affairs. Online. Available at: www.state.gov/r/pa/ho/pubs/8522.htm (accessed 7 January 2008).

Office of the Prosecutor (3 August 2001) 'Arrest of General Enver Hadzihasanovic, General Mehmed Alagic and Colonel Amir Kubura', The Hague, GB/P.I.S./610e. Online. Available at: www.un.org/icty/pressreal/p610-e.htm (accessed 7 January 2008).

Office of the Prosecutor (18 February 2003) 'Haradin Bala, Isak Musliu and Agim Murtezi Transferred to the ICTY Following Their Indictment for Crimes against Humanity and War Crimes', The Hague, FH-CC/P.I.S/729e. Online. Available at: www.un.org/icty/pressreal/2003/p729-e.htm (accessed 28 December 2007).

Okuizumi, K. (2002) 'Peacebuilding Mission: Lessons from the UN Mission in Bosnia-Herzegovina', *Human Rights Quarterly*, 24(3): 721–735.

O'Neill, W.G. (2002) 'Monitoring the Administration of Justice', in *The Manual on Human Rights Monitoring: An Introduction for Human Rights Field Officers*, Oslo: Norwegian Institute of Human Rights.

O'Neill, W.G. (2005) Draft Paper for Review Meeting on 'Role of Human Rights in Peace Agreements', International Council on Human Rights Policy, Belfast, 7–8 March.

Orentlicher, D.F. (1995) 'Settling Accounts: The Duty to Prosecute Human Rights Violations of a Prior Regime', in N.J. Kritz (ed.) *Transitional Justice: How Emerging Democracies Reckon with Former Regimes, Volume 1: General Considerations*, Washington, DC: United States Institute of Peace Press.

Paris, R. (2003) 'Peacekeeping and the Constraints of Global Culture', *European Journal of International Relations*, 9(3): 441–473.

Paulo, M.J. (2004) 'The Role of the UN in the Angolan Peace Process', *Accord*, Issue 15, London: Conciliation Resources.

Penrose, M.M. (1999) 'Lest We Fail: The Importance of Enforcement in International Criminal Law', *American University International Law Review*, 15(2): 321–394.

Perlez, J. (1996) 'Serb Stands Firm in Face of US Effort to Oust Karadzic', *The New York Times*, 18 July. Online. Available at: query.nytimes.com/gst/fullpage.html?res=9503E0DC1F39F93BA25754C0A960958260 (accessed 5 January 2008).

Perriello, T. and Wierda, M. (2006) 'Lessons from the Deployment of International Judges and Prosecutors in Kosovo', Prosecutions Case Studies Series, Centre for Transitional Justice, March. Online. Available at: www.ictj.org/static/Prosecutions/Kosovo.study.pdf (accessed 6 January 2008).

Peskin, V. and Boduszynski, M.P. (2003) 'International Justice and Domestic Politics: Post-Tudjman Croatia and the International Criminal Tribunal for the Former Yugoslavia', *Europe-Asia Studies*, 55(7): 1117–1142.

Petrovic, D. (1998) 'The Post-Dayton Role of the International Criminal Tribunal for the Former Yugoslavia', in M. O'Flaherty and G. Gisvold (eds) *Post-War Protection of Human Rights in Bosnia and Herzegovina*, The Hague/London/Boston: Martinus Nijhoff Publishers.

Pouligny, B. (2006) *Peace Operations Seen from Below: UN Missions and Local People*, London: C. Hurst and Co. Publishers.

President of the ICTR (1997) 'Report of the International Criminal Tribunal for the Prosecution of Persons Responsible for Genocide and Other Serious Violations of International Humanitarian Law Committed in the Territory of Rwanda and Rwandan Citizens Responsible for Genocide and Other Such Violations Committed in the Territory of Neighbouring States between 1 January and 31 December 1994', A/52/582-S/1997/868, United Nations Security Council General Assembly, 52nd Session, Agenda Item 50, 13 November 1997. Online. Available at: 69.94.11.53/ENGLISH/annualreports/a52/9731665e.htm (accessed 5 January 2008).

President of the ICTR (2007) 'Address by Judge Dennis Byron to the United Nations Security Council, Six-Monthly Report on the Completion Strategy: The International Criminal Tribunal for Rwanda, 10 December. Online. Available at: 69.94.11.53/default.htm (accessed 5 January 2008).

President of the ICTY (1995) 'Report of the International Tribunal for the Prosecution of Persons Responsible for Serious Violations of International Humanitarian Law Committed in the Territory of the Former Yugoslavia since 1991', A/50/365-S/1995/728. Online. Available at: www.un.org/icty/rappannu-e/1995/index.htm (accessed 2 May 2008).

President of the ICTY (1996) 'Report of the International Tribunal for the Prosecution of Persons Responsible for Serious Violations of International Humanitarian Law Committed in the Territory of the Former Yugoslavia since 1991', A/51/292-S/1996/665. Online. Available at: www.un.org/icty/rappannu-e/1996/index.htm (accessed 27 December 2007).

President of the ICTY (1997) 'Report of the International Tribunal for the Prosecution of Persons Responsible for Serious Violations of International Humanitarian Law Committed in the Territory of the Former Yugoslavia since 1991', A/52/375-S/1997/729. Online. Available at: www.un.org/icty/rappannu-e/1997/index.htm (accessed 27 December 2007).

President of the ICTY (1998) 'Report of the International Tribunal for the Prosecution of Persons Responsible for Serious Violations of International Humanitarian Law Committed in the Territory of the Former Yugoslavia since 1991', A/53/219-S/1998/737. Online. Available at: www.un.org/icty/rappannu-e/1998/index.htm (accessed 28 December 2007).

President of the ICTY (1999) 'Report of the International Tribunal for the Prosecution of Persons Responsible for Serious Violations of International Humanitarian Law Committed in the Territory of the Former Yugoslavia since 1991', A/54/187/S/1999/846. Online. Available at: www.un.org/icty/rappannu-e/1999/index.htm (accessed 28 December 2007).

President of the ICTY (2000) 'Report of the International Tribunal for the Prosecution of Persons Responsible for Serious Violations of International Humanitarian Law Committed in the Territory of the Former Yugoslavia since 1991', A/55/273-S/2000/777. Online. Available at: www.un.org/icty/rappannu-e/2000/index.htm (accessed 28 December 2007).

President of the ICTY (2001) 'Report of the International Tribunal for the Prosecution of Persons Responsible for Serious Violations of International Humanitarian Law Committed in the Territory of the Former Yugoslavia since 1991', A/56/352-S/2001/865. Online. Available at: www.un.org/icty/rappannu-e/2001/index.htm (accessed 28 December 2007).

President of the ICTY (2002) 'Report of the International Tribunal for the Prosecution of Persons Responsible for Serious Violations of International Humanitarian Law Committed in the Territory of the Former Yugoslavia since 1991', A/57/379-S/2002/985. Online. Available at: www.un.org/icty/rappannu-e/2002/index.htm (accessed 28 December 2007).

President of the ICTY (2003) 'Report of the International Tribunal for the Prosecution of Persons Responsible for Serious Violations of International Humanitarian Law Committed in the Territory of the Former Yugoslavia since 1991', A/58/297-S/2003/829. Online. Available at: www.un.org/icty/rappannu-e/2003/index.htm (accessed 28 December 2007).

President of the ICTY (2004) 'Report of the International Tribunal for the Prosecution of Persons Responsible for Serious Violations of International Humanitarian Law Committed in the Territory of the Former Yugoslavia since 1991', A/59/215-S/2004/627. Online. Available at: www.un.org/icty/rappannu-e/2004/index.htm (accessed 28 December 2007).

President of the ICTY (2005) 'Report of the International Tribunal for the Prosecution of

Persons Responsible for Serious Violations of International Humanitarian Law Committed in the Territory of the Former Yugoslavia since 1991', A/60/267-S/2005/532. Online. Available at: www.un.org/icty/rappannu-e/2005/index.htm (accessed 5 January 2008).

President of the ICTY (2006) 'Report of the International Tribunal for the Prosecution of Persons Responsible for Serious Violations of International Humanitarian Law Committed in the Territory of the Former Yugoslavia since 1991', A/61/271-S/2006/666. Online. Available at: www.un.org/icty/rappannu-e/2006/AR06.pdf (accessed 5 January 2008).

President of the ICTY (2007) 'Report of the International Tribunal for the Prosecution of Persons Responsible for Serious Violations of International Humanitarian Law Committed in the Territory of the Former Yugoslavia since 1991', A/62/172-S/2007/469. Online. Available at: www.un.org/icty/rappannu-e/2007/AR07.pdf (accessed 5 January 2008).

Pugh, M. (2004) 'Peacekeeping and Critical Theory', *International Peacekeeping*, 11(1): 39–58.

Ratner, S.R. and Abrams, J.S. (2001) *Accountability for Human Rights Atrocities in International Law*, 2nd edn; Oxford: Oxford University Press.

Rausch, C. (2006) *Combating Serious Crimes in Post-conflict Societies: A Handbook for Policymakers and Practitioners*, New York: United States Institute of Peace Press.

Reenen, P. v. (2001) 'The Need for Police Capacities and Skills when Arresting War Criminals, Aspects of Proportionality, Subsidiarity and Human Rights', in v.W.A.M. Dijk and J.I. Hovens (eds) *Arresting War Criminals: Special Publication by the Royal Dutch Constabulary*. Nijmegen: Wolf Legal Productions.

Refugees International (2004) 'UNAMSIL Drawdown: Too Soon for Sierra Leone to Stand Alone', 15 March. Online. Available at: www.refugeesinternational.org/content/article/detail/947/ (accessed 1 January 2008).

Reiger, C. and Wierda, M. (2006) 'The Serious Crimes Process in Timor-Leste: In Retrospect', Prosecution Case Studies Series, International Centre for Transitional Justice, March. Online. Available at: www.ictj.org/static/Prosecutions/Timor.study.pdf (accessed 8 January 2008).

Richmond, O.P. (2004) 'UN Peace Operations and the Dilemmas of the Peacebuilding Consensus', *International Peacekeeping*, 11(1): 83–101.

Rieff, D. (1996) 'The Case against the Serb War Criminals', *Washington Post*, 8 September. Online. Available at: www.washingtonpost.com/wp-srv/inatl/longterm/bosnia/stories/wanted.htm (accessed 27 December 2007).

Risley, P. (10 May 2000) 'ICTY Weekly Press Briefing'. Online. Available at: www.un.org/icty/briefing/PB100500.htm (accessed 7 January 2008).

Robertson, G. (2000) *Crimes against Humanity: The Struggle for Global Justice*, London: Allen Lane.

Rozenberg, J. (12 January 2006) 'The Court That Tries America's Patience', *Telegraph*. Online. Available at: www.globalpolicy.org/intljustice/icc/2006/0112patience.htm (accessed 5 January 2008).

Rumin, S. (2007) 'Gathering and Managing Information in Vetting Processes', in A. Mayer-Rieckh and P. de Greiff (eds) *Justice as Prevention: Vetting Public Employees in Transitional Societies*, New York: Social Science Research Council.

Ruxton, G.F. (2001) 'Present and Future Record of Arresting War Criminals: The View of the Public Prosecutor of ICTY', in v.W.A.M. Dijk and J.I. Hovens (eds) *Arresting War Criminals: Special Publication by the Royal Dutch Constabulary*. Nijmegen: Wolf Legal Productions.

Ryall, T. (9 August 2005) Transcript of the International Agency's Joint Press Conference, Sarajevo: OHR. Online. Available at: www.ohr.int/ohr-dept/presso/pressb/default.asp?content_id=35163 (accessed 2 January 2008).

Samuels, K. (2006) 'Rule of Law Reform in Post-conflict Countries: Operational Initiatives and Lessons Learned', Social Development Paper no. 37, Conflict Prevention and Reconstruction Unit, Washington, DC: World Bank.

Schabas, W.A. (2001) *An Introduction to the International Criminal Court*, Cambridge: Cambridge University Press.

Scharf, M.P. (1997) *Balkan Justice: The Story behind the First International War Crimes Trial since Nuremberg*, Durham, NC: Carolina Academic Press.

Schear, J.A. and Farris, K. (2002) 'Policing Cambodia: The Public Security Dimensions of UN Peace Operations', in R.B. Oakley, M.J. Dziedzic and E.M. Goldberg (eds) *Policing the New World Disorder: Peace Operations and Public Security*, Washington, DC: National Defense University Press.

Schocken, C. (2002) 'The Special Court for Sierra Leone: Overview and Recommendations', *Berkeley Journal of International Law*, 20(2): 436–461.

Schvey, A.A. (2003) 'Striving for Accountability in the Former Yugoslavia', in J.E. Stromseth (ed.) *Accountability for Atrocities: National and International Responses*, Ardsley, NY: Transnational Publishers.

Schwartz, H. (1995) 'Lustrations in Europe', in N.J. Kritz (ed.) *Transitional Justice: How Emerging Democracies Reckon with Former Regimes. Volume 1: General Considerations*, Washington, DC: United States Institute of Peace Press.

Second Lt Marin, A.L. (9 January 2003) 'The Spanish–French Battle Group Runs Again', *SFOR Informer 155*. Online. Available at: www.nato.int/sfor/indexinf/155/p12a/t02p12a.htm (accessed 28 December 2007).

Seidel, F. (10 January 1999) Transcript of Joint Press Conference, Sarajevo: Coalition Press Information Centre. Online. Available at: www.nato.int/sfor/trans/1999/t990110a.htm (accessed 28 December 2007).

Sewall, J.O.B. (1994) Implications for U.N. Peacekeeping, *JFQ Forum Winter 1993–1994*. Online. Available at: www.dtic.mil/doctrine/jel/jfq_pubs/jfq0803.pdf (accessed 29 December 2007).

SFOR (9 June 2003) 'SFOR's Detention of Suspected War Criminals', Press Release. Online. Available at: www.nato.int/sfor/trans/2003/p030609a.htm (accessed 28 December 2007).

SFOR (13 August 2003) 'SFOR Conducts Operation to Detain Person Indicted for War Crimes (PIFWC)', Press Release. Online. Available at: www.nato.int/sfor/trans/2003/p030813a.htm (accessed 28 December 2007).

SFOR (26 August 2003) 'SFOR Conducts Operations in the Pale Area', Press Release. Online. Available at: www.nato.int/sfor/trans/2003/p030826a.htm (accessed 28 December 2007).

SFOR (10 January 2004) 'RS and SFOR Conduct Joint Anti PIFWC Operations in Pale', Press Release. Online. Available at: www.nato.int/sfor/trans/2004/p040110a.htm (accessed 28 December 2007).

SFOR (13 January 2004) 'SFOR Search a House in Pale', Press Release. Online. Available at: www.nato.int/sfor/trans/2004/p040113a.htm (accessed 28 December 2007).

SFOR (28 January 2004a) 'SFOR Detain Person Suspected of Supporting PIFWCs', Press Release. Online. Available at: www.nato.int/sfor/trans/2004/p040128a.htm (accessed 28 December 2007).

SFOR (28 January 2004b) 'SFOR Operation Supported by RS MUP in Bijeljina Concludes', Press Release. Online. Available at: www.nato.int/sfor/trans/2004/ p040128b.htm (accessed 28 December 2007).

SFOR (12 February 2004) 'RS Police Allegations/Detention of Tesic and Jankovic', Press Release. Online. Available at: www.nato.int/sfor/trans/2004/p040212a.htm (accessed 28 December 2007).

SFOR (17 February 2004) 'Detention of Jankovic', Press Release. Online. Available at: www.nato.int/sfor/trans/2004/p040217a.htm (accessed 28 December 2007).

SFOR (19 February 2004) 'SFOR Conducts Operations in Pale', Press Release. Online. Available at: www.nato.int/sfor/trans/2004/p040219a.htm (accessed 28 December 2007).

SFOR (3 March 2004) 'SFOR Detain Person Suspected of Supporting PIFWCs', Press Release. Online. Available at: www.nato.int/sfor/trans/2004/p040303a.htm (accessed 28 December 2007).

SFOR (1 April 2004) 'SFOR Conducts PIFWC Operation in Pale', Press Release. Online. Available at: www.nato.int/sfor/trans/2004/p040401a.htm (accessed 28 December 2007).

SFOR (2 April 2004) 'SFOR Operation in Pale – Additional Information', Press Release.Online. Available at: www.nato.int/sfor/trans/2004/p040402a.htm (accessed 28 December 2007).

SFOR (14 May 2004) 'SFOR Detain Milovan Bjelica – Suspected PIFWC Supporter', Press Release.Online. Available at: www.nato.int/sfor/trans/2004/p040514a.htm (accessed 28 December 2007).

SFOR (26 July 2004) 'SFOR Releases Rajko Banduka', Press Release. Online. Available at: www.nato.int/sfor/trans/2004/p040726a.htm (accessed 28 December 2007).

SFOR (31 July 2004) 'SFOR Detains Mile Pejcic', Press Release. Online. Available at: www.nato.int/sfor/trans/2004/p040731a.htm (accessed 28 December 2007).

SFOR (August 2004) 'Multinational Specialized Unit', SFOR Fact Sheet. Online. Available at: www.nato.int/sfor/factsheet/msu/t040809a.htm (accessed 5 January 2008).

SFOR (31 August 2004a) 'SFOR Detains Milovan Bjelica', Press Release. Online. Available at: www.nato.int/sfor/trans/2004/p040831a.htm (accessed 28 December 2007).

SFOR (31 August 2004b) 'SFOR Detains Suspected PIFWC Supporter', Press Release. Online. Available at: www.nato.int/sfor/trans/2004/p040831b.htm (accessed 28 December 2007).

SFOR (7 October 2004) 'SFOR Conducts Unannounced Search in Vlasenica', Press Release. Online. Available at: www.nato.int/sfor/trans/2004/p041007a.htm (accessed 28 December 2007).

SFOR (8 October 2004) 'SFOR Conducts Unannounced Search in Bijeljina', Press Release. Online. Available at: www.nato.int/sfor/trans/2004/p041008b.htm (accessed 28 December 2007).

SFOR (14 October 2004) 'SFOR Conducts Unannounced Search in Sokolac', Press Release. Online. Available at: www.nato.int/sfor/trans/2004/p041014a.htm (accessed 28 December 2007).

SFOR (15 October 2004) 'SFOR Conducts Unannounced Search in Banja Luka', Press Release. Online. Available at: www.nato.int/sfor/trans/2004/p041015a.htm (accessed 28 December 2007).

SFOR (21 October 2004) 'SFOR Conducts Unannounced Searches in Pale', Press Release. Online. Available at: www.nato.int/sfor/trans/2004/p041021a.htm (accessed 28 December 2007).

SFOR interview (2003) Interviews with senior military officers from SFOR conducted by the author in Bosnia-Herzegovina.

SFOR Peace Stabilisation Force (7 June 1999) 'Suspected War Criminal Detained', Sarajevo: Coalition Press Information Office. Online. Available at: www.nato.int/sfor/advisory/1999/p990607a.htm (accessed 28 December 2007).

SFOR Peace Stabilisation Force (2 August 1999) 'Suspected War Criminal Detained', Sarajevo: Coalition Press Information Office. Online. Available at: www.nato.int/sfor/advisory/1999/p990802a.htm (accessed 28 December 2007).

SFOR Peace Stabilisation Force (25 October 1999) 'Suspected War Criminal Detained', CPIC-NR99.005, Sarajevo: Coalition Press Information Office. Online. Available at: www.nato.int/sfor/advisory/1999/p991025a.htm (accessed 28 December 2007).

SFOR Peace Stabilisation Force (20 December 1999) 'Suspected War Criminal Detained', Sarajevo: Coalition Press Information Office. Online. Available at: www.nato.int/sfor/advisory/1999/p991220a.htm (accessed 28 December 2007).

SFOR Peace Stabilisation Force (25 January 2000) 'Suspected War Criminal Detained', No 00.005, Sarajevo: Coalition Press Information Office. Online. Available at: www.nato.int/sfor/advisory/2000/t000125a.htm (accessed 28 December 2007).

SFOR Peace Stabilisation Force (5 March 2000) 'Accused War Criminal Detained', No 00.013, Sarajevo: Coalition Press Information Office. Online. Available at: www.nato.int/sfor/advisory/2000/t000306a.htm (accessed 28 December 2007).

SFOR Peace Stabilisation Force (3 April 2000) 'Accused War Criminal Detained', Sarajevo: Coalition Press Information Office. Online. Available at: www.nato.int/sfor/advisory/2000/t000403a.htm (accessed 28 December 2007).

SFOR Peace Stabilisation Force (22 April 2000) Accused War Criminal Detained, No 00.023, Sarajevo: Coalition Press Information Office. Online. Available at: www.nato.int/sfor/advisory/2000/t000422a.htm (accessed 28 December 2007).

SFOR Peace Stabilisation Force (25 June 2000) 'Accused War Criminal Detained', Sarajevo: Coalition Press Information Office. Online. Available at: www.nato.int/sfor/advisory/2000/t000626a.htm (accessed 28 December 2007).

Sharp, J.M.O. (1997) 'British Views on NATO Enlargement. Conference: NATO Enlargement: The National Debates over Ratification', 1 October. Online. Available at: www.nato.int/acad/conf/enlarg97/sharp.htm (accessed 27 December 2007).

Shitakha, E. (1998) 'From Conventional Peacekeeping to Multidimensional Field Operations', in M. Kapila, N.S. Rodley, K. Boyle and A. Reidy (eds) *Conference Report on 'The Promotion and Protection of Human Rights in Acute Crisis'*, London, 11–13 February 1998. Online. Available at: www.essex.ac.uk/rightsinacutecrisis/report/shitakha.htm (accessed 3 January 2008).

Siegel, R.L. (1998) 'Transitional Justice: A Decade of Debate and Experience', *Human Rights Quarterly*, 20(2): 431–454.

Simons, M. (12 December 2005) '40,000 Protest General's Arrest', *International Herald Tribune Europe*. Online. Available at: www.iht.com/articles/2005/12/11/news/croatia.php (accessed 5 January 2008).

Sismanidis, R.D.V. (1997) 'Police Functions in Peace Operations': Report from a Workshop Organised by the United States Institute of Peace, Washington, DC: United States Institute of Peace.

Sliedregt, E. v. (2001) 'Arresting War Criminals: Male Captus Bene Detentus, Human Rights and the Rule of Law', in v.W.A.M. Dijk and J.I. Hovens (eds) *Arresting War Criminals: Special Publication by the Royal Dutch Constabulary*. Nijmegen: Wolf Legal Productions.

Slovo, G. (2002) 'Making history: South Africa's Truth and Reconciliation Commission', 15 December. Online. Available at: www.opendemocracy.net/democracy-apologypolitics/article_818.jsp (accessed 28 December 2007).

Staff Sgt Simpson, L.M. (25 April 2002) 'MSU Trains Slovenians and Romanians', *SFOR Informer 137*. Online. Available at: www.nato.int/sfor/indexinf/137/p07a/ t02p07a.htm (accessed 28 December 2007).

Stanley, W. and Loosle, R. (2002) 'El Salvador: The Civilian Police Component of Peace Operations', in R.B. Oakley, M.J. Dziedzic and E.M. Goldberg (eds) *Policing the New World Disorder: Peace Operations and Public Security*, Washington, DC: National Defense University Press.

Steadman, S.J. (1997) 'Spoilers Problems in Peace Processes', *International Security*, 22(2): 5–53.

Stephen, C. (2003) Oric Hague Demo, Institute for War and Peace Reporting, 18 April. Online. Available at: www.globalpolicy.org/intljustice/tribunals/yugo/2003/0418 oric.htm (accessed 29 December 2007).

Strain, J. and Keyes, E. (2003) 'Accountability in the Aftermath of Rwanda's Genocide', in J.E. Stromseth (ed.) *Accountability for Atrocities: National and International Responses*, Ardsley, NY: Transnational Publishers Inc.

Supernor, C.M. (2001) 'International Bounty Hunters for War Criminals: Privatising the Enforcement of Justice', *Air Force Law Review*, Winter 2001.

Supreme Headquarters Allied Powers Europe (9 May 1996) 'On Signing of the Memorandum of Understanding between SHAPE and the International Criminal Tribunal for Former Yugoslavia', Press Release (96)74. Online. Available at: www.nato.int/ docu/pr/1996/p96–074e.htm (accessed 29 December 2007).

Teitel, R.G. (2001) *Transitional Justice*, Oxford: Oxford University Press.

Ter Horst, E. (2006) 'El Salvador and Haiti Revisited: The Role of UN Peace Operations, Democracy, Conflict and Human Security: Further Reading (Volume 2). Online. Available at: www.idea.int/publications/dchs/dchs_vol2.cfm (accessed 2 January 2008).

Theissen, G (2003) 'Supporting Justice, Co-existence and Reconciliation after Armed Conflict: Strategies for Dealing with the Past', Berghof Research Center for Constructive Conflict Management. Online. Available at: www.berghof-handbook.net/articles/ theissen_handbook.pdf (accessed 22 December 2007).

Thomas, J. (11 October 2005) Transcript of the International Agency's Joint Press Conference, Sarajevo: OHR. Online. Available at: www.ohr.int/ohr-dept/pressb/default. asp?contentid=35665

Thomas, L. and Spataro, S. (2002) 'Peacekeeping and Policing in Somalia', in R.B. Oakley, M.J. Dziedzic and E.M. Goldberg (eds) *Policing the New World Disorder: Peace Operations and Public Security*, Washington D.C.: National Defense University Press.

Tolbert, D. (2006) 'Session 2: NGOs and Other Experts', Second Public Hearing of the Office of the Prosecutor, The Hague, 26 September. Online. Available at: www.icc-cpi.int/organs/otp/otp_public_hearing/otp_ph2/otp_ph2_HGNGO_2.html (accessed 7 January 2008).

Traynor, I. (12 February 2001) 'Croats Turn on Leaders for Hunting "War Criminals"', *Guardian*. Online. Available at: www.guardian.co.uk/international/story/0,,436733, 00.html (accessed 5 January 2008).

Tutu, D.M. (1999) *No Future without Forgiveness*, New York: Doubleday.

Tutu, D.M. (2000) 'Reconciliation in Post-Apartheid South Africa: Experiences of the Truth Commission', in J. Hopkins (ed.) *The Art of Peace: Nobel Peace Laureates Discuss Human Rights, Conflict and Reconciliation*, Ithaca, NY: Snow Lion Publications.

Udombana, N.J. (2003) 'Globalisation of Justice and the Special Court for Sierra Leone's War Crimes', *Emory International Law Review*, 17(1): 55–132.

United Nations Development Programme (2006) 'Vetting Public Employees in Post-conflict Settings', New York: UNDP, Bureau for Crisis Prevention and Recovery.

United States Institute of Peace (1997) 'Dayton Implementation: The Apprehension and Prosecution of Indicted War Criminals', United States Institute of Peace Special Report from Working Group of Dayton Implementation, Washington, DC: United States Institute of Peace.

Unknown Participant in Workshop 1 (2001) 'Workshop 1: The Need for an International Arresting Team: UN- or not UN-led?', in v.W.A.M. Dijk and J.I. Hovens (eds) *Arresting War Criminals: Special Publication by the Royal Dutch Constabulary*, Nijmegen: Wolf Legal Productions.

UNMIK (26 February 2003) *Foreign Media Monitoring*, Division of Public Information. Online. Available at: www.unmikonline.org/press/2003/wire/feb/imm260203PM.htm (accessed 28 December 2007).

UNMIK interview (2003) Interviews with senior police officers from UNMIK police conducted by the author in Kosovo.

Vallières-Roland, P. (2002) 'Prosecuting War Criminals: A Critique of the Relationship between NATO and the International Criminal Courts', Briefing Paper, Brussels: Centre for European Security and Disarmament.

Vulliamy, E. (2 December 2007) 'How He Slipped into Hiding', *Observer*. Online. Available at: www.guardian.co.uk/yugo/article/0,,2220679,00.html (accessed 5 January 2008).

Ward, K. (2003) 'Might v. right: Charles Taylor and the Sierra Leone Special Court', *Human Rights Brief*, 11(1): 8–11.

Wilkinson, P. (2000) 'Sharpening the Weapons of Peace: Peace Support Operations and Complex Emergencies', in T. Woodhouse and O. Ramsbotham (eds) *Peacekeeping and Conflict Resolution*, London: Frank Cass Publishers.

Wille, C. and Pietz, T. (2006) 'BCPR Strategic Review: Bosnia and Herzegovina, Small Arms Survey, February. Online. Available at: www.undp.org/bcpr/documents/sa_control/BCPRStrategicreview_B&H.doc (accessed 29 December 2007).

Wilson, R. (1997) 'Violent Truths: The Politics of Memory in Guatemala', *Accord*, Issue 2, London: Conciliation Resources.

Woodhouse, T. and Ramsbotham, O. (1999) Encyclopedia of International Peacekeeping Operations, Oxford: ABC-Clio Inc.

Woodhouse, T. and Ramsbotham, O. (2005) 'Cosmopolitan Peacekeeping and the Globalization of Security', *International Peacekeeping*, 12(2): 139–156.

Woods, J.L. (2002) 'Mozambique: The CIVPOL Operation', in R.B. Oakley, M.J. Dziedzic and E.M. Goldberg (eds) *Policing the New World Disorder: Peace Operations and Public Security*, Washington, DC: National Defense University Press.

Homepages from the United Nations' Department of Peacekeeping Operations (DPKO)

DPKO Angola – UNAVEM II: Background. Full text. Online. Available at: www.un.org/Depts/DPKO/Missions/Unavem2/UnavemIIB.html.

DPKO Angola – UNAVEM III. Online. Available at: www.un.org/Depts/dpko/dpko/co_mission/unavem_p.htm.

DPKO Angola – MONUA: Background. Full text. Online. Available at: www.un.org/Depts/DPKO/Missions/Monua/monuab.htm.

DPKO Angola – MONUA: Mandate. Online. Available at: www.un.org/Depts/DPKO/Missions/Monua/monuam.htm.

DPKO Bosnia-Herzegovina – UNMIBH: Background. Full text. Online. Available at: www.un.org/Depts/dpko/missions/unmibh/background.html.

DPKO Bosnia-Herzegovina – UNPROFOR: Background. Full text. Online. Available at: www.un.org/Depts/dpko/dpko/co_mission/unprof_b.htm.

DPKO Bosnia-Herzegovina – UNPROFOR: Profile. Online. Available at: www.un.org/Depts/dpko/dpko/co_mission/unprof_p.htm.

DPKO Cambodia – UNTAC: Background. Full text. Online. Available at: www.un.org/Depts/dpko/dpko/co_mission/untacbackgr2.html.

DPKO Côte d'Ivoire – UNOCI: Mandate. Online. Available at: www.un.org/Depts/dpko/missions/unoci/mandate.html.

DPKO Croatia – UNTAES: Background. Full text. Online. Available at: www.un.org/Depts/DPKO/Missions/untaes_b.htm.

DPKO Croatia – UNTAES: Brief Chronology. Online. Available at: www.un.org/Depts/DPKO/Missions/untaes_e.htm.

DPKO Democratic Republic of Congo – MONUC: DDDRR Activities. Online. Available at: www.monuc.org/news.aspx?newsID=718.

DPKO Democratic Republic of Congo – MONUC: Human Rights Justice Support Unit. Online. Available at: www.monuc.org/news.aspx?newsID=767.

DPKO Democratic Republic of Congo – MONUC: Human Rights Mandates and Activities. Online. Available at: www.monuc.org/news.aspx?newsID=761&menuOpened=Activities.

DPKO Democratic Republic of Congo – MONUC: Human Rights Special Investigations Unit. Online. Available at: www.monuc.org/news.aspx?newsID=769.

DPKO Democratic Republic of Congo – MONUC: Mandate. Online. Available at: www.un.org/Depts/dpko/missions/monuc/mandate.html.

DPKO Democratic Republic of Congo – MONUC: Police Activities. Online. Available at: www.monuc.org/news.aspx?newsID=705.

DPKO East Timor – UNMISET: Branches Human Rights. Online. Available at: www.un.org/Depts/dpko/missions/UNMISETlocal/index.html.

DPKO East Timor – UNMISET: Branches Legal Affairs. Online. Available at: www.un.org/Depts/dpko/missions/UNMISETlocal/index.html.

DPKO East Timor – UNMISET: Branches UN Police. Online. Available at: www.un.org/Depts/dpko/missions/UNMISETlocal/index.html.

DPKO East Timor – UNTAET: Background. Full text. Online. Available at: www.un.org/peace/etimor/UntaetB.htm.

DPKO East Timor – UNTAET: Human Rights. Online. Available at: www.un.org/peace/etimor/fact/fs10.PDF.

DPKO East Timor – UNTAET: Justice and Serious Crimes. Online. Available at: www.un.org/peace/etimor/fact/fs7.PDF.

DPKO East Timor – UNTAET: Law and Order. Online. Available at: www.un.org/peace/etimor/fact/fs6.PDF.

DPKO East Timor – UNTAET: Truth and Reconciliation. Online. Available at: www.un.org/peace/etimor/fact/fs8.PDF.

DPKO El Salvador – ONUSAL: Background. Full text. Online. Available at: www.un.org/Depts/dpko/dpko/co_mission/onusalbackgr2.html.

DPKO El Salvador – ONUSAL: Mandate. Online. Available at: www.un.org/Depts/dpko/dpko/co_mission/onusalmandate.html.

DPKO Guatemala – MINUGUA: Background. Full text. Online. Available at: http://www.un.org/Depts/dpko/dpko/co_mission/minuguabackgr.html.

DPKO Haiti – MINUSTAH: Mandate. Online. Available at: www.un.org/Depts/dpko/missions/minustah/mandate.html.

DPKO Haiti – UNMIH: Background. Full text. Online. Available at: www.un.org/Depts/dpko/dpko/co_mission/unmihbackgr2.html.

DPKO Haiti – UNSMIH: Background. Full text. Online. Available at: www.un.org/Depts/dpko/dpko/co_mission/unsmihbackgr.html.

DPKO Haiti – UNTMIH. Online. Available at: www.un.org/Depts/dpko/dpko/co_mission/untmih.htm.

DPKO Liberia – UNMIL: About UNMIL History. Available at: www.unmil.org/content.asp?ccat=history.

DPKO Liberia – UNMIL: Operations Disarmament Process. Available at: www.unmil.org/content.asp?ccat=ddrr.

DPKO Liberia – UNMIL: Operations Corrections. Online. Available at: www.unmil.org/content.asp?ccat=corrections.

DPKO Liberia – UNMIL: Operations Legal & Judicial Coordination. Online. Available at: www.unmil.org/content.asp?ccat=judicial.

DPKO Liberia – UNMIL: Operations UN Police. Online. Available HTTP www.unmil.org/content.asp?ccat=civpol.

DPKO Liberia – UNMIL: Operations Human Rights. Online. Available at: www.unmil.org/content.asp?ccat=humanrights.

DPKO Liberia – UNOMIL: Background. Full text. Online. Available at: www.un.org/Depts/dpko/dpko/co_mission/unomilFT.htm.

DPKO Mozambique – ONUMUZ: Background. Full text. Online. Available at: www.un.org/Depts/dpko/dpko/co_mission/onumozFT.htm#General.

DPKO Namibia – UNTAG: Background. Full text. Online. Available at: www.un.org/Depts/dpko/dpko/co_mission/untagFT.htm.

DPKO Rwanda – UNAMIR: Background. Full text. Online. Available at: www.un.org/Depts/dpko/dpko/co_mission/unamirFT.htm.

DPKO Rwanda – UNAMIR: Mandate. Online. Available at: www.un.org/Depts/dpko/dpko/co_mission/unamirM.htm.

DPKO Sierra Leone – UNAMSIL: Background. Full text. Online. Available at: www.un.org/Depts/dpko/missions/unamsil/background.html.

DPKO Sierra Leone – UNAMSIL: Disarmament, Demobilisation and Reintegration. Fact Sheet 1. Online. Available at: www.un.org/Depts/dpko/missions/unamsil/factsheet1_DDR.pdf.

DPKO Sierra Leone – UNAMSIL: Human Rights and Rule of Law. Fact Sheet 3. Online. Available at: www.un.org/Depts/dpko/missions/unamsil/factsheet3_HRRL.pdf.

DPKO Sierra Leone – UNAMSIL: Mandate. Online. Available at: www.un.org/Depts/dpko/missions/unamsil/mandate.html.

DPKO Sierra Leone – UNOMSIL: Background. Full text. Online. Available at: www.un.org/Depts/DPKO/Missions/unomsil/UnomsilB.htm.

DPKO Somalia – UNOSOM II: Background. Full text. Online. Available at: www.un.org/Depts/dpko/dpko/co_mission/unosom2backgr2.html.

DPKO Sudan – UNMIS: Mandate. Online. Available at: www.un.org/Depts/dpko/missions/unmis/mandate.html.

UNMIK – Civilian Police – Mandate & Tasks. Online. Available at: www.unmikonline.org/civpol/mandate.htm.

UNMIK – Police & Justice (Pillar I) – Police. Online. Available at: www.unmikonline.org/justice/police.htm#2.

UNMIL (2006) 'UNMIL Statement on Former Liberian President Charles Taylor', 30 March. Online. Available at: www.un.org/Depts/dpko/missions/unmil/Stat300306.pdf.

UNMIS – DDR Achievements. Online. Available at: www.unmis.org/english/ddr-achievments.htm.

UNMIS – Human Rights Office. Online. Available at: www.unmis.org/english/human-rights.htm.

UNMIS – Police Operations. Online. Available at: www.unmis.org/english/police-operations.htm.

UNMIS – Police Reform and Restructuring. Online. Available at: www.unmis.org/english/police-RR.htm.

UNMIS – Police Training. Online. Available at: www.unmis.org/english/police-training.htm.

UNMIS – Rule of Law and Judicial Systems Advisory. Online. Available at: www.unmis.org/english/Rule%20of%20Law.html.

UNOCI – Human Rights. Online. Available at: www.onuci.org/archives/feature_stories/le%20kit/anglais/Human%20Rights.pdf.

UNOCI – Rule of Law. Online. Available at: www.onuci.org/archives/feature_stories/le%20kit/anglais/Rule%20of%20Law.pdf.

UNOCI – Working for Peace in a Country in Crisis. Online. Available at: www.onuci.org/archives/feature_stories/le%20kit/anglais/L%27ONUCI,%20working%20for%20peace.pdf.

(All accessed on 6 January 2008.)

UNSC meetings

United Nations Security Council (24 September 2003) 'Justice and the Rule of Law: The United Nations' Role', Meeting no. 4833, S/PV.4833. Online. Available at: daccess-dds.un.org/doc/UNDOC/PRO/N03/529/99/PDF/N0352999.pdf?OpenElemen.

United Nations Security Council (30 September 2003) 'Justice and the Rule of Law: The United Nations' Role', Meeting no. 4835, S/PV.4835. Online. Available at:daccess-dds.un.org/doc/UNDOC/PRO/N03/535/43/PDF/N0353543.pdf?OpenElement.

United Nations Security Council (6 October 2004a) 'Justice and the Rule of Law: The United Nations' Role', Meeting no. 5052, S/PV.5052. Online. Available at: daccess-dds.un.org/doc/UNDOC/PRO/N04/537/59/PDF/N0453759.pdf?OpenElement.

United Nations Security Council (6 October 2004b) 'Justice and the Rule of Law: The United Nations' Role', Meeting no. 5052, S/PV.5052 (Resumption 1). Online. Available at: daccessdds.un.org/doc/UNDOC/PRO/N04/538/83/PDF/N0453883.pdf?Open Element..

United Nations Security Council (22 June 2006a) 'Strengthening International Law: Rule of Law and the Maintenance of International Peace and Security', Meeting no. 5474, S/PV.5474. Online. Available at: daccessdds.un.org/doc/UNDOC/PRO/N06/400/28/PDF/N0640028.pdf?OpenElement.

United Nations Security Council (22 June 2006b) 'Strengthening International Law: Rule of Law and the Maintenance of International Peace and Security', Meeting no. 5474, S/PV.5474 (Resumption 1). Online. Available at: daccessdds.un.org/doc/UNDOC/PRO/N06/401/01/PDF/N0640101.pdf?OpenElement.

UN reports and handbooks

Annan, K. (2004) 'The Rule of Law and Transitional Justice in Conflict and Post-conflict Societies', S/2004/616. Online. Available at: daccessdds.un.org/doc/UNDOC/GEN/N04/395/29/PDF/N0439529.pdf?OpenElement.

Annan, K. (2006) 'Uniting Our Strengths: Enhancing United Nations Support for the Rule of Law', S/2006/980. Online. Available at: daccessdds.un.org/doc/UNDOC/GEN/N07/212/52/PDF/N0721252.pdf?OpenElement.

Boutros-Ghali, B. (1992) 'An Agenda for Peace: Preventive Diplomacy, Peacemaking and Peace-keeping', A/47/277 – S/24111. Online. Available at: www.un.org/Docs/SG/agpeace.html.

Boutrous-Ghali, B. (1995) 'Supplement to an Agenda for Peace: Position Paper of the Secretary-General on the Occasion of the Fiftieth Anniversary of the United Nations', A/50/60 – S/1995/1. Online. Available at: www.un.org/Docs/SG/agsupp.html.

Brahimi, L. (2000) 'The Report of the Panel on the United Nations Peace Operations'. Online. Available at: http://www.un.org/peace/reports/peace_operations/.

Peacekeeping Best Practices Unit (2003) *Handbook on United Nations Multidimensional Peacekeeping Operations*, New York: UN Department of Peacekeeping Operations. Online. Available at: pbpu.unlb.org/pbpu/handbook/START-Handbook.html.

(All accessed on 6 January 2008.)

United Nations Security Council resolutions

632 (1989) Online. Available at: daccessdds.un.org/doc/RESOLUTION/GEN/NR0/557/69/IMG/NR055769.pdf?OpenElement.

696 (1991) Online. Available at: daccessdds.un.org/doc/RESOLUTION/GEN/NR0/596/32/IMG/NR059632.pdf?OpenElement.

729 (1992) Online. Available at: daccessdds.un.org/doc/RESOLUTION/GEN/NR0/010/88/IMG/NR001088.pdf?OpenElement.

745 (1992) Online. Available at: daccessdds.un.org/doc/RESOLUTION/GEN/NR0/011/04/IMG/NR001104.pdf?OpenElement.

797 (1992) Online. Available at: daccessdds.un.org/doc/UNDOC/GEN/N92/824/85/IMG/N9282485.pdf?OpenElement.

814 (1993) Online. Available at: daccessdds.un.org/doc/UNDOC/GEN/N93/226/18/IMG/N9322618.pdf?OpenElement.

827 (1993) Online. Available at: daccessdds.un.org/doc/UNDOC/GEN/N93/306/28/IMG/N9330628.pdf?OpenElement.

865 (1993) Online. Available at: daccessdds.un.org/doc/UNDOC/GEN/N93/513/77/PDF/N9351377.pdf?OpenElement.

866 (1993) Online. Available at: daccessdds.un.org/doc/UNDOC/GEN/N93/513/89/PDF/N9351389.pdf?OpenElement.

867 (1993) Online. Available at: daccessdds.un.org/doc/UNDOC/GEN/N93/515/30/PDF/N9351530.pdf?OpenElement.

872 (1993) Online. Available at: daccessdds.un.org/doc/UNDOC/GEN/N93/540/63/PDF/N9354063.pdf?OpenElement.

897 (1994) Online. Available at: daccessdds.un.org/doc/UNDOC/GEN/N94/065/62/PDF/N9406562.pdf?OpenElement.

898 (1994) Online. Available at: daccessdds.un.org/doc/UNDOC/GEN/N94/091/22/PDF/N9409122.pdf?OpenElement.

965 (1994) Online. Available at: daccessdds.un.org/doc/UNDOC/GEN/N94/475/84/PDF/ N9447584.pdf?OpenElement.

976 (1995) Online. Available at: daccessdds.un.org/doc/UNDOC/GEN/N95/038/14/PDF/ N9503814.pdf?OpenElement.

1008 (1995) Online. Available at: daccessdds.un.org/doc/UNDOC/GEN/N95/233/40/ PDF/N9523340.pdf?OpenElement.

1020 (1995) Online. Available at: daccessdds.un.org/doc/UNDOC/GEN/N95/348/93/ PDF/N9534893.pdf?OpenElement.

1037 (1996) Online. Available at: daccessdds.un.org/doc/UNDOC/GEN/N96/007/55/ PDF/N9600755.pdf?OpenElement.

1045 (1996) Online. Available at: daccessdds.un.org/doc/UNDOC/GEN/N96/029/87/ PDF/N9602987.pdf?OpenElement.

1055 (1996) Online. Available at: daccessdds.un.org/doc/UNDOC/GEN/N96/118/64/ PDF/N9611864.pdf?OpenElement.

1063 (1996) Online. Available at: daccessdds.un.org/doc/UNDOC/GEN/N96/162/13/ PDF/N9616213.pdf?OpenElement.

1088 (1996) Online. Available at: daccessdds.un.org/doc/UNDOC/GEN/N97/026/19/ PDF/N9702619.pdf?OpenElement.

1103 (1997) Online. Available at: daccessdds.un.org/doc/UNDOC/GEN/N97/085/71/ PDF/N9708571.pdf?OpenElement.

1107 (1997) Online. Available at: daccessdds.un.org/doc/UNDOC/GEN/N97/128/99/ PDF/N9712899.pdf?OpenElement.

1123 (1997) Online. Available at: daccessdds.un.org/doc/UNDOC/GEN/N97/206/88/ PDF/N9720688.pdf?OpenElement.

1144 (1997) Online. Available at: daccessdds.un.org/doc/UNDOC/GEN/N97/375/23/ PDF/N9737523.pdf?OpenElement.

1168 (1998) Online. Available at: daccessdds.un.org/doc/UNDOC/GEN/N98/141/10/ PDF/N9814110.pdf?OpenElement.

1181 (1998) Online. Available at: daccessdds.un.org/doc/UNDOC/GEN/N98/203/28/ PDF/N9820328.pdf?OpenElement.

1184 (1998) Online. Available at: daccessdds.un.org/doc/UNDOC/GEN/N98/207/87/ PDF/N9820787.pdf?OpenElement.

1244 (1999) Online. Available at: daccessdds.un.org/doc/UNDOC/GEN/N99/172/89/ PDF/N9917289.pdf?OpenElement.

1270 (1999) Online. Available at: daccessdds.un.org/doc/UNDOC/GEN/N99/315/02/ PDF/N9931502.pdf?OpenElement.

1272 (1999) Online. Available at: daccessdds.un.org/doc/UNDOC/GEN/N99/312/77/ PDF/N9931277.pdf?OpenElement.

1410 (2002) Online. Available at: daccessdds.un.org/doc/UNDOC/GEN/N02/387/02/ PDF/N0238702.pdf?OpenElement.

1468 (2003) Online. Available at: daccessdds.un.org/doc/UNDOC/GEN/N02/387/02/ PDF/N0238702.pdf?OpenElement.

1509 (2003) Online. Available at: daccessdds.un.org/doc/UNDOC/GEN/N03/525/70/ PDF/N0352570.pdf?OpenElement.

1528 (2004) Online. Available at: daccessdds.un.org/doc/UNDOC/GEN/N04/253/20/ PDF/N0425320.pdf?OpenElement.

1542 (2004) Online. Available at: daccessdds.un.org/doc/UNDOC/GEN/N04/332/98/ PDF/N0433298.pdf?OpenElement.

1565 (2004) Online. Available at: daccessdds.un.org/doc/UNDOC/GEN/N04/531/89/ PDF/N0453189.pdf?OpenElement.

1590 (2005) Online. Available at: daccessdds.un.org/doc/UNDOC/GEN/N05/284/08/ PDF/N0528408.pdf?OpenElement.

1638 (2005) Online. Available at: daccessdds.un.org/doc/UNDOC/GEN/N05/600/30/ PDF/N0560030.pdf?OpenElement.

1739 (2007) Online. Available at: daccessdds.un.org/doc/UNDOC/GEN/N07/206/02/ PDF/N0720602.pdf?OpenElement.

(All accessed on 6 January 2008.)

Index

For Product Safety Concerns and Information please contact our EU
representative GPSR@taylorandfrancis.com
Taylor & Francis Verlag GmbH, Kaufingerstraße 24, 80331 München, Germany

www.ingramcontent.com/pod-product-compliance
Lightning Source LLC
Chambersburg PA
CBHW050410280326
41932CB00013BA/1805

9 780415 575331